FLORENCE

1138 - 1737

Gene Adam Brucker

FLORENCE

1138 - 1737

SIDGWICK & JACKSON

LONDON

Opposite title page: detail from the Visitation *by Domenico Ghirlandaio and pupils, in the church of Santa Maria Novella, Florence*

Title page: the Marzocco, *symbol of Florence's republican independence, as seen in a sculpture by Donatello in the Museo del Bargello, Florence*

Text by Gene Adam Brucker
Additional material by Nello Forti translated by James Ramsey and Geoffrey Culverwell
Copyright © 1983 Arnoldo Mondadori Editore S.p.A., Milan
English translation copyright © 1984 Arnoldo Mondadori Editore S.p.A., Milan

The quotations from *Della Famiglia* by Leon Battista Alberti on pages 48, 50 and 219 are taken from Renée Watkins's translation, *The Family in Renaissance Florence* (University of South Carolina Press, 1969).

First published in Great Britain by Sidgwick & Jackson Limited
First published in Italy in 1983 under the title *Firenze 1138–1737 L'Impero del Fiorino* by Arnoldo Mondadori Editore S.p.A., Milan

ISBN 0-283-99091-0

Printed and bound in Italy by Arnoldo Mondadori Editore, Verona
for Sidgwick & Jackson Limited
1 Tavistock Chambers
Bloomsbury Way
London WC1A 2SG

Contents

The uniqueness of Florence's historical experience

In his classic work, *The Civilization of the Renaissance in Italy,* Jacob Burckhardt wrote: "The most elevated political thought and the most varied form of human development are found united in the history of Florence which in this sense deserves the name of the first modern state of the world." Burckhardt's view of Florence as the premier city of the Italian Renaissance (to quote him again, "in many of their chief merits the Florentines are the pattern and the earliest type of Italians and modern Europeans generally,") was not an original perception. That claim had already been made by the Florentines themselves, who extolled the merits of their city, comparing it with Athens, with Rome, with Jerusalem.

Florentines never tired of emphasizing the achievements of their fellow citizens, beginning with Dante and Giotto in the 14th century, and concluding with such illustrious names as Leonardo da Vinci and Michelangelo, Machiavelli and Guicciardini, in the 16th. Panegyrics of their native city flowed from the pens of Florentine writers such as Leonardo Bruni for example, the 15th-century humanist who in 1428 delivered a funeral oration in honour of a fallen Florentine soldier, Nanni degli Strozzi. Bruni took advantage of the occasion to write a eulogy of Florence, modelled upon Pericles' speech in praise of Athens, "the school of Hellas," at the beginning of the Peloponnesian War. Bruni first described Florence's government as a free republic in which large numbers of citizens participated. The form of this government, he argued, contributed significantly to the high level of achievement which the Florentines had attained. "It is marvellous to see," he wrote, "how powerful this access to public office, once it is offered to a free people, proves to be in awakening the talents of the citizens. For where men are given the hope of attaining honour within the state, they take courage and raise themselves to a higher plane ... And since such hope and opportunity are held out in our commonwealth, we need not be surprised that talent and industry distinguish themselves to the highest degree." Bruni was a classical scholar who believed that the revival of ancient learning was exclusively a Florentine achievement: "Who has called this wholly lost skill of expression back into light, if not our citizens? Who, if not our republic, has brought to recognition, revived and rescued from ruin Latin learning, which previously had been abject, prostrate and almost dead? ... Even the knowledge of Greek letters, which for more than 700 years had fallen into disuse in Italy, has been called forth and brought back by our community ... Finally, the humanistic studies, surely the best and most excellent of studies, those most appropriate for the human race, needed in private as well as public life ... such studies took root in Italy after originating in our city." Now such eulogistic statements were not uniquely Florentine. Every Italian city of any size and reputation – from the great urban centers like Milan and Venice, to small communities like Forlì and Pistoia – had its promoters and its eulogists, who wrote in glowing terms about their city: its growth, its military victories, the strength of its walls, the beauty of its churches and public buildings, the holiness of its saints, the great achievements of its poets and artists, its lawyers and statesmen. What distinguished the Florentine contribution to this encomiastic literature was its volume, and the reputation of the authors, whose works reached a much larger audience than those of writers from other cities.

Florentines were keenly aware of the value of their historians in promoting the city's fame and reputation. Vespasiano da Bisticci, the bookseller who wrote a series of biographies of famous 15th-century Italians, noted that: "The city of Florence owes much to *messer* Leonardo [Bruni] and *messer* Poggio [Bracciolini]. There is no republic nor city state, save the Roman republic, which has been so celebrated as the city of Florence, with two such worthy writers to record its history, a history which was shrouded in the utmost obscurity before they wrote it down. If the Venetian republic, which boasts so many cultured men with achievements both on land and on sea to their name, had had its own exploits recorded, it would enjoy even greater fame and reputation than it already does." Vespasiano concluded his statement with this comment: "And any republic worthy of its name should richly reward the writers that have recorded its history."

From this massive literature in praise of Florence and Florentines, there emerge four or five distinctive themes: the special nature of the city's achievement, her reputation, her superiority over other Italian cities. First there was the aesthetic dimension, the physical beauty of the city and the surrounding countryside: the churches, palaces, squares, streets, villas. A second theme concerns the great wealth amassed by Florentine merchants, bankers and industrialists in their business activities which had taken them to the four corners of the known world – from Scandinavia to central Asia – and had inspired the comment by Pope Boniface VIII that the Florentines were the fifth element of the universe. Burckhardt noted this Florentine penchant for statistics, for measuring the city's wealth and her economic vitality in numerical terms. Giovanni Villani devoted three chapters of his 14th-century chronicle to a statistical survey of the city – with data on population, food consumption, the production of woollen cloth, the income and expenditures of the commune, even a rare and illuminating reference to the number of students who were enrolled in the city's schools. The political achievements of the Florentines also figure prominently in the civic eulogies dedicated to the city. Leonardo Bruni's praise of the republic has already been

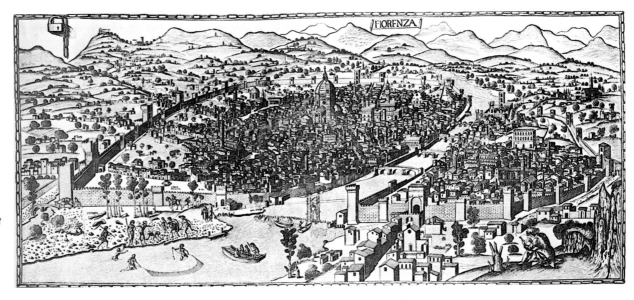

The so-called "chained view" (right), created around 1472 and attributed to the workshop of Francesco Rosselli, is the earliest example of a realistic "portrait" of Florence, depicted with no flights of fancy and no symbolical nuances. The city is shown within the confines of the walls built between 1299 and 1333. Before these, Florence had possessed two other circles of walls during the communal era. The urban nucleus contained by the first set of communal walls was divided into quarters (quartieri), which took their names from the four gates that led into them (Porta Domus, Porta S. Petri, Porta S. Mariae, Porta S. Pancratii). When the city spread across the Arno at the beginning of the 12th century, a series of six new divisions (sestieri) was initiated; one of these (the sesto Oltrarno) lay to the south of the river, whilst the other five (the sesto di S. Pancrazio, di Borgo S. Pietro Scheraggio, di Porta del Duomo, di S. Piero Maggiore), whose emblems, preserved in the courtyard of the Bargello, are shown on the opposite page, lay to the north. Each of these territorial entities exercised its own administrative, economic, military and town planning functions, as well as possessing its own magistrates and its own tribunal and being responsible for the defenses of its own section of wall. This organization of the city into sestieri *lasted until 1343, when a combination of political and military factors made a return to the* quartiere *system desirable. The area to the south of the Arno now became known as the* quartiere *of S. Spirito, while on the northern bank lay the* quartieri *of S. Giovanni, S. Maria Novella and S. Croce.*

mentioned. Not only did Florence share, with Venice, the distinction of preserving her liberty and her republican form of government longer than most other Italian city-states, but her citizens contended that by her efforts alone, republicanism in Italy survived as a viable political force in the Renaissance, in contrast to the despotisms and tyrannies which had replaced popular regimes in other cities.

However, it is in the cultural realm, in literature and the arts, that Florence's achievement has been most highly valued, by her own citizens and by later generations of Italians and foreigners who have made the pilgrimage to the city on the Arno: to her libraries and archives, and above all, to her churches, palaces and museums, to gaze in admiration at the works of her great artists.

Florence's most renowned literary figure was Dante Alighieri whose death was noted by Giovanni Villani with this statement: "… For his many virtues as a citizen, I think it seemly that he be perpetually remembered through the present chronicle, along with all his noble written works, which bear true and honourable witness to our city." When Dante died in 1321, his most illustrious literary successors, Petrarch and Boccaccio, were still boys; their contribution to Italian literature would not be made until decades later, in the second half of the century. In addition to their contributions to the development of Tuscan as a literary language, both Petrarch and Boccaccio were classical scholars; their enthusiasm for the learning of antiquity

stimulated that revival of the *studia humanitatis* that Bruni had described in his funeral oration for Nanni degli Strozzi. Throughout the 15th century, the Greek and Latin classics were the pre-eminent concern of young Florentine intellectuals, not only professional scholars like Bruni and Coluccio Salutati, but also laymen like Cosimo de' Medici and his brother Lorenzo, who studied classical literature with Roberto de' Rossi, who had been the pupil of the Greek scholar from Constantinople, Manuel Chrysoloras. Classical literature became, during the 15th century, the standard educational fare of young Florentine aristocrats so that by the end of the century it was normal for the lawyer Bernardo Machiavelli to send his young son Niccolò (as he reported in his diary) "to master Matteo, the grammar teacher … to learn to read his Donatello," the basic textbook for the study of Latin. If literature, both classical and vernacular, figured very prominently in the Florentine claim to cultural distinction, the achievements of the city's painters, sculptors, goldsmiths and architects were the most important element in Florence's coronation as queen of the Renaissance.

It is the overwhelming visual impact of this artistic heritage that has made such a powerful impression on the imagination and sensibilities of generations of Europeans. In the 18th century, Florence was an obligatory stop on the grand tour of young English aristocrats, and later, of their continental counterparts. With the emergence of mass tourism in the 20th century it is

Florence, together with Rome, that attracts the greatest number of visitors; and it is to the churches and museums that they go to catch a glimpse of Ghiberti's *Doors of Paradise*, Donatello's sculptures in the Bargello and the Museo dell' Opera del Duomo, Botticelli's *Primavera* and *Birth of Venus* in the Uffizi, and Michelangelo's *David* in the Accademia.

Florence seen from abroad

Florentines were not the most objective observers of their city and its historical achievement, but neither were their fellow Italians, who had their own strong attachments to their native towns and who, particularly if they lived close to Florence, often nourished an intense hatred for their neighbours on the Arno. Perhaps the most unbiased observers were foreigners from across the Alps, but the evidence from ultramontane visitors is very scanty before 1500. There was general agreement, among Italians and foreigners alike, that Florence was one of the most beautiful cities in Italy and indeed in Europe. The Venetian ambassador, Marco Foscari, wrote in 1527 that "there is in my opinion no region more sweet or pleasing in Italy or in any other part of Europe than that wherein Florence is placed, for Florence is situated in a plain surrounded on all sides by hills and mountains ... And the hills are fertile, cultivated, pleasant, all bearing beautiful and sumptuous *palazzi* built at great expense and boasting all manner of fine

A drawing by Leonardo shows an area of the countryside surrounding Florence through which the Arno flows. In 1527 the Venetian ambassador Marco Foscari wrote: "There is in my opinion no region more sweet or pleasing in Italy or in any other part of Europe than that wherein Florence is placed, for Florence is situated in a plain surrounded on all sides by hills and mountains ..." These words are matched by the detail taken from a copy of the "chained view" shown on the opposite page (above).

:atures: gardens, woods, fountains, fish ponds,
ools and much else besides, with views that
esemble paintings ... Through the city runs the
.rno, an admirable river, one and a half times
ne width of our own Grand Canal, with tranquil,
mpid and clear water, a river made even more
greeable and delightful by four stone bridges
raddling it. The city has beautiful straight
oads; it is a clean, beautiful, happy place ..."
early a century later (in 1600) a French visitor,
ne Prince de Rohan, waxed lyrical in his praise
f the city: "Florence has spread the concept of
beauty throughout Italy ... It is now at the height
of its glory: filled with beautiful squares, beautiful streets, beautiful palaces, beautiful hospitals
and beautiful churches; more than any other city
in Italy. These features, combined with the
freedom that exists here for all types of people,
and the creative activities of the inhabitants,
have persuaded me to stay here longer than
anywhere else ..."

If the consensus of opinion about the physical
city was unanimously favourable, the judgement
of the Florentines as a people was just as
consistently negative. They were sometimes
admired, they were often feared, but they were
never loved. They were accused of every vice
known to their contemporaries: greed and avarice, inconstancy and faithlessness, pride and
arrogance, and peculiar sexual proclivities. Our
Venetian witness, Marco Foscari, described the
Florentines in these terms: "... They are weak
men: both by nature and by chance. They are
weak because they are naturally timid, because

the air of Florence only produces timid men (...),
or because they engage in trade, manual skills
and similar menial occupations. For in Florence
everyone is a craftsman ... the highest citizens
who govern the state go to their silk *botteghe* and
work the silk for all to see (...) their children are
in the *bottega* all day, in their smocks, carrying
sacks and baskets of silk (...) and performing
other such tasks ... " Factional discord was said
to be endemic among the Florentines, as even
their own citizens acknowledged. Dante accused
them of that disease in the *Divine Comedy*; so did
a host of Florentine chroniclers: Dino Compagni, Giovanni and Matteo Villani, Marchionne
Stefani. The Florentines saw themselves, in their
business and diplomatic relations, as honourable

*Less idyllic are the words of
Giovanni Villani: "The
contado was completely built
over by noblemen who did
not obey the city (...) and the
Florentines ordered their
contado outside to be
expanded and their signory
extended, and for any castle
and fortress that failed to
obey to be attacked ..." In
1125, the price of
disobedience was paid by the
town of Fiesole (shown on
the left in a miniature from
the Rustici codex, 1448),
whose fortress the
Florentines, after a lengthy
siege, "completely destroyed
and demolished right down
to its very foundations."*

The Ponte Vecchio (shown on the right in a drawing by E. Burci from 1864) is Florence's oldest bridge and may have been constructed a short distance below an earlier, Roman one, built in the middle of the first century at the point where a ferry linked the two sections of the Via Cassia. The present bridge has its roots in one dating back to the ninth century, which collapsed during the floods of 1178. The present structure is the one completed by Taddeo Gaddi in 1345. The workshops between the arches were originally occupied by butchers and other tradesmen, but from the end of the 16th century they were reserved for goldsmiths. The rooms at the back of these workshops, supported on wooden beams, were added during the 17th century. Up until the 13th century the Ponte Vecchio provided the only link between the two banks of the Arno (in the lower illustration on the page opposite, we can see a section of the right bank showing the backs of the houses of the Borgo d'Ognissanti before the construction of the Arno embankment or lungarno, *as shown in a drawing by E. Burci). When the city expanded along the river, other bridges were needed. Within little more than 30 years, during the first half of the 13th century, the Ponte Vecchio was joined by the Ponte Nuovo, later called the Ponte alla Carraia (1218-20), and the Ponte Ruba-conte, named after the podestà who had laid its first stone and later called the Ponte alle Grazie (1237), which is shown on the opposite page, above. These two bridges, one built above the Ponte Vecchio and the other below it, were followed in 1352 by the Ponte a Santa Trinita, the last of the four links in the system that joined the two parts of the city until the earlier half of the 19th century.*

and trustworthy, as never violating their contracts or treaties, but their neighbours viewed them in a different light. Here is a not untypical comment by a citizen of Lucca in the year 1388. He had been sent by his government to Siena, whose inhabitants, he reported, lived in fear of Florentine aggression. "They are as sly as foxes," he wrote, and then warned his own government to be on guard against Florentine treachery: "They are cunning in everything they do, and their mischief knows no bounds. I entreat you to take good care, for the wicked Judas, full of evil and simony, sleeps not."

Not loved, then, but feared and resented by other Italians; sometimes respected for their wealth and the military power wealth could buy; sometimes admired for their tenacity and determination in fighting wars. One particularly heroic moment in Florentine military history was the year 1402, when the city was surrounded by the troups of the Duke of Milan. The Florentines refused to surrender to their more powerful enemy who (fortunately for them) died of a fever in the autumn of that year, whereupon his leaderless army melted away and Florence was saved. The Florentines were frequently defeated

in battle: by Siena at Montaperti in 1266, by Lucca at Altopascio in 1326, and Milan in a series of disastrous defeats in the Romagna in the late 1420s. But they rarely lost their wars, which usually ended in a military stalemate and a negotiated peace. The city was not occupied by enemy troops from the beginnings of communal government in the 12th century, until 1530; and only on rare occasions did hostile forces penetrate her frontier defenses to ravage the villages and farms in her dominion. The Florentines were thus remarkably successful in defending themselves against their enemies, and thus in preserving their liberty.

No one could deny the strong Florentine commitment to self-government, to *libertà*, but as critics pointed out, Florentine liberty has to be understood in a very restricted sense. Despite claims by Leonardo Bruni that Florence was governed by a substantial part of her citizens, political power was in fact enjoyed only by a small minority, recruited for the most part from the wealthiest and most prominent families: the Strozzi, the Capponi, the Albizzi, the Medici. Though a few artisans and petty shopkeepers held civic office, most were excluded from

When the river became included within the city walls, the areas of habitation along its banks became the most densely populated of all. This detail of a painting by Bernardo Bellotto (opposite), showing a section of the right-hand river bank near the Ponte a Santa Trinita, provides eloquent testimony to this fact. The relationship between the city and its river had always been a close one, and the Arno was already navigable between its estuary and Florence during Roman times (despite the difficulties resulting from shifting sandbanks and seasonal variations in water levels). At the height of the communal period it was used to transport timbers for shipbuilding from the Casentino to Pisa, whilst from Pisa flat-bottomed barges carried wool, minerals and goods of every type up to Florence. Apart from being an important means of communication, the Arno was also an important source of energy. It powered mills and fulfilled a number of industrial functions, especially the cleaning and dyeing of woollens and textiles. The Florentines were proud of their river and also appreciated its worth as a visual amenity. Through Goro Dati, who was writing in 1422, they were able to boast that they had left an empty space in the middle of the Ponte Vecchio, not for any practical purposes, but purely so that people could gaze up- and downstream and admire the beauty of the banks and the hills in the surrounding area. The Florentines gave their city the allegorical appearance of a beautiful lady (right), as in the miniature by an unknown artist in Convenevole da Prato's codex Robertum Siciliae regiem, *which dates from the mid 14th century.*

politics. This severe limitation on political participation has persuaded some modern historians that Florentine republicanism was essentially a sham, and that power in the city was limited to such a small number of people, that in its essential features, the so-called republic was scarcely distinguishable from the despotisms of Milan or Ferrara. This argument assumed even greater weight after the Medici became the leaders of the Florentine state in 1434. But if only a few Florentines possessed political rights, they were more fortunate than the citizens of the subject towns of Pisa, Pistoia, Arezzo, Volterra and San Gimignano, who were governed by magistrates sent from Florence and who paid heavily, in taxes and in humiliation, for the privilege of being ruled by others. Pisa was conquered by a Florentine army in 1406, but the Pisans were never reconciled to Florentine rule. In 1494 they recovered their freedom and for 15 years they fought desperately to preserve their liberty, before finally succumbing to the superior forces of the Florentines. For the Pisans, and for other Tuscans who lived under Florence's domination, the Florentines were conquerors, tyrants, exploiters, not lovers of freedom.

Florentine liberty was thus reserved for the privileged few: freedom from the rule of foreigners for the residents of the city itself, and freedom to participate actively in political life for only a minority of those residents. And yet, with all these restrictions and limitations, it can be argued that the Florentine political experience was unique in Italy, and that it was very significant historically. The Arno republic was neither the most stable nor the most durable in Italy; that distinction belongs rather to Venice. Like Venice, though, Florence provided its citizens (and not just a handful but rather hundreds) with the opportunity to gain a political education, to listen to and participate in the lengthy deliberations over problems confronting the state – problems of war and peace, finance and justice – and to be involved in the administration of public affairs: as magistrates in the dominion, as officials in charge of the grain supply, as members of the supreme executive, the *Signoria*. No other Italian city, not even Venice, has left so full and rich a record of political deliberation, over so long a period of time: from the age of Dante in the early 14th century to the age of Savonarola and Machiavelli

at the end of the 15th. No other city explored so systematically and deeply the basic problems of government: how to create and maintain institutions that would preserve liberty, how to foster a strong civic spirit, how to persuade citizens to make sacrifices for the good of the whole community. It is no accident that the most creative and original political thinker of the Renaissance, Niccolò Machiavelli, was a

Questionable modifications to the city's layout have partially altered the appearance of old Florence. The bistre drawings of E. Burci, executed around 1845, provide an essential reconstruction of how the city looked before the demolitions that took place during the second half of the 19th century. In the illustration on the left, we can see the walls built by the Ghibellines stretching from Porta San Giorgio to Porta San Niccolò. The section of wall by the Porta San Niccolò was demolished in 1870. Below, the Via degli Archibusieri, now the Lungarno Diaz, leading up towards the Ponte Vecchio.

Florentine, and that his ideas were shaped by his experiences as an official of the republic between 1498 and 1512.

The significance of Florence's political achievement was not recognized by Italian or European opinion, which tended to emphasize the negative rather than the positive aspects of that experience. Her Tuscan neighbours lived in fear of being conquered, or in rage because they had been conquered. Her rivals in other Italian states – Milan, Naples, Venice – were hostile because their political interests often clashed with those of Florence. Foreigners from across the Alps were generally contemptuous of this small republic that was too weak to defend itself without allies. When, for example, Machiavelli visited the French court in 1500 to appeal for help from King Louis XII to assist Florence in recovering Pisa, he noted bitterly that he was not treated with respect by officials at the court, who viewed him as a kind of poor cousin, whose government needed the king more than he needed them. Machiavelli did get his revenge, in a sense, by writing, in *The Prince*, a devastating critique of French policy in Italy after the first

invasion by King Charles VIII in 1494. He showed clearly how the stupidity of that policy led ultimately to the expulsion of the French from the peninsula. But even though he created, in *The Prince*, an enduring image of Louis XII as an inept fool, he was not able to change French policy nor French attitudes towards Florence.

In contrast to contemporary judgements on Florence as a political community, there was general agreement among Italians that the city was the leading cultural center of the peninsula. Not until around 1500, when Rome emerged as the intellectual and artistic capital of Italy, was Florence's primacy challenged; and in the 16th century other cities like Ferrara and Venice were competing successfully with Florence for this position. Pope Pius II, a native of Siena, identified (1460) those Florentines who had achieved renown as poets and scholars: Dante, Petrarch, Coluccio Salutati, Leonardo Bruni. Pope Pius has nothing to say about Florence's achievement in the arts, except to describe the beauty of her churches and palaces. Pius was a humanist, who regarded painters and sculptors as craftsmen – like carpenters and stonemasons – and not as creative artists, whose skills could be compared to those of poets and scholars. There are some scattered hints in contemporary sources of Florentine awareness of the exceptional talents of her artists: for example in the year 1300 the eulogy of the architect Arnolfo di Cambio is inserted in the legislation granting him a tax exemption. Arnolfo was described as "the most renowned and the most expert in church construction of any other in these parts and … through his industry, experience and genius, the Florentine commune … hopes to have the most beautiful and most honourable cathedral in Tuscany."

The painter Giotto was universally recognized by contemporaries as Florence's (and indeed, Italy's) greatest artist of the 14th century. His distinction was acknowledged early by Dante in the *Divine Comedy:*

(…) Cimabue thought
To lord it over painting's field; and now
The cry is Giotto's, and his name eclipsed.
(*Purgatorio*, XI, 93-95)

When Giotto was appointed to the position of governor of the building works of the Florentine

The mills of San Niccolò and (below) the same mills with the weir and the Porta San Niccolò. All that now remains of this ancient view is the impressive gate, erected in 1324. The mills, whose existence was recorded as far back as the 13th century, have been destroyed, and the 15th-century weir has also been removed as a result of measures intended to control the flow of the Arno as it passes through the city.

commune in the 1330s, he received this official accolade from his employers: "It is said that in the whole world no one can be found who is more capable in these and other things than Maestro Giotto di Bondone, painter of Florence. He should be received therefore in his country as a great master and held dear in the city, and he

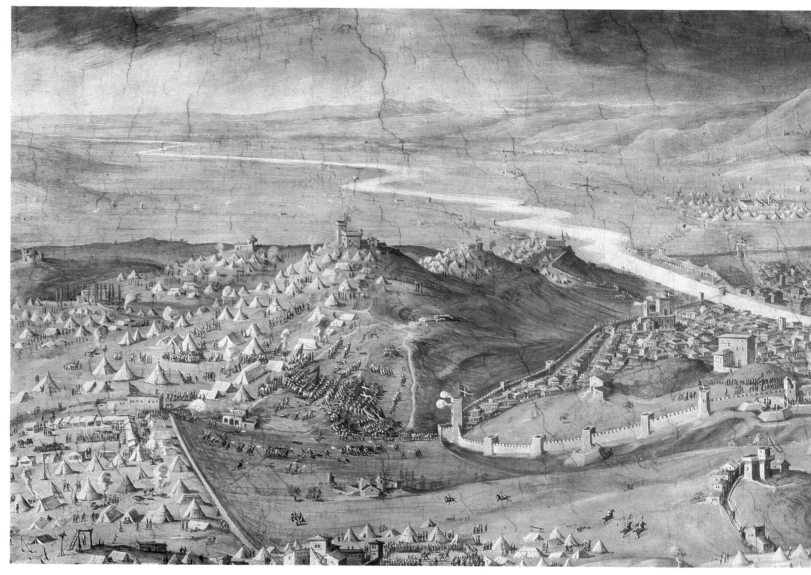

should have cause to live permanently there. For many will profit from his knowledge and learning, and the city's beauty will be enhanced." Boccaccio described Giotto's talents in his *Decameron*: "His genius [*ingegno*] was unsurpassed in its excellence; there was nothing in nature, the mother of all things and the pivot of the universe, that he could not reproduce with his paintbrush. Indeed, so faithful was his reproduction of nature that the objects he depicted appeared not so much similar to the originals, as real in themselves ... And so, having revived that skill which had lain buried and concealed for many centuries, he could most deservingly claim the honour of having made a splendid contribution to Florentine glory ..." Giotto's work was known to Florentines who were neither artists nor professional writers, but who could admire his frescoes, for example, his cycle of paintings of the life of St. Francis in the basilica of Santa Croce. Writing in his diary in around 1400, a merchant named Giovanni Morelli was describing his sister Mea's hands which were, he said, so beautiful that they appeared to have been painted by Giotto.

The quattrocento was Florence's great age of the arts, when the giants appear, and when each decade brought forth a new surge of artistic creativity. And it was in that century that Florence's reputation as an artistic center spread throughout the peninsula and to other parts of Europe. The 15th-century Umbrian artist, Giovanni Santi (the father of Raphael), wrote a poem in which he claimed that so many contem-

This fresco painted by Vasari in 1561-62, in the Sala di Clemente VII in the Palazzo Vecchio, shows the siege of Florence by the imperial armies during 1529-30. The 16th-century city is shown with its greatest architectural monuments already completed. The dominant feature is the dome of the cathedral and the high tower of the Palazzo Vecchio. The Uffizi palace, to be finished in 1580, does not feature, whilst the Palazzo Pitti is shown before the addition of its side wings.

porary Italian painters had achieved renown that they made every other age seem poor by comparison. In the poem Giovanni named some 25 Italian painters as worthy of distinction, of whom 13 were Florentine: Fra Angelico, Fra Filippo Lippi, Domenico Veneziano, Masaccio, Andrea del Castagno, Paolo Uccello, Antonio and Piero Pollaiuolo, Leonardo da Vinci, Ghirlandaio, Filippino Lippi, Sandro Botticelli.

The Florentine "ingegno"

How did contemporaries explain this remarkable efflorescence of artistic genius in the Arno city? Giorgio Vasari, whose *Lives of the Most Eminent Painters, Sculptors and Architects* was an important source for the phenomenon, offered a variety of explanations for Florence's primacy in

the arts. In his biography of Michelangelo, he wrote that " … the Tuscan genius [*ingegno*] has ever been raised high above all others, the men of that country displaying more zeal in study, and more constancy in labour, than any other people of Italy …" Vasari was keenly aware of the value of a tradition of artistic excellence, of standards set by earlier generations of artists, and standards surpassed by their successors. In his biography of Masaccio, he wrote that the most celebrated artists went regularly to the Brancacci chapel to study the frescoes there: "This chapel has indeed been continually frequented by an infinite number of students and masters, for the sake of the benefit to be derived from these works, in which there are still some heads so beautiful and life-like, that we may safely affirm

Top, the Ponte alle Grazie and to the right, the Ponte alla Carraia, as seen in old photographs from the second half of the 19th century. Above, a detail from the "chained view," showing the four bridges which, from the 13th to the 19th century, linked the two areas of the city.

no artist of that period to have approached so nearly to the manner of the moderns as did Masaccio." In another passage, Vasari developed a sociological explanation for Florence's extraordinary achievement: "In that city men are driven on by three things; the first of these is disapproval, which many of them vent on many things and with much frequency, their genius never being content with mediocrity, but seeking what is good and beautiful (…) secondly, industriousness in their daily lives, which means constantly drawing on their *ingegno* and judgement, and being shrewd and quick in their dealings, and knowing how to earn money (…) The third thing (…) is a quest for glory and honour, which is common to Florentines of all professions …"

No word descriptive of the Florentines appears more frequently in Renaissance texts than *ingegno*, quoted with pride by the Florentines themselves, and with some degree of envy and resentment by other Italians. In his treatise on Florentine government, Girolamo Savonarola wrote: "The Florentines are the sharpest of all the Italian people, lively, shrewd and bold in their enterprises, as we have witnessed many times; although they are mainly concerned with trade and of a seemingly tranquil disposition, when the Florentines engage in military matters, or in civil war against their enemy, they become animated and terrifying …" When criticizing Savonarola's utilization of Florentine children as moral guardians and censors in the city, Fra Giorgio da Perugia commented from the pulpit in Santo Spirito: "One wonders how the Florentines, who are regarded as people of considerable skill and sharp wit [*ingegno*], could stoop so low as to conquer children in so vile a fashion, and to seek to rule over them."

Our perception of this distinctive quality of *ingegno* is derived less from Florentine deeds (which are known only dimly to us) than from their words, and above all, from their private and personal writings, which have survived in such abundance. Perhaps as many as 200 private reminiscences from the 14th to the 17th century exist today in Florentine archives and libraries. In no other Italian city, indeed, in no other European city before the 17th century, is a community's private experience so fully and richly recorded. Perhaps more private records survived in Florence than elsewhere because

The Ponte alle Grazie (above), originally known as the Ponte Rubaconte, was given its name because of the small chapel dedicated to the Madonna delle Grazie (Our Lady of Mercy) that was built at its entrance. As can be seen in this old photograph, on each pier at the sides of the carriageway there were small oratories, which were later demolished together with the chapel. Left, a photograph from the second half of the 19th century showing the Porta Romana surrounded by buildings that have since been demolished.

they were spared destruction by war and rebellion (though not by fire and flood); perhaps Florentine families were more concerned to preserve their records than those in other cities. But it is also probable that Florentines, for whatever reasons, were exceptionally motivated to write about themselves, their families, their city, their world.

One such writer was Giovanni Morelli (1371–1444). He belonged to a wealthy family of

merchants and cloth manufacturers established near the Franciscan church of Santa Croce. In his diary, he wrote extensively about his family history, and about individual kinsmen; he wrote too about Florentine public life. But the most remarkable part of his diary is his record of his own experience which, in its openness and candour, has few parallels in the history of European autobiography before the 19th century. The key to Morelli's personal life was the death of his father when he was only three years old. Though his mother survived her husband, she remarried and he felt that he was abandoned by her. The strongest attachment of his youth was to his sister Mea, who gave him some of the emotional sustenance he did not receive from his parents. But Mea died, quite young, in childbirth, and Giovanni had to make his own way in the world. His life seemed to be a series of misfortunes that, in their number and magnitude, remind us of Job in the Old Testament. He fell in love with a Florentine girl from his neighbourhood, but her father forbade the marriage. So he married another girl, not for love but for social and economic motives; and his emotional needs remained unsatisfied. He was very

happy when a son Alberto was born to him, but that joy turned to intense grief when the boy died at the age of nine. In his diary, Giovanni described his feelings of loss, and his efforts to recover from his misery. On the first anniversary of the boy's death, Giovanni prayed to the Virgin and the saints for solace. Falling asleep, he had a dream in which he saw his dead son, accompanied by St. Catherine. The boy told him that he was in paradise, and that Giovanni should not grieve for him. On waking up, Giovanni experienced a profound sense of relief.

Giovanni Morelli's diary provides concrete evidence of a characteristic Florentine trait, not found commonly elsewhere: to express openly and freely one's emotions, likes and dislikes, loves and hates, passions and prejudices. In this private realm of inner experience, Florentines made a particular, unique statement, just as they did in their economic and social relations, in their politics, in their piety, in their poetry and their painting.

·CIUITAS· FLORENTIE

THE CITY STRADDLING THE ARNO

In 1584 the Olivetan monk Stefano Bonsignori drew a map of the city of Florence (1) dedicated to the Grand Duke Francesco Medici – who, seeing it, would ''be flattered to realize himself prince and king of a city so noble and so illustrious as to need no extolling.'' In this map (as indeed in the city as it still is today) one can discern the various stages of Florence's development up to the period of the *granducato*. In the middle is the square Roman colony founded by Caesar in the spring of 59 B.C., during the *ludi florales* (whence possibly the city's name, *Florentia*). This is the ancient heart of the city, the forum which would later become the Mercato Vecchio.

When the city was undergoing a process of urban improvement in the 19th century (1885-95) and numerous changes were occurring, a map (3) was drawn, based on the official building survey (made for fiscal purposes) of 1427. The original Roman square expanded in all directions, beyond the original perimeters. For instance, the Via Torta (curving round the outside of the amphitheater) and the site of the church of San Lorenzo reached so far as the Arno. By the second century the town had already grown more or less into the structure the commune walls were built around in the 12th century, at least as far as the area north of the Arno was concerned. This growth had been determined by the axes linking the consular roads and by the division of land in the countryside (at an angle of some 45° in relation to the

urban grid), and expansion continued along roughly the same pattern in the Middle Ages. In the early Middle Ages the city contracted, the Byzantine walls returning to the original Roman square. The Carolingian fortifications (ninth-tenth century) took in suburbs to the south, towards the Arno, but in the north did not include the Baptistery complex, Santa Reparata, or the bishop's palace (for political reasons); the walls erected at the instigation of the Countess Matilda (1078) enclosed both the Roman colonial area and the Carolingian additions. However, the really significant development, reflecting the city's growth in importance, happened in the following century, with the building of the first commun-

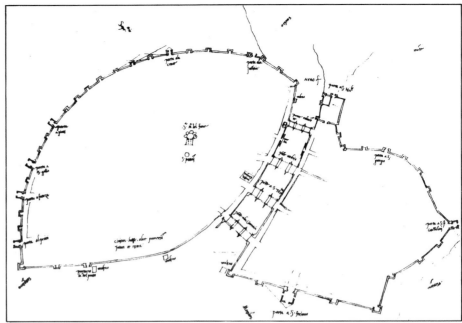

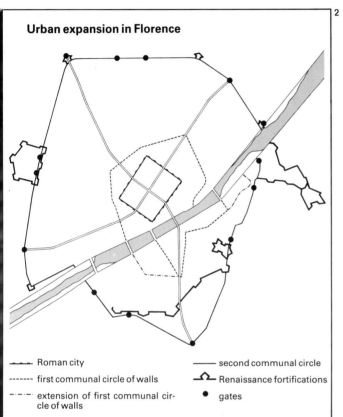

Urban expansion in Florence

Legend:
- —▲— Roman city
- ----- first communal circle of walls
- —·—· extension of first communal circle of walls
- —— second communal circle
- ⬟ Renaissance fortifications
- ● gates

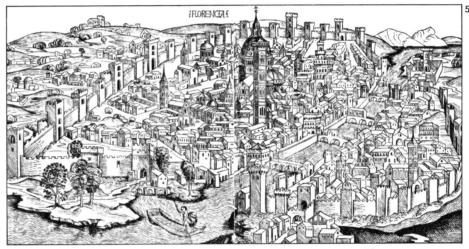

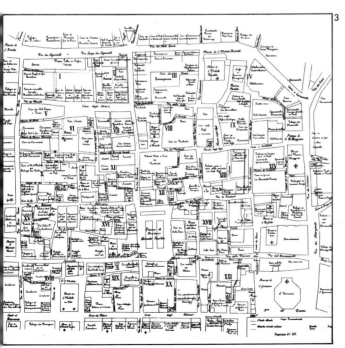

al circle of walls (actually the fifth since the city's foundation). Erected over two years (1173-75), these walls took in the *borghi* (suburbs) that had grown up along the streets leading out of the city, and extended south of the Arno. This section of the city south of the river was then further expanded in the middle of the 13th century, the new fortifications being built with materials removed from private towers (whose height had been restricted "for greater public security," as Giovanni Villani records).

During the prosperous, turbulent period of the commune Florence also continued to expand north of the Arno. For instance the two great medieval monastic churches of Santa Croce and Santa Maria Novella (the one Franciscan, the other Dominican) were outwith the walls. A new circle of walls was begun in 1284. Work was more than once interrupted, but was eventually finished in 1333. The engraving by M. Wohlgemut (5), included in the Nuremberg humanist doctor Hartmann Schedel's *Liber Chronicorum* of 1493, shows this second circle of communal walls. They were an ambitious construction, leaving large areas still to be built up, as can be seen in Bonsignori's map. The population had increased, but shortly afterwards (1348) came the Black Death, which decimated Florence: the population was not to reach the same size again until the 19th century. All the urban changes of the late Middle Ages, the Renaissance, and the *granducato* occurred within this second circle of communal walls. A drawing by Baldassarre Peruzzi (4) dating from 1520 sketches the outline of the walled area on both banks of the Arno, with four bridges crossing the river. This was just as it had been in the 14th century. When the Medici pope Clement VII opposed Emperor Charles V, the imperial German mercenaries took and sacked Rome (1527), prompting the Florentines to rebel against the Medici and reestablish a short-lived republic. Michelangelo was put in charge of the city defenses, and he built bastions in front of the medieval gates and a hastily constructed salient angle on the hill of San Miniato. After a siege lasting 11 months (1529-30) the Medici returned. Alessandro de' Medici's Fortezza da Basso (1534) was a fortress intended to intimidate his newly chastened subjects rather than to impress enemies outside. Later Ferdinando I commissioned the Belevedere fort (1590-95) from Bernardo Buontalenti (known as Bernardino delle Girandole).

The great families

Streets and houses in Florence around 1530, as seen in a painting by Francesco Ubertini known as Bachiacca in Amsterdam's Rijksmuseum. Building activity in Florence enjoyed a period of renewal during the 13th century, when the economic boom enabled the old wooden buildings to be replaced by stone ones. The typical medieval Florentine house, which was inhabited by a family community, developed out of the working area situated on the ground floor; this comprised a vast, vaulted room used as a shop, a workshop or a warehouse, Above, another room with the same ground area acted as bedroom, living room and kitchen, rarely separated by wooden partitions. Sometimes the kitchen was arranged in an overhanging, box-like extension in order to lessen the risk of chimney fires. With the formation of a new family nucleus, the house was enlarged by a further storey, with the result that the building developed into a tall and narrow tower-like structure.

"The history of Florence, even at its most democratic, remains in large measure the history of its principal families ..." This statement, by the distinguished English historian of medieval Italy, Philip Jones, provides the focus for this chapter, and a major theme for this book. This emphasis upon the aristocratic, elitist elements in Florentine experience contradicts a traditional view which held that, in its formative stage, the medieval city was largely populated by peasants seeking freedom from their servile condition, and that it was a "bourgeois" community that ultimately conquered the feudal world outside its walls.

Though an elitist interpretation of urban experience is not palatable to our age of "mass society," so hostile to aristocratic traditions and values, it is supported by massive evidence, both visual and documentary. The great *palazzi* that dominate the Via Maggio and the Borgo degli Albizzi, or that surround the Piazza de' Peruzzi, are surviving testimonials to the great *casate* that built them between the 14th and 16th centuries. The few truncated remnants of the medieval towers that can still be seen near the Ponte Vecchio remind us that, around 1200, the city contained some 200 of these fortified structures, some as high as those surviving in San Gimignano and Bologna. The great monastic basilicas of Santo Spirito, Santa Croce and Santa Maria Novella are lined with family chapels containing the tombs and the coats of arms of long dead members of the Bardi, Tornaquinci, Cavalcanti and Rucellai families. Giovanni Villani, who wrote the most comprehensive record of Florence's early centuries, described in great detail the deeds of the city's dominant families. The vast compilations of ancient documents in the

Archivio di Stato and the Biblioteca Nazionale are filled with references to the great *casate:* property transactions, litigations, records of births, marriages and deaths. At every moment of Florence's history, from the 1100s to the 18th century and beyond, the great families controlled a major portion of the city's wealth, dominated its social order and political life, and funded the cultural activities which gave Florence its worldwide renown.

The origins

The precise origins of the oldest Florentine *casate* are unknown, for they go back to those poorly documented centuries after the Germanic invasions. When, during the Renaissance, genealogists began to construct the early history of these families, some traced their origins to the ancient Romans, others to the Lombards, still others (the Medici, for example) to Frankish knights who had accompanied Charlemagne on his journey to Tuscany at the end of the eighth century. Most of these legends surrounding social origins are fictitious creations, though a few of these families may have descended from Lombard ancestors. Even though documentation is lacking, it can be sugested that most ancient urban *casate,* like the Uberti and the Buondelmonti, were descendants of Tuscan noble families with large estates in the *contado,* and were linked to the ecclesiastical and secular powers that had ruled Tuscany since Carolingian times. These *casate* had been established in Florence long before the rise of the commune in the early 12th century; they formed the nucleus of that group of *maiores* who initially participated with the bishops and the secular powers (representatives of the counts of Tuscany) in the governance of the city and later, by a process that is very scantily documented, created that political association, the commune, which supplanted those older authorities.

When the consular commune was established sometime in the early 1100s, its leadership was recruited from ancient noble houses – the Uberti, Giandonati, Visdomini, Buondelmonti – and also from families of non noble origins. whose members had migrated to Florence some decades earlier. The surviving documents tell us little about the origins of these families; some may have descended from serfs in the post-Carolingian period. By the 11th century, however, they had gained possession of the rights to substantial blocks of rural property, and with this

solid economic base, they moved to Florence, buying urban real estate, building houses and towers, while retaining their possessions in the *contado*. These families migrated to the city from every part of the Tuscan countryside. The earliest Caponsacchi came to Florence in the 11th century from the Fiesole area, establishing themselves next to the Mercato Vecchio. The Scali created their urban base around the monastery of Santa Trinita, having moved there from the zone of Calenzano sometime before 1100. Representative of a later wave of prosperous, landed migrants from the *contado* was the Medici family. Originally from the Mugello district north of the city, the first Medici settled in Florence sometime in the late 12th century,

though it was not until 1216 that one Bonagiunta de' Medici was named in a Florentine document. Throughout the 13th century, Medici moved to the city, establishing their residences near the Mercato Vecchio and the church of San Lorenzo.

The ancient noble families, and the later migrants of non noble origins retained their links with the rural world from which they had come. They retained their estates in the *contado*, their patronage rights in local churches and monasteries, and their connections with the inhabitants of the rural *borghi* and *castelli* in their ancestral zones. They customarily established themselves in Florentine neighbourhoods that were geographically closest to their *contado* bases. There they built or bought towers and houses, creating

Chests (examples from the early 15th century, above, and from the first quarter of the 16th century, left, in the Museo di Palazzo Davanzati, Florence), tables, seats and beds formed the essential equipment for Florentine houses between the Middle Ages and the Renaissance. The furniture was not always owned by its users: it could be loaned, as is verified by the 1424 statute of the guild of Florentine second-hand dealers. From the 14th century on, the proper use of fireplaces (opposite above, the fireplace in the Sala dei Pappagalli in the Palazzo Davanzati, which dates from the end of the 14th century) led to the transformation of the home: wooden dividing walls were replaced by stone ones, while fireplaces and stoves were installed in many of the rooms, thereby influencing the architecture of Florentine palaces during the 15th and 16th centuries, a typical example of which (the Palazzo Medici on the Via Larga, built by Michelozzo Michelozzi for Cosimo the Elder) can be seen in the illustration opposite.

nuclei of possessions, and networks of clients, retainers and supporters who were either brought into the city from their rural bases, or recruited among the residents of their neighbourhood. Their motives for coming into the city were primarily economic. Population growth in the countryside had created pressures on local resources; the city, with its burgeoning population and real estate market, and its expanding commercial and industrial base, offered opportunities for wealth and fortune.

"A lust of ... dominion"

From the countryside, these families brought into the city their social institutions and customs,

and their life style. Above all, they brought with them a strong sense of family identity and solidarity, including such legal practices as property held in common by heirs (*fideicommisum*). They maintained the military traditions of their feudal past, with its emphasis upon knightly status and upon warfare as an honourable occupation. The spirit of the vendetta was yet another social tradition which these *casate* brought into Florence: the source of so much urban conflict throughout the medieval and Renaissance period. And, as Philip Jones has pointed out, the noble families in particular carried into the city "a lust of power and dominion" (Machiavelli, *Discourses*, I, 5).

The participation of Florence's urban aristocracy in mercantile and industrial enterprises did not restrain or limit the violence which characterized its social relationships. In the city, as in the country, the survival of families depended upon the possession of fortified dwellings, and of military resources both material and human. For mutual protection, Florentine aristocratic families banded together into "tower societies," associations of kinsmen from several *casate* who lived in the same neighbourhood, and

Details of paintings by Ambrogio Lorenzetti (above), Fra Angelico (above left) and Gentile da Fabriano (left) show the interiors of bedrooms during the 14th and 15th centuries. This period saw the introduction of hitherto unknown comforts. The bare wooden boards of the medieval bed were softened by a thin mattress filled with cotton, wool or horsehair. As protection against the cold, coverlets filled with goose feathers were introduced, whilst sheets of linen or hempen cloth were a common feature. The platform surrounding the bed consisted of chests used both as seats and as containers for storing linen. Opposite, a corner of the living room under the stairs acts as the workplace for a woman spinning wool in this detail of a fresco by Giotto.

who were linked together by bonds of friendship, marriage and, frequently, economic partnership. Of central importance for these societies were the towers, owned jointly by the members, in which they assembled to defend themselves, or to attack their enemies. Charters pertaining to these societies have survived from the 1170s, but they had been in existence for some years before that. These organizations played a key role in the bitter struggles among the city's leading families during the last decades of the 12th century, and the first half of the 13th (the dugento).

The motives underlying these struggles which convulsed the city, and earned it a reputation as one of the most violent and faction prone in Italy, are very complex. Some scholars have interpreted these conflicts as originating in class differences, specifically between the old feudal aristocracy and its "bourgeois" rivals. This view, however, ignores the fact that noble and non noble families had been integrated into a single elite, bound together by marriage, and by similar economic and political interests. Motives of honour and prestige played an important part in these struggles; through the institution of the vendetta, a quarrel between two men over a trifling incident could easily spread to involve their entire families, and to years of mutual killing and maiming. In this intensely competitive society, men fought for wealth, social status and political power. Their struggles inevitably involved their kinsmen, their friends and clients, their retainers, their neighbours.

According to an anonymous chronicler, the division of Florence into Guelf and Ghibelline factions could be traced to an incident at a wedding banquet in 1216. A dispute broke out between two guests and in the ensuing fracas, *messer* Buondelmonte de' Buondelmonti wounded *messer* Oddo Arrighi de' Fifanti with a knife. *Messer* Oddo belonged to a faction led by the Uberti, Lamberti and Amidei families. To prevent this quarrel becoming a full-scale vendetta, the Uberti party offered to make peace with the Buondelmonti and their allies, the agreement to be sealed by a marriage between *messer* Buondelmonte and an Amidei girl. However, the wife of *messer* Forese Donati reproached the young knight for his craven behaviour, in accepting a bride to avoid a vendetta. She offered him her own beautiful daughter as his bride. When *messer* Buondel-

monte accepted her proposal, the enraged Uberti faction met to plot its revenge. *Messer* Mosca de' Lamberti favoured extreme action and his advice was followed. As *messer* Buondelmonte rode with his bride across the Ponte Vecchio on Easter Sunday 1216, a group of conspirators ambushed him at the site of the statue of Mars, and left him lying dead in the street. In Giovanni Villani's words, "The death of *messer* Buondelmonte was the reason behind the accursed division of Florence into Guelf and Ghibelline factions, and marked the beginning of it (…) Some supported the Buondelmonti and so became Guelfs, while others went with the Uberti, who were at the head of the Ghibellines, and much evil and ruination befell our city as a consequence …"

Writing a century after that event, Villani's account of the rise of the Guelf and Ghibelline parties, as a consequence of a single vendetta, is too simplistic. The Buondelmonti assassination was only one incident in a broader pattern of political polarization in Florence during the 13th century. It does illustrate the familial foundation

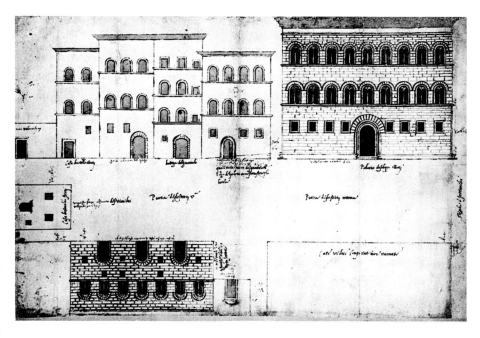

of the factions which, by a process that is not well documented, eventually embraced all of the important *casate* in the city. By the mid 13th century, the two parties had emerged as fully mature associations, with their constitutions and officials, their treasuries, their distinctive emblems, and their ideologies. The Ghibellines, the imperial party, included the majority of the old noble houses with feudal associations (Uberti, Malespini, the counts of Gangalandi). While the pro-papal Guelf party also had its noble contingent (Buondelmonti, Pazzi, Giandonati), its ranks were filled with those non noble *casate* that were deeply involved in the city's mercantile life and, in particular, in papal finance. But a family's decision to join the Guelf or the Ghibelline party was made not so much for economic or ideological motives as for social reasons. The most important factor was the family's particular social network, and the alliances it had previously forged with other families in its neighbourhood. The bonds of *parentado* among the Uberti, Lamberti and Amidei, all living closely together near the church of San Stefano a Ponte, were the critical elements in their association with the Ghibelline party.

The familial foundation of Florentine political life throughout the dugento provides a focus to a history that seems so chaotic. Guelfs and Ghibellines vied for control of the city, allying with their counterparts in other central Italian

This drawing by Benedetto da Maiano (above) shows the Piazza Strozzi with the grandiose palazzo of the merchant Filippo, begun by Benedetto da Maiano in 1489, and, on the opposite side, the Palazzo dello Strozzino, built by Michelozzo and Giuliano da Maiano between 1458 and 1465.
The former is regarded as the finest example of a Florentine Renaissance palazzo. Florence was in the forefront of architecture at the time: it was there that the prototype of the noble palazzo was first introduced, which later spread throughout Italy. Between the 14th and the 15th century the whole appearance of the city was changed as it became embellished with new and impressive buildings. One of many examples of this phenomenon is provided by the Piazza de' Peruzzi, a glimpse of which can be seen on the left in a 19th-century drawing. A widespread feature of architectural exteriors was rustication (opposite), which had a purely decorative function, being used to create interesting plays of light.

towns, and fighting alongside them and their German (Ghibelline) or French (Guelf) allies, to establish their dominion in Florence and in Tuscany. With the death of Emperor Frederick II in 1250, the Guelfs gained control of the city, forcing the Ghibellines into exile. A decade later, after the defeat of the Guelf army at Montaperti (1260), it was the turn of the Ghibellines to occupy Florence and to wreak vengeance upon their Guelf enemies. But their triumph was short-lived, and in 1267 the Guelfs returned to the city in triumph. Though Ghibelline partisans were later allowed into Florence during brief periods of truce, they never again established themselves as a viable political force. The extreme bitterness of this partisan struggle was dramatically demonstrated by the wholesale destruction of Guelf property in city and countryside, by the Ghibellines (1260-66), and a comparable wave of demolition of Ghibelline towers and houses by the vengeful Guelfs when they returned to Florence in 1266. The houses of the Uberti were razed to the ground. Many Ghibellines left the city permanently to live in exile; those who returned had to suffer the loss of much of their property, the prospect of being confined at the whim of their conquerors, and the stigma of having belonged to a defeated and disgraced faction.

The old aristocracy and the popolo

This systematic degradation and impoverishment of the Ghibelline families transformed the character of the city's elite, which had lost an important segment of its ancient feudal element. By the end of the 13th century, this elite contained a larger proportion of families of more recent origins, whose fortunes were largely, though not exclusively, mercantile. The old coalition of aristocratic *casate* had broken down after more than a century of internal strife. Another challenge to the power and influence of the old noble families emerged gradually during the 13th century: in the rise of the *popolo* which first came to power in the 1250s (the regime of the *primo popolo*), and then after a temporary eclipse, created a new political order in the 1280s, the government of the guilds. These guilds were organizations of merchants, industrialists, bankers, lawyers, and other professional and craft groups. They had grown steadily in size,

wealth and political influence, particularly after 1250, parallelling the expansion of the city's population and economy. The leaders of the *popolo* were recruited from families (the Medici, Strozzi, Rucellai, Peruzzi, etc.) that were very active in trade, banking and industry. The rank and file included petty merchants, shopkeepers and artisans who belonged to the middle echelons of the city's social and economic order.

Though many *popolani* had been involved in the factional struggles between Ghibelline and Guelf, as partisans of the Guelf faction, they were increasingly opposed to the incessant violence arising from these conflicts. While recognizing the value of a military caste whose members, trained in warfare, could fight for the commune, they resented the arrogant and lawless behaviour of these prepotent individuals. One measure designed to limit the power of these families focused upon their towers, which were limited to a height of 30 meters (98 feet). But the most dramatic action taken by the government of the *popolo,* which had been established in 1282, was the enactment of the Ordinances of Justice in 1293. Designated by the

Details from Domenico Ghirlandaio's Visitation *(above), Andrea di Bonaiuto's* The Church Militant and Triumphant *(right) and* St. Francis Reviving a Young Boy of the Spini House *(far right), also by Ghirlandaio. In his* Relazione *to the Venetian* Consiglio dei Pregadi, *written in 1527, Marco Foscari says: "In Florence nobody calls himself 'noble,' but everyone, high and low, is called 'citizen.' And because the only governors were those who held the reins of power, the nobles were obliged to enter a guild. The fact that they all call themselves 'citizen' and that they are involved in some guild is a matter of universal satisfaction to the poor and the lowly because it makes them feel equal to the great..."*

A Florentine citizen at table, as seen in a 14th-century Florentine miniature. Below, detail of a fresco by Giotto in the Scrovegni chapel at Padua. A great deal of wine was consumed in Florence, both at home and in hostelries. It appears that in the San Giovanni quarter of Florence alone, no fewer than 62 taverns and 55 wineshops prospered. For family consumption it was the norm to buy no more than one cogno per person per year, which amounts to roughly 400 liters per person.

Ordinances as "magnate," by virtue of their penchant for violence, were 150 families in the city and *contado,* who were thereby deprived of the right to hold major offices in the commune, and who were also subject to special judicial penalties. Each male member of a magnate family had to swear an oath of obedience to the commune, and to provide a surety of 2,000 lire that he would keep the peace. Kinsmen were liable for any fines levied against a magnate. For acts of violence against *popolani,* magnates could be penalized by heavy fines and in extreme cases, by death and the despoliation of their property. The famous Ordinances have been interpreted, by Salvemini and others, as a consequence of a class conflict between a noble landed aristocracy (*magnati*) and a capitalist bourgeoisie (*popolani*). Nicola Ottokar has shown, however, that there were no significant economic or social differences between families designated as *magnati* and *popolani.* It would perhaps be more accurate to interpret the Ordinances as a product of a conflict within Florence's ruling elite, in which one potent coalition of families (*popolani*) sought to weaken a rival group (*magnati*) by keeping them out of office, and by subjecting them to severe and discriminatory judicial penalties.

As a youth, Dante Alighieri (1267-1321) witnessed these events and in his great poem he testifies to the importance, in this society, of both family and party bonds. When he encountered, in the *Inferno* (canto X, 42), the imposing figure of Farinata degli Uberti, the leader of the Florentine Ghibellines at the battle of Montaperti asked the poet:

Say what ancestors were thine.

Dante told him about his family and its party allegiance, and Farinata commented:

Fiercely were they
Adverse to me, my party and the blood
From whence I sprang ...

Dante placed those infamous characters who had betrayed their kinsmen and their party in the last circle of the *Inferno* (canto XXXII). The poet's encounter in *Paradiso* (canto XVI) with the founder of the Alighieri family, Cacciaguida, provides him with the opportunity to describe his own origins with these words:

Say then, my honour'd stem! what ancestors
Were those you sprang from, and what years
were mark'd
In your first childhood?

Cacciaguida tells him that he had been knighted
by the German emperor, Conrad III, whom he
accompanied on the second crusade (1147-50).

Cacciaguida identifies the noble families
which, in his lifetime, had formed the city's social
and political elite: the Ughi, Lamberti, Arriguc-
ci, Amidei, Fifanti, Caponsacchi, Soldanieri. By
Dante's own time, many of these *casate* had died
out, or had been exiled, suffered economic
decline and social derogation. The political

Right, the interior of a pharmacy, as shown in a panel on Giotto's campanile. Below, a row of shops with their characteristic canopy roofs near the Ponte a Santa Trinita in around 1561, as depicted in a fresco by Giovanni Stradano in the Palazzo Vecchio. Workshops were used both for selling and working in. The honesty of shopkeepers was carefully monitored by the guilds, who forbade the establishment of monopolies when goods were in short supply in order to keep prices down. The guilds sometimes imposed the use of brand marks on woollen cloth, which recorded the price at source of the goods as well as the price paid by the shopkeeper and the retail price; they also controlled weights and measures. The guild of doctors and druggists possessed scales of every sort, both great and small, for the weighing of cloves, nutmegs and saffron; these scales had to be checked every three months and compared to the official scales of the commune, with traders being obliged to weigh and sift their wares with scales and sieves provided by the guild. There was a very dense network of shops. In Benedetto Dei's Cronaca Fiorentina, *written in 1472 when there were some 70,000 inhabitants in the city, there is a series of statistics illustrating the importance of the city's trading activities. In that year Florence contained: 270 shops belonging to the wool guild, 83 belonging to the silk guild, 33 large banks "possessing a table and carpet outside," 84 shops belonging to woodcarvers and workers in wood inlay, 66 druggist's shops, 54 stonecutter's and sculptor's shops, 70 butcher's shops, eight shops belonging to sellers of game and poultry, 30 shops belonging to workers in gold leaf and silver wire, and 44 gold- and silversmith's and jeweller's shops.*

"ONE HUNDRED AND FIFTY TOWERS BELONGING TO PRIVATE CITIZENS ..."

1

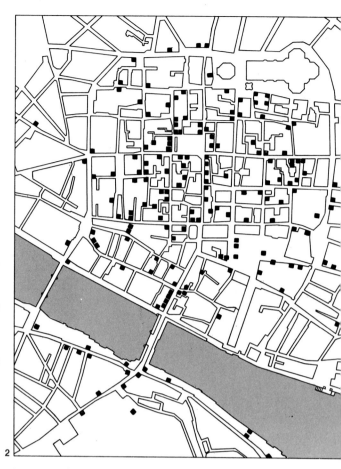

2

3

4

"And in the said small city there were soon about one hundred and fifty towers belonging to private citizens, each one hundred and twenty *braccia,* [old measure used in several Italian cities; this measure varied slightly from city to city] not counting the towers on the walls ... And because of the height of the many towers then in Florence, from outside, both at a distance and close to, it was said to be the finest and most splendid city of its region."

Thus wrote the Florentine Lapo da Castiglionchio to his son. Lapo was a prominent Guelf towards the end of the 14th century, and was the first to see his houses burned down, and to have to flee from the rioting Ciompi (22 June 1378). However, by then the age of private towers (at least, towers 120 *braccia* high) was past. The new democratic constitution of 20 October 1250 (as Giovanni Villani records, "when the people had taken control over *Signoria* and state") forbade towers to exceed 50 *braccia* in height. Passed with the aim of preserving political stability, this law was put into effect between 1250 and 1258, at the height of the Guelf party's power. Two years before (1248), the Ghibellines had had the upper hand, and had knocked down their opponents' towers. Villani mentions the dangerously hasty way these towers were destroyed: "One of the Guelf towers to be demolished was a particularly tall, beautiful one in Piazza di San Giovanni at the top of the Corso degli Adimari, called the torre del Guardamorto (*morto,* dead). It was so named because San Giovanni was where all the dead used to be buried. The Ghibellines shored up the base of the said tower in such a way that, when the props were burnt, it would fall on top of the church of San Giovanni. But as it pleased God, out of reverence and through a miracle of the Blessed St. John, the tower – which was one hundred and twenty *braccia* high – seemed as it fell to shun this holy church, and turned, falling onto the *piazza,* at which all Florence marvelled ..." The shortening of the towers in 1250-58 was followed by further turbulence, and more Guelf towers, *palazzi* and houses were demolished when the Ghibellines regained power after the Battle of Montaperti (1260). The precise number is known to us from a list of claims for damages from the commune when, after yet another reversal of government, the Guelfs were once again in power: 59 towers, 47 *palazzi,* 198 houses, nine workshops, ten *tiratoi* (stretching sheds for woollen cloth), and a warehouse. A third of a century later, the section *De Turribus Exquadrandis* in Giano della Bella's Ordinances of Justice (1293) outlawed the practice of erecting such high edifices. The obsession with towers was finally at an end. The number 150 quoted by Lapo da Castiglionchio tallies with the number recorded as having been demolished. At the end of the 11th century mention is made of no more than five; 35 are recorded around 1180 (though historians believe this figure to be less than a third of the actual total).

The map showing the distribution of towers between the mid 12th century and the mid 13th century (2) demonstrates that the majority was in the oldest part of the city, around the Mercato Vecchio, between the Baptistery and the Arno. These curious buildings (known to have been common also in other cities) belonged to the nobility: they were strongholds, at a time when security and power depended on individual strength. However, there were other motives in building such towers – the memory among the recently urbanized nobility of the towers of their feudal castles, as well as the simple desire for show and ostentation. To begin with at least, the towers were not inhabited (they only became so when they were altered and made smaller in the 14th century). They were places of refuge, connected to the adjacent houses by means of passages, to avoid people having to go into the street. In some cases the owner was a single individual, in others a "tower syndicate." These syndicates, controlled by legislation (dating back to 1137 at least), consisted of groups of aristocratic families who were linked by family ties (*consorterie*) and united by the common purpose of owning a tower. We known of one tower in Piazza di Orsanmichele, for instance, having one side giving onto the square, and the houses of three different "associates" abutting onto the other sides, each with separate access to it. These syndicates then tended to enclose whole blocks with towers – each with its own walls, so the destruction of one would leave others still intact. The artist's impression of such a complex (1) shows how wooden galleries were built on the inside and covered balconies on the outside. The external balconies were used in the feuding we read so much about in medieval chronicles. The regular "scaffold holes," still visible in the towers that have survived, were for the beams that supported these balconies (8). Town planners have noted that certain alleys in the old center which traverse the original Roman *insulae* were made to separate sections of single blocks belonging to different *consorterie*. The variety and picturesque appeal of the towers that still stand today are due more to changes over the years than to any intrinsic architectural value: the walls were solid and severe, with only occasional, narrow openings. The straight or slightly curved door lintel was often topped by a pointed arch of dressed stone, and the windows sometimes feature a similar design. Of the examples given here the first (3), with two ornamental lion's heads, is the tower of the Amidei (known as *La Bigoncia*) at Por Santa Maria. Not far from this tower, at the head of the Ponte Vecchio, on Easter morning 1216, members of the Amidei faction murdered Buondelmonte dei Buondelmonti (who had been betrothed against his will to an Amidei girl, but had then married a Donati). This murder led to the birth of the Guelf and Ghibelline parties, headed respectively by the Donati and the Amidei. The Amidei fought with the Sienese at the Battle of Mon-

8

taperti. Fighting for the Florentines at the same battle were many members of the Gherardini family, whose tower (4) stands in Via Lambertesca. Only two citizens spoke out against the war with Siena, which ended in the bloody defeat of Montaperti: one of these was Cece da' Gherardini. His words cost him a fine; he paid and spoke again; yet again he spoke up, and yet again he paid up. It was only with the threat of the death penalty on the fourth such occasion that he kept his peace.

The tower of the Alberti di Catenaia, the family of the great Leon Battista Alberti, stands between Via de' Benci and Borgo Santa Croce (5). The base of this tower later acquired an elegant *loggetta* with columns, the capitals of which are decorated with crossed chains, the family crest. Guelfs, the Alberti di Catenaia (*catena,* chain) were banished during the reprisals after the Ciompi Revolution, and only a few returned under Cosimo de' Medici. Another Guelf family was that of the Foresi, who produced a number of *priori* and *gonfalonieri*. Their tower in Via Porta Rossa (6) stands beside their house, from which it is, however, separated by a narrow gap. Finally the tower of the Barbadori (7), another Guelf family that produced priors and *gonfalonieri,* stands on the south bank of the Arno, in the Borgo San Jacopo. Like those of the Alberti and the Foresi, it was reduced in height to 50 *braccia* to comply with the law. Though German mines destroyed most of Borgo San Jacopo in 1944, they proved unable to bring down this sturdy, tall tower.

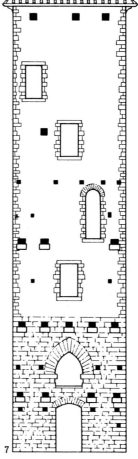

5

6

7

This detail of a marriage feast (left) from the series of paintings by Botticelli dedicated to Nastagio degli Onesti's Boccaccioesque novel recalls the wedding celebrations of the Florentine nobility during the second half of the 15th century. Shared political and economic interests provided the basis for those family links that in Florence ensured the formation of an elite composed of both nobles and non nobles. In fact, the family was of fundamental relevance to the city's political life and explains much of the factionalism that plagued it. Marriage was therefore of prime importance to parents, together with the allied problems of the dowry (which was an indication of the family's wealth and social status), the health of their daughter (whose duty it was to give birth to numerous healthy children) and also her physical appearance. It was with these considerations in mind that Lucrezia Tornabuoni wrote to her husband Piero de' Medici describing Clarice Orsini, the prospective bride of their son Lorenzo: "Hair tending towards the red, a face that is a little on the round side, although her neck is slender; we were unable to see her bosom because the girls here are completely covered up, but it seems to have good features. She has long, slim hands." Below, a noble wedding, as seen in a small panel painting attributed to Sano di Pietro, in a tax record from 1473, preserved in Siena's Archivio di Stato. Opposite, detail from the Story of Patient Griselda, *an anonymous 15th-century painting in the National Gallery, London.*

upheavals of the 13th century had contributed to the decline of several of these once illustrious families, but Dante also saw them as victims of the social dislocations resulting from the massive immigration of lowly people (*gente nuova*) into the city from the countryside:

But then the citizen's blood, that now is mix'd
From Campi and Certaldo and Fighine,
Ran purely through the last mechanic's veins.
O how much better were it, that these people
Were neighbours to you; and that at Galluzzo
and at Trespiano ye should have your boundary;
Than to have them within, and bear the stench
of Aguglione's hind, and Signa's …
(*Paradiso*, XVI, 49-54)

Other writers of the trecento, Boccaccio and Franco Sacchetti among them, made similar derogatory comments about the rustics who had displaced the ancient urban nobility and had corrupted the city's ancient traditions and values.

The displacement of old families by new ones in Florence was a continuous process, in which demographic as well as economic and political forces were at work. Many smaller houses died out in the male line, while others suffered economic losses in Florence's volatile economy. Those losses threatened their political and social status, since these poor families were no longer able to contract good marriages nor retain their politcal influence in the city. The bitter struggle between the Black and the White factions (c. 1300) also contributed to the realignment of

Florence's social order. The leading familes of the triumphant Black faction, led by the Donati, used their influence with the *podestà, messer* Cante de' Gabrielli of Gubbio (1302), who passed sentence of confiscation, exile and death on 600 members of the White party, including Dante Alighieri and Petrarch's father.

As in the Guelf-Ghibelline conflict a century before, these partisan struggles between Blacks and Whites were as strongly influenced by personal and family hatreds, as by political considerations. Describing the origins of the Black-White struggle, the chronicler Dino Compagni wrote that the Donati were angered by the pretensions of the upstart Cerchi (leaders of the White faction), who had bought a palace in their neighbourhood from the ancient feudal house of the Conti Guidi. The Donati launched an attack against their rivals, and thereby plunged the whole city into civil war. Stories of family vendettas, culled from the private memoirs of the period, reveal the intensity and longevity of these feuds. The lawyer Donato Velluti (c. 1370) discovered among his family papers the record of his father's participation in a vendetta against the

Mannelli family. That feud had begun in 1267 when Gino di Donato Velluti had been assassinated by a Mannelli. This murder was avenged by Donato's father Berto who, together with a group of kinsmen, killed Lippo Mannelli in 1295. Although the commune forced the two families to make a peace treaty, their mutual hatred did not die out until 50 years later, when Donato arranged for the cancellation of a judicial penalty against one of the Mannelli. In June 1350, Luca di Totto da Panzano, scion of the noble house of the Firidolfi, wrote in his memoirs: "I went to Prato to kill Carlo di Baldovinetto Gherardini." Luca and his kinsmen and clients attacked Gherardini and his allies in a parish church. After setting fire to the church, Luca's band of men fought with their enemies until sunset, "watched by more than 5,000 people, both from Florence and the *contado* ..."

The Black Death of 1348 wrought far more damage on the city's great families than all their vendettas over the centuries had done. The plague killed between one third and two fifths of the city's population, which had fallen from 90,000 in 1340 (the date of an earlier epidemic) to

no more than 50,000 in 1352. Some families lost more than half of their male relatives; Donato Velluti counted 19 dead and only 12 survivors among his male kinsfolk. Writing in 1374, Foligno di Conte de' Medici appealed to his heirs, "do not merely conserve your possessions, but conserve the heritage we acquired in times past; we are a great state, and would have been greater still, but we are declining through the plague which is robbing us of good men, which we used to have in such abundance." Many plague victims from the city's leading families died without heirs, their property bequeathed to convents and to the city's charitable institutions. The pestilence of 1348, and the later visitations of 1363, 1374, 1383 and 1399-1400, to list only the major epidemics of the late trecento, changed not only the demographic but also the economic configuration of the city.

Not only had many of the great *casate* declined in size and wealth after the Black Death; they also suffered a loss of political status. One result of the mid-century demographic and economic crisis was an upward surge of men from obscure and lowly origins into the upper echelons of the

As can be seen in this detail (above) from the Adimari Chest, painted during the 15th century, women's dresses for important occasions featured long trains. These trains became the target of clerical disapproval, as well as attracting the attention of the lawmakers, who sought to limit their length. St. Bernardino of Siena accused the train of making women look like animals "muddy in winter, dusty in summer." It was an appendage that seemed to him to be "a stupid woman's broom, an infernal censer." The penalties for those transgressing the sumptuary laws involved large fines laid down in special registers, such as the one shown here on the right, formerly in the Archivio di Stato, Florence.

city's guilds and business firms, and into the *Signoria,* the supreme executive of the commune. Not since the 1280s and 1290s, when the guild commune was first established, had so many of these *gente nuova* moved into the city's economic and political elite. They competed with, and often pushed aside, members of the old aristocracy, who did not qualify in the scrutinies for the major civic offices, and who withdrew from active roles in the entrepreneurial world. The low point – in power, prestige and morale – for the great Florentine families was reached at the time of the Ciompi Revolution, when the city was governed (July-August 1378) by the Florentine cloth workers and other salaried labourers. For a brief moment these workers were in a position to rule over and to inflict punishment on their former masters.

Although the Ciompi were defeated (September 1378), their regime was replaced by one controlled by lesser guildsmen, who were hostile to the great Guelf aristocratic families which had dominated the city's economic and political life for more than a century. Between 1378 and 1382,

many members of these families lived abroad in exile, their property confiscated, their families dispersed. Some, like Buonaccorso Pitti, participated in conspiracies against the commune; others attempted to survive in Florence by maintaining a low profile and avoiding any involvement in politics.

The consolidation of aristocratic power

A revolution in January 1382 destroyed the guild regime and created the conditions for the restoration of the power and prestige of the great families which, in the subsequent years, consolidated their position as the dominant group in Florentine society and politics. Never again was the supremacy of this aristocratic elite seriously threatened by the people. The Ciompi Revolution had taught these families some important lessons. They learned to restrain, if not to eliminate completely, their penchant for feuding. They developed techniques and rules for resolving their conflicts in the public arena, for example, in the electoral scrutinies, rather than in street battles. "Nowadays vendettas take place in the *palazzi;* there are no more street battles

with knives," commented Barna di Valorino Curiani in a letter to his father (c. 1400). Having gained firm control of the state, the great families collaborated to increase its power, so that it could suppress any challenge to its authority, whether internal or external.

In the records of the 1427 *catasto,* the monumental tax record that included demographic and economic information on 10,000 Florentine households, the economic pre-eminence of Florence's great families is fully documented. The richest man in the city, Palla di Nofri Strozzi, owned property valued at more than 100,000 florins. The 100 richest Florentine households possessed one fourth of the city's entire wealth. Their income came from real estate, in city and countryside, from investments in communal bonds (*monti*), and from companies engaged in banking, commerce and industry. Palla Strozzi's inventory of his property included 54 farms (*poderi*), 30 houses, a banking firm with a capital investment of 45,000 florins, and a large amount of communal bonds. In contrast to the enormous wealth of these men,

Among the many Florentine confraternities that combined devotional activities with charitable works, a special place is reserved for the Arciconfraternita della Misericordia, *founded in 1240 and still active today, whose members (far right: a group of* incappucciati, *hooded men, in a painting by Ridolfo del Ghirlandaio, now in the Bigallo) were dedicated to the assistance of the sick and injured and the burial of abandoned corpses. The confraternities, which received large amounts of money in the form of legacies, were also important economic entities. The Orsanmichele confraternity was able to lend 1,000 florins in 1375 for the construction of the cathedral, with the same amount going to the* Studio Generale. *The other illustrations show charitable works depicted in frescoes by the School of Ghirlandaio in the church of San Martino dei Buonomini: burying the dead and visiting the sick (opposite) and, on this page, visiting prisoners (above) and offering hospitality to pilgrims (right).*

1,500 Florentine heads of households owned no property, and another 1,600 were so poor that they were exempt from taxation. Giovanni di Bicci de' Medici's fortune (80,000 florins) was large enough to pay the annual salaries (40 florins) of 2,000 labourers in the woollen cloth industry. Such was the discrepancy in the wealth and living standards of Florence's richest and

poorest inhabitants in the early quattrocento.

Seven years after the compilation of the *catasto,* Palla Strozzi was forced into exile, and Giovanni de' Medici's son Cosimo had become the dominant political figure in Florence. A revival of factional conflict between two family coalitions, one led by Rinaldo degli Albizzi (Palla Strozzi's ally) and the other by Cosimo de' Medici, had resulted first in Cosimo's expulsion (1433) by the Albizzi faction, and then, a year later (October 1434), in his triumphant return. Once in power, Cosimo and his associates imposed sentences of exile upon some 90 of their political enemies, and fined or excluded from office another 80. Among the families who suffered most severely from these penalties were the Albizzi, Altoviti, Bardi, Brancacci, Castellani, Gianfigliazzi, Guadagni, Peruzzi and Strozzi. Many of the proscribed citizens, like Palla Strozzi, died in exile; others were eventually allowed to return to Florence, but did not possess the political influence or social status that their forebears had enjoyed prior to 1434.

Had Cosimo de' Medici's enemies killed him when they had him in their power (September

The lives of the saints are a familiar element in Florence's vast artistic heritage. In the painting illustrated above, Pesellino, a 15th-century painter, tells of St. Anthony of Padua's miraculous rediscovery of the moneylender's heart in his strongbox. Paolo Uccello, in a detail from his Episodes in a Hermit's Life *(below), however, seems to be musing on the values of asceticism. The religious sentiments of the Florentine* people also found expression in the proliferation of churches and religious foundations. The miniature from the Chigi codex of Villani's Cronica *(below right) shows the foundation of the church of Santa Croce.*

1433) his family's place in Florentine history might have remained as obscure as it had been for the previous two centuries. Prior to the early 1400s, there was little to distinguish the Medici from a hundred other Florentine families of similar background and status. They had regularly been represented in the highest offices of the commune since the late 1200s; they were active as merchants, moneylenders, cloth manufacturers. They intermarried with other families in their quarter of San Giovanni, between the Mercato Vecchio and the church of San Lorenzo. A large lineage comprising several branches and between 20 and 30 households, the Medici were not as cohesive, politically and socially, as some other prominent *casate,* like the Castellani and the Peruzzi. In the 1390s and early 1400s, some of the Medici were involved in conspiracies against the regime; Antonio de' Medici was executed for treason (1397), and several others were deprived of their right to hold office. The fortunes of the family revived after 1410, however, with the emergence of Giovanni de Bicci de' Medici as one of the city's richest bankers, who had close ties with the Roman curia. While carefully avoiding the political limelight, Giovanni assembled a powerful coalition of kinsmen, friends and clients, who remained loyal to his son Cosimo after his death in 1429.

Many of Cosimo's contemporaries, most notably the rulers of other Italian states with whom he had personal contacts, believed that he was the *de facto* ruler of Florence, even though the city preserved its traditional republican institutions. But Nicolai Rubinstein has demonstrated conclusively that after 1434, Florence was governed, as it had been in the past, by a coalition of families, of whom the Medici under Cosimo's leadership was the most prominent. This ruling group included many of the city's most illustrious *casate* (Pitti, Ridolfi, Capponi, Soderini, Guicciardini, Pandolfini, Tornabuoni), and also some families (Martelli, Ginori, Pucci) which had been neighbours and clients of the Medici prior to 1434. As head of the Medici bank, Cosimo had large resources at his disposal which could be used, if necessary, to achieve his political objectives. Though he could not control the appointment to all of the offices in the Florentine state, he was able to help friends and clients by a judicious exercise of power which was primarily personal.

In this climate the great Florentine families flourished as never before in the city's history. Those *casate* in the regime enjoyed their secure place in the political and social order. The bitter rivalries among families, so characteristic of past ages, were for the most part restrained by the regime's leadership, which developed an efficient system of distributing the offices and honours that it controlled. Families that had

In Giovanni Villani's Cronica *we read: "As for the churches that there were then (1338) in Florence and her environs (...) we find that there are one hundred and ten, amongst which there are fifty-seven parish churches, five abbeys with two priors and eighty monks, twenty-four nunneries with five hundred ladies, ten orders of friars (...) and from two hundred and fifty to three hundred chaplain priests." Above, the consecration of the cathedral, S. Maria del Fiore, by Pope Eugenius IV.*

been penalized for their opposition to the Medici (the Albizzi, Peruzzi, Guadagni, Castellani, and some of the Strozzi) did not share in these benefits, but they were a small and impotent minority, their leaders forced to live abroad in exile or, if allowed to return to Florence, to accept disqualification from civic office.

The life style of the aristocracy

The mentality of this dominant elite is reflected in Leon Battista Alberti's *Della Famiglia*, written during the 1430s. Alberti belonged to one of Florence's most illustrious families, that had suffered exile and discrimination for many years, but was finally rehabilitated in the late 1420s. Throughout the book, Alberti reveals his pride in his family's antiquity and its record of distinguished service to the commune. His purpose in writing the book was to keep alive the honour and glory of the Alberti: "... I ask you young Albertis to ... seek the well-being, increase the honour, magnify the fame of our house." If the Alberti hoped to avoid the fate of other Florentine *casate* that had fallen into poverty and

Three delicate portraits of women by Florentine artists: above, a drawing by Lorenzo di Credi (1459-1537); far left, a sanguine drawing by Cecco Bravo (1607-61); left, a drawing attributed to Bachiacca (1495-1557). Opposite, the Lady of the Primroses, *a sculpture by Verrocchio (1435-88) on which some people believe Leonardo also worked. The finely-chiselled features of the subject may be those of Lucrezia Donati, the mistress of Lorenzo the Magnificent.*

disgrace, its members should follow the traditions and practices of their ancestors. Above all, they should cultivate a strong sense of family unity. Brothers should live together in their father's house, keeping the patrimony intact. Kinsmen who had suffered misfortune should be helped by their more affluent relatives. Alberti also preached the personal virtues of thrift, moderation, self-discipline and efficiency. Time, in his view, was a precious commodity, always to be used rationally, never to be wasted.

No decision involving the family was more important than matrimony; the *parentadi* (marriages) arranged among the great families were the cement that bound together this elite. Alberti devoted several pages of his book to the problem. From his mother and other female relatives, the prospective bridegroom should receive a list of all well-born maidens of good upbringing in the neighbourhood. Then he should "act as do wise heads of families before they acquire some

property – they like to look it over several times before they actually sign a contract. It is good in the case of any purchase and contract to inform oneself fully and to take counsel. One should consult a good number of persons and be very careful in order to avoid belated regrets." Marriage arrangements were a major theme in private correspondence; men writing to kinsmen in distant cities would report regularly on the lengthy and often frustrating negotiations concerning a prospective wedding. In 1469 Marco Parenti wrote to his brother-in-law, Filippo Strozzi, in Naples, about the search by Filippo's brother Lorenzo for a Florentine bride: "He is much impressed with one of Francesco del Benino's daughters, and with one of the Vigna girls. Their background is not akin to yours, however, and they are not beautiful (...) The first thing they will want to know in Naples is whether the bride is a gentlewoman. Indeed, her background must be such as to be utterly unimpeachable (...) should anyone be so bold as to challenge it." Parenti then identified some of the eligible girls: the daughter of Bartolomeo Gianfigliazzi (beautiful and noble but poor), the daughter of Federigo Sassetti (less beautiful but possessing a larger dowry), the daughters of Francesco Baroncelli, Luigi da Quarata and Luca Capponi, each with specific merits and defects. After prolonged negotiations, Lorenzo eventually married Antonia di Francesco Baroncelli.

Dowries were a critical element in every marriage, and their size was an important index of a family's wealth and social status. To provide dowries enabling daughters to contract proper marriages was a preoccupation of every Florentine father of the aristocracy. To marry beneath one's rank was a mark of dishonour, to be avoided at all costs. Fathers who had sired several daughters were in a particularly difficult situation, unless they were very rich. They might receive some dowry money from relatives (as Leon Battista Alberti strongly recommended), or from charitable foundations, or they might be forced to place some of their daughters in a convent. In 1425 the Florentine government established a *monte delle doti*, a financial institution which enabled fathers to invest money for their daughters' dowries. A sum of 100 florins (later, 60 florins) deposited in a girl's name and retained in the *monte* for 15 years, yielded 500

The Florentine engravings on these pages, which date from the second half of the 15th century, show some of the most popular musical instruments of the period: the lute, the portable organ and the viola da braccio. As the arts flourished, so did secular music, becoming more widespread and more sophisticated, providing a suitable accompaniment to the dancing and relaxation of an increasingly refined society. A product of the street and the piazza, the love ballad and the roundelay began to be heard within palazzo walls, echoing through halls and gardens. Verses inspired by popular poetry and accompanied by music enjoyed a period of extraordinary brilliance in Florence.

Some realistic portraits of Florentine men, both famous and unknown. Below, a charcoal drawing by Fra Bartolommeo (1475-1517) and right, a study of a man's head by Benozzo Gozzoli (1420-97).

florins. This *monte* was a great boon to Florentine fathers who, with a modest investment on behalf of their infant daughters, could provide them with a dowry that would attract suitors of the appropriate rank.

If the size of dowries was a mark of family status, noted in the diaries and letters of the time, so too were the private palaces that were being constructed in increasing numbers during the Medici period. It has been estimated that 100 new or remodelled palaces were built in the city during the 15th century. Distinguishing these palaces from earlier models (e.g. the palaces of the Spini, Mozzi and Castellani) were their monumentality and their distinctive aesthetic qualities. These palaces were constructed on

sites formerly occupied by several houses and shops, which were either razed or their parts incorporated into the remodelled structures. The palace commissioned by Cosimo de' Medici on the Via Larga (now Via Cavour) became the prototype for many of these Renaissance palaces. Begun in 1444 and completed about 1460, the Medici palace was built in the classical style from plans developed by the architect Michelozzo. While the Medici palace was under construction, other Florentine aristocrats were making plans for their own palaces. Giovanni Rucellai began to construct his palace on the Via Vigna Nuova in the 1440s, Luca Pitti some time after 1450, the largest and most magnificent of them all (at a cost of 40,000 florins) by Filippo Strozzi in 1489. This unprecedented boom in palace construction transformed the physical character of the city, and represented a very significant dimension of the city's economy in those decades.

Michelangelo wrote that "a splendid residence is the source of much honour, being more conspicuous than mere possessions alone, and bears witness to our noble birth …" The grandiose palace dominating its street, decorated with the family's coat of arms, was the most visible and enduring monument to a family's distinction. To ensure that these palaces would remain in the family's possession, their owners inserted elaborate provisions in their testaments. Many aristocratic families also built or remodelled villas on their rural estates, to which they retired during the summer months to escape the heat and discomfort of the sweltering city. The Medici were particularly active in villa construction and decoration. In addition to the ancestral villa, Cafaggiolo, in the Mugello, Cosimo and his heirs acquired and restored villas nearer the city: at Careggi, at Poggio a Caiano, and near Fiesole. Yet another important category of aristocratic building was the family chapel in which the bodies of family members were interred. The Rucellai buried their dead in their neighbourhood church of San Pancrazio, and in the Dominican basilica of Santa Maria Novella. The Capponi found their final resting place across the Arno in the Augustinian church of Santo Spirito, in Santa Felicita and in San Iacopo sopr'Arno. As a burial for his family, Andrea Pazzi commissioned Brunelleschi to build a chapel in the cloister of Santa Croce. Neither Andrea nor Brunelleschi lived to witness the completion of this marvel of early Renaissance architecture.

The aristocratic impulse to make these imperious statements of family wealth and prestige had been restrained, in earlier times, by political and religious scruples. The church's hostility to wealth and its display was articulated with particular force by Franciscan preachers, who warned their audiences that their acquisitiveness would imperil their souls. Under the republican regimes that had governed Florence prior to 1434, civic policy was consistently hostile to such gestures, prohibiting for example the construction of family tombs in the cathedral, and restricting expenditures for weddings and funerals. During the Medicean period, however, these events became opportunities for ceremonies calculated to aggrandize the reputations of the families. The rituals surrounding the death,

Left, the deeply-lined face of the wealthy merchant Pietro Mellini, as portrayed in a marble sculpture by Benedetto da Maiano, dated 1474. Below, a portrait of Giovanni Tornabuoni, as seen in a fresco in the Church of Santa Maria Novella by Domenico Ghirlandaio, executed between 1485 and 1490.

mourning and burial of prominent citizens became increasingly elaborate and costly; more expensive, too, were the tombs built in the family chapels to commemorate the deceased. Wedding celebrations followed a similar pattern. Few Florentine weddings of the 15th century could surpass, in sumptuousness, that of Giovanni Rucellai's son Bernardo to Nannina, the daughter of Piero di Cosimo de' Medici, on 8 June 1466. The wedding feast was held in a pavilion adjacent to Giovanni's palace in the Via della Vigna Nuova. Giovanni described the setting as "the finest and most beautiful ever to grace a wedding banquet; there was dancing and merrymaking in the pavilion, and tables were laid for both a midday and an evening meal." Some 500 guests dined and danced at the celebration, which cost Giovanni Rucellai 6,638 lire (1,185 florins). The bride brought to her husband a dowry of 2,500 florins; among the wedding gifts were eight calves, capons, quails, fish, barrels of wine and, for the bride, 25 gold rings.

Giovanni Rucellai's life (1403-81) may serve as a model for the Florentine elite in this age, when it enjoyed its greatest prestige and prosperity. and when it was most supremely confident of its power. Giovanni's family was among the most distinguished in its quarter of Santa Maria Novella. Since the time of Dante, the Rucellai had played a leading role in the city's economic and political life, engaged in trade, banking and cloth manufacture, filling the major communal offices. Giovanni's own career was quite typical of his family and his social order, though it did

have its unique features. Orphaned at the age of three, he launched his business career during the turbulent years of conflict prior to the triumph of the Medici. In 1428, he had married the daughter of Palla Strozzi, a leading opponent of the Medici. He paid a heavy price for this *parentado* after 1434, being excluded from civic office and from the honours and perquisites enjoyed by the ruling group. Still, Giovanni's business prospered and by 1458, he was the third wealthiest man in Florence. With the marriage of his son to a Medici girl in 1461, he became acceptable to the regime's leadership, and eligible for the major offices. His last years, however, were clouded by economic difficulties, and the loss of a substantial part of his once large fortune. As was true of so many Florentines of his class, the pattern of his life was characterized by vicissitude.

Giovanni Rucellai was not trained in the classical studies that were in vogue during his lifetime, but he was deeply interested in the moral and ethical problems that so preoccupied the humanists of his generation. His passion was not literature but building, and his construction projects were among the most elaborate and

We know that the Renaissance brought about a new relationship between man and nature. The desire to be able to look over the countryside and let one's gaze roam over hills and woods, led to a new link being established between garden and landscape. The high walls that enclosed the hidden medieval flower garden were torn down and architects introduced new theories concerning the ways in which the space around houses could be adapted to the needs of the inhabitants and arranged so as to provide all the amenities necessary for open-air life. The result of this research was the "architectural" garden, a perfectly arranged and balanced space, based on a simple linear design that would provide the necessary link between the house and its surroundings.

expensive of his time. As early as 1448, he was planning to construct a chapel, either in San Pancrazio or Santa Maria Novella, that would be a replica of the Holy Sepulcher in Jerusalem. In the 1450s he commissioned Leon Battista Alberti to construct a façade for Santa Maria Novella; it was completed in 1470. While work on these projects proceeded, Giovanni was acquiring property adjacent to his house in the Via della Vigna Nuova, to build a family palace and loggia in the new classical style perfected by Alberti. Giovanni also owned a country villa at Quaracchi near Peretola, and he purchased another at Poggio a Caiano, which he later sold (1479) to Lorenzo de' Medici. Writing (1464) in his *Zibaldone,* Giovanni listed all of these building enterprises that he had been able to complete. Fortune had smiled on him and he had become wealthy: "I have been lucky enough to have earned my fortune, and also to have spent my money wisely, which is no less a virtue than earning itself is. I feel that to have spent my money judiciously has brought me greater honour and contentment than to have merely earned it." Thus did this Florentine patrician sum up his life and accomplishments. He communicated his

deep sense of satisfaction that he lived in Florence with these words: "This is reputed to be the worthiest homeland not only in Christendom, but in the entire universe."

The aristocracy under the principato

The buoyant mood of the Florentine elite in the Laurentian period (1469-92) was expressed in an inscription placed in one of the panels of a fresco cycle painted by Domenico Ghirlandaio in the Cappella Maggiore of Santa Maria Novella. These frescoes were commissioned by the rich banker, Giovanni Tornabuoni, a friend of the Medici. In the panel depicting the annunciation, by the archangel Gabriel, of the birth of St. John the Baptist, was inserted this inscription: "In the year 1490, this most beautiful city, renowned for its power and wealth, for its victories, for the arts and its buildings, enjoyed great prosperity, health and peace."

Two years later, Lorenzo de' Medici was dead, and 30 months after his death, his son Piero was expelled from Florence. The collapse of the Medici regime inaugurated a period of political and social instability which did not subside until

Opposite above, detail of the Italian-style garden of the Villa Ambrogiana, as seen in a painting by Utens; below, a pergola in a 15th-century garden, as shown in a woodcut dating from 1492. On this page above, the river and its banks. Above left, detail of a miniature painted for one of Boccaccio's tales. Above, a section of the Arno banks beneath the walls, at a spot known as sardigna. *It was used as a place to dispose of the carcasses of domestic animals and refuse from butcher's shops, thereby fulfilling a basic requirement of hygiene for the city and its environs (detail from the "chained view" of Florence).*

Duke Cosimo de' Medici gained control of the city in 1537 and established a hereditary *principato*. Throughout this period, the great Florentine families were sharply divided and fragmented. Some *casate* remained loyal to the exiled Medici; others participated in the new republican regime created in 1494 and were strongly influenced by the Dominican friar, Girolamo Savonarola. Citizens from several of the city's most prominent families were passionately devoted to the friar, while others despised him and sought to achieve his downfall. The chronicler Parenti wrote (1497) that civic opinion concerning Savonarola was so mixed "it divided fathers and children, husbands and wives, and siblings. Young men between the ages of 18 and 30 differed greatly on this issue." The restoration of the Medici in 1512 exacerbated the conflict between their partisans and those citizens who had been closely associated with the defunct regime. Allegiance to republican institutions and traditions was widespread among Florentine aristocrats in the early cinquecento, as witnessed by the writings of Niccolò Machiavelli and Francesco Guicciardini.

A Medici partisan, Lodovico Alamanni, wrote (1516) a very astute analysis of the Florentine scene after the Medici restoration. Alamanni's letter to the head of the regime, Lorenzo di Piero de' Medici, contained suggestions for transforming Florentine citizens into courtiers who would accept Medici rule: "… The Florentines do not condescend to pay homage to anyone, not even those who would command respect. They only pay their respects to the magistrates, and even then with great reluctance. They are therefore far removed from court manners, in a way few others are; however when they are away from their native city they are quite different. I think this may derive from the fact that in days of old they thought it inconvenient to doff their hats; and the reluctance on their part to perform this courtesy became a habit, and this habit became part of their nature. I believe when they are away from their native land and away from that custom, they have little trouble in conversing with princes.

"Such behaviour will never be changed in old people; they are not to be feared, for they shun novelty. Young people however could easily shed this habit and adopt court manners, if the prince should request it. In order to achieve this,

he should behave in the usual way and select all those young men in our city who are worthy of esteem, and send his emissaries to them to summon them to his presence whereupon he would inform them that he was prepared to offer them a suitable stipend. No one would refuse this offer, and once they had entered into his service, they would be discouraged from these citizens' habits, and their manners moulded into a more courtly mode of behaviour, as practiced by all the other subjects."

Alamanni's evaluation of the Florentine situation was prescient; he predicted accurately the future role of the great families. Reluctantly at first, but then with increasing willingness, the aristocracy accepted its subservient role under a succession of Medici rulers: Lorenzo, Cardinal Giulio (later Pope Clement VII), Alessandro and finally Grand Duke Cosimo. The career of Francesco Guicciardini illustrates this pattern. Descended from one of Florence's most illustrious *casate,* Guicciardini was a dedicated republican who wrote (1512): "Before I die I would like to see an ordered republican way of life in our city, and to see Italy freed from the yoke of all barbarians and from the tyranny of these iniquitous priests." Yet he accepted service with the Medici, and after the collapse of the last Florentine republic in 1520, he curried favour with them by persecuting the leaders of that regime. It was often necessary, he observed in his *Ricordi,* for men to live under the rule of tyrants, and to adjust their lives to that situation. If a tyrant is "bloodthirsty and brutish," then one should flee into exile, "but when, either through prudence or necessity (...) the tyrant behaves with respect, an accomplished man should strive to be grateful (...) and not hunger for change unless forced to, because then the tyrant shall cherish him and seek to give him no cause to think of change."

Not every Florentine aristocrat accepted the *pax medicea.* The leader of the opposition to Cosimo's rule was Filippo Strozzi, once a Medici partisan, who had married the daughter of Piero, the son of Lorenzo the Magnificent. Filippo had been a close associate of the Medici pope, Clement VII, but after that pontiff's death in 1534, his fortunes declined. He joined the band of exiles who had fled from the city after the fall of the republic in 1530. In the summer of 1537, some 200 exiles and their hired mercenaries

Scenes from the tales of the Decameron, *taken from the de' Gregori edition of 1492. The culture, habits and attitudes of Florentine society are accurately mirrored in this, Boccaccio's greatest work. A free and easy approach to life, in which man was an active participant, ever-eager for knowledge and fresh experiences, characterized the spirit of the new era and the new middle class that developed between the tail end of the Middle Ages and the first stirrings of the new, humanistic civilization. The illustrations shown here were engraved more than a century after the creation of Boccaccio's masterpiece, and therefore largely reflect clothes and settings from the end of the 15th century. However, through the human comedy of the famous book, there is evidence of an undeniable feeling of continuity in Florence between two great historical eras, as well as a sense of their gradual integration.*

moved toward Florence, with the intention of assaulting the city. They were defeated in the battle of Montemurlo, their leaders captured and brought to Florence for execution. Filippo Strozzi was imprisoned and eventually committed suicide. Only a handful of republican exiles survived this disaster, and they were never again able to threaten seriously the Medici control of their native city.

The public execution of the exiled leaders in the Piazza della Signoria was a warning to potential dissidents of the price of rebellion. And the building and fortification of the Fortezza da Basso was yet another reminder to the Florentine aristocracy of its powerlessness against the Medici regime. But Cosimo knew the value of the carrot as well as the stick and with his situation more secure, he was willing to entice the aristocracy into his service. Members of the city's leading families sat in the *Magistrato*

Supremo, the executive committee that was responsible for many aspects of administration. Aristocrats also served as governors of towns and fortresses in the territory, and as diplomats and military captains. It is true that Cosimo and his successors chose foreigners and citizens from the dominion (Arezzo, Pistoia, Pescia, Colle, etc.) for positions of authority in the government, as *auditori* and *segretari* and as officials in the ducal household. But in the magistracies and civic offices that had survived from republican times, the old families were predominant.

Nowhere in Florence is the evidence of this aristocracy's wealth and status under the *principato* more palpable than on the Via Maggio, lined with magnificent palaces that were constructed or remodelled in the 16th and 17th centuries. Sixty woollen cloth *botteghe* were razed to make room for these palaces of the Corsini, Biliotti, Corbinelli, Ridolfi, Ricasoli. The money to construct and furnish them, and to maintain the life style appropriate to their architectural grandeur, came from many sources. Income from offices and ducal gifts supplemented the revenues from rural estates. Throughout the cinquecento and in the early seicento, the Florentine aristocracy invested heavily in commercial and industrial enterprises. The most aggressive capitalist of his age was Duke Cosimo, who invested money in real estate in the city and the dominion, in mining and stone quarrying, and in commercial enterprises in Tuscany and abroad. Not until the economic crisis of the 1620s and 1630s did Florence's aristocracy withdraw from entrepreneurial activity to become primarily *rentiers.*

To preserve their wealth and status, Florentine aristocratic families developed complex strategies, involving marriage and inheritance. It became customary, within aristocratic households, for only one male and one female child to marry. This practice guaranteed that the family patrimony would not be fragmented, but would be passed on intact to the eldest son who in turn would arrange for his eldest male child to be the exclusive heir to his urban palace and rural estates. Younger sons who, in a contracting economic climate, could not hope to make their fortunes in business were discouraged if not prohibited from marrying. These bachelors either lived in the family palace with their older brother and his family, or they received an

income or a share of the family patrimony enabling them to establish a separate ménage. But on their death, their property reverted to the children of their eldest brother. In this more rigid social milieu, daughters of aristocratic families fared poorly. Already in the 15th century, the escalation of dowries had placed many families under severe financial pressure. "The most difficult thing in life," wrote Francesco Guicciardini, "is to provide a suitable marriage settlement for one's daughters." With the median price of dowries in aristocratic marriages about 10,000 *scudi* in 1600, most fathers could afford to marry off only one of their daughters. The remainder were placed in convents with little or no regard for their sense of religious vocation. The plight of the abbess of Monza in Manzoni's *I Promessi Sposi* (*The Betrothed*) was similar to that of thousands of Florentine girls in these centuries.

THE FLORENTINE PALAZZO

"What is behind all this vying for renovation to be witnessed throughout Italy? How many towns that were built of wooden planks when we were children are now all marble?" Thus Leon Battista Alberti writes about the architectural revival of his day. In Benedetto Dei's *Cronica Fiorentina* we find that in the 20 years between 1450 and 1470 "thirty *palazzi* were erected in Florence." Spurred by the desire for comfortable, beautiful, and grand houses, the Florentine traders and bankers now also found themselves rich enough to realize such ambitions. Coinciding with the new wave of humanism in the city, in which scholars, patrons, and artists worked side by side, this revival of secular architecture then spread to other cities. The result was that pride and glory of Italy, and of Florence in particular, the Renaissance *palazzo*. A group of architects working in Florence produced the prototypes which were subsequently copied and adapted throughout the rest of Italy and even farther afield: Filippo Brunelleschi with the Palazzo Pitti, Michelozzo with the Palazzo Medici, Leon Battista Alberti with the Palazzo

Rucellai, Giuliano da Maiano with the Palazzo Antinori, his brother Benedetto with the Palazzo Strozzi (rather extravagantly described as "the most beautiful Renaissance *palazzo* in Florence"), and Giuliano da Sangallo with the Palazzo Gondi.

It has been shown elsewhere (cf. page 38) how the Florentine townscape was at one time dominated by the towers. Something of the original military function of the towers is still detectable in the *palazzo* (vestigial, almost allegorical traces also remaining in the public *palazzi* such as the Bargello and the Palazzo della Signoria). The aristocratic home of the Davizzi in Via Porta Rossa (10), completed around 1330 (and now named after Bernardo Davanzati, who bought it in 1578), exemplifies the evolution of the fortified *palazzo* immediately prior to the fearful time of the Black Death (1348), the loggia under the roof being a 16th-century addition. This was the typical raw material of 15th-century architectural taste and tradition. Yet there were now different social requirements. The Davizzi had warehouses on the ground floor of their house, and this was no longer deemed desirable by the next century: buildings had begun to be more "specialized," and the flavour of the medieval city, in which house and workshop, private life and work, coexisted, was changing.

The quattrocento *palazzo* also tended to occupy an entire block, thus reuniting areas previously split into smaller sections, and ironically fulfilling the intentions of the former "tower syndicates." Luca Pitti exploited his position in government to demolish a large number of houses on the site on which he wanted to build his *palazzo;* and it is fascinating to study the details of the sketch possibly by Aristotile da Sangallo (7) of a projected transformation and expansion of the houses of the Gaddi – a typical medieval architectural "allotment" complex – in Piazza Madonna degli Aldobrandini. The Palazzo Pitti was started after 1457 by Luca Fancelli, but it was designed by Brunelleschi. Work was halted through lack of funds in about 1470. Then in 1549 Eleanora of Toledo bought it, altering and extending it to its present state. The Utens lunette detail (6) illustrates the Brunelleschian archetype. The most striking feature is the rustication (1), which Florentine architects used with great skill for special effects of composition,

chiaroscuro, and wall thickness. The balustrades marking each different floor level were then replaced by simple cornices, though these still remained an important compositional element (the new style also dispensed with the engaging random projections of all kinds that were so popular in the Middle Ages (a typical 16th-century house in Via de' Coverelli (2), however, again features such details). The Palazzo Pitti in the painting by Utens is topped by a loggia under the roof; later a classical entablature was to be preferred. A famous example of this feature is the one by il Cronaca (5) on the *palazzo* commissioned from Benedetto da Maiano by the merchant Filippo Strozzi in 1489. Strozzi was here taking advantage of a law passed by Lorenzo de' Medici exempting anyone who built houses within five years from 40 years' communal taxes.

Of fundamental importance in the composition and structure of the Florentine Renaissance *palazzo* were the windows and the courtyard. The windows broke up the façade with harmonious regularity; in the Palazzo Pitti

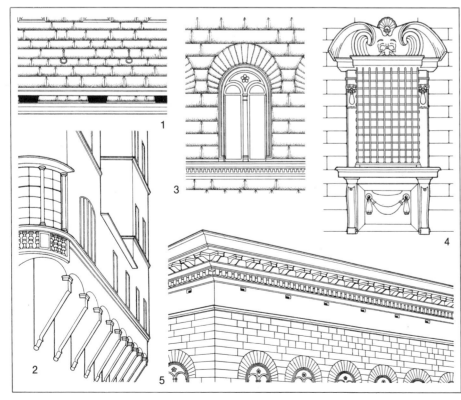

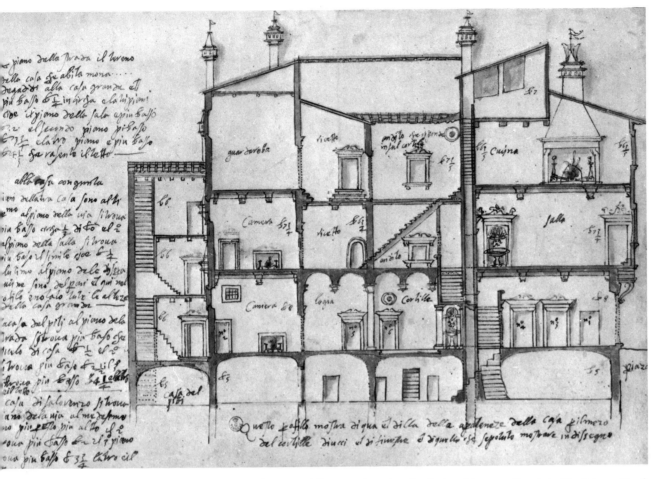

7

shows the courtyard of the Medici palace designed by Michelozzo. The Palazzo Horne (9), dating from the end of the 15th century, is an interesting example of asymmetric design, with the staircase to one side – although Florentine visual harmony reasserts itself in the heavily corniced doors and the well opening in the wall. A characteristic feature of the new *palazzo* style were the benches along the façade, and the bronze fixtures for tying up horses, attaching torches, and displaying flags. However, the essence of the new style and its permanent fascination lie in the strict mathematical harmony of the design, and the gradual elaboration of a certain classical ''poetry.'' The *palazzo* built by Bernardo Rossellino for the Rucellai (1446-51), to a design by Leon Battista Alberti (11), reintroduces the Roman element of horizontal ''layers,'' distinguished one from another by the use of different orders (Tuscan, Ionic, and Corinthian). The rustication is relatively smooth and delicately modulated, the windows are round-arched with double lights, with elegant pilasters supporting the various architraves, the last of which develops into a full-scale entablature and cornice. The composition is an example of compact architectural logic which reflects supreme rational clarity.

Although intended primarily as a building of individual social prestige, the *palazzo* nevertheless represents a remarkable achievement in the overall history of Florentine culture.

the dressed stones of the window jambs and round-arched lintels are uniformly aligned; elsewhere the voussoirs stand out and the embrasures feature delicate twin lights (as in the *palazzo* (3) designed by Michelozzo for Cosimo the Elder in Via Larga – c. 1444-64). After a time the classical architrave and pediment (either a triangle or a broken arch) were favoured: for example, the windows of Bernardo Buontalenti's Palazzo Nonfinito (4) in Via del Proconsolo. The courtyard formed the center of the *palazzo* and usually displayed harmonious symmetry, with a portico arcading on the ground floor and *logge* or windows on the upper floors, all counterbalancing each other. In the middle there would often be a fountain. Illustration (8)

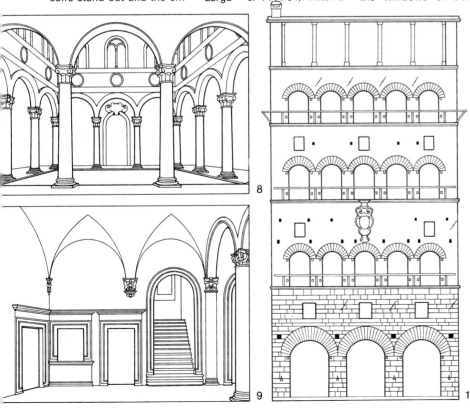

8

9

11

10

Overhanging architectural elements in Via Toscanella, in the Oltrarno district. Below left, arches in Chiasso Baroncelli. Below right, the Via dei Girolami, spanned by cross arches. Such overhangs, which allowed great gains to be made on the basic ground area of a house, had become so common that, according to Villani, at the beginning of the 14th century the tax levied on them produced 7,000 florins, almost four per cent of the city's entire tax revenue. In order to prevent the abuse of such structures, regulations were introduced to control their depth and their height above the ground. Bridges and arches, however, were intended to act as a means of communication between the houses or merely to serve as buttresses.

By means of their wealth, social rank and access to office, members of the great Florentine families were able to perpetuate and reinforce their sense of being an exclusive, hereditary elite, a "noble" class. Although they did not possess titles of nobility, they were convinced that they were as "noble" as the *marchesi, conti* and *baroni* in Milan or Ferrara or Naples. Theirs was a *nobiltà civile*, which they enjoyed by virtue of the fact that their ancestors for generations had held high office in the republic. The argument was advanced by several Florentine writers in the late cinquecento and early seicento, for example, by the historian Scipione Ammirato (1615): "… If we examine the great republics, such as that of Florence, we will see that no noble family should consider itself inferior to another. Even if the family has not been part of the *Signoria*, or has not lived according to courtly principles as is the custom, or as is seemly at the court of a king or great prince, it may at least be able to number among its ancestors *gonfalonieri, priori, commissari*, members of the *Dieci di Balìa*, and similar figures by no means inferior to these. Such office holders will have been in a

court as *conti* or *marchesi*. It was not until 1750, when Florence was under the rule of the Hapsburgs, that nobility was legally defined, with the old families being registered in special *Libri d'Oro* (Golden Books). Thus, after more than two centuries, the members of the great Florentine families were fully integrated into the ranks of the European nobility.

position of authority over non noble persons, and even though the power they enjoyed would not have been absolute, they would at least have been equals and not subjects (as at the court of a king or prince)."

Cosimo I contributed to this "aristocratization" by establishing (1562) the Order of Santo Stefano, a crusading order modelled on the chivalric fraternities of Europe's monarchies. Admission to this order conferred noble status; it could be obtained either by purchasing a *commenda,* or by claiming *nobiltà civile.* That status could be demonstrated by furnishing evidence that one's ancestors had held high civic office either in Florence or in the major towns of the dominion. The great Florentine families provided one third of the 900 members of this knightly order, the remainder being recruited from the dominion towns and from abroad. For some aristocratic families, the title of knight of Santo Stefano was insufficient recognition of their noble status. In 1623 four members of the Strozzi family with connections at the imperial court obtained the title of "count of the Holy Roman Empire." Others purchased fiefs in the dominion, which entitled them to be invested at

The economy

A foreign merchant, leading his packhorses into Florence at some time in the 1170s, would have noticed immediately the recently constructed circle of walls (begun in 1172 and completed four years later) that had enlarged the enclosed urban space to 80 hectares. As he moved through the fortified gate of San Lorenzo, on the city's northern boundary, and then along the Borgo San Lorenzo, he would see evidence everywhere of intensive construction: houses and towers, churches and monasteries, streets and *piazze*. This building boom was stimulated by the expansion of the city's population which, since the early decades of the 12th century, had spilled out beyond the old circle of walls, which ran just north of the cathedral. Making his way slowly through crowds that filled the narrow streets, our merchant would see on his right the collegiate church of San Lorenzo, one of the major Florentine buildings of the Romanesque style. Once through the Porta del Duomo, he would have encountered the cathedral complex: the recently built Baptistery (but without its marble sheath that was added later); the episcopal palace; and the old cathedral church of Santa Reparata, only half the length of the grandiose basilica that replaced it in the 14th century. Moving south towards the Arno, our traveller reached his final destination, the Mercato Vecchio, where he would sell or exchange his cargo of goods for either money or other commodities that, in some other market in some other town, he would endeavour to sell at a profit.

The ancient site of the Mercato Vecchio was obliterated in the late 19th century, to make room for the vast square now called the Piazza della Repubblica. Old photographs reveal its basic outlines, though the market's physiognomy has changed significantly over the centuries. The site of the ancient Roman forum, its function as a medieval market, has been documented as early as 1030. For many years before that date it had served the urban population and the adjacent rural districts as the region's major market. Its specific nature and activity in the 1170s can only be surmised, since no records have survived to reveal its operations. Crucial to the market's activity was the sale and exchange of foodstuffs from the countryside: grain, wine, oil, meat, poultry, vegetables. These products were the city's life blood. It is possible that some commodities were already being bought and sold in other locations, as the grain market was later transferred to Orsanmichele. Our foreign merchant may have brought a cargo of spices from Venice, or some quality cloth from Milan, or metalware to sell in the Mercato Vecchio. The trade in woollen cloth was a staple of commercial exchange, second only to foodstuffs in value and importance. Luxury items from the Levant were expensive and rare, and would not have represented a significant share of market activity. More important were the products made and sold by local artisans: hosiers, shoemakers, tanners, weavers, metalworkers. Facilitating the buying, selling and trading were the moneychangers, who traded in a bewildering variety of coins that circulated in medieval markets.

The evidence for the resurgence of commerce in the early medieval centuries in Italy is extremely sparse; the fragmentary sources provide only fleeting and cursory hints, in the eighth and ninth enturies A.D., of trade and traders, for the most part in the towns of the Lombard plain (Pavia, Milan, Cremona, Piacenza, Venice). In the post-Carolingian era, coastal towns – Genoa,

Pisa, Naples, Amalfi – have left traces in the sources of their participation in the buoyant Mediterranean trade, and their struggles against Moslem ships and sailors based in Spain and north Africa. Pisan and Genoese galleys ferried crusaders to the Holy Land at the end of the 11th century; thereafter, both cities were heavily involved in Levantine commerce. While the documents reveal this trend of intensified commercial activity throughout the peninsula from the ninth to the 11th century, they contain scarcely any reference to Florence's role in this economic expansion. By contrast, Lucca's merchants are mentioned frequently in the documents as early as the tenth century. By the early 1100s, Florentines had finally broken through whatever barriers had restricted their commercial activity. They had participated with Pisa in a war against Moslem pirates (clear evidence of their involvement in Mediterranean trade), and in 1117 received a pair of porphyry columns as a trophy. Yet throughout the 12th century Pisa was Florence's superior, both demographically and economically. Pisa's prosperity was dramatically

displayed by the construction of her splendid complex of ecclesiastical building – cathedral, baptistery and campanile – in the 11th and 12th centuries, whose grandeur and beauty surpassed any comparable Florentine structure built before 1300. Though no accurate demographic data survives for the two cities from these centuries, it is probable that Florence did not surpass Pisa in population before 1250.

As a river town on the Via Cassia, Florence did possess certain geographical assets, although it was not located on the major north-south route connecting Lombardy and Rome. The major pilgrimage road from northern Europe was the *via francigena,* which passed through Lucca and crossed the Arno at Fucecchio, west of Florence. Another main Roman road, the Via Flaminia, ran along the Arno valley north of Arezzo, crossing the river at Pontassieve and reaching Bologna after traversing the Apennines. The Arno was not an ideal route between the sea and Florence. River traffic was impeded by artificial barriers and shifting deposits of sand, and by seasonal fluctuations in water depth. The

swamps that covered large tracts in the Arno valley west of Florence were yet another impediment to rapid communication. The Apennines were not a serious barrier to Florence's relations with the north, but the journeys over those curving mountain roads were certainly arduous. The visitor who came to Florence was not attracted there by the ease and facility of the journey.

If Florence was a less than perfect site for a commercial center, it was also seriously deficient in the raw materials that supplied the basic needs of medieval society. The hilly terrain so characteristic of the Tuscan landscape limited the production of grain, the basic element in the medieval diet, though it did foster the cultivation of grapes and olives. By the mid 13th century, the urban population of perhaps 70,000 was already too large to subsist on the surplus yield of the *contado,* and in years of poor harvest, grain had to be imported from abroad. Tuscany's forests were soon depleted by the expanding city's voracious appetite for building materials which, by the 14th century, largely consisted of stone

and brick. No significant deposits of iron ore were to be found in Tuscany; it had to be imported from the island of Elba. The woollen cloth industry did not use the wool from local sheep, which was too poor in quality, but relied instead on imported fleeces. The city did however possess two crucially important ingredients for that burgeoning industry: an ample water supply for washing, fulling and dyeing; and a large workforce, immigrant men and women from the countryside, whose labour produced, according to Villani's estimate in 1336, 80,000 bolts of cloth valued at 1,200,000 gold florins.

The woollen cloth industry was the foundation of Florence's demographic and economic growth in the late Middle Ages, and thus the primary cause of the city's emergence as one of Italy's, and Europe's largest and wealthiest urban centers. Like so much of the early history of the city's economic development, the origins of this industry are not well documented. Poor quality cloth from Tuscan wool had been produced for local consumption for centuries, and sold or bartered in the marketplaces of the city and the surrounding towns. Cloth of superior quality for rich laymen and clerics was imported from France, the Low Countries and Spain. Some of that cloth was brought to Florence to be refined, dyed and resold, by merchants who were organized into the guild of the Calimala. At some time around the year 1200, Florentine entrepreneurs began to organize the production of fine cloth made from imported wool. Certain techniques for improving the quality of this cloth may

have been brought into the city by the monks of the Umiliati order, who established their convent of Ognissanti and their cloth workshops adjacent to the Arno. This industry grew rapidly during the 13th century. Florentine cloth of superior quality competed effectively in European and Levant markets with that produced in other parts of Europe. The production of woollen cloth was a very complex operation, involving 26 separate steps: from washing, cleaning and combing the wool; to spinning, dyeing, carding and weaving it into cloth; to the final stages of washing, drying, stretching and trimming it before it was ready for sale. The key figure in the industry was the *lanaiolo*, who provided the capital to purchase the wool, furnished the shop and tools and hired the labour for the early stages of production, then arranged for the wool (and later the cloth) to be passed to the *sottoposti*, who performed the specialized tasks in the manufacturing process.

Established some time in the early 13th century, the *Arte della Lana* (the wool guild) soon became one of the most powerful corporations in the city. In league with the other guilds, it formed the government of the *primo popolo* in 1250, and later the communal regime of 1282. Throughout the late 13th and 14th centuries, its influence in Florentine political and economic life was always significant, sometimes decisive. From its headquarters adjacent to Orsanmichele, the guild supervised the activities of the city's *lanaioli*. It controlled guild membership and levied taxes on its members. It established high standards for cloth production, to protect

The families who, from the 14th century on, had moved into the city, attracted by the advantages to be derived from industry and commerce, did not generally relinquish the lands and estates of their ancestors and the sure supply of produce that they represented. There were strong links between the city and the country, with the two areas coexisting in peaceful harmony. Grain, fruit and wine (above, a 14th-century miniature showing a grape picker at work) were the most important products of the Florentine countryside. Farms and agricultural buildings were often attached to the villas of the nobility; an example of this can be seen in a detail from a painting by Utens, which shows the farm buildings and labourers' cottages of the Villa di Collesalvetti (above left).
Another typical rural building can be seen in the background of Benozzo Gozzoli's Procession of the Magi *(opposite).*

FLORIN AND LIRA, GOLD AND SILVER

The devaluation of money is an ancient evil. Charlemagne's monetary reforms introduced the monometallist use of silver, and he minted the denarius; 240 of these coins could be obtained from a pound of silver. The lira (from the Latin *libra,* pound) thus evolved as a convenience for accounting purposes, allowing the figure 1 to stand for 240 denarii. Under Charlemagne this lira was worth 390 grams of pure silver. In the Ottonian period (7) the silver content of the denarius had been reduced, and the lira stood at 275 grams of pure silver. There were then various other coinages and types of money in circulation. In the mid 12th century the lira varied from 103 grams of pure silver (the imperial Milanese lira) to 20 (the Venetian). A century later the silver content of the lira (still

anchored to sound money that should not be devalued. In a way the minting of the gold florin was an attempt to give concrete reality to that non-existent article, the lira: made of 3.54 grams of gold, it represented the exact value of the Florentine lira at the then current rate of exchange between gold and silver. The florin was an exceptionally sound currency, "for centuries fulfilling the role that would later be carried out by sterling and the dollar." (Sapori). However, as we shall see, the lira continued to decline in value. The word *fiorino* (literally, little flower) already existed: in the 12th and 13th centuries the Florentines had coined silver *fiorini* (3), with a fleur-de-lis on the obverse (equalling 12 denarii). On the reverse, the gold florin bore an image of St. John, the patron saint of the city (ex-

1

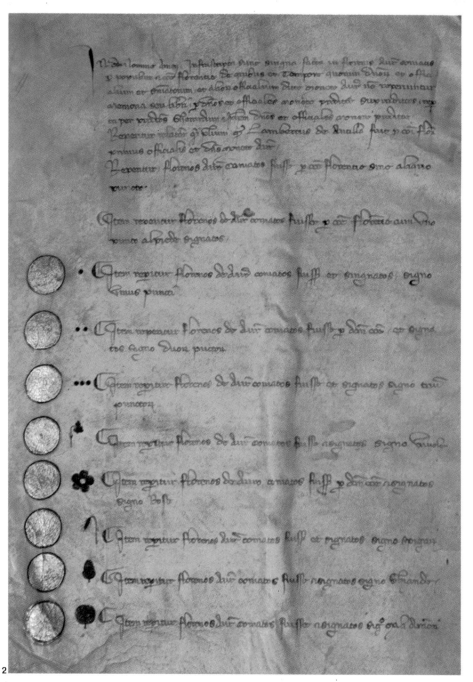

4

6

3

5

an imaginary accounting coin) had fallen lower still: 70 grams in the case of the Genoese and Milanese, 35 in the Florentine, and 20 in the Venetian. An important stage in the history of money was then reached, with the minting of gold coins, and thus the move to bimetallism: the Genoese with the *genovino* and the Florentines with the florin in 1252, then the Venetians with the ducat (1284). Armando Sapori writes: "given the monetary instability of this period it was vital that the economy – especially in the domain of international exchange – be

amples of gold florin: (4) 13th century; (5) 14th century; (6) 15th century). Florence was justifiably proud of her fine gold coin, which retained its value right through to the fall of the republic. Giovanni Villani described it as "almost the common currency of Christendom," and one poet saw it as a paragon of feminine beauty. The coiners who minted the florin had their own guild. In the Archivio di Stato in Florence there is a "constitution and statues of the guild and university of coiners." On the binding of this document there is a painting (8), possibly by a

Silver content of the lira (an accounting coin equivalent to 240 denarii) in grams of pure silver

	Carolingian reform (780-790)	Early Ottonian period (961-983)	Mid 12th century (1150)	The return to gold (1252)
400				
390 — Charlemagne's lira				
300				
275 — Ottonian lira				
200				
100				
103 — Imperial Milanese lira				
85 — Lucca lira				
75 — Genoese lira				
70 — Milanese and Genoese lira				
50 — Pavia lira				
35 — Florentine lira				
25 — Veronese lira				
20 — **20** — Venetian lira				

follower of Giotto, of St. John the Baptist with three gold disks – florins – on either side of him. Above is the inscription *Monetieri del Chomune* (Moneychangers to the Commune). Overseeing the mint were two officials holding six-monthly terms of office, one from the *Arte di Calimala* (the merchants' guild) and the other from the exchange. After 1324 the appointment of such officials was the responsibility of the *Consiglio della Mercanzia* (trade council), assisted by two members from each of the five major trade guilds. These officials had to put down a very considerable sum as security. Eight goldsmiths, appointed annually, were employed to test and weigh each florin: those which they passed being put into a bag with their seal (*suggello*); these were the *fiorini di suggello*. Those that were worn out were withdrawn and cut up, to be valued according to their gold content. By means of these precautions the florin remained sound, and some 29 other versions came to be copied from it by popes, kings, princes, and other cities. At first the florin bore no indication of the date when it was struck. The coiners then started introducing marks (violets, an ear of corn, a horseshoe, miter, etc.) which soon became difficult to keep track of. Thus in 1317 Giovanni Villani and Ghirardo Gentili, the officers of the mint, instituted a record, the *Fiorinaio* (2), recording various features, including all the date marks. Later the *signori della zecca* (gentlemen of the mint) took to stamping coins with their own crests. It is hardly necessary to stress how important this precise control of the

8

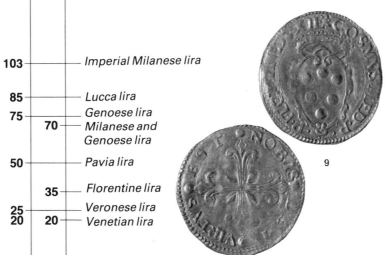

9

city's gold coinage was in its general trading and financial dealings (illustration (1) shows a 15th-century engraving of a Florentine bank). Meanwhile the silver accounting coin, the lira, continued to decline. Originally the florin had been worth one lira; in the decade from 1315 to 1325 it was already worth more than three (10); by the end of the century it was close to four; in 1530 it had come to be worth seven. The following year the florin was abandoned in favour of the gold *scudo* (9), and later that in turn gave way to the *zecchino gigliato* (sequin), which was also known as a *fiorino*.

The value of the florin in terms of silver lire (accounting coins)

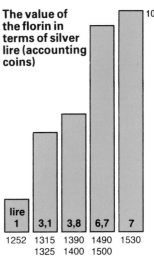

lire 1	3,1	3,8	6,7	7	10
1252	1315 1325	1390 1400	1490 1500	1530	

the quality and reputation of its product. To ensure a regular supply of the raw material required for cloth production, it purchased oil and dyestuffs, and made these available to its members. It financed the construction of wash houses and stretching sheds (*tiratoi*). Guild statutes regulated economic relationships among *lanaioli,* and between them and their workers. The guild court settled disputes over contracts and debts, and penalized *lanaioli* who had violated guild statutes. The guild's most difficult and sensitive task was maintaining its authority over the subordinate workers in the cloth industry. The guild statutes that prohibited any organization of those workers, or any strikes against *lanaioli,* were rigidly enforced. Guild officials regularly fined workers who owed money to their employers, who refused to work at the established wage or piece rate, or who were found guilty of violating rules governing their labour. These repressive regulations aroused strong resentment among *sottoposti,* who sporadically but unsuccessfully attempted to limit the guild's control over their activities. Though occasionally challenged, the power of the *Arte della Lana* was never broken so long as the cloth industry remained an important element in the Florentine economy.

The Florentine cloth industry, which ranked in size and capital investment among the largest in Europe from the 13th to the 15th century, was heavily dependent on the availability of imported wool, and on a ready market for its finished cloth. These requirements were provided by a large and active corps of merchants, predominantly Florentine, who bought the raw materials in England, Flanders, and Spain, and who sold the cloth in every part of Europe and the Mediterranean where they were established. Since the early 12th century, Florentine merchants were already trading outside the peninsula; their numbers, and the scope of their activities, expanded rapidly in the 13th century. They were to be found in the markets of the Spanish cities of Barcelona and Valencia, in the southern French towns of Montpellier and Toulouse, in every major seaport on the Mediterranean littoral. Moving across the Alps, the Florentines joined in the great diaspora of Italian merchants who traded in market centers in England, France, the Low Countries and Germany, and in the Champagne fairs, buying and selling wool,

Miniatures from the codex known as Il Biadaiolo *(The Harvester) in the Biblioteca Laurenziana in Florence, which show grain transactions taking place in shops and in the market during the first half of the 14th century. According to Giovanni Villani, the city's daily wheat requirements at the time averaged 140 bushels, around 1,120 sacks, for a population of about 90,000 people, "without taking into account the fact that most of the rich and noble and well-to-do citizens, together with their families, spent four months of the year in the countryside around Florence." Recent calculations (Fiumi) conclude that the daily per capita consumption of bread was about 700 grams (25 oz), the equivalent of roughly 240 kilograms (529 lb) of wheat per year. In addition, again according to Giovanni Villani, in 1338 there were 146 bakeries in the city.*

cloth, grain, wine and many other commodities. In major cities like London, Paris and Bruges, they joined forces with merchants from other Italian towns to form *societates mercatorum*. These associations established rules to regulate their commercial activities, and to negotiate for special privileges with foreign princes and urban governments.

The distribution of wheat in Orsanmichele (left), as shown in the Biadaiolo *codex. Here, on the spot where there was already an oratory dedicated to St. Michael (San Michele), Arnolfo had built a loggia to house the grain market in 1290. The present building (above), however, is of later date. Work was begun on a larger version in 1337, after the earlier building was destroyed in a fire. The arcade of the loggia was closed up in 1380, when the building became used for religious purposes, but at the same time two very high stories were added to it, which were completed in 1404, to be used as grain stores in case of emergency.*

Above, cultivated fields at the gates of the city, as depicted in an early 18th-century landscape. Opposite, a shepherd in the countryside, from Alessio Baldovinetti's Nativity *(15th century). The beautiful Tuscan countryside, which inspired so many great Florentine painters, played a very important role in the city's economy. The many well-to-do families who during the 14th century would spend several months a year on their estates, clearly show the amount of attention paid to agriculture, which provided an important source of revenue. Villani tells us that every year the city opened its gates to some 4,000 oxen and calves, 70,000 sheep and wethers, 20,000 goats and she-goats, and 30,000 pigs. This would mean an average consumption of some 38 kilograms (84 lb) of meat per person per year.*

The great companies

While some Florentine merchants engaged in international commerce operated independently, most belonged to partnerships (*compagnie*) which became their characteristic mode of collecting substantial sums of capital, and engaging in large-scale trade. The earliest examples of *compagnie* are found in Siena in the early 13th century; the *gran tavola* of the Bonsignori was one of the largest commercial and banking enterprises in Europe before its collapse in 1298. By the middle of the 13th century, Florentine merchants were organizing their own *compagnie,* and developing their distinctive form and character. They were predominantly though not exclusively family partnerships, the members linked together by ties of blood and marriage. They were always limited to brief time periods, from two to five years, though frequently the partners would form a new *compagnia* immediately after the dissolution of the old one. Their headquarters were located in Florence, where the senior partners supervised the firm and its affairs. Many of these firms established branches in other Italian and European cities, where their partners engaged in the varied commercial and banking operations that brought large profits to themselves and their associates.

From the 1280s until the 1330s, the Florentine companies established and maintained their dominant place in European international trade. The names of these companies reveal that they were made up of the city's great *casate:* Acciaiuoli, Alberti del Giudice, Albizzi, Antellesi, Ardinghelli, Bardi, Baroncelli, Buondelmonti, Cerchi, Del Bene, Frescobaldi, Gianfigliazzi, Peruzzi, Pulci, Scali, Spini, Strozzi. In the size, wealth and scope of their enterprises, the Bardi and Peruzzi firms loomed over the others; together, they formed the greatest concentration of private capital that medieval Europe had known. The capital of the firm of Tommaso d'Arnoldo de' Peruzzi *e compagni* formed in 1310 was 103,000 gold florins: that of the Bardi companies of these years was even larger, even though no precise figures are available. Between 1300 and 1325, 25 Peruzzi were partners in one or more of the companies; another 24 partners belonged to other Florentine *casate:* Baroncelli, Soderini, Da Filicaia, Raugi, Villani. The records of the Peruzzi companies contain the names of 142 salaried employees (*fattori*) who worked in the main Florentine office, or in one or more of the branches. The specific locations of these *fattori* define the area of the Peruzzi company's mercantile network: Pisa, Venice, Naples, Barletta, Palermo, Tunis, Rhodes, Cyprus, Majorca, Avignon, Nice, Paris, Bruges and London.

The account books of the Peruzzi company, and of those other firms whose records survive, reveal the dimensions of this mercantile activity. These firms imported the woollen cloth, and the bales of raw wool, that nourished the Florentine cloth industry. Their *fattori* arranged for the transport of these commodities, overland on packhorses through France to the Provençal ports, and thence by sea to Genoa or Pisa, before finally arriving in the Arno city. Then the bales of finished cloth were loaded onto horses and transported to Pisa for shipment to Spanish and African ports, or sent across the Apennines to Venice, where they were shipped to the ports of the eastern Mediterranean. Some of that cloth might have been taken on caravans destined for China, when the Asiatic trade routes under the

Mongol rulers were still open. In addition to raw materials and manufactured products associated with the woollen cloth industry (which included oil, dyestuffs, and alum), the Florentine companies also traded heavily in food products: grain, wine, oil, livestock. In 1336, Pope Benedict XII in Avignon learned that Armenian Christians were experiencing a famine. He instructed the Bardi company's branch in Avignon to arrange for the transport of grain to Asia Minor, to feed those Christians who were threatened by the Turks. Using bills of exchange, the Bardi purchased cargoes of wheat worth 10,000 florins in Naples and Bari, and arranged for its transport to Armenia.

An age-old scourge, famine claimed many victims during the Middle Ages and at other times in history. It was caused by many factors: excessive rains, drought, late frosts, periodic explosions in the insect and rodent population and the depredations of invading armies. Hunger lurked constantly in the background. Efforts at relief, even when they existed, were always inadequate. Feeding the poor was a moral imperative even before it became one of the basic precepts of the church. These illustrations from the Biadaiolo *codex in the Biblioteca Laurenziana show this laborious work of charity being carried out in Florence: they show grain being distributed amongst the needy in Orsanmichele (above left) and beyond the city walls (above right).*

Trading in commodities was a major source of activity and profit for these companies; trading in money was another. A very elaborate system of exchange had been developed within the international mercantile community, to facilitate the transfer of money from one place to another without actually transferring specie. A typical bill of exchange involved the advance of money in one city, e.g. Florence, and its repayment in another city, e.g. Bruges, in another currency.

These exchange transactions involved not only the transfer but also the extension of credit, and the arrangement for interest payments that technically did not violate the church's rules against usury.

The account books of these companies, studied and edited with exemplary care by Armando Sapori, reveal the technical expertise which Florentine merchants had developed by 1300. While men from other Italian cities, from Asti and Pavia, from Pisa and Genoa, had pioneered these mercantile skills, the Florentines perfected them and, by the late 13th century, were the acknowledged masters of international commerce. They invented double entry bookkeeping and the prototype of the modern cheque; they developed methods of insuring ships and their cargoes. A clear signal of Florence's primacy was the coining (1252) of the florin, the first gold coin to be minted in large amounts in Western Europe since Carolingian times. The florin quickly became the standard coin for international trading, though it was later rivalled by the Venetian ducat, first minted in 1284. The gold florin, with its image of the city's patron saint, John the Baptist, circulated throughout the European continent and the Mediterranean basin. It was a symbol of Florence's wealth and of the integrity of its merchants and their government. The entire structure of international business was ultimately based on this trust, on the belief that contracts would be honoured, that money loaned would be repaid, that violations of the rules would be punished. Companies like the Bardi and the Peruzzi enjoyed greater trust than smaller firms or individual merchants, because their resources were so vast and their reputation was so high. So solid and impregnable did these great firms appear that they received thousands of florins in deposits, which they invested in their enterprises.

The unfortunate fate of these great companies is a testimonial to the uncertainties of international mercantile activity in these years. The lives and fortunes of these merchants were in constant peril, threatened by dangers both natural and man-made. Cargoes sent by sea could be lost by shipwreck or through the depredations of pirates. Overland shipments could be pillaged by bandits, or seized by officials claiming the right of reprisal, or the failure to pay tolls. Merchants were continually guessing about fluctuations in

In 1348, along with the rest of Europe, Florence was devastated by the Black Death. A description of this terrible disease takes up the first pages of Boccaccio's masterpiece, the Decameron, *and also provides an explanation as to why the ten young people, who while away their time telling the famous hundred stories to each other, have fled to the countryside, hoping to avoid contamination.*

The illustration from the Lucca codex of Giovanni Sercambi's Croniche *(top) portrays an allegorical representation of the Plague: sinister winged creatures armed with scythes cutting people down. There is a similar idea behind the portrayal of the Black Death of 1348 in a miniature from the same codex (above).*

the prices of commodities, and about future shortages. They guessed, too, about the political conditions in those regions where they traded: whether (for example) a new prince would be more or less favourable to their activities than his predecessors; whether the costs of business licenses and tolls would rise or fall. The policies of princes towards foreign merchants was an important variable in international commerce. The vicissitudes of these policies is well illustrated by the fortunes of Italian merchants in France during the reign of King Philip the Fair (1285-1314). In the early years of his rule, Philip had employed these merchants, most notably the Franzesi of Florence, as his bankers, mint masters and tax collectors. Together with other

Italian companies, the Franzesi lent large sums of money to the king to subsidize his military operations in Aquitaine and Flanders. But as the king's financial situation deteriorated after 1300, these men suffered severe losses at his hands. Heavy taxes were imposed on them; they had to buy licenses to engage in trade. In 1303 and again in 1311, their goods were seized by royal order, and released only after the payment of heavy fines. When the Franzesi brothers, Biche and Mouche, died in 1307, their property was confiscated on the excuse that they owed money to the crown. Italians lost their posts in the royal administration, although many companies (e.g. the Bardi, Peruzzi, and Scali) continued to maintain branch offices in Paris and in certain other French towns.

The process of producing silk is illustrated in miniatures from the Precetti dell'Arte della Seta *(Rules of the Silk Guild), which dates from the end of the 15th century and is now in the Biblioteca Laurenziana in Florence. Working clockwise from top left, acquiring the raw silk, spinning it, dyeing it, and unravelling the skeins to prepare the bobbins. Opposite, twisting the thread and on this page below, weaving it.*

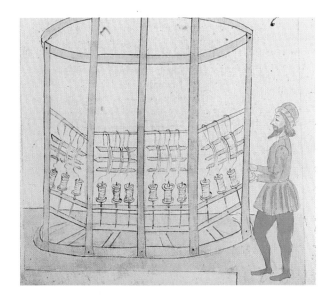

Although the Tuscan textile industry had its center in Lucca, by the mid 13th century Florence had its own silk workers' guild linked, with its own statutes, to the guild of Por Santa Maria. From this period on, the Florentine silk industry went from strength to strength and, by the end of the century, when the guild numbered as many as 100 or 150 members, the fine textiles of Florence – sendal and taffeta – were competing with fabrics from the East.

dramatic events in his chronicle: "... they supplied all the king's expenses, and met other requirements. The Bardi thus found themselves, once the king had returned from the war, faced with an unpaid debt of £180,000, and the Peruzzi with a similar debt of £135,000. All in all, the deficit rose to more than 1,365,000 florins, a vast sum, the price of an entire kingdom." Himself a partner in the Buonaccorsi company, which was a casualty of this collapse, Villani blamed the disaster on the greed of the Bardi and the Peruzzi: "... It was their great folly and cupidity that drove them to buy like madmen, lending their money, and that of other people, to just one person. The said money came mostly from deposits made by both Florentines and foreigners alike. This was a very hazardous position

With a large network of branch offices that stretched from England to Cyprus, the Bardi and Peruzzi companies were not seriously damaged by the losses which they incurred in France under Philip the Fair. But 20 years later, their mercantile empire collapsed when King Edward III of England defaulted on his huge debt to them. Together with other Florentine and Italian companies, the Bardi and Peruzzi had been intimately involved in royal finance in England since the 1270s. Every firm based in London, and involved in the wool traffic, inevitably had financial dealings with the crown, particularly by loaning money to the king, who in turn would guarantee repayment of the loans by pledging future tax revenues. To ensure that those taxes would be collected, and their proceeds applied to these debts, the Italian merchants often accepted positions as tax collectors for the king. Although repayment was sometimes delayed, the merchants could normally expect to recover their loans with interest, as long as they remained in the king's favour. But that favour could only be preserved if the Italians agreed to make additional loans to the impecunious ruler. If they refused, they could lose their outstanding loans and their other property, and face imprisonment.

This was the dilemma confronting the Bardi and Peruzzi companies in the mid 1330s, when King Edward III was collecting money for his war against Philip VI of France. He turned to his Italian associates for the huge sums required for assembling his army and arranging for its transport to Flanders. Giovanni Villani described the

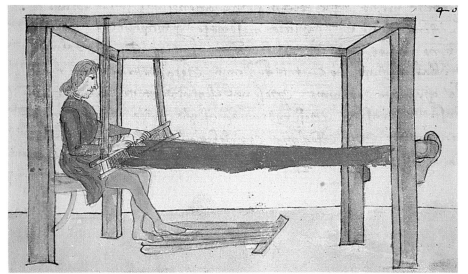

for them, and indeed our city, to be in (...) With the fall of these two banking companies, which were two bastions of power and strength, handling the business of much of Christendom, all other businessmen became the object of suspicion and mistrust."

The collapse of the Bardi and Peruzzi companies in the 1340s set off a chain reaction of business failures in Florence. The city's economic difficulties worsened after 1348, when the Black Death decimated its population and labour force. There were no safe havens to which frightened citizens could flee to escape this terrible scourge. The plague swept through the peninsula and beyond the Alps, disrupting trade routes and industries, and reducing the market for Florentine goods and services by a third. The

It was during the 14th century, however, that the silk industry really developed. Florentine cloths and gold brocades were so sought-after that, in 1391, King Sigismund of Hungary sent an embassy to Florence to acquire fine brocaded materials for himself and his queen. The raw silk at this time was still being imported from the East, but during the 15th century mulberry bushes and silkworms were introduced by the Florentines with very favourable economic consequences.

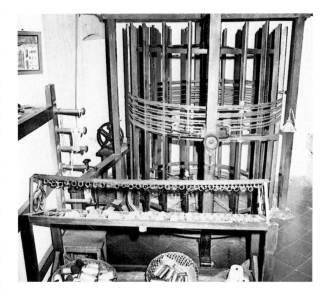

Sixteenth-century machinery still in working order at the Antico Setificio in Florence. Right, an upright warping machine, designed by Leonardo da Vinci, for the creation of special types of braid. Below, a loom. Opposite, a niche dedicated to builders, smiths and woodworkers on the exterior of Orsanmichele, created by Nanni di Banco after 1413. The upper section contains carvings of the four Crowned Saints, whilst the bas relief below shows architects and sculptors at work.

difficulties confronting those merchants who survived the plague were described by Giovanni Morelli, in his account of his father Pagolo's ordeal, following the plague visitation of 1363: "The said Pagolo, young, innocent, alone, with no help or counsel other than that of his friends in this time of great mortality, devastated by the death of his loved ones and much afraid for his own life, found himself in a terrible predicament. Thousands of florins were due to him, but many of his debtors had died (…) This was a dreadful situation, coming as it did at such a time."

These disasters of unprecedented magnitude did not however destroy the Florentine mercantile empire. Replacing the bankrupt companies on the international market were other Florentine firms, some that had existed in the shadow of the Bardi and Peruzzi, others formed by new men and new capital. Though its markets and its production were much reduced, the textile industry did recover, requiring the

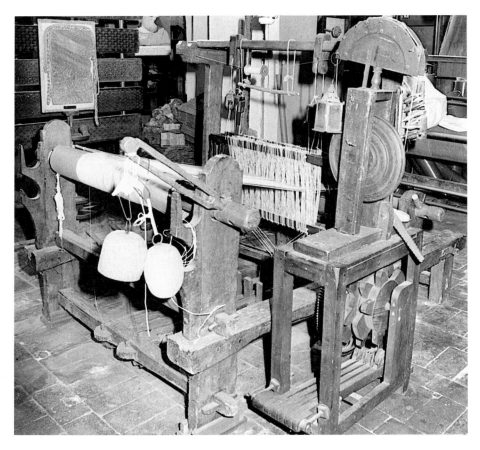

services of merchants – in England, France and Spain – to obtain raw wool, and there and elsewhere (in Naples, Hungary, the Balkans, the Levant) to sell the finished cloth and the other products of Florentine *botteghe*. In Avignon, where the papal court had been established since 1309, 13 Florentine companies participated in the fiscal affairs of the curia in the 1350s. In 1369, 106 Florentine mercantile companies were recorded as being engaged in trade at the port of Pisa. None of these firms was as large as the giants that had collapsed, but a few – the Alberti, Strozzi, Ricci – did achieve a substantial volume of business and of profit. The successes of these Florentine firms were achieved despite very unfavourable conditions in international trade: endemic warfare throughout much of Europe which threatened trade routes; depredations of pirates at sea and brigands on land; taxes, confiscations and monetary devaluations by rapacious princes. Florence's mercantile community abroad was particularly threatened in the late 1370s, when the commune was at war with the papacy. In 1376, Pope Gregory XI ordered the expulsion of Florentine merchants from every Christian state, and authorized the seizure of their property. Though this peril ended in 1378 with a peace agreement between Florence and the papacy, the succeeding decades were times of almost continuous warfare for Florence: against Giangaleazzo Visconti of Milan, against King Ladislas of Naples, against Genoa, and in the 1420s, against Filippo Maria Visconti of Milan.

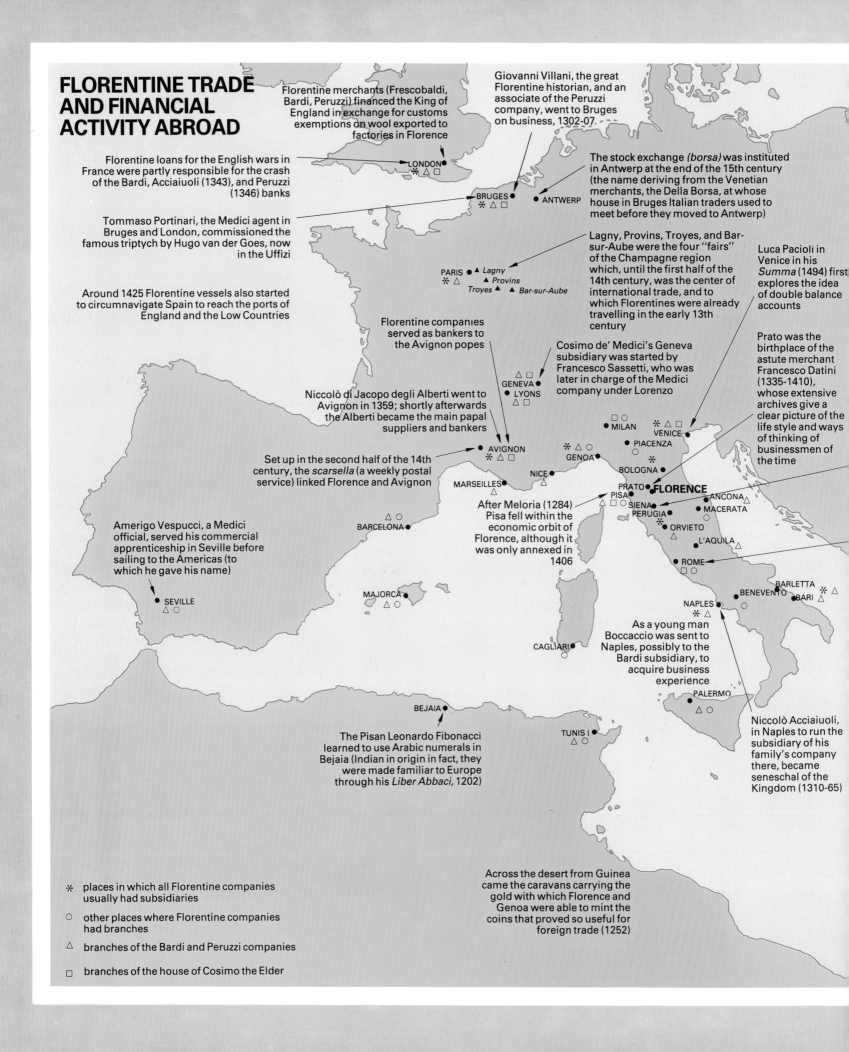

FLORENTINE TRADE AND FINANCIAL ACTIVITY ABROAD

Florentine merchants (Frescobaldi, Bardi, Peruzzi) financed the King of England in exchange for customs exemptions on wool exported to factories in Florence

Giovanni Villani, the great Florentine historian, and an associate of the Peruzzi company, went to Bruges on business, 1302-07

Florentine loans for the English wars in France were partly responsible for the crash of the Bardi, Acciaiuoli (1343), and Peruzzi (1346) banks

The stock exchange (borsa) was instituted in Antwerp at the end of the 15th century (the name deriving from the Venetian merchants, the Della Borsa, at whose house in Bruges Italian traders used to meet before they moved to Antwerp)

Tommaso Portinari, the Medici agent in Bruges and London, commissioned the famous triptych by Hugo van der Goes, now in the Uffizi

Lagny, Provins, Troyes, and Bar-sur-Aube were the four "fairs" of the Champagne region which, until the first half of the 14th century, was the center of international trade, and to which Florentines were already travelling in the early 13th century

Luca Pacioli in Venice in his Summa (1494) first explores the idea of double balance accounts

Around 1425 Florentine vessels also started to circumnavigate Spain to reach the ports of England and the Low Countries

Florentine companies served as bankers to the Avignon popes

Cosimo de' Medici's Geneva subsidiary was started by Francesco Sassetti, who was later in charge of the Medici company under Lorenzo

Prato was the birthplace of the astute merchant Francesco Datini (1335-1410), whose extensive archives give a clear picture of the life style and ways of thinking of businessmen of the time

Niccolò di Jacopo degli Alberti went to Avignon in 1359; shortly afterwards the Alberti became the main papal suppliers and bankers

Set up in the second half of the 14th century, the scarsella (a weekly postal service) linked Florence and Avignon

After Meloria (1284) Pisa fell within the economic orbit of Florence, although it was only annexed in 1406

Amerigo Vespucci, a Medici official, served his commercial apprenticeship in Seville before sailing to the Americas (to which he gave his name)

As a young man Boccaccio was sent to Naples, possibly to the Bardi subsidiary, to acquire business experience

The Pisan Leonardo Fibonacci learned to use Arabic numerals in Bejaia (Indian in origin in fact, they were made familiar to Europe through his Liber Abbaci, 1202)

Niccolò Acciaiuoli, in Naples to run the subsidiary of his family's company there, became seneschal of the Kingdom (1310-65)

Across the desert from Guinea came the caravans carrying the gold with which Florence and Genoa were able to mint the coins that proved so useful for foreign trade (1252)

Place labels: LONDON · BRUGES · ANTWERP · PARIS · Lagny · Provins · Troyes · Bar-sur-Aube · GENEVA · LYONS · MILAN · VENICE · PIACENZA · AVIGNON · GENOA · BOLOGNA · NICE · MARSEILLES · PRATO · FLORENCE · PISA · SIENA · ANCONA · MACERATA · PERUGIA · ORVIETO · L'AQUILA · ROME · BARCELONA · SEVILLE · MAJORCA · BARLETTA · BENEVENTO · BARI · NAPLES · CAGLIARI · PALERMO · BEJAIA · TUNIS

* places in which all Florentine companies usually had subsidiaries

○ other places where Florentine companies had branches

△ branches of the Bardi and Peruzzi companies

□ branches of the house of Cosimo the Elder

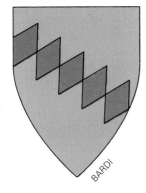

BARDI

PERUZZI

GIANFIGLIAZZI

ALBERTI

MEDICI

The map on the left, showing the normal bases of Florentine subsidiaries and a few basic facts and figures, gives some idea of the extent of international commerce. As Armando Sapori observes, this "is even more impressive when one considers the relatively short space of time over which these links were developed: the Florentines started serious trading at the beginning of the 13th century; by the mid 14th century

the outburst of expansion was over, though enough had been established to ensure them a leading – albeit not a totally dominant – position until the 16th century." The names of the companies concerned, which engaged in both trade and finance, imports of various goods and exports of manufactured articles, and money lending whenever opportunity for profit presented itself (though the risks too were

great), do not only evoke the city's economic past but its history as well: Acciaiuoli, Alberti del Giudice di Catenaia, Albizzi, Amieri, Ardinghelli, Bardi, Baroncelli, Bonaccorsi, Buondelmonti, Capponi, Cerchi, Corsini, Datini, Da Uzzano, Del Bene, Dell'Antella, Falconieri, Frescobaldi, Gianfigliazzi, Guadagni, Magalotti, Medici, Mozzi, Pazzi, Peruzzi, Portinari, Pulci, Rimbertini, Scali, Soderini, Spini, Strozzi, Tor-

nabuoni, Velluti. The arms of some of these families are shown above. As we know, the Bardi and Peruzzi became involved in disastrous loans to the King of England (Florence imported a great deal of high quality wool from England). On the failure of Edward III's campaign in France, the Florentine banking houses crashed. A tragic letter from the *Signoria* (1358) says of those members of the Bardi family who were still in Italy: *"facti sunt de locupletibus pauperes et ageni."* Villani recorded the figure of unreclaimable loans as 900,000 florins owing to the Bardi, and 600,000 to the Peruzzi. Less well known is the fact that the balance was settled in transactions undertaken under Richard II (1391). The Gianfigliazzi, who were unusual in confining themselves exclusively to banking, lent money to the La Tour in the Dauphiné. So binding were the guarantees and concessions they made, that when they left the country the prince was placed in financial embarrassment, and Philip VI de Valois was able to buy the Dauphiné for 120,000 florins, an annuity and repayment of the debt, thereby uniting the region to France. The Alberti del Giudice di Catenaia looked after much church finance, facilitating the collection of revenue, with transfers of capital by letter from the various markets where they operated to the papal camera, and receiving the *portagium* in payment, even though no cash had actually been transported. The Medici are familiar enough, but it is worth noting here their attempt to monopolize the alum market – for which, as we learn from the discoverer of this mineral in the Tolfa hills (in papal territory), the Turks every year "extorted more than 30,000 ducats from the Christians." By agreement with the pope, the Medici acquired control

of the mining and sale of Tolfa alum hoping to supplant the Turks in this field (alum was vital to the woollen cloth industry). But England, Burgundy, and Venice refused to cooperate. The anti-Medicean Sixtus IV switched the concession to the Centurione and the Genoese Doria family.

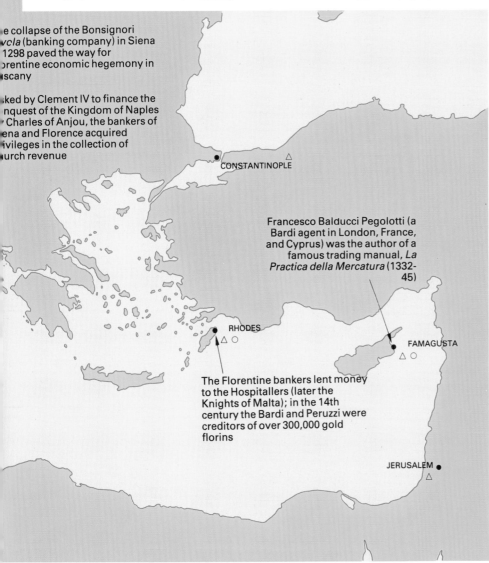

e collapse of the Bonsignori *vcla* (banking company) in Siena 1298 paved the way for orentine economic hegemony in scany

ked by Clement IV to finance the nquest of the Kingdom of Naples Charles of Anjou, the bankers of ena and Florence acquired ivileges in the collection of urch revenue

CONSTANTINOPLE

Francesco Balducci Pegolotti (a Bardi agent in London, France, and Cyprus) was the author of a famous trading manual, *La Practica della Mercatura* (1332-45)

RHODES

FAMAGUSTA

The Florentine bankers lent money to the Hospitallers (later the Knights of Malta); in the 14th century the Bardi and Peruzzi were creditors of over 300,000 gold florins

JERUSALEM

These wars disrupted trade routes and markets and required the imposition of heavy taxes on Florentine citizens. In 1402, a disgruntled merchant wrote to a business associate in Majorca: "There is no business here; everyone has to pay money to the commune to pay for this accursed war against the duke [Giangaleazzo Visconti]. We can send nothing out of our *contado,* because everything goes to him."

Profile of the Florentine merchant

It is possible to sketch a profile of the Florentine merchant who lived and worked abroad, thanks to thousands of mercantile letters which are extant in the city's archives and libraries, supplementing the information contained in account books, in public records and in mercantile manuals which were copied and disseminated in Italian business communities from England to North Africa and the Levant. In Prato, there exist 125,000 letters exchanged between Francesco Datini (1348-1410) and his business associates in Italy, Spain and France. This is by far the largest cache of mercantile letters from a single source to have survived prior to the 18th century.

Training for a mercantile career began early. Boys were first taught the fundamentals of reading and writing, and at the age of about ten, were sent to *scuole d'abbaco* to learn business arithmetic. In his early teens, a boy would be apprenticed to a merchant in Florence, where he would learn the technical aspects of the business. In his later teens, he would then be sent to a Florentine branch abroad: London, Bruges, Paris, Barcelona, Naples, Barletta, Famagusta. In 1397, Francesco Datini sent to his branch in Valencia "a young man who has been dealing with our accounts. He writes very well, and keeps excellent books; besides this, he also has a knowledge of Latin, a skill which is often sought after." In addition to mastering the intricacies of foreign commerce, the young merchant would also be learning the language and customs of the region, so that he could communicate with local merchants and officials. Promotions within the firm would come with experience. At some point in his early career, the young merchant would have to make a decision, either to remain with his company, or transfer to another firm, or become an independent entrepreneur. The latter option was the most risky, but it appealed to adventurers like Buonaccorso Pitti who travelled and traded through France, Germany, England, Flanders, Slavonia and Hungary, before finally returning permanently to Florence. From Ancona in 1408, one Remigio Lanfredini wrote to his brother in Florence that he planned to associate himself with "some great merchant, either Genoese or Venetian," intending to trade either "in the Eastern Empire or Alexandria or Syria or Pera ... or Constantinople or Kaffa ..."

The merchant engaged in international trade had to absorb a vast amount of information

At the base of the cathedral campanile, begun by Giotto in 1334 and continued by Andrea Pisano and Francesco Talenti, two superimposed bands of bas reliefs (now replaced by casts, with the originals preserved in the Opera del Duomo) provide an encyclopedic panorama of life as seen through medieval eyes.
The first band of panels, created by Andrea Pisano and possibly based on a design by Giotto, record man's progress from the Creation to civilization through arts and science. Amongst other subjects, there are emblematic representations of sculpture (left), painting (center), architecture (above), agriculture (opposite left), weaving (center) and metalworking (right).

The second band of bas-reliefs, completed by followers of Andrea Pisano, completes the series. They represent planets, because of their supposed influence on mankind; the virtues; the liberal arts (astronomy, music, geometry, grammar, rhetoric, logic, arithmetic) and, finally, the seven Sacraments, the crowning glory of man's existence.

about commodities, prices, tariffs, exchange rates, trade routes, and markets. Mercantile letters sent between a company's Florentine headquarters and its branches were filled with information on business conditions, and about any political or military events that could affect trade. When received, this information might be kept secret if it was to the firm's advantage, or it could be communicated to business associates and friends, who could be relied on to use it discreetly and who in turn would be expected to share any valuable news gleaned from their correspondence. Two examples illustrate the genre. In November 1396, the Avignon *fattore* of Francesco Datini, Boninsegna di Matteo, wrote to his employer in Florence about the commercial opportunites in Milan: "... Milan is a good trading city: most of our goods come from there, and we do more business there than anywhere else. Milan is on good terms with Genoa, Venice, Florence and Pisa; one may do business at a reasonable profit there." In December 1431, Francesco Davizi sent this information to Matteo Strozzi in Florence: "The wars between the French and the English are the cause of a great deal of trouble for both countries – this year the English have conquered back some of the land they lost at the time of Joan of Arc, but at considerable cost ... more than a million ducats, and 1,500 English lives. It would be easier for the English to abandon these disputed territories, or else they will utterly destroy their country.

Please God peace may reign once more."

In whatever city outside Italy these merchants resided, they constituted a very exclusive elite. They were both literate and numerate in a society where most people could not read, write or calculate. Jacob Burckhardt was among the first to recognize the significance of this mastery of numbers among Italian merchants, and of its profound influence upon their modes of thought. The Florentine merchant was trained to measure and to calculate, to make decisions after a careful evaluation of all of the relevant factors. He was trained to be flexible and pragmatic in his business affairs, and in other areas of his life and work. He was part of that tiny minority of Europeans who first developed a rational approach to human experience.

It was common practice for Florentine merchants to remain in one foreign city or region for several years, taking advantage of their special knowledge of local conditions, and of their ties with the political establishment. "I have been in Venice for more than 45 years," Bernardo Davanzati wrote to his son (1393), "and have done business with many generations of people, buying and selling much merchandise ..." Clusters of Florentine merchants were to be found in every major European court, providing credit and merchandise for princes and the members of their entourage, and serving frequently as officials and advisers in the government. That role did not please some citizens, who regarded

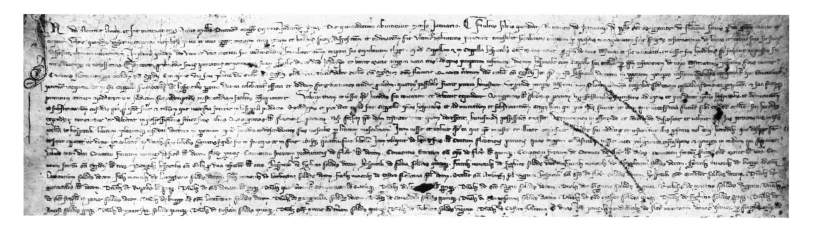

service with princes as a betrayal of their republican values. From Ferrara, where he was employed by Niccolò d'Este, Donato dell' Antella wrote a justificatory letter to his friend, Forese Sacchetti (c. 1415): "Forese, you must not be surprised at my approaching this gentleman, whom I have been acquainted with and whose servant I have been for many a year, to seek his help and counsel ..." But some merchants endeavoured to remain free of the intrigues and entanglements of foreign courts. Alessandro Ferrantini wrote from London to Matteo Strozzi (1434): "My business is trade, and I am not concerned with lords and communes. For me to be involved in anything like this would only be folly, for I have never engaged in such matters. I would look a fool either talking about or practicing such things; people would accuse me of attempting to dabble in philosophy." Ferrantini readily admitted that his business affairs required him to meet with English princes and courtiers, who were eager to receive news from the continent. For that reason, he asked Strozzi to send him relevant information that he could communicate to his contacts at Westminster.

The benevolence of local rulers was essential for the well-being of Florentine merchants abroad, who could not rely on their own government to protect them. When, for whatever reason, the local authorites could not maintain order, foreign merchants were in particular danger. Giovanni di Lando complained (1393) about the lawlessness in Rome during the absence of the papal court. "We can do nothing at present; without the court we have no choice but to leave Rome after the ill treatment foreigners have to endure every day. I am one of those who have to suffer constantly at the hand of marshals,

captains and anyone inclined to inflict such treatment. There is always someone ready to make trouble for poor foreigners ..." The Florentine commune did negotiate commercial treaties with some foreign states, that provided some security for their merchants. And if their citizens were maltreated by a foreign prince, they could request that reprisals be taken against his subjects who resided in, or travelled through, Florentine territory. However, these legal stratagems were not always effective in protecting merchants who had fallen into disfavour, as did Jacopo del Bene with the lord of Faenza, Astorgio Manfredi, in 1395. Jacopo was thrown into prison for a debt that he allegedly owed to Manfredi. Ill with fever in his underground cell, Jacopo sent a desperate plea for help to his friend, Luigi Milanesi, in Florence: "I entreat you to go to Fulignato and ask him to come here; beg him to have me released from this place, where I fear I may die!" Jacopo was still in prison three months later, when he wrote to his brother Riccardo: "I am still in prison, it must be for my sins. If you ever have children, never let them be incarcerated to mend their ways, for here one becomes murderous, cruel and mad."

Imprisonment for debt was a constant worry for merchants who lived abroad, and whose commercial ventures wre clouded by so much uncertainty. Even the most cautious and prudent merchant could not foresee every contingency that might result in business losses, bankruptcy, incarceration, or death. The insecurity deriving from their business affairs was intensified by their awareness of being alone and vulnerable in an alien land, resented for their wealth which, in the eyes of many of their hosts, was gained through usury and monopolies. Once profits

Above, a page of the will made by Folco Portinari on 15 January 1287. The protection of the legal rights of heirs was very precisely formulated in Florence. It was the custom for the father of a family to specify in his will who was to act as guardian for any underage children. If, however, no precise stipulation had been made, it was up to one of the podestà's clerks, or the court of the local sestiere, to name the person responsible, should the mother so request.

The person appointed was obliged, under oath, to act solely in their charge's interest, their first duty being to draw up an inventory of the goods, both fixed and moveable, that formed part of the inheritance. The confraternities were common recipients of bequests and legacies. The detail of a fresco from the workshop of Ghirlandaio in the church of San Martino dei Buonomini (right) shows a nun and a notary busy drawing up an inventory of an inheritance willed to the Compagnia dei Buonomini, the confraternity set up by St. Anthony in 1442 with the main aim of distributing alms to indigent families.

FLORENCE 1338: SOME ROUGH STATISTICS

Four famous chapters in Giovanni Villani's *Cronica* give information which allows us to sketch a rough statistical picture of Florence as it would have been around the end of the 1340s. The writer was well placed to find out facts. Born in about 1280, he was quickly introduced to the life of commerce in the famous and powerful Peruzzi company (acting as their *fattore* or steward in Bruges; he also became a partner). At the same time he was equally well informed about the machinery of government: in the 1330s he held various administrative posts, was twice a prior, and worked in embassies. His public career then seems to have come under a cloud, and his business interests would appear to have suffered. He died during the Black Death in 1348.

The period Villani writes about are the years 1336-38, a time of war. The *signore* of Verona, Mastino della Scala, had extended his territory to include Brescia, Parma, Lucca, and Treviso. Florence had offered the Veronese 360,000 florins for Lucca, in an attempt to halt their advance beyond the Apennines. When this offer was rejected war ensued (10 March 1337), with Venice, Florence, the Visconti, the d'Este, the Gonzaga, and John and Charles of Bohemia all allied with one another. With the restoration of peace just under two years later, Florence (already holding Arezzo, Pistoia, and Colle Valdelsa) acquired Pescia, Altopascio, and part of the territory of Lucca, although not the city itself. Not long before, the Florentine commune had built its second circle of city walls (1333); Villani had been treasurer of this project, and on the termination of this post he was accused of embezzlement, though he was able to prove his innocence. The miniature (1) from Pietro del Massaio's edition of Ptolemy's *Geography* dates from 1469, although Achille Ratti (later Pope Pius XI) suggested it was modelled on a drawing dating from the beginning of the century. The walls depicted here are, at any rate,

those of 1333. At this point in its history Florence's population, according to Villani, stood at about 90,000. This and other figures enable us to construct a graph (2) demonstrating the great population explosion of the 13th century, peaking in 1338 or possibly even later still. The figures for 1351 illustrate the devastation wrought by the Black Death, and the subsequent partial recovery. The population increased to 70,000 once more, to remain more or less the same until the end of the republic.

Diagram (6) is a breakdown of the population according to occupation and status, using Villani's facts reduced to a representative 500 inhabitants. Perhaps the most striking feature is that a third of the population made its living by the wool trade. The *Cronica* explicitly mentions that there were between about 300 and 500 more male than female baptisms per year; however, this may be deceptive, since baptism in San Giovanni was a way of gaining Florentine citizenship, which for those in the suburbs and surrounding countryside would have been more important for their sons than for their daughters.

A businessman through and through, Villani is very detailed on financial matters: the revenue of the commune is carefully recorded to total 306,500 florins. It is difficult to gain a precise idea of what such a sum represents. For instance, a few years later (1334) the King of France bought the Dauphiné for 120,000 florins; the accounts of the Bardi company for 1 July 1318 registered a turnover of 873,638

Approximate rate of population development in Florence

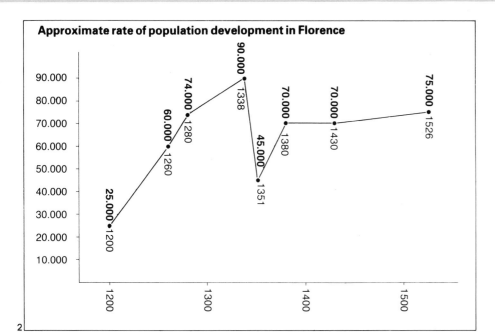

Food consumption in Florence

	data recorded by G. Villani	modern equivalents	annual availability per capita
grain	140 *moggia* bushels)	—	240 kg
wine	55,000 *cogna* per year	223,740 hl	248 l.
beef and veal	4,000 per year	780,000 kg	8,4 kg
geldings and sheep	60,000 per year	600,000 kg	6,5 kg
goats	20,000 per year	300,000 kg	3,3 kg
pigs	30,000 per year	1,800,000 kg	19,6 kg

Ordinary expenditure in 1338

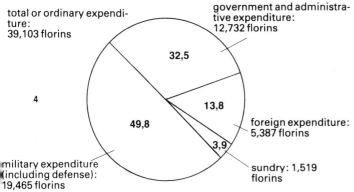

total or ordinary expenditure: 39,103 florins

government and administrative expenditure: 12,732 florins

4

foreign expenditure: 5,387 florins

sundry: 1,519 florins

military expenditure (including defense): 19,465 florins

florins. Sixty-three per cent of revenue (5) went on warfare (and this was still insufficient: for the two · wars against Mastino della Scala and Castruccio Castracani loans were taken out – both voluntary and enforced – worth 800,000 florins). Ordinary expenses took up 12.8 per cent. There thus remained 24.2 per cent for "communal works that cannot be reduced to simple numbers." The sum ₍the commune was run on (less than 40,000 florins) was distributed according to dia-

gram (4): almost half on military expenditure (including defense); about a third on government and administration; and the rest on foreign policy and sundry items including "the annual *palio di sciamito* (flag race) of San Giovanni." The government expenses (13,000 florins) referred to went mainly on honorariums for civil servants and on salaries: for the *podestà*, the *capitano del popolo,* officials of the judiciary, notaries, archivists, the senior public officials with their assistants and servants

("their families" as Villani calls them), and then *donzelli* (pages), menials and "bell ringers for the two towers," and finally "the trumpeters, six town criers for the *commune,* drummers, bagpipes, *cennamelle* (a variety of bagpipe), and bugles, ten in all with silver trumpets." The chart showing what was eaten (3) gives some indication of the availability of individual commoditfes annually per capita: 240 kg (530 lbs) of grain, 248 l. (54 gal) of wine, and 40 kg (88 lbs) of meat.

General accounts for 1338 (in florins)

revenue	expenditure		
306,500	193,050	39,103	74,347
	on warfare 63%	ordinary 12.8%	balance 24.2%

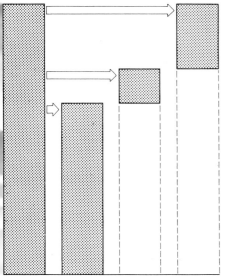

In 1338, out of 500 people representing a cross section of the whole population of Florence ...

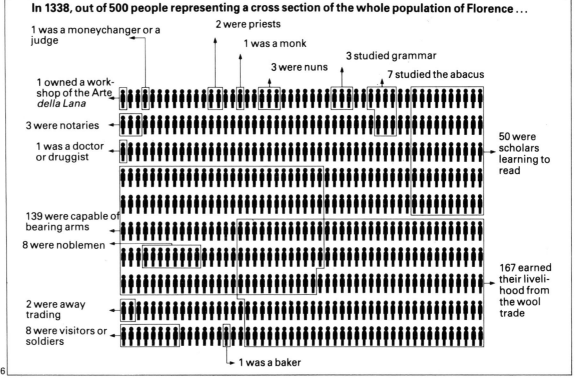

1 was a moneychanger or a judge

2 were priests

1 was a monk

3 were nuns

3 studied grammar

7 studied the abacus

1 owned a workshop of the Arte *della Lana*

3 were notaries

1 was a doctor or druggist

50 were scholars learning to read

139 were capable of bearing arms

8 were noblemen

167 earned their livelihood from the wool trade

2 were away trading

8 were visitors or soldiers

1 was a baker

6

were realized from trade, there were always difficulties in transferring the money back to Florence. "This happens in almost every country," Rosso Orlandi commented in 1396, "citizens who might have gained from a foreigner's earnings resent his taking this money elsewhere, and, if it is in their power to do so, will prevent him, and gladly take that money away from him …" Datini, a man prone to deep pessimism, wrote (1398) that "land and sea alike are riddled with thieves, and man is mostly ill disposed towards his brother."

To protect himself and his property, the international merchant had to rely on his own skills and knowledge and also the support he might receive from his fellow nationals who, in

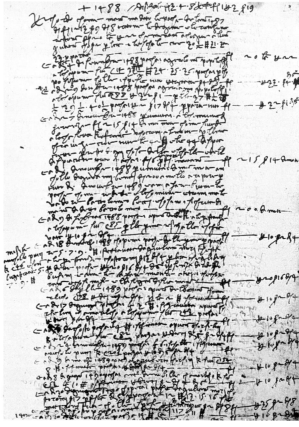

In the church of Santa Trinita there is a chapel belonging to the Sassetti, a famous family of Florentine merchants. In the frescoes covering the chapel walls, which are the work of Domenico Ghirlandaio, is depicted one of the family's most illustrious members, Francesco Sassetti, who was an agent of the Medici and a friend of the humanists. The merchant, accompanied by his son, is shown to the left of Lorenzo the Magnificent, on whose right stands Antonio Pucci. Far left, a wing of the Portinari triptych, the work of Hugo van der Goes, showing St. Thomas and St. Anthony. The kneeling figure is Tommaso Portinari, the great Florentine businessman, manager of the Medici interests in Bruges, and banker to Charles the Bold and the Emperor Maximilian. Behind him kneel his children. Left, a page from the Libro Debitori e Creditori di Rinieri di Rinaldo Peruzzi e di Amerigo suo Figliuolo ed Erede *(Book of Creditors and Debtors of Rinieri di Rinaldo Peruzzi and of Amerigo his Son and Heir), drawn up between 1488 and 1502 (Archivio di Stato, Florence). For almost five centuries, Florentine and Italian businessmen in general occupied an unrivalled position in the economic life of the West, contributing to the establishment of the middle class and the development of a secular, urban culture. Yves Renouard wrote that they provided the essential basis for contemporary commercial and financial skills, whilst their rationalism and their desire to please gave an important boost to those Renaissance ideas and ethics that still play such an important role in the modern world.*

times of difficulty, banded together to defend each other's interests. The ideal merchant, as depicted in mercantile manuals and correspondence, was shrewd, cautious and laconic. "I would ask you henceforth to be more circumspect and cautious," Rosso Orlandi wrote to Piero Davanzati (1396), "may I remind you of the saying 'he who knows a lot and spends a lot will soon be in trouble,' and another proverb which says 'he who deals in facts does not utter a word, but keeps his lips sealed.'" The merchant's most precious asset was his reputation for honesty and integrity. To preserve that reputation, merchants acted quickly to condemn any breach of trust, any violation of the mercantile code to which they all subscribed. Merchants who absconded with the assets of others were prosecuted relentlessly in the courts. Their goods, if found, were confiscated, and they were subject to imprisonment. The records of the *Mercanzia*, the merchants' court in Florence, are replete with documents concerning the business failures of merchants both foreign and native, and the penalties meted out to those involved in these disasters.

The international merchant's life could never be calm and tranquil; he lived perforce in a constant state of anxiety. That was in part due to the vicissitudes of his business affairs, and in part to his living in a society that still viewed his activities with suspicion and distrust. In the minds of many, probably the majority, of 15th-century Europeans, there was something dishonourable about the merchant's calling. That sentiment, pervasive in medieval culture, had never died out, even in mercantile communities like Florence and Venice. It was kept alive by preachers, who criticized the greed and avarice of merchants, and by nobles who claimed that warfare was the only honourable profession for men. The church's prohibitions against usury were never clear and unambiguous, and the most scrupulous merchant, at some time in his career, might be guilty of violating the rules, particularly if he engaged in moneylending and exchange. When, in 1398, an associate of Francesco Datini learned that the Prato merchant was planning to set up a bank, he wrote him a warning letter: "I hear you intend to establish a banking company, and I must tell you that I feel you are ill-advised, for this is not as profitable a trade, nor as honourable or pleasing to God as being a

A Florentine merchant-banker, shown holding his scales and linear measure, in a woodcut from the end of the 15th century.

The Stock Exchange at Bruges, a renowned commercial center in Flanders, showing the buildings housing Florentine and Genoese merchants.

Confirmation of the very lively nature of the mercantile class is provided by the manual entitled The Practice of Commerce, *written by Balducci Pegolotti, a Florentine entrepreneur who between 1318 and 1321 ran the London branch of the Bardi company, Europe's largest banking and trading concern during the 13th and 14th centuries. The book, two pages of which, taken from an edition now in the Biblioteca Riccardiana, are reproduced on the left, was the indispensible vademecum of contemporary traders, containing information on the uses of international exchanges and coinage, as well as metrological data. In their search for maritime outlets, the Florentines in 1421 acquired the port of Leghorn which up until then had been a Genoese possession, buying it, along with the port of Pisa, for the sum of 100,000 florins. Opposite, a galley in Leghorn harbour, as depicted in an engraving by Stefano della Bella dated 1634. The port of Leghorn was expanded during the 16th century and it became the greatest Florentinne entrepôt of the Medici era, its growth being further encouraged by the system of bonded warehousing, the introduction of which gave the city its great commercial prosperity as an international trading center.*

merchant." More than a century later (1515), Filippo Strozzi noted that in Rome and Naples, there was still a widespread feeling in aristocratic circles that a mercantile career was dishonourable. Filippo was criticized for his plan to form a company in Naples and only his appointment as *depositarius* of the apostolic camera made his banking activities in Rome acceptable to high-born members of that community.

The Medici bank

At some time in the 1380s, an obscure Florentine from a well-known if not distinguished family, Giovanni di Bicci de' Medici (1360-1429), received his first employment in the Roman branch of a company headed by his relative, Vieri di Cambio de' Medici. He soon became a partner and manager of that office, and on Vieri's retirement in 1393, he formed his own company. Four years later, Giovanni moved to Florence and established a banking firm there, keeping the Roman office under a managing partner. In 1402, he founded yet another branch in Venice, and in that same decade, he opened two woollen cloth *botteghe* in Florence. He created his first banking company across the Alps in 1426; other branches were opened later in Avignon, Bruges and London. When Giovanni died in 1429, he bequeathed to his sons Cosimo and Lorenzo a fortune estimated at 180,000 florins.

Giovanni's enormous wealth came primarily from the Roman branch of the Medici bank, which since the 1390s had been involved in papal finance. Since the late 13th century, Florentines had been active in the lucrative business, even though they had to share it with merchants from Siena, Lucca, Pistoia and Bologna. During the 70-year residence of the papacy in Avignon (1309-76), Florentine bankers, most notably the Alberti, gradually edged out their rivals and achieved a quasi monopoly of papal financial business. After the outbreak of the Great Schism, they fell out of favour with the Roman popes, Urban VI and Boniface IX. However, they recovered their influence, and the lion's

nguille o buratelch la

Ariento lauorato vecchio

share of papal financial business, in the early years of the 15th century. Giovanni de' Medici had been a close friend of the antipope John XXIII, while he was a curial official. When the latter was elected pope in 1410, Giovanni was appointed *depositarius camerae apostolice,* an office which gave him special responsibilities in handling papal business, and also exceptional privileges. Though obligated to lend money to the papal camera, the Medici were guaranteed repayment from papal revenues, and they received a fee from nearly every financial transaction involving the papacy. The Medici bank was involved in collecting papal revenues from all of Christian Europe, in paying *condottieri* in the papal armies, in making loans to the apostolic camera, to other curial officials, to cardinals and their dependents, to clerics who came to Rome on business, to pilgrims. When a German bishop-elect arranged for the payment of common services to the camera, or when a *signore* in the Papal States paid his *censo,* the Medici bank received its share of those financial transactions. The privileged position of the Medici in papal finance continued for most of the 15th century, and did not finally end until the pontificate of Sixtus IV (1476-84).

The Medici branch in Rome was consistently the most profitable segment of the company's operations; Professor de Roover has calculated that it produced more than half of the profits during Cosimo's lifetime. Cosimo was one of the most astute entrepreneurs of his age, combining in his person all the qualities – intelligence, shrewdness, realism, foresight – that had traditionally characterized the most successful Florentine entrepreneurs. While managing the operations of his network of companies, he was also, after 1434, deeply involved in Florentine politics. In supervising the operations of his various enterprises (in 1451 these included the main office in Florence, six foreign branches, one silk and two wool shops), he relied heavily on his partners, who managed these operations directly. Cosimo possessed a distinct flair for choosing reliable men to serve as factors and partners in his organization. Many of these men came from Florentine families – Bardi, Benci, Martelli, Portinari, Sassetti, Tornabuoni – who profited handsomely from their connection with the Medici.

Under Cosimo's astute direction, the network

Shops in a Florentine street with the typical sloping roofs over the entrance, as seen in a drawing from the beginning of the 17th century by Taddeo Zuccari. Below, shops in the Mercato Vecchio as they still appeared in 1870, when this drawing by Edoardo Borrani was executed. Opposite, counters within shops of the 14th century, as portrayed in the Libro delle Gabelle Fiorentine *(Book of Florentine Taxes) by Antonio Ventura, now preserved in the Biblioteca Riccardiana.*

of Medici companies blanketed much of Christian Europe and the western Mediterranean. Only in the Levant did the Medici, perhaps sensitive to papal opposition to trading with the infidel, fail to develop a strong presence in the second half of the 15th century. Elsewhere, their factors and agents arranged for transfers of money and credit between northern Europe and Italy. They made loans to kings, princes and prelates in London, Bruges, Rome and Naples. From London and Bruges, they arranged for the shipment of textiles in the Florentine galleys that, since the 1420s, were engaged in the Atlantic trade. They also provided luxury products – fine woollen cloth and silk brocade, spices and jewels – for the courts in London, Paris, and Naples. The Medici branch in Bruges obtained paintings by Flemish artists for Italian buyers, and recruited singers in the Low Countries for the choir of San Giovanni Laterano in Rome. Medici agents in northern Europe also received commissions from their masters in Florence to search for rare copies of classical authors: Livy, Pliny and Suetonius, among others.

The business operations of the Medici

reflected accurately the strengths and weaknesses of Florence's economic structure in the 15th century. The Medici fortune was based on banking and exchange operations, which were indeed lucrative, but which depended to a large degree on the good will and the prosperity of the "great men" in Rome and in other major European cities. That fortune, and others of similar provenance, contributed to the great concentration of wealth in a few Florentine households, but it did not directly promote the prosperity of the rest of the population. It has been argued that through their building projects, the Medici and other rich citizens did support large numbers of artists, craftsmen and labourers. But the *catasto* records show that most artisans lived at no higher than the subsistence level, and that a large portion of the population was abysmally poor. Florentine industry was geared to the production of luxury goods, which were highly prized by wealthy Europeans. The demand for these expensive products was however limited and erratic. In retrospect, the Florentine economy of the 15th century was like an exotic plant, flourishing under very unique conditions, but unable to survive sustained adversity.

The decline of the Medici bank in the last decades of the 15th century was a grim portent for the city's economy, of which it was so integral a part. The story of that crash has been well told by Professor de Roover, the distinguished historian of the bank. Already at the time of Cosimo's death in 1464, the Medici branches in London and Bruges were in serious difficulty, partly due to poor management and partly as a consequence of a perennial trade imbalance between Italy and the North. Like the Bardi and the Peruzzi a century earlier, these branches had loaned money to impecunious princes, specifically to King Edward IV of England and Duke Charles the Bold of Burgundy. Lorenzo de' Medici was too preoccupied with affairs of state to devote much attention to business affairs, which he entrusted to Francesco Sassetti, a man of limited entrepreneurial talent. The war between Florence and Pope Sixtus IV (1478-81) was very damaging to Medici business interests, because it cut off the revenues and profits from Rome. Lorenzo was in such grave financial difficulties during this war that he took money from the inheritance of his two nephews, who were his

Left, a fantastical view of Florence, from Maso Finiguerra's 15th-century Cronaca Illustrata. *The figure represents Julius Caesar, who, according to one ancient tradition, was the founder of the city. Opposite, the heraldic device of the Rucellai family, on the façade of the church of Santa Maria Novella. Giovanni di Paolo Rucellai was the man who, during the second half of the 15th century, financed the construction of the upper part of the church's façade, commissioning Leon Battista Alberti to carry out the work.*

wards, and probably (the evidence is inconclusive) also seized public funds to prop up his private fortune. But these infusions of capital did not improve his economic situation, which continued to deteriorate. When Lorenzo died in 1494, the Medici bank was on the verge of bankruptcy, and the expulsion from Florence of his son Piero in 1494 was the definitive blow to the bank founded by his great-grandfather Giovanni.

From crisis to stasis

The difficulties of the Medici bank in the last years of the 15th century were experienced, in some degree, by every sector of the Florentine economy. Banking was perhaps the most seriously depressed of the city's economic activities, but international trade and the cloth industry were also in a prolonged slump. The French invasion of 1494 was an ominous event for Florence and the rest of Italy. It signalled the beginning of half

a century of intermittent warfare, with very adverse consequences for the populace: disrupted trade routes, depressed industries, high rates of taxation to meet the costs of military activities, depredations by soldiers. In 1480, during Florence's war with Pope Sixtus IV, a Florentine cleric, Manente Buondelmonti, explained in his tax declaration why some of his rural property had not yielded a profit: "The said mill (…) was sacked by our own men, and all the harvest taken. Our stores, buildings and land have been damaged and we have lost everything we worked for during this year: our prospects for the year to come are therefore not good. The parish church and all the houses are nearly deserted, occupied only by soldiers who drank all our wine, about 50 barrels' worth …" Similar

laments appear with increasing frequency in the Florentine fiscal records after 1494, when foreign and native troops moved around the Tuscan countryside, looting, ravaging, burning, killing. These were years of unparalleled misery for the unprotected peasants and villagers of the Florentine dominion.

The recovery of Pisa in 1509 gave Florence only a momentary respite from its heavy tax burden and its vulnerability. In that same year, the imperious Pope Julius II began an assault, first on Venice, and then on the French, who had occupied Milan since 1500. Warfare spread throughout the Lombard plain, then into Emilia and the Romagna, and finally, in 1512, into Tuscany. A Spanish army moved towards Florence, routing the republic's army at Prato, and

The guild of moneychangers, vital to the commercial life of the city, was one of Florence's seven major guilds. The moneychangers sat behind a counter or "bank," which was covered by a carpet, a symbol of distinction; they thereby became "bankers," holding deposits and registers in which merchants opened accounts and executed financial transfers. Above left, a bank depicted in the church of San Francesco at Prato.
Above, the shrine of the guild of moneychangers in Orsanmichele, with a statue of its patron St. Matthew attributed to Ghiberti.

The cover of a Registro di Gabella *(tax register) dating from 1648, now preserved in the Archivio di Stato in Siena. The distinction between banker and merchant was rather blurred in 14th- and 15th-century Italy. Banks were, in fact, also trading establishments, with bankers continuing to act as merchants.*

sacking that town only ten kilometers (6 miles) from the city. The restoration of a Medicean regime (September 1512) brought a measure of peace to the region, and some modest prosperity to its inhabitants.

Once again under Medici control, Florence enjoyed a few years of peace and prosperity before experiencing the most agonizing ordeal of its history: the siege of the imperial armies that culminated in its capitulation (August 1530). During these years, two Medici popes, Leo X (1513-21) and Clement VII (1523-34) provided unique opportunities for a select group of Florentine bankers to make their fortunes in Rome. Filippo Strozzi, married to Leo X's niece, Clarice, was named depositor of the apostolic camera in 1515. Strozzi was the most favoured of

the Florentine bankers operating in Rome during the Medici pontificates, but members of other prominent families – the Altoviti, Antinori, Gaddi, Salviati, Soderini, Tornabuoni – were also involved in banking and tax farming in the Roman curia. Although these merchants profited handsomely from their connections with the Medici, they had to make risky loans to these popes, who were perpetually short of money. The sack of Rome by an imperial army in 1527 threatened the economic viability of the Florentine bankers at the curia, who also lost influence there after the death of Clement VII in 1534. The dramatic decline in the fortunes of Filippo Strozzi drove him into political opposition to Duke Cosimo, and then to defeat in battle, imprisonment and suicide. Although

some bankers like the Altoviti continued to play a substantial role in papal finance under Pope Paul III and his successors, the great age of Florentine banking in the Eternal City had come to an end by 1534.

The perils encountered by Florentine merchants in Rome, who witnessed the pillaging and looting of that city by imperial troops, was matched by their relatives in Florence during the Last Republic and particularly during the siege in the last year of that doomed regime. In 1527 a lethal epidemic had struck the city, killing several thousand of its residents. Those who survived were heavily taxed to pay for mercenaries, the repair of fortifications, and grain supplies. The imperial forces surrounding the city ransacked monasteries and country villas, burned peasants' cottages, cut down trees for firewood, and killed livestock for food. They cut off the supplies from the *contado* for the beleaguered city, whose starving residents finally surrendered to their enemies on 12 August 1530. Returning to Florence from his country villa after the siege had ended, Francesco Guicciardini recorded his impressions: "The misery that has befallen the city and the *contado* and the devastation are almost unmentionable, and greatly exceed anything we could ever have imagined. The people are powerless. Houses for miles around Florence and in many other parts of the dominion have been destroyed; only a few farmers have survived and there are almost no poor left at all. There is very little grain to live on this year, and little to hope for in the year to come. In short, this is an unbelievable calamity for this province to have to endure."

The economy of both city and territory recovered rapidly after 1530, when peace finally came to Tuscany after 35 years of turmoil. The population of Florence in 1552 was 60,000, the highest level since the 14th century. The woollen cloth industry, on which the livelihood of thousands depended, produced more than 30,000 bolts per year. Florentine merchants sold that cloth, and the other products of the city's *botteghe,* in markets throughout Europe and the Levant. Grand Duke Cosimo I pursued what may be called a "proto-mercantilist" policy. He reorganized the city's guilds, encouraged old industries and developed new ones in the city and the territory, and established a new port city at Leghorn. Cosimo and his successors realized the importance of economic prosperity for the stability of their government, and their policies were designed to keep Tuscany peaceful and productive. For most of the 16th century they were remarkably successful.

There is little evidence, from the 16th century, that Florence's entrepreneurial class had become

Illustrated on these pages are different methods of transporting goods and people used between the 14th and 16th centuries.
Above, provisions for an army being transported by cart during the 14th century (Biblioteca Marciana).

Below, a riding party, and goods being carried on the back of a mule (miniatures from the second half of the 14th century).
Opposite above left, a carriage drawn by four horses, from a 1599 painting by Giusto Utens. Above

right, a message being despatched in the 14th century (from an Italian miniature in the Aeschlimann Collection).
Below, a Pisan ship being loaded (from the Douce Manuscript in the Bodleian Library, Oxford).

less active in business, or less motivated by a desire for profit, than before. It is true that some members of old mercantile families were, like Machiavelli and Guicciardini, more attracted to public service, while others preferred a quiet life in their country villas to the bustle of the *botteghe* and the moneychangers' tables. But Florentines had pursued such vocations since Dante's time. It was still customary, in the late cinquecento, for adolescents from prominent families to be trained for a mercantile career, and for many to pursue that career in Florence and abroad. Two nephews of Francesco Guicciardini, Lodovico and Giovanbattista, lived and traded in Antwerp until their death; another merchant, Vicenzo, established his permanent residence in London. Still another nephew, Girolamo, remained in Florence where he made his fortune in textile manufacturing, invested heavily in real estate, and played an active role at the court of Duke Cosimo. The Gondi and the Guadagni were deeply involved in trade and banking in Lyons, where some became permanent residents and members of the local nobility. Giuliano di Piero Capponi (d. 1565) was the head of a very prosperous enterprise, involved in cloth manufacturing in Florence and Pisa, and in international trade and banking, with branches and investments in Naples, Antwerp, Seville, London and Lyons.

In 1609, the Venetian ambassador Francesco Badoer wrote about Florence: "There is a great

On the subject of Florence at the end of the 13th century, Giovanni Villani says: "Within, she was well laid out and furnished with many fine houses, and there was continual building going on, with improvements being made to make the houses rich and luxurious, their exteriors revealing splendid evidence of every improvement." A picture of later building work in Florence is offered by the illustration opposite, showing a detail of the Building of the Tower of Babel, *a fresco by Benozzo Gozzoli in Pisa's* Camposanto. *Fifteenth-century masons belonged to the guild of master craftsmen in stone and wood, whose emblem, modelled by Luca della Robbia, can be seen above left. There were frequent portrayals of building work: above, the reconstruction of the walls of Arezzo (detail of the sarcophagus of Bishop Tarlato, created by Giovanni and Angelo di Ventura from Siena) and, left, a tablet from a register of the* Ufficiali dei Casseri *dating from 1440 (Archivio di Stato, Siena).*

FLORENCE'S WOOL INDUSTRY

The most important business in Florence was the wool industry. Evidence of this is afforded by a document dating from the late 14th century, in the archives of Francesco di Marco Datini, a merchant from Prato, which has samples of material attached (5). A large part of the population was involved in the wool business, including the importation of the wool itself, the various stages of production, and then the selling, both at home and, more importantly, abroad. All this generated wealth and led to the creation of a highly complex organization. There were two main branches of the wool industry: either partially worked cloth was imported to be finished off – dyed carded, woven and marketed – or the whole cycle was started from the beginning, with the fleece itself.

Shipping conditions in the Mediterranean improved around the beginning of the 13th century, allowing Italy to import medium-quality wool from Spain and Portugal, and wool of poorer quality from North Africa. Many wools from Portugal and north-west Africa were called *lane di garbo* (literally, honest wool) after the Islamic sultanate of the Algarve which had been reconquered in 1253. Around 1280, and even more so 30 years later, Florentine traders were able, thanks to loans made to England, to import English wools: and it was due to the superiority of these wools that Florentine cloth was better than that of Flanders and northern France. It is no accident therefore that we see the word *Inghilterra* (England) in the miniature (1) from the 14th-century *Libro delle Gabelle* by Antonio di Ventura, showing a sheep

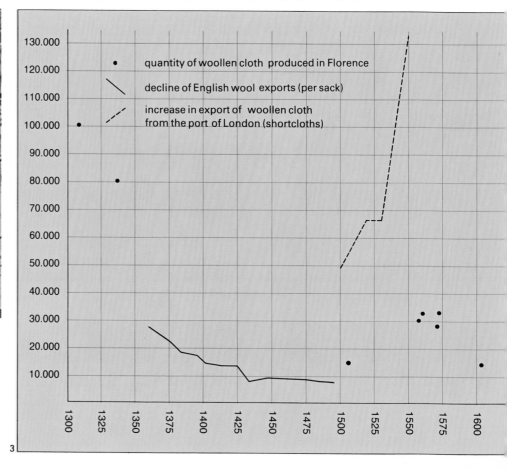

2

individual pieces and production as a whole – was more valuable. In graph (3) some 14th-century production figures are compared with much later figures, seen in the light of two developments relating to England: the decrease in English wool exports, and their increased exportation of woollen cloth; the production center of the international market had shifted. As Alfred Doren quite rightly observed, with the Florentine wool industry, medieval capitalism reached its peak.

1

Giovanni Villani records that the 20 *fondaci* of the Calimala (the guild of the great cloth merchants and refiners) imported 10,000 articles per year, at a value of 360,000 florins; and that the 200 workshops produced 80,000 articles having a total value of 1,200,000 florins (i.e. between the years 1336-38).

being sheared. This precious wool had to be carried by sea to the Tyrrhenian ports or, even more expensively, by land through France: thus within some 30 years the amount of cloth produced diminished (3), along with the number of businesses (7). At the same time, however, the end product – both

quantity of woollen cloth produced in Florence

decline of English wool exports (per sack)

increase in export of woollen cloth from the port of London (shortcloths)

3

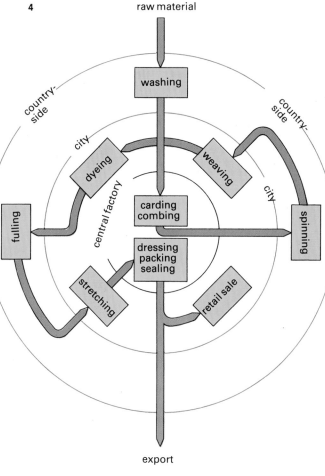

4

raw material

countryside · city

washing

dyeing · weaving

fulling · central factory · carding combing · spinning

dressing packing sealing

stretching · retail sale

countryside · city

export

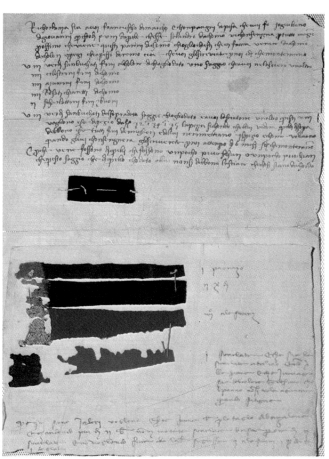

5

The *lanaiolo* (the general term for someone in the wool business) with capital at his disposal, whether his own or borrowed, was both a tradesman and a production entrepreneur. He would buy the raw materials (the wool and dyeing substances, woad and alum) and market the finished product once the wool had passed through the various stages of cloth production. During this process he would have recourse to workers directly answerable to him, working at home sometimes with their own equipment, as well as independent artisans, but he would always remain in charge and would always retain ownership of the wool, as it progressively became transformed into cloth. Of interest also is the geography of the industry (4), with much to-ing and fro-ing between three distinct centers of production – the actual factory of the *lanaiolo,* the city at large, and the countryside. The imported wool would first arrive at the *laverie* (wash house), on the Arno to be washed; it would then proceed to the factory to be carded and combed; out to the country to be spun; back into the city for weaving and dyeing; once again into the country to be fulled and then back to town finally to be stretched in the *tiratoi* (stretching sheds). Many pictures of old Florence (2) show the *tiratoi* of the *Arte della Lana* along the Arno (demolished in 1859). To end the process the cloth would once more return to the factory for the final packing, checking, and sealing (as a guarantee of quality). It would then be retailed in shops (6) or exported.

Sociological studies have been made of the various classes of worker involved in the wool industry – the great success of which was due as much to the availability of cheap labour as to the wit and enterprise of the merchants. Those who spun, carded, and combed the wool relied entirely on their own two hands to make an uncertain living: these formed the proletariat of the Ciompi Revolution. The spinners and weavers worked in their own homes, and sometimes themselves employed workers and apprentices. Nevertheless they remained financially dependent on the *lanaiolo:* the looms were borrowed or sold on a pro rata basis of payment by instalments of work, or else they were pledged to the *lanaiolo* in return for work. Those employed in finishing off and treating the cloth were somewhat better off thanks to their expertise (and such jobs were often handed down from father to son). The twin commercial poles of capital and labour met in the jobs of those who dyed and stretched the cloth: "capital made its way into their workshops either from the capitalists themselves, from the guild or city, or else from the workers, in the form of savings. Only for this category of worker was there opportunity for breaking out of the working class into the upper echelons of the capitalist society" (Doren).

6

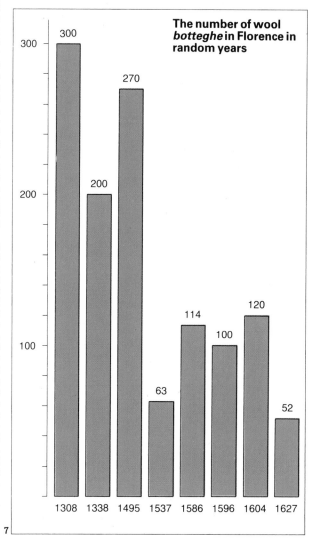

The number of wool *botteghe* in Florence in random years

Year	Number
1308	300
1338	200
1495	270
1537	63
1586	114
1596	100
1604	120
1627	52

7

Sixteenth-century paintings by pupils of Vasari in the Palazzo Vecchio celebrate man's work by means of pictorial images that also provide comprehensive documentation of contemporary techniques. The tasks being carried out by men in a woollen works (below) are depicted by Mirabello Cavalori in the studiolo of Francis I. The same room also contains a painting by Giovanni Maria Butteri showing the interior of a glassworks (right).

deal of activity. The population, which numbers about 70,000, is very industrious, although its energies are concentrated more on the manufacture of wool than anything else. This business is handled by gentlemen who are involved in trade all over the world, making their city one of the foremost centers in Europe." Badoer saw signs of a change in the mentality of the entrepreneurial class, however: "It is true that for some time now merchants have been turning into noblemen, with young men spending their time on court pursuits ..." The new ruler of Florence, Grand Duke Cosimo II, preferred to see the nobility as "knights rather than merchants ..." Within a decade of that report, the decline of the industrial and mercantile sectors of the Florentine economy had become precipitous. Woollen cloth production, which in the 1570s had still averaged 30,000 pieces of cloth per year, had fallen by 1620 to less than 10,000, and by 1650, to a mere 5,000. This trend was parallelled by a steady reduction in investments in interna-

tional trade and banking. The colonies of Florentine merchants that for centuries had clustered around every major European market center, had all but disappeared by the middle of the 17th century.

Much ink has been spilled by economic historians seeking to explain this downward trend, which was not confined to Florence, but embraced the entire peninsula, including those former mercantile giants, Venice and Genoa. All of Europe experienced an economic slump in the 1620s and 1630s; it was an age of generally poor harvests and famines, of periodic outbreaks of plague, of destructive wars, and of reduced levels of trade and industrial activity. Florence never recovered its former role in the European economy, which increasingly was dominated by Dutch and English entrepreneurs. Textiles produced in northern Europe were cheaper than those manufactured in Florence, where guild restrictions and burdensome taxes contributed to the high costs of production. In the unfavourable

economic climate, the incentives to pursue a mercantile career or to invest in a cloth *bottega* were much reduced. The attractions of the court outweighed the thirst for profit that had motivated generations of young Florentines for more than five centuries. The economy became progressively more provincial and agrarian, resembling in some respects that which had existed in the early 11th century, before the city began its spectacular rise to the heights of Europe's economic order.

Also in the studiolo *is a painting of a goldsmith's workshop (above left) by Alessandro Fei del Barbiere, which is an imaginary representation of Benvenuto Cellini in the act of creating the crown of the grand dukes. On the ceiling of the Sala di Penelope, also in the Palazzo Vecchio, there is a fresco of a weaving scene, the work of Marco Stradano, which shows Penelope working at her loom, surrounded by women busy spinning and embroidering.*

A school for self-government

In his analysis of the Italian city-state of the Middle Ages, the English historian Daniel Waley considered the fortunes of self-governing communes, which eventually were transformed into *Signorie*. These republican regimes, he wrote, gave their citizens "a certain 'political education,' but the school broke up in disorder and hence one must doubt whether the pupils had learned their lessons." This chapter will suggest that, in Florence at least, the pupils, the citizens, did indeed learn their lessons. Their experience, recorded and analyzed by their historians and theorists, above all Machiavelli, was destined to have a profound influence upon European political thought.

The formation of the urban commune was the most significant political development in Italy during the 11th and early 12th centuries. The commune became the typical form of political organization in the northern and central parts of the peninsula, replacing the traditional authorities that had governed those provinces since the disintegration of the Carolingian empire in the ninth century. The circumstances that resulted in the creation of these communes were similar everywhere. The first prerequisite was an expanding, dynamic urban society, pulsating with the tides and pressures of demographic expansion in the surrounding rural areas, and responding to new economic opportunities in its region and beyond. Its leaders were men with estates and connections in the feudal world outside the city walls, men who had been involved in the governance of their towns, together with the representatives of imperial or episcopal authority. The birth of communes frequently occurred when those traditional powers were weak and faltering, unable to perform effectively the ser-

vices, primarily those of defense, that had been their responsibility. In the pre-communal era, assemblies of leading citizens in these towns had met irregularly, to give counsel and assistance to these authorities. This tradition of cooperation and participation in municipal affairs had gradually developed in the towns during the 11th century; it provided the framework for the emergence of those new associations, the communes, which sprang up everywhere in Italy from the Alps to the Tiber.

In Tuscany as elsewhere in northern and central Italy, the rise of the communes was facilitated by the bitter struggle between the papacy and the Holy Roman Empire, a conflict that had its origins in the controversy over investiture in the late 11th century. Pope Gregory VII (d. 1085) and his successors had challenged the right of the emperors to invest bishops and abbots with their offices and the estates pertaining to them. The secular authority in Tuscany, Countess Matilda, was a strong supporter of the papacy and when she died in 1115, she left her property to the Holy See. But her pro-papal stance had undermined her own authority, which derived from the imperial power. During these unsettled times, the Tuscan communes emerged to assume, very gradually, the public duties and responsibilities that had formerly been exercised by imperial officials. The first Tuscan town known to have elected consuls, executive officials of the commune, was Pisa in 1085. Arezzo followed in 1098, Pistoia in 1105, Lucca in 1115.

In its political as in its economic development, Florence was somewhat retarded by comparison with its neighbours. Not until 1138 is there a reference in the sources to the existence of four

Shortly after the middle of the 16th century, the military architect and stage designer Baldassare Lanci recreated the teeming heart of Florence in a theatrical backdrop. The scene represented the Piazza della Signoria, the historical center of the city, dominated by Florence's most important and majestic building, successively called, as its function altered, the Palazzo del Popolo, the Palazzo dei Priori or della Signoria, and, finally, the Palazzo Vecchio.

created to assume these legislative responsibilities. The membership of the 12th-century commune was restricted to a small group of prominent citizens, *boni homines.* Their social rank was aristocratic, their economic interests landed, their background and training military and knightly. Within their ranks, accepted as their political equals, were men with legal training, judges who were qualified to serve as consuls and in other administrative offices. In this early commune, there were few merchants, though their numbers increased as the city's economy expanded.

Although the evidence for the functioning of the commune in this pristine stage is fragmentary, a plausible pattern of development can be constructed from documentation for other towns. This involved a progressive enlargement of responsibilities, a broadening of jurisdiction, and a burgeoning self-confidence and audacity exhibited by these officials in their relations with representatives of imperial and ecclesiastical authority. Initially, the consuls were preoccupied with settling disputes among members of the commune, with defending their rights against aggressors, and with internal security. Gradually, the scope of their activities widened, to include the apportionment of taxes, the organization of the communal army and, most significantly, decisions concerning war and peace. By the end of the 12th century, the commune had become the dominant if not the exclusive power in the city, and it was aggressively seeking to extend its authority over the territory outside its walls. In its subjection of the *contado,* the commune sometimes achieved its objectives by persuasion and compromise, and sometimes by force. Bishops surrendered their jurisdiction over their lands, as did many nobles and rural communities. Communal armies conquered the neighbouring towns of Fiesole and Prato. By 1200, the Florentine commune had extended its control over its entire *contado,* and was willing and able to challenge neighbouring cities: Siena, Pistoia, Pisa, Lucca, Arezzo.

Like other Italian city-states, Florence was motivated by economic and military considerations to dominate her hinterland: to ensure control over local food supplies and trade routes, and over the manpower and resources of the rural population. For decades after the death of Countess Matilda in 1115, the imperial power in

consuls – Burellus, Florenzitus, Broccardus, Servolus – as the first communal officials in this embryonic phase of self-government. It is likely that consuls had been chosen for some years before that date by members of the commune, who had taken an oath to act collectively in support of their interests. The fragmentary documentation of communal origins in Florence reveals a structure similar to that of other towns e.g. Pisa and Bologna, from which these institutions were undoubtedly borrowed. The consuls were elected yearly by the members of the commune assembled in a *parlamentum,* which could also vote on legislative proposals submitted, for its approval. Sometime during the later 12th century, a smaller legislative council was

CHARLO

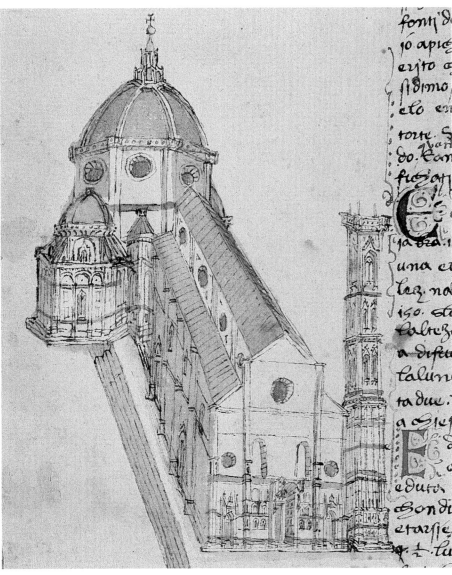

Tuscany did not constitute a serious obstacle to Florentine expansion. Emperor Henry V (d. 1125) was preoccupied with German affairs, as were his immediate successors. Their Tuscan officials were unable to sustain imperial authority in the region. Finally, in the 1150s, the Hohenstaufen emperor, Frederick Barbarossa (d. 1190), made a determined effort to regain control of the Italian portions of his empire. He fought tenaciously, but ultimately without success, to subdue the Lombard towns led by Milan, and supported by the papacy. He also reorganized the imperial administration of Tuscany, appointing officials to collect taxes and administer justice. Henry VI was a formidable ruler, who maintained a tight control over his Italian posses-

sions, but his premature death (1197) created a power vacuum in the peninsula. Florence joined other Tuscan towns in organizing a league to defend themselves against imperial authority. The city also completed the reconquest of those parts of the *contado* that had been lost, and became involved in sporadic conflicts with Siena and Pisa.

The maturing commune

The passage from the 12th to the 13th century was momentous in the history of the Florentine commune: it marked the transition from its primitive, formative stage to its mature and more complex phase. The public records reflect this

The old cathedral (above left), dedicated to St. John and the new one (above), Santa Maria del Fiore, represented the religious heart of the city (shown here in two drawings from the Rustici codex). The decision to erect a newer and much vaster cathedral was precipitated by the growth in the city's population. When the commission was entrusted to Arnolfo di Cambio in 1294, the republic stipulated that the edifice be constructed "with the greatest lavishness and magnificence possible..."

The Palazzo del Bargello, the most significant civil building in Florence after the Palazzo della Signoria, both in terms of size and importance, was built as the seat of the capitano del popolo *in 1255 and became the seat of the* podestà *five years later, the first occupant in that role being the Ghibelline* podestà *Guido Novello. The building changed roles once again in 1502, when it played host to the Council of Justice (also known as the* Consiglio di Ruota)*, a predominantly civil tribunal; finally, in 1574, it was taken over by the* bargello *(the city's chief guardian of law and order), whereupon it became a prison and place of execution. Nowadays the Palazzo del Bargello houses Florence's National Museum, one of the most important establishments of its type in the world because of its collection of sculptures and art objects.*

change dramatically. The lacunae in the 12th-century sources are, after 1200, filled by clusters of executive and legislative documents, supplemented by some chroniclers, from which it is possible to construct a more detailed record of the city's political experience.

When the members of the Florentine commune assembled in a *parlamento* in the year 1200, they formed a group of several hundred citizens, possibly more than a thousand. That figure reflected the steady demographic growth of the city, now surrounded by its second girdle of walls. The commune's administrative structure had also been expanded, in response to this demographic trend and to the progressive enlargement of the commune's responsibilities. Many of these tasks were performed by the citizens whose energies were divided between public and private affairs. Increasingly, however, the administrative routines were performed by men, frequently lawyers and notaries, who had developed particular skills that qualified them for such tasks as, for example, the assessment and collection of taxes, or the provisioning of grain for the city. Citizens were expected to

participate regularly in the deliberations that preceded every important communal action taken by the consuls or other official bodies. Had any record of these deliberations survived for the decades around 1200, they would have revealed the broad range of problems that concerned communal officials: public order, military and diplomatic affairs, taxation, regulation of prices and wages and, more broadly, the supervision of economic activity. These civic deliberations would also have expressed the intense patriotism of citizens who regularly voted to levy taxes on themselves for public purposes and who supported decisions to launch wars in which they fought as soldiers. More difficult to detect, in these civic deliberations, would have been the factional conflicts that divided and weakened the commune in these turbulent years.

These divisions were rooted in feuds among the city's leading noble families, competing for wealth, status and power in this dynamic society. In an attempt to dampen these internal struggles, in about 1200, the commune changed its executive office from the consulate to the *podestà*. That constitutional transformation had already

The courtyard of the Palazzo del Bargello, which possesses an almost theatrical quality, is bounded on three sides by an arcaded portico; on its fourth side an uncovered staircase leads up to the upper loggias. The latter contain objects, sculptures, relief works and coats of arms of the different podestà *and* Ruota *judges, reminders of the building's glorious past.*
Right, 16th-century lantern holder of wrought iron in the shape of a cornucopia. Below, a view of the loggia on the upper level. Below right, the staircase and the central well.

occurred in other towns; the shift from a multiple to a single executive was nearly universal in Italian city-states in the early 13th century. The *podestà* was not a native Florentine but a foreigner, a noble with some legal training, usually chosen from Lombard towns. His term of office was normally fixed for one year although in exceptional circumstances, his tenure could be extended. He was the city's chief magistrate, the head of the judiciary and of the police force, which he brought with him from his native city. In time of war, the *podestà* led the Florentine army into battle. In no sense was he a dictator or a tyrant; he was required to observe the communal statutes and the enactments of the legislative councils. As a professional, the *podestà* was expected to govern the city efficiently and, as an outsider, to be unattached to any civic faction.

Guelfs, Ghibellines and the rise of the popolo

The regime of the *podestà* in Florence coincided with the intensification of factional conflict among noble lineages and their clusters of

THE GUILDS: CORPORATION POLITICS

The feast day of St. John the Baptist (to whom the Baptistery is dedicated) was and still is also the great feast day of the city of Florence. The occasion (24 June) enabled the city to enjoy flaunting its own importance and individuals to display their pride in their citizenship. Three days before the event the herald of the *podestà* would announce that everyone over the age of 15 should be prepared to carry a votive candle to St. John on the eve of the feast day (the candlemakers would sell some 20,000 candles for the occasion). As protection from the summer sun teams of workers would erect a cloth "sky,"

After the first quarter of the 14th century the custom developed of the magistrates offering, in this procession on the eve of the feast day, a *bravio* or *palio* – a valuable strip of silk attached to a pole. Care was taken to ensure the most sumptuous piece of cloth should be that of the *podestà,* and that the value of the others should equally correspond to their position in the hierarchy. The feudal lords and country communes also took to offering *palii* to St. John. Borne by riders on horseback, these appeared to be more to the glory of Florence than an offering of homage to the saint. Illustration (2)

city. The supreme magistracy, the *Signoria dei priori,* was at first held by the three trading guilds of the *Calimala* (1, the crest of the *Calimala,* painted on the back of a Byzantine mosaic), the wool business (the *Arte della Lana*), or the exchange (1282). This soon extended to the three other guilds, the *Por Santa Maria* (the silk workers), the doctors and druggists, and the furriers. It then also became open to the guild of judges and notaries (these seven guilds now constituted the greater guilds). Then a further five "middle grade" guilds were admitted, and finally too nine lower guilds. In the course of only 11 years there thus evolved the organization of the 21 "political" guilds. As well as those already mentioned, these in-

a canopy decorated with the commune lily and the coats of arms of the guilds, 12 meters (39 feet) high, suspended from ropes attached to hooks in the walls of the houses. On the eve of the feast day the clergy made a solemn procession through the city bearing the relics of all the churches; this was followed by a procession for the offering of the candles for vespers, with the priors and the guilds proceeding among popular companies demonstrating their skills.

shows part of a painted chest dating from 1417, with the Baptistery, the cloth "sky," and the offerings of *palii*.

The professional corporations which took an active part in these celebrations also played a fundamental role in the economic and political life of the city. The guild was a universal medieval phenomenon, but in Florence it acquired peculiar characteristics. As Sapori commented, from an economic point of view "it had a degree of rigidity that might

well have reduced rather than increased economic growth. On the one hand specific restrictions were imposed to prevent new members being admitted, and on the other, production was indirectly controlled through a mass of regulations governing every stage of the production process." Given such restrictions it is surprising that there should ever have been the flourishing industrial life that in fact did develop. However, in practice the rules were not al-

ways obeyed. In the archives of the *botteghe* one finds accounting records of fines paid for engagement in forbidden free competitive trade.

While Florentine economic history with its dynamic individualism would appear to contradict the normal egalitarianism of the corporations, at the political level it is certain that syndication of trade interests (into the corporations or guilds) was what enabled the merchant classes to gain power in the

cluded (3) the sword makers and armourers, the locksmiths, the cobblers, the strapmakers, the leatherworkers and tanners, the linen workers and second-hand dealers, the smiths, the carpenters and stonemasons, the timber merchants, the bakers, the goat butchers, the vintners, the oil merchants, and the innkeepers. As political bodies these guilds included members having no connection with the relevant trades: the aristocratic Dante Alighieri enrolled in the guild of doctors and druggists in order to gain a political platform. However, the *capitudini* (chief councils) of the guilds did not govern directly: the priors of the commune were elected from among the guild members. There were then other guilds apart from the 21 political corporations so far mentioned (which formed a bastion "circa honorem et defensionem, exaltationem et pacificum et tranquillum statum dominorum priorum et vexilliferi justitiae et totius populi florentini" – for the honour and defense, the aggrandizement and the peaceful and calm life of the lord priors, the *gonfaloniere di giustizia*, and all the people of Florence).

Sources quote a total of 73 guilds. Many never had any political function; others were linked to the political guilds as autonomous or junior members; and various professional groups moved from one guild to another. They constituted a whole world in themselves – a fascinating, dynamic organization within which conflicts of interests and political ambitions were embodied and fought out. The glaziers and bellfounders for example, though a corporation, had no political muscle; the papermakers were a "subsidiary"

of the doctors and druggists; the goldsmiths were initially amalgamated with the furriers, then with the *Arte di Por Santa Maria*; the mint workers formed only a corporative guild with the gold and silver refiners; the guild of the woodworkers included both timber merchants and humble pole manufacturers, basket makers and saddlers who were later amalgamated (though as autonomous members) with the joiners and cabinetmakers who produced the famous Florentine *cassoni* (long, low chests); the swordmakers joined the armourers (originally just the makers of cuirasses) to create a political guild that also embraced the producers of helmets and greaves. The farriers and the smiths were separate, the very ancient smiths' guild being something of an exception in that it gave apprentices a recognized position. Those who manufactured industrial equipment such as looms were a guild with no political rights, along with the weavers; in a similar position was the guild comprising turners, crockery producers, and the woolwinder makers. The clock makers, a small body of highly skilled craftsmen, were claimed by both the smiths and the locksmiths, but eventually became part

of the latter. Painters began in the guild of doctors and druggists (who sold the materials for paints), but then founded their own Company of the Glorious Evangelist St. Luke. Other merely professional guilds were formed by the boot makers, the candlemakers, combined with the producers of gut strings for musical instruments, the barbers and country surgeons, and the cooks. The pursemakers were at first part of the guild of doctors and notaries but then joined the glove makers. The soap manufacturers were temporarily associated with the oil merchants, the grain merchants, the cheese producers, and the sellers of earthenware bowls. Much against their will, the fishmongers were put under the butchers. Spice merchants had to join either the butchers or the doctors and druggists, according to the type of spice they sold, but they later came under the oil merchants, whose guild also covered the salt merchants and the *caciaioli* (producers of a salty cheese called *cacio*). The innkeepers' guild at first only included the important landlords, but later came to include everyone (including women) who took in strangers, provided they were not thieves, murderers, forgers, or prostitutes.

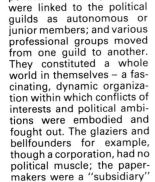

CALIMALA MERCHANTS

SWORDMAKERS AND ARMOURERS

STONEMASONS AND CARPENTERS

JUDGES AND NOTARIES

LOCKSMITHS

TIMBER MERCHANTS

MONEYCHANGERS

COBBLERS

BAKERS

WOOL WORKERS

STRAPMAKERS

GOAT BUTCHERS

POR SANTA MARIA (SILK)

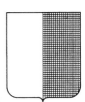

LEATHERWORKERS AND TANNERS

VINTNERS

DOCTORS AND DRUGGISTS

LINEN MERCHANTS AND SECOND-HAND DEALERS

OIL MERCHANTS

FURRIERS

SMITHS

INNKEEPERS

supporters. These officials were unable to control the violence that erupted after the assassination of Buondelmonte Buondelmonti in 1216, and the polarization of the city's political community into rival factions of Guelfs and Ghibellines. These factions assumed an ideological dimension, with the Guelfs supporting the Roman papacy and, more generally, the authority of the church, while the Ghibellines looked to their titular leader, Emperor Frederick II, to create an effective imperial regime in Italy. Guelf and Ghibelline factions arose in other Italian cities, fighting each other for dominance in their communities, and forming alliances with their counterparts in nearby towns. The Florentine Ghibelline party gained a temporary victory over their Guelf enemies in 1238, when imperial authority in Tuscany revived after Frederick II's victory over a coalition of Lombard Guelfs at Cortenuova. The Florentine commune was forced to accept the right of the emperor to ratify its choice of *podestà;* in 1246 that office was filled by the emperor's illegitimate son, Frederick of Antioch. Two years later (February 1248), the Guelfs abandoned the city

This page contains illustrations of some of the most significant documents in the history of the Florentine republic, now in the city's Archivio di Stato. Left, the page bearing the names of the first priores artium *(guild priors), from 1282. Below left, the first page of Giano della Bella's Ordinances of Justice (1293), an official work by means of which the political power of the mercantile and entrepreneurial middle class was consolidated and the reins of power passed into the hands of the seven major guilds.*
Below right, the Incipit *of the statute of the commune of Florence's* podestà *(1325). The first* podestà *whose name we know is Gherardo Caponsacchi, elected in 1193. A single magistrate who took the place of the collegiate magistracy that had existed during the consular era, the* podestà, *elected from year to year, probably by noble citizens, must have been able to abuse his position, in view of the fact that from the beginning of the 13th century it was decided to elect men from other cities, who would be more likely to act impartially in dealing with Florence's fierce factional rivalries. In the election of men to other political and administrative offices, similar attempts were made to eliminate favouritism and other abuses. This was the purpose of the electoral ballot pouches (opposite above), which contained the names of citizens that would be drawn at random by someone uninvolved with the election.*
Opposite below, the coats of arms of the podestà *and other high-ranking magistrates were carved in stone and jealously preserved, as can still be seen on the walls of the courtyard in the Palazzo del Bargello.*

to their rivals. Imperial control of Florence ended, however, when a Guelf army defeated a Ghibelline force near Figline, southeast of the city, shortly before Frederick II died in southern Italy (December 1250). In Florence, the citizenry organized a new regime of the *popolo* in which for the first time in the city's history, merchants, cloth manufacturers and other guildsmen gained a preponderant role in the commune, excluding most nobles from civic office.

The establishment of the regime of the *primo popolo* (1250-60) was a political act reflecting the economic and social changes within the city: demographic growth, the expansion of commercial, industrial and craft activity, and the emergence of new business and professional groups. Through their professional and craft organizations, the guilds, these merchants and artisans developed a sense of their common interests. They formed military associations in their neighbourhoods, to protect their homes in times of civic strife, and to march together against the city's enemies in time of war. During the first half of the 13th century, at the height of the Guelf-Ghibelline rivalry, the *popolo* was gradually increasing in size, self-confidence and organizational experience. The crisis of 1250 enabled it to seize power.

The regime of the *popolo* did not abolish the office of *podestà,* but instead added a new official, the captain of the *popolo,* and a new council of the *popolo,* to the commune's institutional structure. To house the captain and his retinue, charged with the specific responsibility of defending the *popolo,* the commune built a palace that still stands in the center of the city (now called the Bargello). This regime was no less bellicose than its predecessors. It fought a series of wars to recover those parts of the *contado* that had escaped the commune's jurisdiction in the 1240s; it also fought against Siena and Pisa, ruled by the Ghibelline factions. Initially, the Florentines and their Guelf allies from other Tuscan towns were victorious. However, at the battle of Montaperti (September 1260), a Guelf army that included a large Florentine contingent was routed by a Sienese force, reinforced by German mercenaries and a group of Florentine Ghibellines. After that devastating defeat, the Ghibelline party regained control of Florence, expelling the Guelfs and confiscating their property. But in the spring of

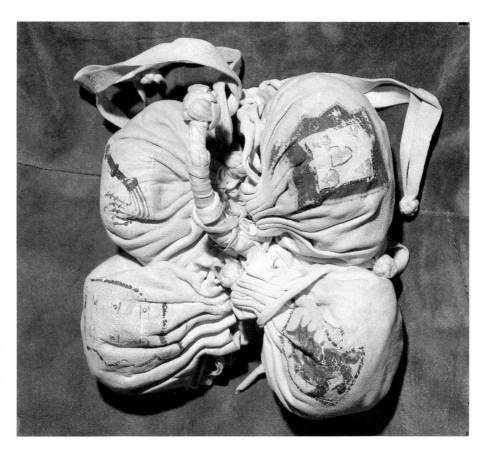

and to create a new regime dominated by the guilds.

Civic office in this regime of the *popolo* was reserved for guild members. The city was divided into six districts (*sesti*), each represented in the new executive magistracy (*priores artium*) by a guildsman from one of the 21 recognized guilds. A new group of priors was chosen every two months. The majority of the priors came from the largest and wealthiest guilds: the *Calimala* (cloth refiners), *Lana* (woollen cloth manufacturers), *Cambio* (moneychangers) and *Giudici e notai* (judges and notaries). In addition to their general executive authority, the priors were also responsible for the formulation of legislative proposals. The records of this legislation (*Provvisioni*) and of the deliberations and votes on the proposals (*Libri Fabarum*) have survived; they constitute a valuable source for the political history of the guild commune.

The establishment of the guild regime represented a defeat for the old Guelf aristocracy. The division between the guild community and those Guelf families was not so wide nor so permanent

The character and enterprise of the Florentines was described by Benedetto Varchi in his Storia Fiorentina *in the following words: "I have very often marvelled at how it is possible for many of those men who from boyhood are employed for very little money as porters to carry bales of wool or to lift baskets of silk, and, in short, act as little more than slaves standing the whole day and much of the night at the spindle and spinning wheel, to display, when and where necessary, such greatness of spirit and such noble and elevated thoughts. They venture not only to discuss, but also to carry out those very many fine things, with some of them talking and some of them acting ..."*
We can see the faces of some of these citizens in an anonymous 14th-century fresco dedicated to the Madonna della Misericordia *in the Loggia del Bigallo (opposite and below) and in the bas-relief on the campanile of the cathedral, a work by Andrea Pisano that depicts the celebration of a marriage (left).*

1276, the Ghibellines abandoned the city when an army of exiled Guelfs and French troops appeared before the city walls. Florence was again under the control of the Guelfs.

The Guelf regime established in 1267 had close ties with the Roman papacy, and with the King of Naples, Charles of Anjou. The Angevin ruler held the office of *podestà* from 1267 until 1282, though he was rarely in the city and normally exercised his office through vicars. This French presence in Florence was strongly favoured by the leaders of the Guelf party, who lived in fear of attack by their Ghibelline enemies. In 1273 Pope Gregory X failed in his efforts to reconcile the two factions. Pope Nicholas III sent his nephew, Cardinal Latino, to Florence in 1279 on a peacemaking mission, and the Guelf leadership was persuaded to allow some Ghibelline exiles to return home. Florence's guild community was increasingly troubled by the disorders fomented by the aristocratic factions, and resentful of the interference in their city's politics by Angevin and papal officials. When, in 1282, the Sicilian people successfully rebelled against Angevin rule in their island, the Florentines took advantage of King Charles' difficulties to expel his officials

the end of factional strife. The Guelf magnates remained a potent force in communal politics, through their control of the *Parte Guelfa* (with its own constitution, treasury and militia), and their network of clients and supporters within and outside the city. In 1295 the magnates succeeded in driving their enemy, Giano della Bella, into exile. Despite the penalites imposed by the Ordinances of Justice, their partisan feuds became more violent and disruptive. By the late 1290s, the struggle between magnates and *popolo* was overshadowed by the rivalry between the two factions headed by the Donati and the Cerchi. Through their identification with feuding factions in Pistoia, the Donati party became known as the Blacks, and the Cerchi as the

as to preclude social and economic contacts and intermarriage between these groups. And though the leaders of the guild regime viewed the magnate families with suspicion, they needed their military expertise for the wars then being fought against Arezzo and Pisa. In 1293, however, the guild regime, led by a nobleman named Giano della Bella, enacted the Ordinances of Justice, which imposed severe restrictions and penalties upon the 150 lineages designated as magnate. Members of these families could not serve as priors; only a limited number of civic offices was open to them, However, the enactment of these ordinances did not signify the permanent triumph of the guild community, nor

Whites. Complicating this partisan struggle was the intervention of Pope Boniface VIII, who supported the Blacks and who hoped to exploit the divisions in Florence to impose his will on the city.

We know the details of this dramatic struggle between the Blacks and the Whites from the chronicle of a White partisan, Dino Compagni, and from the writings of Dante. In 1301 the White faction, under the leadership of the

On Easter Sunday in 1216, a wedding turned into a funeral when the bridegroom, Buondelmonte Buondelmonti, was murdered by a group of conspirators belonging to the Amidei, Uberti, Lamberti and Arrighi families. Their ostensible motive was a banal vendetta brought about by the young man having broken off an earlier engagement, but the real reason lay in a bitter and longstanding contest between two family groups for political supremacy in the city. The murder marked the city's division into two factions, the Guelfs and the Ghibellines, whose names originated from a corruption of the names of two German political groupings. The terms were, in fact, derived from the names of the Bavarian House of Welf (the Guelfs) and the castle of Waibling belonging to the Hohenstaufen, the former being in favour of the papacy and the latter opposed to it. Their struggle stained the streets and fields of Tuscany with blood, leading to skirmishes and outright war: for example, at Montaperti in 1260, when the Florentine Guelfs were defeated disastrously by the Sienese Ghibellines and their exiled Florentine allies, and at Campaldino in 1289, where there was a battle between the Florentine Guelfs and the Ghibellines of Arezzo in which Dante and Corso Donati both fought (opposite above, a miniature depicting the Battle of Campaldino, from Villani's Cronica, *and a view of the plain on which it was fought).*
The three emblems shown on this page sum up this turbulent period in Florentine history: above left, the arms of the Guelfs over the doorway of the old Zecca (mint); below, a Ghibelline seal in the Bargello; left, the coat of arms of the people of Florence on the campanile of the cathedral.

Cerchi, gained control of the commune. Pope Boniface VIII then sent a French prince, Charles of Valois, to Florence with a military force, ostensibly to pacify the city. But Charles, like the pope, was committed to the Black cause, and he allowed that faction's leader, Corso Donati, to return to the city (5 November 1301), even though he was under a communal ban. The triumphant Blacks then wrought vengeance upon their enemies, burning their houses and forcing hundreds into exile. Together with other Whites, Dante, who had held office as prior in 1301, was condemned to death for treason. He found refuge initially in Arezzo, as did a Florentine notary named *ser* Petracco, father of Petrarch, who was born there in 1304. Communities of exiled Whites settled in several Tuscan towns, joining forces with local Ghibelline parties, and seeking revenge for their expulsion from their native city.

The presence of the Whites in Siena, Arezzo and other Tuscan towns represented a serious threat to the Black Guelfs in Florence, since these exiles were continually seeking aid from their Ghibelline allies in Italy and across the Alps in Germany. They appealed in vain to the emperor-elect, Albert of Hapsburg (d. 1308) to invade Italy and restore imperial authority there. His successor, Henry VII of Luxembourg, was more sympathetic to their petitions. Henry VII crossed the Alps in October 1310, received the submission of some but not all Italian cities, and moved south toward Tuscany. Florence refused to submit to Henry, who placed the city under the imperial ban. When the emperor arrived at

The emblem of the Guelf party bore a red eagle sinking its talons into a green dragon. In reality, these were the arms of Pope Clement IV, whom the Guelfs, scattered and defeated following their rout at Montaperti (1260), turned to for help. The Guelfs, Villani tells us, "were graciously received by the said Pope and provided with money and other assistance; and the Pope, because of his love for Florence's Guelf party, expressed his wish that it should always bear his own arms on its flag and seal, which was and still is a vermilion eagle on a green dragon against a white field, and this they carried and maintained afterwards, and do so even to this day." Above, the episode as painted by Vasari in the Salone dei Cinquecento in the Palazzo Vecchio.

Opposite, detail showing knights against the background of a turreted castle, from an engraving entitled David and Goliath *by an anonymous Florentine artist and attributable to around 1480 (Galleria degli Uffizi, Gabinetto dei Disegni e delle Stampe).*
Left, a lively engraving by Antonio Pollaiolo entitled Battle of Naked Men *dating from about 1470.*
The world of armed conflict became a subject for both study and inspiration among artists of the Florentine Renaissance.

Pisa, he was greeted by exiled Florentine and other Tuscan Ghibellines, who urged him to attack the rebellious city. But Henry first travelled to Rome to receive the imperial crown (June 1312), and then came north to besiege Florence. The city resisted his assault, and Henry was forced to lift the siege and establish winter quarters at Pisa. After receiving military reinforcements from Germany, the emperor again marched south toward Rome, to recover that city from the army of King Robert of Naples. But near Siena he became ill and died (August 1313); his leaderless army disintegrated and Florence's Guelf regime was secure.

Henry VIII's legacy to Tuscany was two decades of bitter strife between Guelfs and Ghibellines. Florence's control of her western territory was challenged, first, by the Ghibelline *signore* of Pisa, Uguccione della Fagiuola, and then by his successor, Castruccio Castracani, lord of Pisa and Lucca. In 1313, Florence's Guelf leaders had granted extensive military and political authority in the city to King Robert of Naples for a five-year period. But this Neapoli-

tan connection did not prevent Florence's army from suffering a major defeat at the hands of Uguccione's troops at Montecatini (August 1315). A decade later, Castruccio overwhelmed another Florentine force at the battle of Altopascio near Lucca (September 1325). The desperate Guelf regime turned again to Naples for help. The commune elected King Robert's son, Duke Charles of Calabria, as its *signore* for a ten-year period. He was made supreme military commander of the Florentine army, and he also received the right to appoint the *podestà* and the priors. Thus, to defend itself against the military threat posed by Castruccio, the Guelf regime had surrendered most of its authority to a foreign prince, whose physical presence, with a large military retinue, was an indication of his determination to rule the city. But Florence's enemy, Castruccio, died of a fever in September 1328, and two months later, Charles of Calabria also died. Fortune had thus delivered the city from its enemy and its oppressive protector.

The Florentine Guelfs responded to these events by promulgating certain institutional

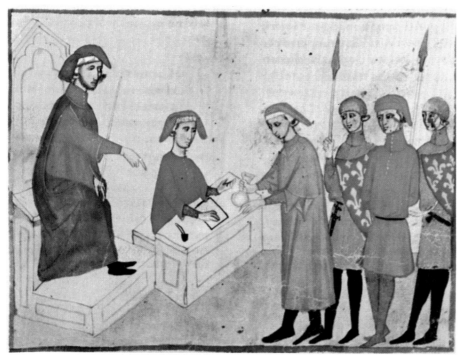

When his powers were at their peak, the podestà *was the supreme executive organ of the commune. His main function was a judicial one, exercised either directly or through his judges. In these illustrations from Villani's* Cronica *(Biblioteca Vaticana, Chigi codex), the* podestà *is shown fulfilling his role as judge. Top, the* podestà Cante de' Gabrielli *of Gubbio in the act of passing a sentence of death by decapitation on certain citizens of the White faction. Above, the exaction of a fine, in pursuance of the Ordinances of Justice.*

reforms (December 1328), designed to stabilize their control of the city. Most important was the establishment of a fixed procedure for periodic scrutinies of the guild membership, to select those eligible for office. These reforms contributed to the establishment of a more stable regime, whose members were recruited largely from Florence's leading Guelf families: merchants, bankers, industrialists, lawyers. This political elite governed the city in the 1330s, when Florence was at the height of its wealth, power and prestige.

Three witnesses

Witnessing, indeed participating in, the creation of the guild commune were three citizens who have left records of their views concerning Florentine political experience in this dynamic and turbulent age. The three were *ser* Brunetto Latini (c. 1220-94), notary and rhetorician, Dante Alighieri (1265-1321), and Dino Compagni (1260-1324), merchant, civic official and chronicler. These men knew each other. In the *Inferno*, Dante encounters Latini and speaks of him with great warmth:

The dear, benign, paternal image, such
As thine was, when so lately thou didst teach me
The way for man to win eternity:
And how I prized the lesson, it behoves,
That ... my tongue should speak.
(*Inferno,* XV, 83-87)

Brunetto Latini was a Guelf, who was exiled during the Ghibelline interlude of 1260-66. Both Dante and Dino Compagni belonged to the White faction, but the chronicler was not as prominent or as partisan as the poet, and thus avoided exile. For all three witnesses, the central problem of communal government was partisan conflict, its causes and its cures.

In canto XV of the *Inferno*, Dante ascribed to Latini a well-known mythical explanation for the Florentine predilection for factionalism, which continually threatened to destroy their city. The seeds of discord were sown when Florence was founded by the Romans, who incorporated natives of Etruscan Fiesole into the new colony:

But that ungrateful and malignant race,
Who in old times came down from Fiesole,

Ay and still smack of their rough mountain-flint,
Will for thy good deeds show thee enmity.
Nor wonder; for amongst ill-savour'd crabs
It suits not the sweet fig-tree lay her fruit.
Old fame reports them in the world for blind,
Covetous, envious, proud. Look to it well:
Take heed thou cleanse thee of their ways …
(*Inferno*, XV, 61-69)

In his treatise *On the Government of Cities*, however, Latini saw discord as a universal problem of government, which required constant vigilance and human ingenuity to control. Latini's ideas derived in part from his readings of classical authors, Aristotle and Cicero, and in part from his own experience as a civic official. He shared the political and social values of the majority of his fellow-citizens. Living in a city was the best kind of human experience; self-government by an elite was the highest form of political life. To participate in civic politics was, for the individual, the most noble and rewarding form of activity. Good government required good laws and good officials, men who were mature, knowledgeable and articulate, for Latini valued rhetorical skills highly in politics.

Ser Brunetto Latini formulated his political principles as a set of guidelines for a newly elected *podestà,* whose successful administration depended on his fulfilling his duties properly. In his inaugural address to the citizenry, the *podestà* should state firmly and unambiguously his commitment to government by law, and his determination to enforce the laws impartially. He tells the citizens, "I have come not to gain money but to acquire praise, esteem and honour for myself and my retinue." Recognizing that civic factions will seek to gain advantage over their rivals by befriending the *podestà,* Latini advises him to have no social contact with any citizen. For such contacts were occasions for the solicitation of favours and the offer of bribes. The *podestà* had to demonstrate to everyone, by his actions as well as his words, that he was above party faction. *Ser* Brunetto was keenly aware of the destructive passions that seethed in every Italian urban community, threatening to destroy communal institutions. He had witnessed in his lifetime the collapse of communal regimes and their replacement by despotisms in such cities as Verona and Ferrara. Nevertheless, *ser* Brunetto believed that communal government was viable,

The violent element of the law was intended to act as a deterrent to the citizenry. Hanging, the application of red-hot pincers, and being strung up by a rope, as seen in these illustrations from Sercambi's Cronica, *which dates from the beginning of the 15th century (Archivio di Stato, Lucca), were just some of the cruel methods used. They were sometimes also used as a barbarous means of reprisal against conquered enemies.*

125

The rise of the commercial and entrepreneurial classes led to the establishment of a new political order, known as the rule of the primo popolo, *promulgated on 20 October 1250. One important innovation lay in the installation of a* capitano del popolo, *who, assisted by a council of 12 elders, cooperated with the old* magistracy of the podestà *in order to curb it and champion the interests of the newly emergent classes. Right, the first page of the statute appointing the* capitano del popolo *of the commune of Florence in 1322. Below, an illuminated page from the* Libro dei Lasciti alla Compagnia dei Capitani *(Book of Bequests Made to the Company of Capitani), showing the Madonna di Orsanmichele. Both documents are now in Florence's Archivio di Stato.*

if the citizens were properly instructed concerning the benefits of self-rule, if the laws and institutions of the commune were good, and if worthy officials were chosen to enforce those laws and preserve those institutions. The treatise of the Florentine notary could have served as the model for Ambrogio Lorenzetti's frescoes on good government (1338-39) in the Palazzo Pubblico of Siena.

Ser Brunetto's perspective on city-state politics was informed by intimate experience, but his treatise was a synthesis of principles and values on which communal government was based. Dino Compagni's view, on the other hand, was more direct and immediate than that of the notary; his chronicle is the most graphic portrayal of Italian civic experience that has been preserved from the communal age. Dino was a merchant of respectable but not noble lineage, well regarded (so he reported) by his fellow-citizens. In 1289 he was selected for an important civic responsibility, "because he was a good and wise man." Strongly committed to the *popolo*, he played an instrumental role in the establishment of the guild regime (1292), which enacted legislation "to inspect the funds of the commune, to make the *Signorie* [magistracies] answerable to one another, and to ensure that the weak are not oppressed by the powerful." His hero was Giano della Bella, who was responsible for the passage of the Ordinances of Justice against the magnates. Dino was a partisan of the White faction led by the Cerchi. His hatred of the Blacks, and of their leaders, the Donati, was palpable. A primary motive for writing his chronicle was his desire to leave a record for posterity of the malevolence of the Blacks, "who through their pride, wickedness, and quest for civic office, divided this noble city, disgraced its laws and so swiftly bartered the honours their forebears had taken such pains to acquire over time."

Dino's special gift as a writer is his ability to convey a sense of social experience in that crowded city, where physical proximity fostered close and intimate ties, but also intense hatred. Every Florentine belonged to a cluster of social groupings and associations, some familial, others geographical (neighbourhoods, parishes), others professional (guilds), still others political (Guelfs, Ghibellines, *popolani, magnati*). Each new day provided a different occasion for the expression and articulation of these allegiances: a change in the staff of the *Signoria*, a tax assessment, an execution, a wedding or funeral. Dino described the following incident which took place at a funeral to which members of the rival Donati and Cerchi factions had been invited: "…Citizens sat on the floor and knights on benches, and those Donati and Cerchi who were not knights happened to be sitting on the floor opposite one another. One of them rose to his feet suddenly, to adjust his clothing or for some similar reason. Members of the rival group, instantly suspicious, got up and drew their swords. The other faction followed suit and a brawl ensued, and the other people present had to break up the fight."

The most divisive issue in the city, according to

Dino Compagni, was the administration of justice. Rare were those officials who, like Brunetto Latini's *podestà*, rendered judicial decisions in accordance with the law. More commonly, so Dino reported, citizens who held office were influenced by self-interest or by the claims of their friends and relatives: "If a friend or a relative should be imprisoned, they would arrange with the magistracies and officials for the crime to be concealed, so that they should go unpunished." Dino observed a consistent pattern of maltreatment and abuse of poor and weak citizens by those who were more powerful and influential, who viewed this form of exploitation almost as a birthright. Such arrogant behaviour aroused deep resentment among the *popolani*,

The capitano del popolo *possessed very real powers: the whole citizen militia was personally organized by him and divided into 20* gonfaloni, *each with its own multicoloured banner. The illustrations on this page, taken from Giovanni Sercambi's* Cronica *(Archivio di Stato, Lucca), show two moments in the organization of Florence's military forces: the hiring of troops (above) and the handing over of the baton of command to a captain (below).*

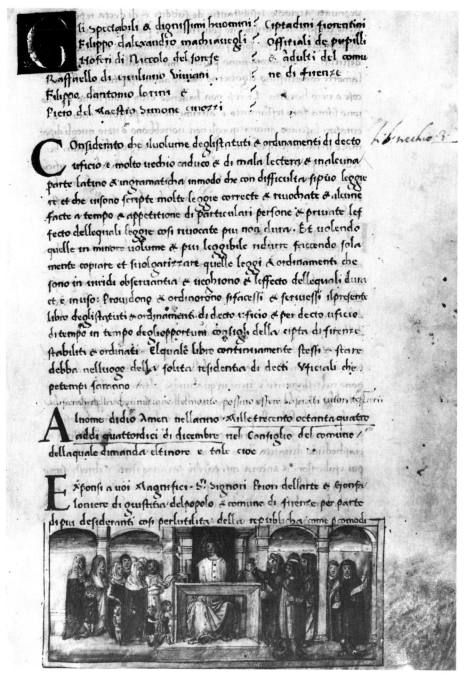

A special office dealt with the guardianship of underage orphans. The statutes of the Ufficiali dei pupilli (officials in charge of underage wards), which dealt with the matter, were drawn up in 1384 and have survived in a replica from 1503 (above), now in the Archivio di Stato, Florence.

and was primarily responsible for the enactment of the Ordinances of Justice. A primary source of civic discord could thus be traced to behaviour patterns characteristic of the city's elite. But the *popolo* were not always innocent victims of upper class ill-treatment. In 1295 a throng of *popolani*, angered by a decision rendered by the *podestà*, seized their arms, forced the official to flee, and ransacked his palace. When Giano della Bella sought to restrain this outbreak of lawlessness, the *popolo* turned against their former leader and allowed the authorties to sentence him to death *in absentia*.

Dino Compagni's perceptions of the causes of civic strife were partly sociological, partly moral. Virtuous and honourable men sought to preserve the commune; evil men, motivated by greed and jealousy, connived to destroy it. Dino's views on politics were fundamentally secular. Men created their political world and they were ultimately responsible for its operation. Divine providence is scarcely mentioned in his chronicle though on one occasion, almost as an afterthought, he makes a pious reference to *"la giustizia di Dio"* (divine justice). We do not know whether, in those years when Dante Alighieri shared political responsibilities with Dino and his fellow citizens, the poet also embraced a secular view of politics. He was an active member of the commune: he fought in the Florentine army that defeated the Aretini at Campaldino; he was a member of the *Signoria;* he spoke in council meetings and went on embassies to Rome and elsewhere. The events that led to the expulsion of the Whites, and to his own condemnation and exile, made a profound impression on Dante. Until the day of his death he proclaimed his innocence of the charges against him and in the *Divine Comedy* he revenged himself on his enemies. Conversing with the glutton Ciacco, he recounts the defeat of the Whites and alludes to the vices that had

In Florence, as elsewhere, there were men responsible for the upkeep of the city's defenses, and the small painting (opposite right) in the Archivio di Stato, Siena shows two inspectors at work.

Tuscan art of the 14th and 15th centuries is rich in scenes relating to the civil administration of cities. The illustration above left from Sercambi's Cronica *(Archivio di Stato, Lucca) relates to discussions concerning the adoption of an estimate. Above right, a small painting from the 1430* Libro delle Balestre *(Archivio di Stato, Siena) showing employees of the commune drawing their salaries.*

Below right, a small painting by Biccherna dated 1340 (Archivio di Stato, Siena) shows a tax collector and a taxpayer, portrayed with a slight tinge of irony in the disproportionate size of the two figures.

infected the city and inflamed the emotions of the Florentine people.

Avarice, envy, pride, three fatal sparks,
have set the hearts of all On fire.
(Inferno, VI, 75-76)

And, in the 26th canto, he speculates on the ultimate fate of his native city.

Florence, exult! for thou so mightily
Hast driven, that o'er land and sea thy wings
Thou beatest, and thy name spreads over hell.
Among the plunderers, such as the three I found
Thy citizens; whence shame to me thy son,
And no proud honour to thyself rebounds.
But if our minds, when dreaming near the dawn,
Are of the truth presageful, thou ere long
Shalt feel what Prato (not to say the rest)
Would fain might come upon thee; and that chance
Were in good time, if it befel thee now.
(Inferno, XXVI, 1-10)

During his years of exile, Dante developed his political ideas which are expressed most clearly in his treatise *De Monarchia*. He rejected completely the values of the civic world into which he had been born for an idealized vision of a world government under the rule of a single prince: the Holy Roman Emperor. When Henry VII came to Italy in 1310, Dante addressed a passionate letter to him as the saviour of Italy. To his fellow Florentines, he wrote a scathing indictment: "You who transgress laws both human and divine, whose avarice and cupidity without limit have made you prone to every crime ..." Only by submitting to imperial rule could Florence avoid destruction. Her communal regime was illegitimate, created in defiance of imperial authority; the Florentines were guilty of usurping powers that God had given to the emperor. Though

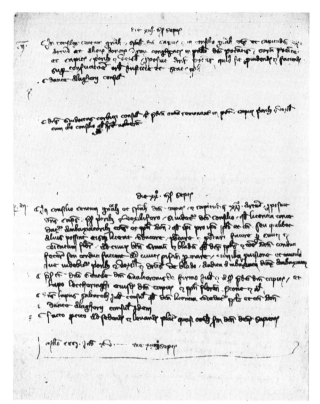

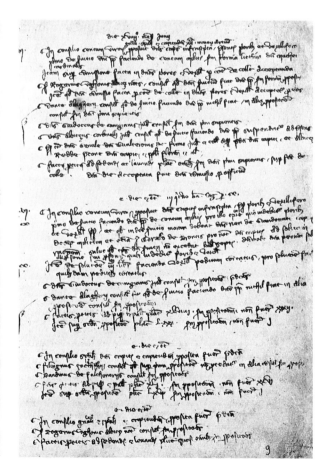

Above far left, the name of Dante (indicated by a small pointing hand) appears in the tenth line of the register of members of the guild of doctors and druggists. Left and below right, two documents of 1301 from the Libri Fabarum, *in which Dante's name again appears; the second relates to the poet's intervention in the Council of One Hundred against sending help to Pope Boniface VIII to fight the Santafiore di Maremma. Below far left, Giotto's nomination as supervisor of Florence cathedral on 12 April 1334 (Archivio di Stato, Florence). Opposite above, detail of the* Paradise *attributed to Giotto in the chapel of the podestà in the Palazzo del Bargello. It includes a likeness of Dante, as well as many other historical figures, amongst them Brunetto Latini and Corso Donati. Between the 13th and 14th century, politics and culture together played a major part in the lives of many great Florentines. Bitten by the political bug, the poet was its most famous victim. When, following the promulgation of Giano della Bella's Ordinances of Justice in 1293, the only men admitted to the priorato were those enrolled in guilds, the poet, in order to conform to the law, entered the guild of doctors and druggists, the one that most nearly matched the qualities of an intellectual. Dante became priore in 1300, at a time of grave tensions, but his political activities were short-lived. After the triumph of the Blacks, which followed the entry into Florence of Charles of Valois, a close ally of Boniface VIII, Dante, who was a White, was tried* in absentia *and banished from the city. He never saw Florence again.*
Opposite below, a shield bearing the fleur-de-lis of the Valois family.

bitterly disappointed by the failure of Henry VII's enterprise, Dante never altered his conviction that peace would come to Florence, and to Italy, only after the restoration of imperial authority in the peninsula.

The time of troubles

The early decades of the 14th century, so filled with political turmoil, were also years of prosperity and growth. In his summary of the "state of the city" in the late 1330s, Giovanni Villani had marvelled at the external signs of wealth: "… At this time churches, cathedrals and magnificent monasteries of all kinds were erected; besides this there was no citizen, great or small who had not built a magnificent and wealthy dwelling." With dramatic suddenness, this opulent and expansive age was succeeded by a "time of troubles," which persisted for more than half a century. The pestilence of 1340 killed 10,000 Florentines, that of 1348 perhaps 30,000. Accompanying the plagues were failed grain harvests, food shortages, and the ravages of bands of soldiers that roamed over the countryside, preying upon the rural inhabitants, and even threatening the fortified towns. Not since the anarchic period of the ninth century had life in Tuscany been so grim and perilous.

These conditions contributed to the turbulence of Florentine politics in these years. The city's financial resources had been drained by a lengthy and futile campaign to conquer Lucca in the 1330s. In an attempt to stave off the bankruptcy of the Bardi and Peruzzi companies, a group of prominent citizens, including some magnates, arranged for a French military leader, Walter of Brienne, to be named *signore* of the city (September 1342). The dictatorship of the Duke of Athens, as Walter was called, did not long survive; he was driven out of Florence (August 1343) by a coalition of magnates, *popolani* and artisans. Within weeks of this uprising, conflict broke out between magnates and *popolani*, which resulted in the military defeat of the magnates (September 1343). The regime established in the aftermath of these disorders was broadly representative of the guild community. Communal offices were shared by the old *popolani* families, by upwardly mobile men from new families, and by artisans and shopkeepers from the 14 lower guilds. Magnates

had only minimal representation in the regime; they were excluded from the *Signoria* and other major offices. Also barred from office were the thousands of cloth workers and other labourers who belonged to no guild.

The institutions of this guild regime had evolved gradually since the 1280s; they had become stabilized and with only minor alterations, were to survive until the fall of the republic in 1530. Executive authority was vested in the nine-man *Signoria* (one *gonfaloniere di giustizia* and eight priors) who held office for a two-month period. Assisting and advising the *Signoria* were two colleges: the 12 *buon'uomini* and the 16 *gonfalonieri di compagnia*. Voting together, the *Signoria* and the colleges promulgated executive decrees and proposed legislation tthat was sub-

mitted for approval to the two legislative councils of the *popolo* and the commune. These councils numbered approximately 200 citizens each; their tenure of office varied from four to six months. The councils could not initiate legislation but could only approve, by majorities of two thirds, provisions submitted to them. Before proposing legislation or making any policy decisions, the *Signoria* frequently asked for advice from the

Scenes of factional conflict. Top left, fighting on the roofs; top right, Corso Donati (second from the left) on the day of Calendimaggio *(May Day); above, the incident when Ricoverino de' Cerchi's nose was severed. Far left, Corso Donati freeing the prisoners (5 November 1301).*

colleges and other magistracies, and also from individual citizens. While the *Signoria* and the colleges possessed broad executive authority, a number of special civic magistracies had jurisdiction over specific areas of administration: for example, over grain supplies, the recruitment and pay of mercenaries, the scrutiny of treasury records. The administration of justice and the maintenance of public order were the responsibility of foreign magistrates (the *podestà*, the captain of the *popolo*, the executor of the Ordinances of Justice), who came to Florence with their retinues for terms of six months.

Most civic offices were filled, not by direct election but by an indirect process of scrutiny and sortition. Periodically, all citizens eligible for specific offices (e.g. the *Signoria*) would be scrutinized by a special electoral commission, and those receiving a majority of two thirds were declared eligible for that office. Their names were placed into leather pouches and office holders selected by lot from the *polizze* (cards) inside. An elaborate system of controls was created to prevent the monopolization of offices by particular families. This electoral system was designed to maintain a balance of power among districts of the city (which was divided into four quarters and 16 *gonfaloni*, among socio-economic groups, and among lineages. But factions and parties did emerge, despite stringent legislation against their formation, and the scrutinies were subject to manipulation by these *sette*. The most profound division within the commune in the second half of the 14th century pitted a cluster of old families, which dominated the Parte Guelfa, against segments of the guild community which contained a large number of *gente nuova*. The *Parte Guelfa* sought to intimidate its opponents by identifying certain citizens as suspected Ghibellines, thus making them ineligible for civic office.

These internal tensions were a persistently disruptive force in Florentine politics, varying in intensity with changing circumstances. Invariably, they became more acute in times of crisis, during a war or famine or economic slump. Still, the regime was able to survive these crises and to maintain its control over the city and the subject territory. It was remarkably successful in rebuilding the shattered fabric of society after the Black Death: burying the dead, restoring public order, supervising the massive redistribution of the property of plague victims. The Florentine poor, who lived precariously on their earnings in the cloth factories and from menial labour, were a constant threat to public order. In times of famine and unemployment, the commune bought grain to feed them. If they rioted to protest at food prices or working conditions, they were dispersed by the authorities who seized and executed their leaders.

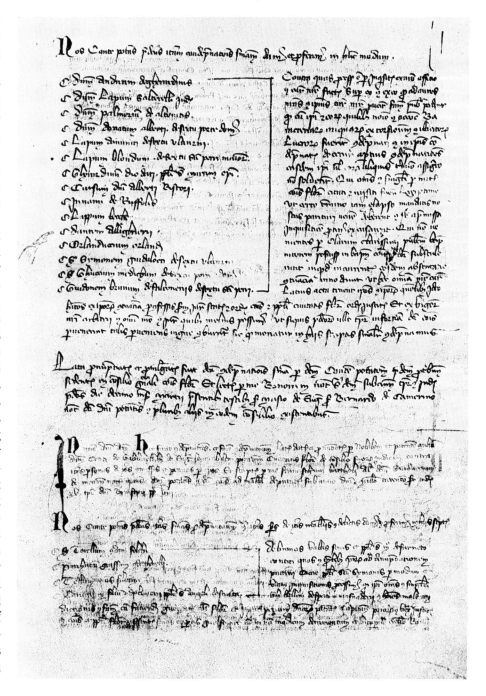

Above, Dante's indictment, as seen in the records of the Black capitani *(Archivio di Stato, Florence), formed part of the rivalry between Blacks and Whites. This factionalism erupted into open conflict on 1 May 1300 (the day known as* Calendimaggio*).*

Above, the lily of Florence in a birth tray attributed to Masaccio (Staatliche Museen, Berlin). Opposite, the façade of the Palazzo Vecchio, as seen in detail from the Confirmation of the Rule *by Domenico Ghirlandaio in the church of Santa Trinita. Begun in 1299 in order to provide a seat for the priors, the palace was built on the site of houses belonging to the Uberti family, "rebels against Florence, and Ghibellines." As can be seen in the painting, the building during the 15th century was not dissimilar to its modern appearance: instead of the stairway there was a dais at whose left-hand corner stood the* Marzocco, *the seated lion bearing the shield with the lily, the symbol of the Florentine* popolo.

The 1370s were particularly troubled years for the Florentine commune. The cloth industry was depressed, creating widespread unemployment and unrest. Factional discord intensified, as the *Parte Guelfa* and its rivals fought for control of the regime. In 1375, a group of citizens hostile to the *Parte Guelfa* launched a war against the papacy, whose officials in the Papal States were accused of threatening Florentine independence. Many cities in papal territory rebelled; an infuriated Pope Gregory XI placed Florence under interdict and in January 1377, he returned to Rome from Avignon to lead the struggle against Florence and her allies. Guelf partisans in the city intensified their campaign against "Ghibellines," who were held responsible for starting the papal war. Tensions created by these tactics, and by the fiscal and psychological pressures of the conflict, erupted into violence in June 1378. Led by the *gonfaloniere di giustizia,* Salvestro de' Medici, the war party passed legislation penalizing leaders of the *Parte Guelfa,*

while a mob burned their palaces. Civic peace was restored briefly before disorders broke out again in mid July. Thousands of artisans and workers assembled and marched to the Palazzo della Signoria, and in an atmosphere of escalating violence, forced the *Signoria* to leave the palace (22 July). A new regime was then established, led by the wool carder Michele di Lando; it included representatives from three new guilds numbering some 13,000 men: *sottoposti* and labourers in the cloth industry, who had formerly been excluded from the communal government.

This regime of the Ciompi (as the cloth workers were called) survived for only six weeks before it was overthrown. During its brief life, the city was governed by a special magistracy (*balìa*) which sought to restore order and to gain popular support for the regime. Its task was complicated by the disruption of the city's economy; many *botteghe,* particularly those producing cloth, had been closed down by their proprietors during the disorders of June and July. This shutdown of the cloth industry created widespread unemployment and misery among the workers, whose leaders sought to force the regime to pursue a more radical policy. These tactics aroused the fears of wealthy citizens, and also of artisans and shopkeepers, who distrusted the motives and objectives of the Ciompi leaders. On 31 August, armed guildsmen fought and defeated the Ciompi in the Piazza della Signoria. Their leaders were forced into exile, and the new guild of the cloth workers was disbanded. A contemporary witness, Guido Monaldi, wrote: "... Every good citizen would have been chased out of his home, and the cloth worker would have taken everything he had."

The Ciompi Revolution has been interpreted by some historians as a manifestation of urban class conflict in late medieval Europe, and as a portent of the future struggles between capitalists and workers in the modern industrial age. Others have viewed the revolt in a more conservative sense, as an effort by the *popolo minuto* to join the guild community and to share in its corporate values and privileges. The regime established after the downfall of the Ciompi was based on that corps of guildsmen: merchants, manufacturers, artisans and shopkeepers. Its efforts to restore stability were hampered by economic difficulties, by threats from abroad,

and by deep divisions within the city. Ciompi exiles periodically organized conspiracies that were suppressed, while Guelf extremists also plotted to overthrow the guild regime. Discord among the leaders of the government ignited a political crisis (January 1382), which led to its downfall, and its replacement by a more conservative regime in which old Guelf families gradually regained their former power and influence.

The Renaissance republic

The events of the 1370s revealed deep rifts within Florence, and the vulnerability of the city's communal institutions. During those troubled times, Florence might have succumbed to the rule of a despot, as had happened to so many Italian cities – including neighbouring Pisa, Siena and Lucca – in similar circumstances. But Florence preserved her communal government; indeed, the city's commitment to republicanism grew steadily stronger in the late trecento and early quattrocento. The republic was strengthened by a surge of patriotic fervour that was stimulated by the wars (1389-1402) with the *signore* of Milan, Giangaleazzo Visconti, whose efforts to extend his authority over all of Tuscany were strongly resisted by the Florentines. Chancellor Coluccio Salutati (d. 1406) was the republic's most eloquent spokesman in those years. Salutati interpreted the conflict between Florence and the Visconti prince as a struggle between the forces of freedom and liberty on one hand, and of tyranny on the other.

The threat of Milanese domination undoubtedly strengthened the Florentine determination to preserve their free government; those years of war also imposed heavy burdens, and created discord, among the citizens. Nearly every year a conspiracy to overthrow the regime was discovered; some were organized by the Ciompi, others by members of prominent families (the Alberti, the Medici, the Ricci) who were hostile to the regime. After 1382, political power in the city centered around a group of old Guelf families – the Albizzi, Peruzzi, Capponi, Soderini, Rucellai, Strozzi, Guasconi being among the most prominent. Recruited from these dominant families was a cadre of leaders (Maso degli Albizzi, Rinaldo Gianfigliazzi, Niccolò da Uzzano, Gino Capponi) who were involved con-

*Opposite, the immense
Salone dei Cinquecento
(Hall of the Five Hundred)
in the Palazzo Vecchio
measures 53 meters by 23
(172 feet × 75 feet) and, as
can be seen in the plan of the
first floor (below), it
occupies the center of the
building. It was built by il
Cronaca for meetings of the
Maggior Consiglio, set up as*

*part of the political reforms
instituted by Savonarola in
1494.
It also houses a sculpture by
Michelangelo (opposite
below), entitled the* Genius
of Victory.

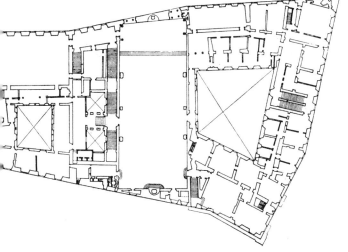

tinuously in the city's political life, even when they were not in office. The influence of these leaders was based upon their family status, their networks of clients and supporters, and their personal reputation and prestige. Devoting almost all of their time and energy to politics, they became experts in the arts of government, in wielding power. Although they did not change the constitutional system, they became adept at manipulating it to maintain their control of the regime. In terms of its institutions, the Florentine republic remained a government of the guild community, with its *Signoria,* its colleges, its legislative councils, its magistracies. But in terms of power, the republic was controlled by a small group of leading citizens, whose rule could be described as oligarchic.

After the death of Coluccio Salutati in 1406, the role of the republic's leading spokesman was filled by the humanist Leonardo Bruni. A native of Arezzo, Bruni came to Florence to study law but then shifted his scholarly interests to the *studia humanitatis.* He worked for several years in the papal curia before returning to Florence in 1415; he was elected chancellor in 1427. His

earliest writing on Florence, the *Laudatio Florentinae Urbis* (1403-04) was a panegyric of the city, her citizens and her government. He elaborated on these themes in his history of the Florentine people, which traced the city's past from its Roman origins to his own time. Strongly influenced by his study of Roman history and of classical political theory, Bruni interpreted Florentine history as a continuous struggle of free men against tyranny.

Most Florentines, even those who were on the fringes of the political community, would have subscribed to the republican ideals formulated by Leonardo Bruni. Evidence for this support abounds in their histories and diaries (for example, in Gregorio Dati's *L'Istoria di Firenze*), in their public and private correspondence, and in the records of their deliberations on political issues confronting their government. Those debates, or *pratiche,* constitute a valuable source for the political thought of Florence's civic leadership in the early quattrocento. Its basic principles can be summarized thus. Florentines were deeply committed to preserving their city's independence from foreign domination, and a

*The room shown above was
the refectory of the priors, at
whose table, apart from the
Signoria, nobody else,
except the notary, was
allowed to sit. The very fine
15th-century washbasin is
surmounted by the
republican lily, which was
not even changed when the
room was put at the disposal
of Eleanora of Toledo, the
wife of Cosimo I de'Medici.
The name "Room of
Esther," by which it is
known today, derives from a
large painting depicting
Esther and Ahasuerus.*

The massive bulk of the Palazzo Vecchio, crowned by Guelf merlons, from which rears up the daringly constructed tower, surmounted by Ghibelline merlons, is a synthesis of Florentine art and history. Below the gallery rest the colourful coats of arms of the republic: the red lily on a white background (the Guelf city), the red and white of the cities of Florence and Fiesole, the papal insignia (crossed keys), that of the Signoria with the motto Libertas, *those of the Guelf faction (the eagle impaling the dragon), of the Ghibelline city (white lily on a red background), of Charles of Anjou and, out of range of the photograph, those of the* capitano del popolo *(red cross on a white background) and of Robert of Anjou.*

republican form of government. They accepted the principle that only guild members had political rights, and that within the guild community, some citizens had a greater claim to offices (and so a greater voice in government) than others. They were in agreement that the common good (*ben comune*) took precedence over private interest. They believed in the social value of active, strong government, which regulated most aspects of their lives; they did not have a well-developed sense of a private realm from which the state was excluded. A corollary to this principle was the general acceptance of the state's right to demand sacrifices of its citizens, primarily in the form of taxes and public service, and not (as in the past) as foot soldiers and cavalry in the communal army. Finally, Florentines believed in the supreme importance of law as the regulator of human affairs, and in the critical importance of the equitable enforcement of the law. A prominent member of the political elite, Agnolo Pandolfini, asserted bluntly in one debate that "if justice is abandoned, then everything will collapse, for it is the only reason whey the poor, who are so much more numerous, do not devour the rich."

With rare exceptions, Florentines who enjoyed political rights would have accepted these principles as basic to their perception of a well-ordered polity. There was, inevitably, disagreement over the interpretation and application of these principles, and over specific questions of policy. Some citizens preferred a regime with a small, exclusive group of officeholders (*governo stretto*); others favoured a more broadly based polity (*governo largo*). Some advocated the grant of extensive authority to the *Signoria* and executive commissions (*balìe*); others, fearful of such concentrations of power, sought to limit the authority of the executive. Nor was there a consensus over the methods and scope of consultation, and over the degree to which citizens could express dissent. While admitting that diversity of opinion was inevitable in a heterogeneous community like Florence, some citizens were fearful that too much public controversy might lead to anarchy. It was universally recognized that civic discord was a constant threat to the stability of the regime. In their deliberations, citizens frequently referred to events in Florentine history (the dictatorship of the Duke of Athens, the Ciompi Revolution) when the city's freedom was threatened by internal conflict. They noted too that once-free cities in their own dominion (Pisa, Arezzo, Volterra) had lost their liberty through their internal divisions. The perils of civic discord were clear enough to all; but the control of that malaise was very difficult.

The Medici regime

In the formative years of the guild republic, violence and its control through the judicial administration was the primary source of internal conflict. This problem never disappeared from the civic agenda, but with the gradual (though incomplete) pacification of Florentine society, it was overshadowed by other problems, notably, the competition for civic office and the distribution of the fiscal burdens. The fisc was the most controversial issue in Florentine politics throughout the 15th century. Fiscal legislation was frequently rejected in the legislative councils, and the debates on those proposals were often bitter and acrimonious. In addition to the revenue from gabelles levied on food and raw materials, the commune relied heavily upon forced loans (*prestanze*) to pay for the costs of government and particularly for military expenditures. A complex system was developed to

The earliest images of the Palazzo Vecchio: in a fresco, above, commemorating the expulsion of the Duke of Athens in 1343 (note the defensive fortifications at the entrance) and right, on the tablet commemorating St. Zanobi, both of which are now preserved in the building that they depict. Left, the profile of a man's head on the exterior wall near the entrance, carved by, it is traditionally believed, Michelangelo, working with his chisel held behind his back whilst deep in conversation with a friend.

A detail from the "chained view" (above) shows work being carried out on controlling the waters of the Arno at the outskirts of the city. Below, the courtyard of the Palazzo Davanzati, one of Florence's important 14th- *century private residences. On one of the capitals of the pilasters (above left) there are male and female heads, which some people maintain display the features of the Davizzi family, the original owners of the palazzo.*

allocate these *prestanze,* based on the collective judgement of neighbours concerning the wealth of particular households in their *gonfalone.* But this arbitrary method could be manipulated by influential citizens to protect themselves and their friends, and to damage their enemies. So intense was the criticism of this method by those who believed that they were unjustly treated that a radical new system, the *catasto,* was implemented in 1427. Since assessments under the *catasto* were based on declarations of assets provided by individuals, they were presumably more equitable. But the utilization of the *catasto* did not eliminate discontent over fiscal policy; indeed, the system was abandoned in the late 1430s, and the old method of assessment restored.

The resentment aroused by the alleged inequities of the fisc was only one factor in the process of political disintegration that culminated in the establishment of a new regime controlled by the Medici. Since the outbreak of war with Filippo Maria Visconti, *signore* of Milan (1423), the republic was in a state of permanent crisis. The burdens of war weighed heavily upon an overtaxed citizenry; complaints

of fiscal and military mismanagement were voiced with increasing frequency. After Florence formed an alliance with Venice (1425), the citizens hoped for a rapid triumph over their Milanese enemy. But the war ended in a truce (1428) not victory, and civic discontent intensified. With the fragmented political community, two factions formed: an oligarchic party led by members of the Albizzi and Peruzzi families; and a rival group led by Cosimo de' Medici. These factions were divided not by issues of ideology or policy; they were competing for control of the regime. Florence's unsuccessful attack upon Lucca (1431) resulted in more intense strife between the factions. That led by Rinaldo degli Albizzi moved first against the Medici and their allies (November 1433), exiling Cosimo to Venice. But a year later (September 1434), a pro-Medicean *Signoria* recalled Cosimo, and then attacked the Albizzi and their partisans, driving them from the city. A new regime under Cosimo's leadership was established, which gave Florence a remarkably stable government for 60 years.

Cosimo de' Medici's genius as a political leader lay in his superb sense of limits. He had a deep understanding of the nature of his fellow citizens; he knew that he could not govern Florence as a *signore*. He could not dismantle the constitutional system that had survived for 150 years. The key to preserving the Medici's authority in this republican polity was control over officeholding. Cosimo and his allies devised an elaborate system of electoral mechanisms to ensure that Medici partisans would always have majorities in the important civic offices: the *Signoria* and the colleges, the magistracies in charge of war and internal security. Cosimo presided over a coalition of prominent citizens, some from old aristocratic lineages, others from

Left and above, intimate scenes of a daily life are portrayed in details of the frescoes by Andrea di Buonaiuto and his pupils in the Cappellone degli Spagnoli, part of the Dominican complex of Santa Maria Novella: they depict the life and customs of Florence during the mid 14th century.

parvenu families (the Martelli, Pucci, Ginori) who constituted the ruling elite. Controlling the important patronage for the whole city, he was ultimately responsible for distributing favours and benefits to his friends and clients, adjudicating between rivals, restraining the more avaricious, placating the dissatisfied. To his enemies (Rinaldo degli Albizzi, Palla Strozzi, Ridolfo Peruzzi), Cosimo was ruthless but not bloodthirsty. He sent his opponents into exile, allowing them to return only when they had ceased to be a threat to the regime.

Though Cosimo was a statesman of great intelligence and skill, his mastery of Florentine politics was never total. He could not end the wars with rival Italian states until the conclusion of the peace of Lodi in 1454. Those wars were a serious drain upon the Florentine economy, and they caused hardship and discontent in every stratum of society. In 1458, the city was seething with unrest, and the regime's leadership was in disarray. The lawyer, *messer* Girolamo Machiavelli (who was later sent into exile) called for major political reform, specifically, the restoration of free and open debate in the councils, a more just and equitable administration of public affairs, and the promotion of trade and industry within the dominion. To restrain a flood of criticism which threatened its authority, the Medici leadership convened a *parlamento*, an assembly of the entire political community dominated by their supporters. This *parlamento*

The miraculous transplant of a Negro's leg to replace one lost by a white man, as performed by two saints, Cosmas and Damian, who were doctors by profession. The episode is here portrayed by Fra Angelico in a painting now in Florence's Museo di San Marco. Perhaps because of the achievements of these two saints, Cosimo de' Medici chose them to be the patrons of his family. Their figures, recognizable by the red, fur-trimmed hats worn by those involved in the healing profession, appear in almost all the paintings commissioned by Cosimo.

The Medici coat of arms: in the border of a tapestry (below), in a block of porphyry (right), modelled in gilded stucco (below right). The palle *within the shield, which represent pills, possibly a reminder of some unverified family connection with medicine (indeed, the name Medici means "physicians"), vary in number over the years from six to 12. Under Cosimo I, the coat of arms was embellished by the addition of the grand ducal crown and, later, after it was granted to Piero, Cosimo's son, by Louis XI of France, the lily was added as well.*

approved the creation of a special *balìa* with extraordinary executive powers. The *balìa* acted quickly to reinforce the regime, by exiling some dissidents (and thus warning others to conform), and by bringing the branches of the administration – fiscal, judicial, police – under the tighter control of the executive power. Eight years later (1466), another crisis broke out shortly after Piero de' Medici succeeded Cosimo as head of the regime. Sensing that Piero was weaker than his father, ambitious men within the regime's leadership – Luca Pitti, Niccolò Soderini, Agnolo Acciaiuoli and others – challenged his authority, hoping to profit personally from his downfall. But Piero outwitted his rivals, first by negotiating an agreement with Luca Pitti, then by recruiting a strong military force to defend the regime. Piero also knew that he could rely on the support of a Milanese army that was poised on Florence's frontier, ready to move into the city if that were necessary to preserve the Medici regime.

Lorenzo de' Medici, *Il Magnifico* (the Magnificent), became the "first citizen" of Florence in 1469, when his father Piero died. He was just 20 years old, and in the early years of his political career, he relied heavily on the support of his ally, Galeazzo Maria Sforza, *signore* of Milan. He gradually gained experience and confidence, learning the difficult political skills of managing men, and creating for himself that public persona which later became an element of the Laurentian myth. The most serious challenge to his authority occurred in 1478, when he and his brother Giuliano were attacked in the cathedral by assassins employed by the Pazzi, bitter rivals of the Medici, and encouraged by Pope Sixtus IV. Giuliano was killed in this assault, and Lorenzo barely escaped with his life. But the Pazzi conspiracy failed when the Florentines refused to respond to the appeal of Jacopo de' Pazzi: *"Popolo e libertà!"* (people and liberty.) Jacopo and his co-conspirators (including the archbishop-elect of Pisa, Francesco Salviati) were hanged from the windows of the Palazzo della Signoria. Buoyed by the popular support of Florentine crowds, Lorenzo strengthened his control over the city and the government.

After the Pazzi conspiracy, the paramount concern of Lorenzo and his associates was to tighten their hold over the regime through institutional reforms (the creation of the Council

of Seventy), and through greater control of the fisc and the administration of justice. More actively than either Cosimo or Piero, Lorenzo intervened directly in political affairs. Many of his instructions and decisions were communicated orally, and most of the petitions addressed to him were presented in person, though a few written appeals have survived in the archives. From this documentation and from other sources, a picture of Lorenzo's activity as politic-

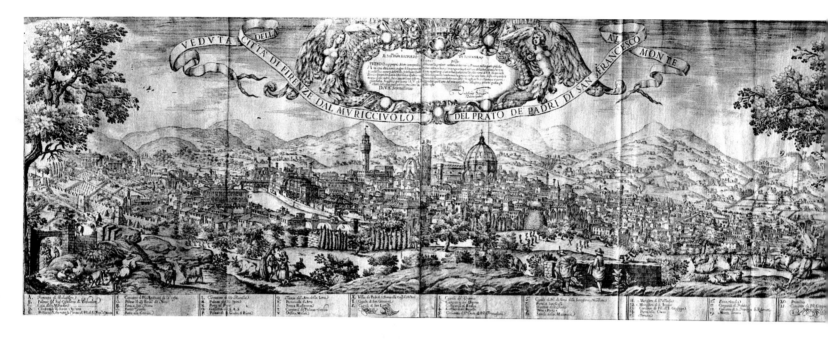

al leader and patron emerges. There was constant communication between *Il Magnifico* and his closest associates; important and difficult problems were invariably referred to him by the *Signoria* and other civic magistracies. This is not to say that Lorenzo made decisions about every political issue. Yet everyone in Florence knew that he could intervene if he chose to do so, and that his intervention would be decisive. Lorenzo was the master broker for the whole city, indeed for the whole Florentine dominion. He accepted this burdensome role, which gave him a sense of power not unlike that enjoyed by a Sforza or an Este prince. He clearly enjoyed some aspects of his patron's role: arranging marriages between prominent families, acting as arbiter in litigation over an inheritance or as the legal guardian of orphaned children. He took pleasure, too, in recommending Florentine artists to princes, and in making suggestions to Filippo Strozzi about the decoration of his new palace.

Il Magnifico was the most intelligent and skilled statesman of his generation, more aware than most of his contemporaries of the fragility of the political system that he had inherited and had learned to manipulate. His basic political instincts were conservative. He realized that his family's wealth and reputation were the foundation of his own power, and much of his energy was devoted to promoting family interests. His primary objective was the preservation of the regime under Medici control. As Cosimo had

done, Lorenzo mollified and placated friends and clients, to ensure their continued support. He arranged marriages within his inner circle to reinforce the bonds of obligation that held the regime together. He sensed the limits of his authority, and the politcal and economic dangers that threatened his power. There was resentment of Medici rule on the part of certain members of the old aristocracy but this was only latent. The Florentine economy was not thriving in the late quattrocento; the city could not long sustain the costs of protracted warfare. Realizing the need for external sources of support, Lorenzo worked assiduously to obtain a cardinal's hat for a Medici, to give the family a solid base in the Roman curia. He cultivated the Milanese connection, first with Galeazzo Maria Sforza, and then with his successor Lodovico il Moro. With great skill, he played the role of mediator among Italian states to maintain the fragile balance of power and the peace on which his regime depended for survival. His was a virtuoso performance, even though its effects were temporary, and ultimately futile.

Niccolò Machiavelli

In the last chapter of his Florentine history, Niccolò Machiavelli described the death of Lorenzo *Il Magnifico* (April 1492), an event that, in retrospect, assumed momentous significance for Florence and for Italy. For it presaged the

A view of Florence from around 1650 in an engraving by Valerio Spada. Opposite, two tondi on the ceiling of the Salone dei Cinquecento in the Palazzo Vecchio, the work of Vasari and his assistants, which present allegories of the city's districts. Above, the districts of Santa Maria Novella and San Giovanni, represented by old warriors resting on shields decorated with the relevant symbols: a gold sun on a blue ground and the Baptistery of San Giovanni. Below, the district of Santo Spirito with its emblem of a gold cross on a blue background, and the district of Santa Croce, distinguished by the white dove on a blue background Both paintings also contain the Marzocco, *i.e. the lion bearing the shield, young boys holding aloft the roundels from the Medici coat of arms, and putti waving the banners of the* gonfaloni, *into which each district was divided. Flora scatters flowers from above, whilst the tiny putti resting on top of the shields signify fertility.*

end of the Medici regime, and the beginning of those foreign interventions that led ultimately to the domination of the peninsula by Spanish arms. "As from his death the greatest devastation would shortly ensue, the heavens gave many evident tokens of its approach; among other signs, the highest pinnacle of the church of Santa Reparata was struck with lightning, and great part of it thrown down, to the terror and amazement of everyone (…) and hence, soon after the death of Lorenzo, those evil plants began to germinate, which in a little time ruined Italy, and continue to keep her in desolation." Two years after Lorenzo's death, a powerful French army under King Charles VIII crossed the Alps, moved through Lombardy into Tuscany and precipitated a political revolution in Florence. Lorenzo's son and successor, Piero de' Medici, fled from the city, and a new republican

regime was established, its character and structure strongly influenced by the Dominican friar, Girolamo Savonarola.

Machiavelli was born in 1469, in the same year that Lorenzo de' Medici had assumed the leadership of the Florentine state. Scarcely any evidence survives concerning his childhood and adolescence, and in his voluminous writings he never referred to his early years. He received a standard classical education, which qualified him for employment in the Florentine government. A few weeks after Savonarola had been executed in the Piazza della Signoria, Machiavelli was chosen to be a *segretarius* in the office of the *Dieci di Balìa,* the civic magistracy responsible for diplomacy and military affairs. Much of his work related to the Florentine campaign to regain control of the rebellious city of Pisa, a goal that was finally achieved in 1509. Machiavelli was also very active in Florentine diplomacy; he was

145

sent on missions to France and Germany, to the Roman curia, and to Cesare Borgia. He witnessed the problems and crises of his own republican regime, struggling for survival in a world dominated by stronger states. He learned about military affairs at first hand, since he was primarily responsible for the organization and training of a militia recruited from the Florentine dominion. His diplomatic missions gave him the opportunity to meet and to judge the European rulers who were involved in Italian politics: King Louis XII of France, Emperor Maximilian, King Ferdinand of Aragon, Pope Julius II. Though Machiavelli's political ideas were strongly influenced by his reading of Roman history, they were formed, too, by his personal experiences as an official of the Florentine republic during these troubled

"Acting on a prearranged sign, just as the priest who was singing the Mass received Communion, Franceschino de' Pazzi, who was walking through the church beside Giuliano de' Medici, attacked and killed him. Then Stefano, chancellor to Iacopo (de' Pazzi), together with others, attacked Lorenzo, but their courage failed them and they merely wounded him in the shoulder; he, for his part, began to move away and, having taken out a dagger to defend himself, with a band of people gathering round, began to make for safety, but his companion Francesco Nori died in the furore; finally Lorenzo, with the help of those around him and of the priests, was led alive to the sacristy and, with the door closed, he was kept from harm" (Guicciardini). The conspiracy, organized by those who could not tolerate the pre-eminence of the Medici, was intended to dispose of its most important members and was put into effect in April 1478 in the church of Santa Maria del Fiore (the cathedral). It failed, however, because of the botched attempt to murder Lorenzo, whose power was actually increased. To quote from Guicciardini again: "This scuffle (...) gave him such a reputation and acted so much to his advantage that it could be described as a very fortunate event for him; it killed his brother Giuliano, with whom he would have had to divide the family inheritance, which would have been a bone of contention; his enemies were gloriously and publicly disposed of, together with all the gloom and suspicion that existed in the city; the people took up arms on his behalf and, doubting that he was still alive, ran to his house demanding to see him, and he appeared at the window to the great joy of all present, and at the end of the day he was acknowledged as master of the city ..."

and historically important years.

Machiavelli had witnessed at first hand the extraordinary career of Savonarola, the Dominican friar who had emerged as a major force in the political life of the republic that had been established in late 1494 after the expulsion of the Medici. Savonarola's prophetic sermons, in which he warned the Florentines of impending doom, had attracted large crowds of citizens, many of whom were convinced that the friar was truly the *vox Dei*. Savonarola identified the French king, Charles VIII, as God's agent, whose mission it was to cleanse Italy of corruption. The friar's political plan contained these features: a military alliance with France, a restored republic based on the Venetian model, the exclusion of the Medici from the city, and a sustained campaign of moral reform. He was remarkably successful in mustering support for these policies, but he also encountered strong opposition from many quarters, within and outside the city. His most formidable opponent was Pope Alexander VI, whom he had attacked as the Antichrist. By the spring of 1498, Florence was deeply divided into two rival factions: the *frateschi* who fervently supported Savonarola, and the *arrabbiati*, who wished to be rid of him. That division was reflected in a *pratica* held in late March, to consider whether or not to authorize the ordeal by fire, involving the friar's Dominican supporters and their Franciscan rivals. Speaking in favour of Savonarola, Giovanni Cambi said: "Either he is a man of God or an evil man. If he is truly from God, we should pay him honour and respect, and do our utmost to avoid bringing God's wrath down upon him, for as a true servant of God he should escape the wrath of the Lord and his own flagellation." But sceptical voices challenged this view of the friar as a man of God. Thus, Carlo Canigiani: "In Florence he thought it best to talk of war and money. The other matter he felt was better discussed in Rome, where saints were canonized." And Filippo Giugni: "Fire seems rather a risk, one I would be personally reluctant to take. He could, with less danger to himself, immerse himself in water and if he were not to be immolated, I would be among the first who would beg his forgiveness. To go into the fire will mean certain death, I feel."

It is likely that Machiavelli came to the Piazza della Signoria to witness the ordeal by fire that

Opposite above: the medal coined by Pollaiolo to commemorate the Pazzi conspiracy, bearing the profile of Giuliano de' *Medici. Opposite below: the two dolphins that appear on the Pazzi coat of arms by Donatello. Above, the Palazzo Pazzi in an* *engraving. Below, the Pazzi coat of arms by della Robbia, on which the Medici* palle *have been superimposed.*

Some of the many villas of the Medici, as seen in paintings by Giusto Utens in the Museo Firenze com'era. Above, the villa of Poggio a Caiano, acquired by Lorenzo the Magnificent, rebuilt to designs by Giuliano Sangallo between 1480 and 1485 and extended by his son Giovanni de' Medici, later to become Pope Leo X; it is arguably one of the most splendid of the Medici summer residences. Above right, the villa of Seravezza, built by Bartolomeo Ammannati in 1555 for Cosimo. Below, the villa of Cafaggiolo, built by Michelozzo in 1432. Opposite, portrait of a young man with a medal of Cosimo the Elder, an oil painting by Botticelli dating from 1474 (Galleria degli Uffizi, Florence).

never took place, with the result that a frustrated citizenry turned against Savonarola, perceiving him not as a man of God but rather as a charlatan. His trial and execution (May 1498) was a victory for the pope and for the *arrabbiati*. Machiavelli had no sympathy for the friar, whose claims to divine inspiration he ridiculed. The secretary's view of politics was totally secular. If God existed for Machiavelli, he was a very distant being, quite indifferent to the fortunes of men. His hostility to Savonarola's efforts to establish a "republic of Christ" in Florence derived from this secular perspective. The friar's policies had divided the city into irreconcilable factions, and, as disarmed prophet, his designs "were at once frustrated when the multitude ceased to have faith in him; for he was destitute of the means either to compel belief, or to inspire confidence" (*The Prince*, Chapter VI).

Like Brunetto Latini and Leonardo Bruni, Machiavelli believed that a republic was the best form of government, since it provided men with the opportunity to live in freedom, and to develop their talents fully. But his reading and experience had taught him the difficulties involved in creating a viable republican polity. By their nature, men were "ungrateful, fickle, timid, dissembling and self-interested" (*The Prince,* Chapter XVII); egocentric and avaricious, they did not possess the requisite qualities for self-government. With such unpromising human material, how could republican regimes be established and maintained? In his study of Roman history, Machiavelli found some answers

to this problem. He perceived in Romulus, the founder of Rome, those qualities of *virtù* that were so important for the establishment of a well-ordered republic. Romulus and his successors enacted laws that taught the Romans how to govern themselves, and how to train their children to be good citizens. This civic education was supremely important for Machiavelli. Young Romans were taught that the republic's needs always took precedence over individual interests. They were trained to be prepared to sacrifice their property and their lives for the honour and glory of the republic. This image of Roman citizens fighting to defend their city and to preserve its honour made a powerful impression on Machiavelli. He compared it with the situation then prevailing in Florence and elsewhere in Italy, where citizens no longer fought to defend their states, but relied on mercenaries. This absence of a military spirit was, for

Machiavelli, the most striking evidence of political corruption in Italy, which made the peninsula so weak and vulnerable.

At the end of the first book of his Florentine history, Machiavelli described the sorry state of Italian arms, as a prelude to his discussion of the origins of his native city, "that it may be clearly understood what was the state of the city in those times, and by what means, through the labours of a thousand years, she became so imbecile." In Machiavelli's view, the Florentines inherited little of the valour and prowess of their Roman forebears. For 700 years, the Romans managed to restrain their internal divisions, before their republic was destroyed. The Florentines, however, became so addicted to these conflicts that they never succeeded in controlling or eradicating them. The roots of this civic malaise lay deep in Florence's social fabric, in the social and economic differences among its citizens. Inevitably, as Machiavelli points out, tensions arose between those in power and the *popolani*, the latter wanting to live according to the law, and the former to dictate the law. Machiavelli admitted that the *popolani* were victims of noble aggression, and that they were justified in restraining their power and arrogance. But, he argued, they went too far in their campaign against the *grandi*, by excluding them from civic offices and, in some cases, sending them into exile. This extreme policy alienated the nobility, who were no longer willing or able to serve in the Florentine army or in public office.

During those years when Machiavelli was an official of the republic (1498-1512), the city was torn by internal conflict, which weakened its efforts to recover Pisa, and to defend itself against its enemies. Savonarola's influence on the city's politics did not end with his death; his supporters (the *frateschi* or *piagnoni* as they were called) were committed to the friar's political plan, specifically, the Great Council established in 1494, the French alliance, and opposition to the Medici. The most serious division within the republic focused on the issue of participation. Most aristocrats favoured a regime with a narrow social base (*governo stretto*), while citizens of lesser rank and status advocated an enlarged political community (*governo largo*), which included all guild members: artisans and shopkeepers as well as merchants, industrialists and *rentiers*. Machiavelli was himself partial to this type of regime, convinced that a broad social base contributed to the stability of republics. His friend, Francesco Guicciardini, believed that the governance of Florence should be restricted to the aristocratic families, who alone possessed the knowledge and experience to govern well. This controversy had run like a thread throughout Florence's history; it remained, in the 16th century, a divisive and unresolved issue.

All of Machiavelli's writing is pervaded by a profound sense of pessimism. In 1512, he lost his position as *segretarius* when the Medici were restored to the city and he never again held an important post in the Florentine government. His appeals to the Medici for employment were consistently ignored and until his death he was forced to live with the burden of that misfortune. He died in 1527, at the time when the Florentines rebelled against Medici rule; he did not live to witness the heroic though ultimately unsuccess-

ful attempt of his fellow-citizens to restore their republic. When he died, Machiavelli's ideas were known only to a handful of his Florentine friends. In his wildest fantasies, he could not have dreamed that one day his name would be known throughout the world, and that his works would be read by millions.

Machiavelli's writings created a revolution in European political thought. He demystified the state, stripping away its religious and sacramental trappings, and exposing as its core the exercise of power. Politics were firmly rooted in the human realm, and thus subject to men's feelings, passions, impulses. Though he laboured to formulate rules of political conduct, Machiavelli was acutely aware of the unstable nature of politics, a perennial struggle between human will and spirit (*virtù*) and the external forces outside man's control (*fortuna*). To suc-

Savonarola's blunt and violent eloquence, tinged with threatening prophecies, struck at religious and political corruption. After the downfall of Piero de' Medici, the friar led a short-lived "demo-theocratic" republic (1494-98). Excommunicated when his monastery was attacked (above, the bell which sounded during the assault), Savonarola was handed over to the Signoria. After being tried and condemned to death, he was hanged and burnt together with two of his fellow friars. The event is recalled in this painting (left) in the Museo di San Marco in Florence.

ceed in that struggle, to dominate *fortuna*, men had to exploit fully all of their talents and resources: reason, will power, instinct. This was Machiavelli's most important teaching to his contemporaries, and to future generations.

Cosimo I de' Medici, a poor and neglected descendant of an offshoot from the Medici dynasty, may be regarded as the founder of the Tuscan state (opposite, a statue of Cosimo on horseback by Giambologna which stands in the Piazza della Signoria).

Having checked a final attempt to restore republicanism by means of his victory at Montemurlo (1538), Cosimo, a highly ambitious and energetic man, obtained the title of Grand Duke from Pope Pius V (below, the papal bull of

1569 which granted him his title). His son, Ferdinando I, favoured a pro-French policy, and it was against this background that he married Christine of Lorraine in 1589, an event shown in the small painting by Biccherna reproduced above.

EXCISE, VALUATIONS, LOANS, LAND SURVEYS

In Florence, as elsewhere in medieval Europe, the state collected the funds it required mainly through indirect taxation. However, Florence also experimented with direct taxation and, to an even greater extent, with public debt. There are many fascinating records of medieval fiscal policy; of particular interest, for instance, is the list of offerings in kind owed to the commune by the people of the *contado* (surrounding countryside) in 1302 (3).

Interesting too is the picture of a tax office at the end of the 14th century, showing a treasurer and a scribe (2), from the cover of a Sienese register (Biccherna). Giovanni Villani gives a precise itemization of the communal revenues for the years 1336-38. This happened to be a period when the *estimo* (a form of direct tax) was not being applied. From the attempted classification of these sources of revenue it can be observed that duties on transit and consumption (8) brought in 60.9 per cent of the total, while direct taxation (in practice, the *estimo* of the country dwellers) accounted for only 9.9 per cent. Of some interest too is the record of income from the ten main kinds of tax (6):

of a total of slightly more than 300,000 florins, the gate tolls proved the most lucrative, with over 90,000 florins (this was the tax on economic goods passing through the city walls); next, worth approximately two thirds of the previous tax, was the duty on wine. Duty on other transactions and commodities took fourth, sixth, and seventh places. The last two sources of revenue require some comment. "Penalties for shortfall on enrolment figures" refers to what Villani describes as "revenue from missing cavalry or infantry men" – the penalties payable by the constables for having fewer men than they had contracted to enlist and for which they had been paid. The last tax, levied on projecting buildings, was a duty raised on buildings that had projecting parts overhanging the street. Revenue from indirect taxation proving inadequate (and clearly such duties bore hardest on the poor, as ever), the *estimo* was introduced during the 13th century. This tax was raised on inheritances, and was based on "estimates" of each person's wealth; in reality, however, these "estimates," as Raymond de Roover points out, were "aimed less at determining the real wealth of individuals than at reaching a figure that would make a convenient quota for collecting the amount due from each quarter, *gonfalone,* or parish. The arbitrariness and inequity of this system inevitably produced protests and tension. Reformed in 1285, it was then abolished in 1315. In 1325 it was reintroduced on a basis of sworn declarations, and with the interesting innovation that, while taxes on property were proportional to the estimated value, professional incomes were assessed on a progressive scale. However, after the departure of Charles of Anjou (Duke of Calabria, son of King Robert of Naples, and father of Queen Joanna I),

who had been elected lord of Florence that year, the *Signoria* burnt all the fiscal records collected under his regime. The Florentine oligarchy always tried to depend as little as possible on direct taxation, for obvious reasons. Subsequently the *estimo* was reintroduced and reabolished according to circumstances.

When money was needed beyond what could be raised by the means so far discussed, state loans were taken out. These could be either voluntary or enforced. Thousands of registers of such loans survive; illustrations (4) and (5) show two covers of state loan registers, that of the 14th *prestanza* of the Lion Rosso *gonfalone* – a subdivision of the Santa Maria Novella quarter – from 1349, and that of a loan made in 1408 to the Ferza *gonfalone,* in the Santo Spirito quarter. At first these loans, which were raised for extraordinary expenditure (especially war), were repayable by concessions from ordinary sources of revenue. Yet this meant that the state was in danger of spending all its revenue on repayment of loans, and so the public debt was eventually consolidated (1343). This sparked off a theological debate on the morality of a policy whereby the state paid interest on public debt (in this controversy the Franciscans were the "permissives"

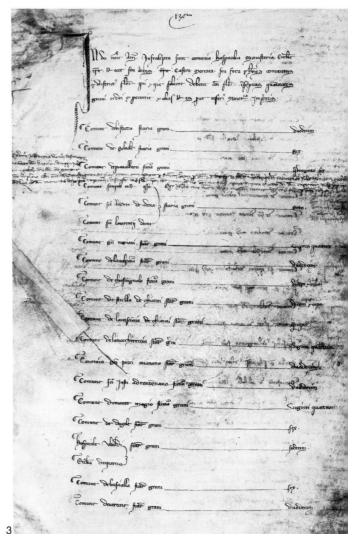

5

against the stricter Dominicans and Augustinians). Meanwhile the delay in interest payments lowered the market value of these "gilts" – to 60 per cent in 1427, 35 per cent in 1431, and 20 per cent in 1458. At the same time the very attitude of the state, which was always short of cash, contributed to this fall. In 1358 it offered 300 florins in public debt bonds for 100 in cash, in an attempt to lure lenders. In 1427, to meet the expense of the extremely costly war with Milan (a war of mercenaries and *condottieri,* thus a war of economic strength), the so-called *catasto* (land tax) was introduced. The person responsible for introducing this tax was the father of Cosimo the Elder, Giovanni di Bicci (1), who thereby established the basis for the future political supremacy of the Medici family. The *catasto* was seen as a great popular victory: the common folk had the satisfaction of seeing, as one chronicle puts it, "those who previously

Sliding scale of taxation for the *catasto* of 1481

income in florins	percentage of tax
—50	7
50/75	8
75/100	11,5
100/150	14
150/200	16
200/250	18
250/300	20
300/400	21
+ 400	22

7

declaration of means had to be renewed periodically, and on the whole it was. In his study of the Medici bank Raymond de Roover publishes a list of those who paid over 50 florins in the *catasto* of 1457: only 11 names figure, the last paying 51 florins, 15 *soldi,* and ten *denari.* Top of the list is Cosimo di Giovanni with Pierfrancesco Medici, who paid 576 florins, 15 *soldi,* and one *denaro.*

The ten major sources of income in Florence during the years 1336-38

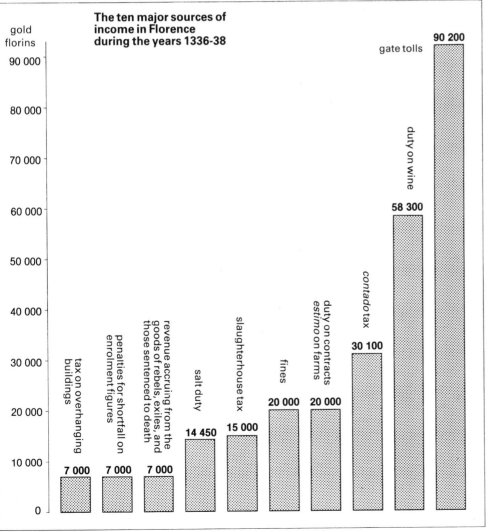

gold florins: 90 000, 80 000, 70 000, 60 000, 50 000, 40 000, 30 000, 20 000, 10 000, 0

- tax on overhanging buildings — 7 000
- penalties for shortfall on enrolment figures — 7 000
- revenue accruing from the goods of rebels, exiles, and those sentenced to death — 7 000
- salt duty — 14 450
- slaughterhouse tax — 15 000
- fines — 20 000
- duty on contracts *estimo* on farms — 20 000
- *contado* tax — 30 100
- duty on wine — 58 300
- gate tolls — 90 200

Percentage breakdown of the revenue of the commune of Florence in 1338

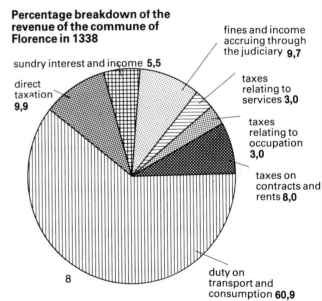

- sundry interest and income **5,5**
- direct taxation **9,9**
- fines and income accruing through the judiciary **9,7**
- taxes relating to services **3,0**
- taxes relating to occupation **3,0**
- taxes on contracts and rents **8,0**
- duty on transport and consumption **60,9**

8

paid twenty florins now paying three hundred." As a form of taxation it was based on a remarkably modern fiscal mentality. Everyone liable for it had to complete a declaration with the relevant authorities listing their properties, their government stock, and their trade investments both in Italy and abroad. As we find from the records, in certain cases balance sheets of companies of which the taxpayer was an associate also had to be appended (and as a result, in secret company books we read of forged accounts, "for love of the *catasto*"). This

Next, way behind, are the heirs of Giovanni d'Amerigo Benci, paying 132 florins, 10 *soldi,* and eight *denari.* For the *catasto* of 1481 (7) the rate of taxation had become progressive: below 50 florins of taxable means the rate was 7 per cent; between 50 and 75 it was 8 per cent etc. up to 22 per cent for 400 or more florins of taxable means. With the expulsion of the Medici in 1494 (due to the cowardliness of Lorenzo the Magnificent's son Piero in his relations with Charles VIII), the Florentines lost no time in abolishing the *catasto.*

The formation of the Florentine dominion

From his reading of ancient and contemporary history, and from his own experience, Machiavelli was acutely aware of the critical role of warfare in the political life of human communities. In his *History of Florence,* he balanced his treatment of the city's internal politics with a detailed account of its military affairs. He understood that the commune's political evolution was profoundly influenced by its efforts, first to dominate its *contado,* and then to extend its rule over the whole province of Tuscany. From its first tentative moves towards self-government in the early 12th century, the city was almost continually engaged in conflict with the feudal nobles whose castles dotted the rural landscape outside its walls, with rival towns, with German emperors and their armies. Those wars fostered a sense of civic pride, whose symbol was the *carroccio,* the military cart adorned with communal banners, that accompanied the Florentine army into battle. The fiscal burdens of war served as a stimulus for administrative growth, for developing more effective methods of tax collection, for exercising greater control over the resources of the community. Finally, those burdens also contributed to political crises, which often resulted in abrupt changes in the city's political order.

The chronicle accounts of the commune's early military exploits are descriptive; they record the bare facts of a castle siege, the conquest of a rural village, the rout of an army from Pisan or Pistoia. These discrete events formed part of a broader pattern of Florentine expansion, the motives for which are clear, though rarely articulated. In that violent and chaotic world that gave birth to the Italian city-states, only the strongest and most aggressive communities sur-

vived as independent entities. Every town that aspired to self-government had to gain control of its *contado,* for economic and strategic reasons. The *contado* produced the food and raw materials that fed the town's inhabitants; through the *contado* ran the trade routes that nourished its commercial and industrial enterprises. The *contado* also contributed manpower for the city's armies, and sites for the castles and fortifications that protected it from its enemies. The larger and stronger city-states like Florence were not content with establishing their authority over their *contadi;* they looked beyond their diocesan boundaries, continually seeking more territory, more subjects, more revenue, more security. The limits to their aggrandizement were reached only when they encountered a city-state strong enough to repulse their territorial ambitions.

The growth of the Florentine territorial state was an untidy historical process, characterized by sharp vicissitudes, by spurts of expansion followed by retreat and retrenchment. Influencing this development were two sets of variables, one internal and the other external. Among the internal factors were the size and resources of the urban population, the varying intensity of demographic, economic and political pressures for territorial growth, and the military organization that achieved the conquests of the castles, towns and villages beyond the city walls. The tempo of expansion was also conditioned by the volatile political and military situation in central Italy. The most important external variable was the presence (or absence) of a strong foreign power in the peninsula: the German emperors in the 12th and 13th centuries; the French and Spanish monarchs in the 16th. With these variables as guidelines, it is possible to identify four distinct phases of Florentine territorial expansion. The first, embracing the 12th century, was characterized by the effective establishment of the commune's control over its *contado*. The next phase, during the 13th and 14th centuries, witnessed the bitter rivalry between Guelf and Ghibelline factions, and the sporadic intervention of papal and imperial authority in Tuscan affairs. During the third phase, from about 1330 to 1494, the absence of a potent imperial force in Italy fostered the development of strong regional states whose centers were the peninsula's great cities: Florence, Venice, Milan, Rome, Naples. The beginning of the fourth phase was marked by the French invasion of 1494, which ended Italy's immunity from foreign intervention and inaugurated three centuries of her domination by

Europe's great powers. It was during that period that the Florentine state reached its historical limits with Grand Duke Cosimo's conquest of Siena in 1555.

The documentation of this first phase of Florentine expansion is as scanty and uninformative as that concerning the emergence of communal institutions, the consulate and the assembly. Both developments involved efforts by the city's elite, its *boni homines,* to achieve autonomy and to dismantle the decaying structure of traditional authority represented by the German emperors and the Florentine bishops. There is evidence of a Florentine army attacking a feudal castle in the *contado* as early as 1107, even before the city's consulate can be documented. The most potent feudal lords in the region were the

"In the year of our Lord 1107, our city of Florence having grown and increased greatly in population and power, the Florentines resolved to extend their contado *further and broaden their* Signoria, *and to wage war on any castle or fortress that might not yield to them"* (Giovanni Villani). *The first expansionist phase was followed by others that lasted right up until the end of the 15th century, made easier by the absence of any firm imperial power to prevent the formation of regional states. Florence's greatest territorial expansion, however, was achieved in 1555 following the conquest of Siena by Grand Duke Cosimo. Opposite, how miniaturists depicted Tuscan arms and soldiers between the 13th and 14th centuries. From the left (working clockwise): the capture of a fortress (13th century); a Florentine skirmish into the Pisan* contado *in 1362; soldiers from Lucca at the recapture of the castle of Pietrabuona from the Florentines (1362); the* condottiero *Giovanni Acuto (the Englishman John Hawkwood), who later joined the Florentines, in Tuscan territory with papal troops, 1375 (from the* Croniche del Sercambi *in the Archivio di Stato, Lucca). Left, a bird's-eye view of part of Tuscany in a map drawn by Leonardo da Vinci in 1502. In the foreground is the city of Volterra, fought over for a long time by Florence, Pisa and Siena and conquered by the Florentines in 1472.*

Conti Guidi and the Conti Alberti; castles belonging to these families were the first targets of communal assaults. By the middle of the 12th century, the nascent commune had conquered and demolished several castles belonging to these lords, and forced them to submit to its jurisdiction. In 1107 Monte Orlandi was besieged and taken; in 1113, Montecascioli; in 1135, Montebuoni; in 1146, Quona. Of these ancient fortifications only a few ruins have survived, but they must have resembled the tower, still extant, of Montegrossoli in the Chianti region, which was conquered by a Florentine army in 1182. Not all of the commune's territory was taken by force; many castles and rural villages voluntarily accepted Florentine jurisdiction. Some lands were acquired through purchase, others by usurpation with only a veiled threat of coercion. In every case, the motivation was the same: to extend the city's control over more land and people, as sources of food, military manpower and taxes.

We know very little about the organization of these Florentine armies that periodically made forays outside the city walls to attack their enemies. Military service was probably mandatory for all able-bodied males who resided in Florence. Those who could afford to maintain a horse fought in the cavalry, while the mass fought on foot with swords and spears. Led by the consuls, these armies went into the field only in summer before the harvest, for short periods of a few weeks or at most two months. Though it cannot be proven, it is likely that these citizen

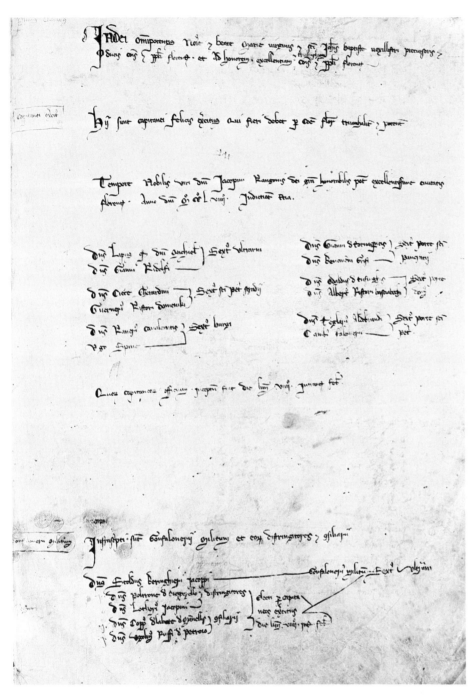

soldiers were paid for their military service. In addition to their assaults on the castles of feudal nobility, these armies also attacked nearby towns. Prato was besieged and demolished (though later rebuilt) in 1107, Fiesole in 1125. In 1168 the *borgo* of Figline on the upper Arno came under the commune's control, and in 1182 Empoli was incorporated into the dominion. Other more distant cities – Pistoia, Siena, Pisa, Lucca – came into contact, and conflict, with Florentine forces during the course of the 12th century, though these conflicts were neither very lengthy nor very destructive.

Contributing significantly to this process of territorial expansion and consolidation was the failure of Florence's sovereign rulers, the German emperors, to maintain a stable and effective presence in Tuscany. The town of San Miniato al Tedesco, west of Florence, was the provincial capital of the empire, but its officials were too weak to control the territory. Emperor Frederick Barbarossa (1152-90) was determined to restore imperial authority to Italy, but the chosen battlefield for his enterprise was Lombardy not Tuscany, whose communal governments were free to pursue their territorial objectives. But Frederick's son, Henry VI, was more strongly drawn to Italy than his predecessors, since he had married the heiress to the Kingdom of Naples. He restored a degree of imperial authority in Tuscany, forcing communes like Florence to surrender some of their conquests. In 1187, the commune received a charter from the emperor confirming its authority within the city walls and in the adjacent outlying areas. But the imperial power in Tuscany declined after Henry's early and unexpected death in 1197. Florence celebrated the event by conquering and demolishing the town of Semifonte near Certaldo in 1202.

The reign of Emperor Frederick II (1211-50), which coincided with the outbreak of the Guelf-Ghibelline rivalry, opened a new chapter in Florence's external affairs. Throughout the 12th century, the commune's Tuscan policy was certainly geared to expansion, but only in its immediate environs. Its relations with other Tuscan cities were occasional and sporadic, while beyond the province's borders, it had few interests or preoccupations. After Henry VI's death, the commune joined a league of Tuscan cities, formed to defend themselves against a potential revival of imperial power. The creation

On 4 September 1260, the Guelfs of Florence and the Ghibellines of Siena, backed by the cavalry of Manfredi, King of Sicily, and by the Florentine exiles under the leadership of Farinata degli Uberti, met in battle at Montaperti in the valley of the river Arbia. It was a bloody defeat for the Florentines, whose blood, according to Dante,

"colour'd Arbia's flood with crimson stain." The preparations for the battle are documented in the Libro di Montaperti *(Archivio di Stato, Florence), the first page of which is illustrated above; the book is composed of records, registers and various papers concerning the military and administrative offices of the Florentine army; the*

documents relate to the period from 9 February to the eve of the battle, 3 September. Opposite, one of the gates in the walls of Florence, the 14th-century Porta a San Frediano, as depicted in a detail from the altarpiece painted by Filippino Lippi for Tanai de' Nerli (church of Santo Spirito, Florence).

Above, the Florentines at the walls of Siena during the war that reached its climax at Montaperti. Giovanni Villani relates that in the retinue of their army the Florentines took their carroccio (the military cart adorned with "the standard of arms of the commune, *which was half white and half vermilion") and the bell known as the* Martinella, *both of which were lost during the rout. Among Florence's allies on that occasion was Volterra (below, in an illustrated map by Jacopo Angelo Fiorentino, 1472), as well as* *Pistoia, Prato, San Gimignano and Colle Val d'Elba. Another traditional rival of Florence was Pisa, shown here (above right) in a detail from an anonymous painting in that city's church of San Nicola.*

of that alliance foreshadowed an era of intense diplomatic contacts among Tuscan towns, and with cities in distant provinces: Emilia, Romagna, Lombardy, Piedmont. With the spread of the Guelf-Ghibelline virus, these connections multiplied, covering the peninsula, and even the lands beyond the Alps, with a dense network of diplomatic ties. In the 1220s and 1230s, when the struggle between Frederick II and the popes was most intense, the Florentine commune maintained close relations with the Roman curia. After Frederick II's death in 1250, the city's Guelf commune forged ties with the Angevin rulers of Naples, and their cousins, the Capetian (and later Valois) kings of France.

The most dramatic reversal of Florentine fortunes occurred halfway through this century, after the death of Frederick II. Since the emperor's victory over the Lombard towns at Cortenuova (1237), his officials succeeded in establishing effective imperial control over Tuscany, limiting the authority of the communes, and exercising direct rule over their *contadi*. But the city threw off the Ghibelline yoke within weeks of the emperor's death, and the regime of the *primo popolo* quickly recovered those lands

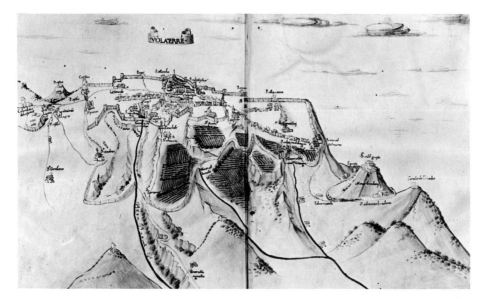

that the commune had surrendered to imperial authorities. As though unleashed from bondage, the new regime embarked upon a series of military campaigns against neighbouring cities that were still controlled by Ghibellines. Florentine armies attacked Siena and Pisa, and then Pistoia, Poggibonsi and Volterra. Each town was forced to submit to Florentine occupation and control (Pistoia, Poggibonsi, Volterra), or to accept peace terms dictated by the Arno commune (Siena, Pisa). In four years, Florence had nearly doubled the size of her dominion, and had established herself as the greatest power in Tuscany. As Giovanni Villani tells us, the year 1254 was known by the Florentines as *l'anno vittorioso* (the victorious year) because the military exploits of the army had brought victory and great honour to the city.

Montaperti

Only a few years after this *anno vittorioso*, Florence suffered the most dramatic and humiliating defeat in her history, at Montaperti, where on 4 September 1260 a Sienese Ghibelline army overwhelmed a much larger force of Tuscan Guelfs. Chroniclers, both Sienese and Florentine, described that historic battle in detail, and their narratives can be supplemented by the *Libro di Montaperti* (the Book of Montaperti), the official Florentine record of the army, that was decimated by the Sienese and their German allies.

The battle of Montaperti was an episode in the perpetual struggle between Tuscan Guelf and Ghibelline factions that had kept the region in turmoil since 1215. The Florentine Guelfs had established their temporary hegemony in the province in the early 1250s, but their Ghibelline enemies were encouraged by the military victories in the south of Frederick II's illegitimate son, Manfred, who was crowned King of Sicily in Palermo in 1258. A group of Florentine Ghibellines, under the leadership of Farinata degli Uberti, fled to Siena and encouraged their allies in that city to resist Florence, and to enlist support from Manfred. A contingent of German cavalry arrived in Siena in the summer of 1259, bolstering the local Ghibelline forces and raising their hopes for victory over their Guelf rivals. In May 1260, a Florentine army attempted a surprise attack on Siena, but it was repulsed. A second force, reinforced by Guelf contingents

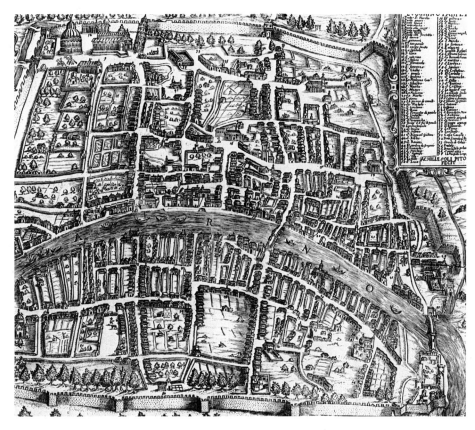

Pisa had enjoyed its greatest moment of glory during the 12th century, when, following the decline of Amalfi, its great maritime trading rival, it sided with those who supported imperial authority in Italy. However, before the century was even over, the city's conflicts with Lucca, Genoa and Florence (the latter was seeking an outlet to the sea via the Arno) had led to the start of its gradual decline. Its turbulent history of clashes with Florence (below, an illustration from Giovanni Sercambi's Croniche *showing the* Florentines attacking the city) culminated in the city's surrender in 1406 after a lengthy siege. Having lost its independence, Pisa then enjoyed an economic upsurge during the granducato *of the Medici* (above, a map of the city during the 17th century).

"TWO BALES OF PINK CLOTH…"

1
2

3

The modest simplicity of Florence's early days came to be romanticized and nostalgically evoked later. Cacciaguida reminds Dante in the *Paradiso* (canto XV) of a Florence that was "chaste and sober, and abode in peace./She had no armlets and no head-tires then;/No purfled dames; no zone, that caught the eye/More than the person did." More will be said later about the finery of Florentine women. Villani adds another few descriptive touches to this picture, recalling the Florentines who "clad both themselves and their womenfolk in plain cloth, and many wore furs without any lining. The ladies wore simple footwear and "those of high rank were content with a narrow skirt of plain scarlet," while "the common women" went "dressed in plain Cambrai green." In contrast Villani looks unfavourably on the "outlandish dress, neither beautiful nor honest" of the younger generations. Between the late 13th and the early 14th century there was indeed, in Florence as elsewhere, a greater degree of luxury in dress: an indication of prosperity, or at least of improved conditions of life. Then there were also, of course, the simple vagaries of fashion – just like nowa-

days. Much later Leonardo was to declare that clothing should "envelop the body with simplicity and grace, without artificial folds."

Colour was greatly appreciated, and new dyes came into use at this time. Pink cloth was very popular in Florence. Cosimo de' Medici used to say that "two bales of pink cloth" made a gentleman – the sensible, well dressed *borghese*. Only in the 16th century did the fashion for black gradually spread (Venetian in origin, but subsequently more Spanish in taste). By the following century it dominated all other colours. Male attire in the Middle Ages was full-length and loose, with long sleeves. It developed directly from the dalmatic of the late Roman Empire. It then slowly became shorter, evolving into a knee-length tunic (13th-century male dress (1) from a print by the Maestro del Bigallo), growing ever tighter and more close-fitting until help was needed to put it on. A pouch hung from a belt around the waist (there were no pockets until the 16th century), and the shoulders were padded with cotton wool. In place of the knee-length stockings attached to the *femoralia* (drawers) that had been worn with the long tunic, the

shorter tunic required a hose that went up to the groin and was held up by laces tied to the smock above (15th-century male attire (5), from a painting by Botticelli). This proving somewhat immodest, tights were introduced.

Florentine male headgear consisted of a round padded cloth hat with a stylish pointed "tail" falling past the

left cheek and onto the left shoulder, which either hung straight down or was wrapped around the neck – thus forming a hat and scarf in one. This was already old-fashioned by the 15th century, and had been replaced by a cap – relatively tall and shaped like the base of a cone – with a brim turned up at the back, and straight in

front. Vasari painted the Grand Duke Cosimo I with hose, breeches, and a large fur-lined jacket (8). This is typical of the late 16th century – the fur lining providing protection against the cold (if one could afford it) in unheated houses. It was at this point, then, that furs began to be imported – the native Italian wolf and squirrel furs

4

5

6

skin, but warns, "the face quickly becomes coarsened and the teeth black, and women age prematurely." Facial hair was removed (as Boccaccio relates, the hairdressers would "flay their ladies, plucking their brows and foreheads, softening their cheeks and neck, removing individual hairs"); the fashion was for blonde hair, set in fantastic styles, sometimes with the aid of wigs (women's hairstyles (7) in the frescoes by Tura at Schifanoia, Ferrara). Female attire also was clearly descended from Roman fashions (female figure from a Pisan crucifixion (2), first half of the 13th century); it then became softer in line, emphasizing the waist and freeing the neck and shoulders (young women (3), from a 14th-century fresco in Santa Maria Novella). Women later started using wadding to accentuate the shape of their hips, and corsets to lift the breasts. The bust was in full fashion by the 16th century: this can be seen in

dress in cold weather. Illustration (6) shows a 15th-century Florentine lady: she is in fact Lucrezia Tornabuoni, wife of Piero de' Medici and mother of Lorenzo the Magnificent, painted by Ghirlandaio; the line of her dress recurs in more modest fashion in the woodcut illustration to *Nencia da Barberino*, a poem attributed to Lorenzo de' Medici. The girl's headgear in this picture shows the kind of wide-brimmed straw hat worn in summer to protect the complexion – the famous Florentine *paglia* (9). Just as there was no longer a free Italy by the end of the century, there no longer seemed to be a distinctively "Italian" style of dress. The following complaint by Francesco Sansovino was common in the 16th century: "the Italians, forgetting they were born in Italy, and following ultramontane fashions, have changed their dress along with their thinking, trying to appear French one minute and Spanish the next…"

no longer being deemed elegant enough. Cosimo is bearded, in keeping with the fashion of the day. At the beginning of the 14th century men tended to be clean-shaven; it was the French and German mercenaries who brought in the fashion for beards (an import from the northern barbarians, some said). The 15th century was clean-shaven to begin with, and hair was worn long. Later, beards reappeared, either free flowing or trimmed in different styles. Female fashions meanwhile evolved through various styles. Cennino Cennini in *Il Libro dell'arte* (c. 1390) gives instructions on painting the

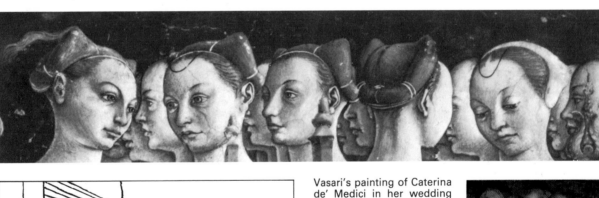

7

8

9

Vasari's painting of Caterina de' Medici in her wedding dress (10). Prior to this, however, there had been the delicate elegance of international gothic (birth tray (4), with a painting of the *Judgement of Paris*) and early Renaissance fashions: embroidery, lace and trimmings of all kinds; the sleeves detached from the dress (a French fashion introduced in the 15th century) and laced with strings and ribbons of precious material such as gold or silver brocade, in colours matching the dress; and the train, which provoked the ire of preachers, and whose length was regulated by sumptuary laws. "In mid 15th-century Florence," we are told by F. Cognasso, "the dress worn in the home was the *gamurra*," a woollen garment worn over a shirt; and over this in turn would be worn the *cioppa*, an overgarment with a train and wide sleeves. This was how women would

10

Henry VIII's descent into Italy (1310-13), welcomed by Dante in the hope that it would lead to the restoration of imperial rule and thereby bring peace and an end to factional rivalries, had the opposite effect of leading to an upsurge in fights between Guelfs and Ghibellines. The pictures on these pages, taken from the 14th-century Balduino codex (State Archives, Coblenz), apart from the last one, which comes from a Chigi codex in the Vatican, portray certain events from the period: the king's entry into Italy from Mont Cenis; his coronation in Rome; his encounter with the Florentines; the capture of San Giovanni Valdarno; the arrival of the emperor at San Casciano; Henry's death at Buonconvento.

from other Tuscan towns – Lucca, Pistoia, Prato, Arezzo, Volterra, San Gimignano – was assembled in August. The size of that Guelf army has been estimated at 70,000, of which 16,000 were Florentines; not since Roman times had a military force of that magnitude been seen in central Italy. The Florentine host established its camp near the castle of Montaperti, 12 kilometers (seven miles) east of Siena. And there, on the morning of 4 September, the Sienese and their Florentine and German allies, numbering

perhaps 25,000, attacked and vanquished the vastly superior Guelf army. Some 10,000 died in the battle, and 20,000 more were taken prisoner and led back to Siena, where many died in prison.

For the Sienese, the victory at Montaperti was – and remains – the most glorious moment in their city's history, when their ancestors fought against overwhelming odds to defeat their proud and arrogant neighbours. The Florentines, however, were persuaded that their defeat was

From Dino Compagni: "Louis of Savoy, sent as ambassador to Tuscany by the emperor, arrived in Florence; and he was treated with little honour by the noble citizens, who acted contrary to their duty. He asked them what ambassador should be sent that they would honour and obey as they would their lord: their reply, delivered

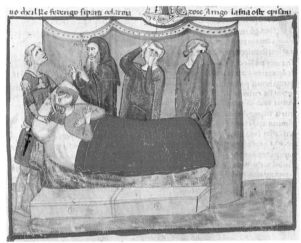

hand in which he bore the standard, killing him." When the banner fell to the ground, the Florentine cavalry fled in disorder, leaving the infantry to be butchered by the Sienese and their German allies. In the *Inferno*, Dante describes the Ghibelline Farinata degli Uberti very sympathetically, but he reviles Bocca degli Abati as a despicable traitor:

But, passing midst the heads, my foot did strike
With violent blow against the face of one.
"Wherefore dost bruise me?" weeping he exclaim'd.
"Unless thy errand be some fresh revenge
For Montaperti, wherefore troublest me?"
(...) another cried,
"What ails thee, Bocca? Sound not loud enough
Thy chattering teeth, but thou must bark outright?
What devil wings thee?" – "Now," said I, "be dumb,
Accursed traitor! To thy shame, of thee
True tidings will I bear."
(*Inferno,* XXXII, 77-81, 106-111)

on behalf of the Signoria *by Betto Brunelleschi, was that 'never would the Florentines bow their heads to any lord.'" "The Florentines," Compagni goes on to say, "revealed by their every act that they were hostile to the emperor, calling him cruel and a tyrant (...) And their banners read: 'Honour to the holy church, and death to the King of the Magna.'"*

the result not of Sienese valour but of the treachery of Florentine Ghibellines in their army. According to Giovanni Villani's account, the Ghibellines in the Florentine host had secret communications with Farinata degli Uberti and his friends in Siena, promising to betray the Guelfs in battle. When the Sienese assault began, the standard-bearer of the Florentine cavalry, Jacopo de' Pazzi, was treacherously attacked by *messer* Bocca degli Abati, "who wounded the said *messer* Jacopo and severed the

Though incomplete, the *Libro di Montaperti* provides the most detailed and accurate record of a Tuscan army in the 13th century. Florence's urban population contributed approximately 7,000 men to the force: 1,500 cavalry, 4,000 infantry, 1,000 crossbowmen, 1,000 archers. The *contado* provided another 5,000 infantry and 3,000 sappers (*guastatores*). Several hundred mercenary cavalry were recruited from Emilia and Romagna, and the army also included foot soldiers from Tuscan towns allied with Florence. All of these troops, native and foreign, were paid. The mercenary cavalry received the highest salaries (eight florins per month), while the infantry received very modest stipends: between one and two *soldi* per day. It has been estimated that the total cost of this army was 35,000 lire per month. Though the largest and richest city in Tuscany, Florence could not long sustain expenditure of that magnitude, which explains why military campaigns were normally of such brief duration.

At Montaperti, the great majority of the combatants were not professional soldiers but citizens who left their occupations in town and countryside, to mount a horse, to wield a sword or pike, to carry a crossbow and to experience either victory or defeat and possibly death. This pattern of military organization continued in Tuscany with little change for nearly a century, though the number of foreign mercenaries – Italian, German, and particularly French – did increase gradually. By the 1280s, Florence

Montalcino, because of its strategic position, was a bone of bitter contention between Florence and Siena during the 13th century and, although its commune sided with Florence, it was forced to surrender to Siena after the rout of the Florentines at Montaperti in 1260. Surrounded since the 12th century by walls, which were strengthened and fortified on several occasions, it underwent and survived a siege by Charles V in 1553, an event recorded in a small painting of the same year by Biccherna (left).

Above, a Florentine cannon in the Museo Nazionale del Bargello. Its rear end bears a representation of the planet Jupiter and its four satellites, which were discovered by Galileo in 1610 are named sidera medicea *(stars of the Medici).*

maintained a permanent mercenary force of several hundred cavalry, which formed the nucleus of its army. These troops were organized into companies, led by experienced commanders, most of whom were recruited from neighbouring provinces: Umbria, Emilia, Romagna. However, the citizen contingent, both cavalry and infantry, continued to be an important part of these military forces mustered for either defense or offense in Tuscany. When Emperor Henry VII moved into Tuscany in 1311 and laid siege to Florence, his army of nearly 20,000 was challenged by a Florentine force of equal size, comprising both city and *contado* contingents, and a corps of Catalan mercenaries. A decade later (1323) Castruccio Castracani, the *signore* of Lucca threatened Prato just 8 kilometers (five miles) from the city, whereupon the Florentine people and cavalry (so Villani reported), "having locked up their *botteghe* and left their guilds, rode reluctantly to Prato. Each guild sent people on foot and on horseback, and many Florentine houses, both noble and *popolani*, sent armed bands of men on foot at their expense ... at Prato the following day the Florentines could boast of 1,500 cavalrymen and a good 20,000 foot soldiers ..." The Florentine army that was soundly beaten by Castruccio at Altopascio (1325) included some 500 urban cavalrymen and 15,000 infantry recruited from both city and countryside.

The arrival of an embassy at a city, as depicted in a small painting by Biccherna from 1498 (Archivio di Stato, Siena).

che si facelle che tanto factenea quanta a none. Come fre comincia
guerra tra ilconte diuirtu el coe difirenza:

Perche ogni male uuol giunta Pensando ladiuina bonta caued
ueduto che plamoria mandura aluata e aicontato no essisi iauta

Dimilano caualcazono insultazono dicoztona azdendo e deruba

qualchato legenti del duqha dimilano fuoza deltza o difioz
archa ad: y aprile i.1397. sidistesso le diche genti uezso pz

come fire latriegua tra il duqa dimilano colla legha:

mro era del fole faciendo suo corso oe suoi razzi nel secno deltauzo.

The balance between citizens and foreign mercenaries in Florentine armies shifted decisively towards the latter by the mid 14th century. Altopascio was the last major battle in which significant numbers of Florentine citizens bore arms and lost their lives in combat, though a few still fought in the war against Pisa in the 1360s. This transition to a wholly mercenary armed force was not due, as Machiavelli believed, to a decline in civic patriotism and to moral degeneracy. Italian warfare had become more professional, requiring a greater degree of skill. Foreign professionals were available for recruitment in large numbers during the second half of the 14th century; they crossed the Alps during lulls in the Anglo-French wars, and many, like the English captain John Hawkwood (known as Giovanni Acuto), remained in Italy for years, employed regularly by Florence and by other Italian states. These governments continued to employ Italian soldiers in their armies, supplementing them with contingents from France, Spain, Germany and Hungary. Many of these foreign mercenaries were organized into companies which sometimes fought for pay and, when unemployed, ravaged the unprotected countryside. By the end of the 14th century, however, these companies had largely disappeared from the Italian scene, to be replaced by a more stable and permanent military system controlled by the *condottieri*. The quattrocento was the great age of these military leaders, some of whom, like Francesco Sforza, used their military prowess to become heads of state.

Territorial consolidation

The foreign mercenaries who filtered into Italy during the 14th century, in search of employment and booty, did not come as part of potent and conquering armies. The Luxembourg prince, Henry VII, was the last imperial ruler whose military force was sufficiently great to intimidate some (though not all) Italian states. After his death in 1313, claimants to the imperial throne – Ludwig of Bavaria, Charles of Bohemia, Frederick of Hapsburg – occasionally crossed the Alps on their way to Italy, but their "invasions" were more ceremonial than military. They came to receive the Lombard crown in Milan, and the imperial crown in Rome, and to replenish their

*At the end of the 14th century Florence was threatened from the north by a war that lasted 12 long years. Giangaleazzo Visconti, Duke of Milan, dreamed of extending his domains to include Tuscany and Umbria, having conquered the Scaliger Signoria of Verona and Vicenza, as well as that of the Carraresi in Padua. The Florentines began to seek new allies to prevent themselves being encircled: they entered into an agreement with the French king, they formed a league with Venice and signed an alliance with the new emperor, Robert of Bavaria. Almost nothing came of these precautions, however, and Giangaleazzo overran Bologna, also establishing a firm foothold in Tuscany and Umbria by seizing Pisa, Siena, Perugia and Assisi. Florence now lay within the grasp of the Milanese leader, who had already ordered a new crown for his investiture as King of Italy. History, however, was not on his side and at Melegnano, on 3 September 1402, Giangaleazzo suddenly died (possibly of plague or tertian fever). His removal from the scene freed the Florentines who, as Machiavelli pointed out, would have lost had it not been for his death.
The* Croniche *of Giovanni Sercambi (Archivio di Stato, Lucca) contain a series of miniatures depicting various events in the war, some of which are illustrated here. Opposite, a confrontation between the troops of Florence and Milan amidst the fluttering banners bearing their respective insignia (top); the conquest of Cortona by the Milanese forces in 1397 (center); the signing of a truce between Milan and the League (below). Right, the meeting between the delegates of Milan, Venice and Florence in 1400.*

coffers by selling imperial charters and other regalian rights. For nearly two centuries, Italy was to be free of any serious foreign interference in her political and military life. City-states like Florence took advantage of this opportunity to consolidate and expand their territories and to develop their administrative structures. These structures, so admired by Burckhardt as "works of art," were the most advanced and elaborate systems of government in all of Europe.

Since the early 13th century, Florence's territorial interests were inextricably tied to the fortunes of the Guelf and Ghibelline parties in Tuscany, and elsewhere in the Italian peninsula. When, by 1280, the Guelfs had finally established their hegemony in Florence and other Tuscan towns, they relied heavily on Rome and Naples, the papal curia and the Angevin court, for political and military support. That support was critical during Henry VII's invasion, and later when Uguccione della Faggiuola and Castruccio Castracani attempted to establish Ghibelline states on Florence's western frontier. Castruccio's fortuitous death in 1328 ended this period of Florentine dependence on papal and Angevin power; thenceforth, the Guelf regime was strong enough to defend its territory, and to embark upon an ambitious campaign of expansion. To gain control of Arezzo and Lucca, Florence became involved in a complex series of negotiations involving the Visconti *signore* of Milan, Mastino della Scala of Verona, the Rossi lords of Parma, and the Venetian republic. Arezzo did fall into Florentine hands, but not

Lucca. It is one of the great ironies of Tuscan history that the Arno city was never able to conquer her smaller and weaker rival on the Serchio river. It was the bitter disappointment over the failure of the Lucca campaign that precipitated the invitation to the Duke of Athens (1342) to become the Florentine *capitano di guerra*. In the disorders that accompanied the duke's expulsion a year later, the subject towns of Pistoia, Arezzo, Volterra, Colle and San Gimignano were lost.

The guild regime that governed Florence from the 1340s until the Ciompi Revolution maintained a cautious and defensive posture in Tuscany. Abandoning the expansionist policy of the 1330s, it sought to maintain good relations with its neighbours, contracting a series of leagues for mutual defense against the marauding bands of soldiers that plagued the province in these years. Florence did fight a major war with Pisa (1362-64) to obtain favourable commercial rights for her merchants. A more aggressive policy of territorial aggrandizement was pursued by the oligarchic regime that was established in 1382, partly in response to the threat to Florentine security posed by the *signore* of Milan, Giangaleazzo Visconti. This shrewd and astute prince forged a powerful state in Lombardy in the late 1380s, and then began to move south into Tuscany. With consummate diplomatic skill, he exploited the local resentments against Florence in Pisa, Lucca and Siena, establishing regimes favourable to him in those cities. In the summer of 1402, Giangaleazzo's army occupied Bologna, completing the encirclement of Florence. The city might well have been forced to submit to the superior power of the Visconti ruler if he had not died of fever (September 1402) at the critical moment. Had Giangaleazzo succeeded in creating a powerful and united state embracing most of the imperial territory in the peninsula, the history of Renais-

Left, detail from a fresco by Piero della Francesca depicting Hercules' Victory over Cosroë *(church of San Francesco, Arezzo), which, although dealing with a classical theme, depicts 15th-century arms and armour. Right, representation of a horseman under arms, known as* Military Valour, *on a panel sculpted by Andrea Pisano in the first half of the 14th century in the campanile of Florence cathedral. Below, detail from the* Intervention of Micheletto da Cotignola, *from the* Battle of San Romano *series by Paolo Uccello (Musée du Louvre, Paris).*

sance Italy would have followed a very different course.

From their struggle with Giangaleazzo, the Florentines learned that their security depended fundamentally on their own resources. No trust could be placed in alliances with other states, since experience had demonstrated their unreliability. None of the Guelf powers that had supported Florence in the past – the papacy, Naples, France, Hungary – had provided any effective assistance to the republic against Giangaleazzo. Rather than promote friendly relations with other Tuscan towns, the best strategy was to absorb them into Florence's dominion, thereby removing the danger of their occupation by enemies like Giangaleazzo. Initially, the main thrust of Florentine expansion had been southward, beginning with the reacquisition of Arezzo (1384), and the submission of Montepulciano (1390). After Giangaleazzo's demise and the disintegration of his state, Florence turned westwards, towards Pisa and the Tyrrhenian sea. After a lengthy siege, Pisa was occupied by Florentine troops in October 1406; the Arno city had obtained a secure port for its merchants. The conquest of Pisa was not welcomed by the other

Marco Foscari, Venetian ambassador in 1527, tells us: "The city of Florence is very well fortified (...) although the walls are built in the old way, fairly high and lack any deep trenches or counterscarps or interior earthworks; the walls, nevertheless, are four Florentine braccia tall, which equal six of our feet. And they are encrusted within and without ex lapidibus quadratis from their mountains, which are somewhat similar to tufa, and inside they are filled with gravel mixed with lime mortar (...) which they need two days to make a small hole in, using wedges, so that experienced people are of the opinion that it would take some days to destroy those walls with artillery..." Left, the Belvedere fortress, built by Buontalenti in 1590-95.

maritime powers on the Tyrrhenian coast, and the republic was soon embroiled in conflict with Genoa and King Ladislaus of Naples. But Florence kept her foothold on the sea, and expanded it through the purchase of Leghorn in 1421. In the 1420s, she launched a series of galley fleets that made voyages to England, the Low Countries and the Levant. This ambitious and costly undertaking was designed to establish Florence as a major maritime power, rivalling Genoa and Venice.

By the 1420s, Florence's territory had reached limits that, save for minor acquisitions, were not exceeded until Duke Cosimo's conquest of Siena in 1555. The western boundary followed the Tyrrhenian coast from the mouth of the Cecina river 40 kilometers (24 miles) south of Pisa, to the river Serchio on the north and, additionally, the town of Sarzana near La Spezia. Lucca's territory intruded into the dominion north of Pisa but the Apennine foothills from Pescia to Pistoia and north of the Mugello were all controlled by Florence. The southern frontier followed the Cecina river south of Volterra, running just north of Siena and then southeast towards Lake Trasimeno. In the early years of

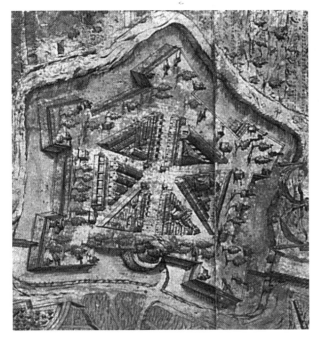

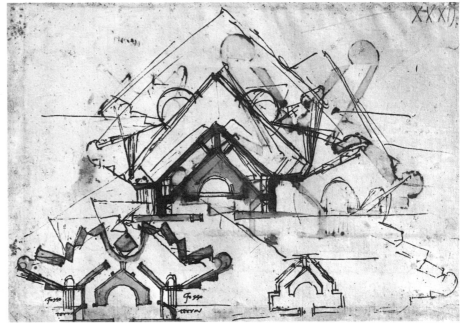

the 15th century, Florence had pushed her eastern frontier beyond Casentino and the Valdichiana, incorporating the towns of Cortona, Borgo Sansepulcro and Bagno di Romagna into her territory. Florence's dominion in 1427 embraced some 11,000 square kilometers (about 4,200 square miles), in which there lived some 260,000 people.

The governance of this dominion was a complex system that had gradually evolved since the 13th century. Supreme authority was vested in the organs of central government in Florence: the *Signoria,* the colleges, the legislative councils. A cluster of civic magistracies (the *Cinque del contado e distretto,* the *Otto di Guardia,* the *Ufficiali dell'estimo del contado*) bore responsibility for particular aspects of territorial administration. An army of officials, all citizens, was sent to the towns and rural districts as agents of the central government. They administered justice, enforced legislation, and collaborated with local officials in the collection of taxes and the maintenance of public order. In the early 15th century, there were more than 100 of these officials, each provided with a staff of judges, notaries, guards and messengers. An official of the highest rank, e.g. the *podestà* of Pisa, might have a retinue of 50 or 60, while a minor official, the *podestà* of Uzzano in the Valdinievole, would be supported by a small staff of four or five. In all of the towns and rural districts of the dominion,

*Opposite below: the Porta Romana, a massive keep of 1326. On this page above left, the Fortezza da Basso or "lower fort" (detail from the map by Bonsignori), planned by Antonio da Sangallo and erected in 1535.
Right, a sketch by Michelangelo for fortifying the Porta al Prato.
Below, detail of the walls from the "chained view" (1472).*

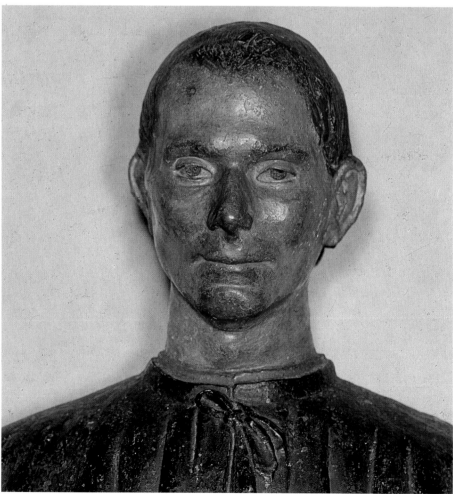

local people were chosen for local offices, with responsibility for certain administrative tasks. Thus, the apportionment of taxes among *contado* residents, and the maintenance of roads and bridges, were usually left to these local officials in the towns, the rural communes and the leagues of the dominion. This administrative system was not highly centralized nor uniform, although in the 15th century, the central government made sporadic attempts to introduce a greater degree of order and rationality to the government of the dominion.

The administration of her territory was a serious and enduring problem for the republic in the 15th century, as demonstrated by the copious legislation, executive decrees and statutes devoted to the subject. The dominion's importance as a fiscal resource, and as a defense bulwark, was fully appreciated by citizens who were responsible for state security. A conception of the ideal relationship between rulers and subjects, between the city and its subject territory, emerges from the frequent debates held in the Palazzo della Signoria. In this vision, Florentine officials governed the territory with firmness and integrity, thereby winning the respect and affection of the inhabitants. Recognizing the benefits of peace and justice which they received, the subjects were obedient to their Florentine rulers, paying their taxes without complaint, and remaining loyal to the republic against all enemies, foreign and domestic. How far this ideal was from reality can be seen from the remarks of the Florentines themselves, in their deliberations on territorial policy. In these debates, Florentine subjects were frequently described as miserable, impoverished creatures, exploited by rapacious officials, overwhelmed by the exactions of usurers. There is evidence from other sources to suggest that this negative evaluation of territorial administration was accurate. The 1427 *catasto* provides irrefutable evidence of the relative poverty of the countryside, by comparison with the city itself. With 16 per cent of the population of the territory, Florence possessed two thirds of the total wealth. The rural population (not including the subject towns) comprised 62 per cent of the total, while possessing only 18 per cent of the taxable property.

Part of this striking difference in wealth was due to the basic structure of the Tuscan economy, but contributing to the dominion's impoverishment were specific policies of the central government. To protect the city's textile industries, the state imposed severe restrictions on cloth production in the territory. In times of famine, grain from the dominion would be requisitioned and transported to Florence to feed its population. During the period of Florence's most intense involvement in warfare (from c. 1375 to c. 1450), the central government imposed very heavy taxes on its subject towns and rural areas, and also required them to provide troops to guard the frontiers and defend the fortresses. In the petitions sent by subject towns to the Florentine authorities, the most common theme was this tax burden, which was so heavy that the local inhabitants could not pay the assessments. Another frequent complaint was the exaction of usurers, some Jews and others Florentine citizens, who lent money at exorbitant rates to the poor residents of the territory, and also to towns and rural communes. When the financial

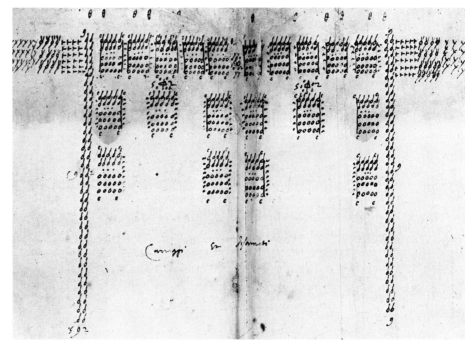

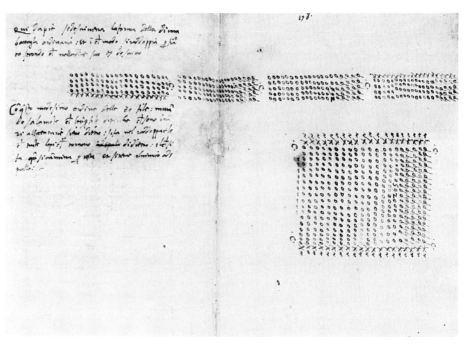

burdens of taxation and usury became too great, desperate *contadini* fled from the territory, thus reducing the number of taxpayers and cultivators of the land.

Numerous, too, were the complaints about the malfeasance of Florentine officials in the territory. They were charged with being as rapacious as wolves, robbing their subjects of "their pastures, their rights and their property." A law enacted in 1415 referred to "the illegal, unjust

Modern political thought has its roots in two outstanding figures of the Italian Renaissance: Niccolò Machiavelli and Francesco Guicciardini. Both men were Florentines and both were historians and writers, men of theory and practice, who held important political office; Machiavelli was the republic's secretary for war

and internal affairs, while Guicciardini was a diplomat and military expert in the service of two Medici popes, Leo X and Clement VII. Opposite, the frontispiece of Machiavelli's History of Florence *(above left); the coat of arms of the Guicciardini family (above right); wooden bust of Niccolò Machiavelli*

(below). On this page, woodcut showing Guicciardini at his desk (above left); two original drawings by Machiavelli for his Arte *della Guerra, a treatise on military technique (top and above).*

and iniquitous extortions, exactions and bribes" of certain officials, whose greed had overcome their sense of honour and propriety. Even though the laws stipulated that the actions of every territorial official were subject to scrutiny, and every complaint investigated, few officials were ever found guilty of malfeasance. A detailed accusation was made in 1461 against Lorenzo Altoviti, the captain of Barga in the Garfagnana region on Florence's northwestern frontier, by certain residents of that town. If these charges can be believed (and they might have been exaggerated), Lorenzo was totally unfit for his post. He insulted the native girls who had come to Barga to the fair of San Pellegrino, "pinching the buttocks of the young Lombard women in such a fashion as to heap shame upon himself, were it not for the fact that the captain of the guard said that he held the *Signoria* in very high esteem ..." It was also alleged that Lorenzo travelled around his jurisdiction with a gang of local *bravi*, disturbing the peace. During Mass on the feast day of San Cristofano, he denounced a friar who was in the pulpit: "Come down from there, friar, and attend to some different business, for as far as I can see, you are nothing but a madman!" So outrageous was his behaviour that: "locals and foreigners alike made fun of him, saying to the people of Barga, 'If this is your captain, then you must be very badly governed

indeed. Why do you not go to your lords to complain of his follies?'"

This document reveals that the sensibilities of the territorial subjects were an important element in their attitude towards their Florentine rulers, and that official behaviour which offended their pride and sense of honour could lead to alienation and even, in extreme cases, to rebellion. Excessive fiscal burdens may have been the major cause of revolts in the territory, but other, less tangible grievances also played a part: for example, resentment over the cancellation of traditional privileges and the violation of ancient customs. During the republic's wars with Giangaleazzo Visconti, the duke sent agents into Florentine territory to foment rebellions, the most serious being the revolt of the *Cancellieri* of Pistoia in 1401. Florentine control of the Apennine region on her northern frontier was always unstable, the inhabitants prone to rebellion. The Aretine *contado* and the Casentino were other districts that did not willingly accept Florentine rule. Volterra rebelled twice in the 15th century, first in 1429 and again in 1472. But nowhere in the territory was hostility of Florence as intense as in Pisa, whose citizens never forgot their history of independence, and never forgave the Florentines for conquering them in 1406.

Pisa is a good illustration of the problems of Florentine territorial administration in the quattrocento. After its conquest in 1406, the city was in a very poor state: its economy wrecked, its population depleted. Florentine policy toward its captive city was initially very harsh. Heavy taxes were levied on the inhabitants to pay for the repairing and manning of the fortifications; and more than a hundred Pisans were forced into exile as being particularly hostile to Florentine rule. These measures were later seen by Florentines themselves as counter-productive, as the Pisan economy continued to stagnate. The creation of the galley fleets in the 1420s was one aspect of a changing policy towards Pisa which was designed to stimulate her economy. By mid century there were distinct signs of revival, resulting in part from investments by Florentine capitalists, most notably the Medici, in Pisa and her *contado*. In 1473, Lorenzo de' Medici arranged for the transfer of the Florentine Studio to Pisa, which benefited from the influx of students. Yet, though Pisa's economic fortunes had certainly improved under Florentine rule,

When the Guelf party became firmly established in Florence, the imperial eagle was banned and replaced by the lion, the animal that was the heraldic antithesis of the eagle, which had been chosen by the primo popolo *as their own emblem. The whole city became decorated with effigies of lions. They appeared on Guelf towers and adorned the banners of* compagnie popolari *and family coats of arms (left, the coat of arms adorning the Palazzo Davanzati). In the Loggia dei Lanzi, two stone lions seem to be guarding the steps (opposite, detail of a lion from the classical era), and other likenesses of the animal appear on the pillars and the interior cornice of the vaults. But Florence also bred real lions, like the ones who lived in cages in the city center, according to the chronicler Giovanni Villani: "In the said year (1332), on the 25th day of July, St. Jacob's day, two lion cubs were born of the commune's lion and lioness, which lived in a cage by San Pietro Scheraggio; and they survived and afterwards grew up; and they were born live and not dead as writers in books on the nature of beasts tell us (...) and it was held to be a great marvel that on this side of the sea lions should be born that lived, and such a thing has never been recorded until the present (...) It was believed by many that this was a sign of good fortune and prosperity for the commune of Florence."*

the city's inhabitants eagerly seized the opportunity to rebel against their overlords in 1494, when Pisa was occupied by a French garrison. A year later, the Pisan ambassador Burgundio Leoli appeared before the French king, Charles VIII, to request that his city remain free of Florentine domination. In his speech, Leoli developed the argument that was to become the standard Pisan view of its subjugation: "Complaining bitterly, the people of Pisa, a city which had extended its empire as far as the Orient by means of many noble victories and which had been one of the most powerful and glorious cities in Italy, were driven to extreme desolation through the cruelty and avariciousness of the Florentines, who had held them in such iniquitous and atrocious servitude for 88 years."

For 15 years, from 1494 to 1509, the Pisans tenaciously resisted the Florentine military forces that sought to reconquer their city. Their leaders desperately sought aid from other powers, promising to accept the rule of France, and later of the German emperor Maximilian, to avoid the restoration of Florentine rule. Though some prominent Pisans were apparently willing to negotiate a settlement with Florence, the urban masses and the Pisan *contadini* were determined to resist reconquest. The Florentine republic spent millions of florins in military efforts to recover the city. On two occasions, in 1499 and again in 1500, Pisa was surrounded by enemy forces and her surrender seemed inevitable. But the mercenaries in the attacking armies failed to press their advantage, which so

Charles VIII of France descended into Italy in 1494 in pursuit of his claim to the throne of Naples. He stopped in Florence, and his passage through the city (opposite below, a contemporary painting of the event by Francesco Granacci) was described thus by Guicciardini: "The king entered Florence with his whole army at arms: first the ranks of infantry, armed with lances, crossbows and scoppietti, by far the majority of whom were Swiss; then came the horses and the fully-armed soldiers, a truly beautiful sight because of their great numbers, the appearance of the men and the beauty of the arms and the horses, with their rich coverings of cloth and gold brocade; finally came the king in full armour as conqueror and triumphant victor over the city, a very beautiful sight in itself, but little enjoyed by the people, who were filled with fear and terror." After conquering Naples, the king was obliged to leave that city because of the war being waged against him by the anti-French league, opening the route for his retreat with the Battle of Fornovo (below).
In 1527, the lansquenets of Charles V laid waste to the countryside, despite sporadic displays of opposition. The emperor returned in 1529 and laid siege to Florence (opposite above, the siege of the city in a painting by Vasari). Outside the city, the Florentine troops of Francesco Ferrucci were defeated at Gavinana on 3 August 1530 (above). The city surrendered on 12 August that same year.

infuriated the Florentine authorities that they executed (October 1499) the commander of their army, Paolo Vitelli. In 1500, a French and Swiss military force abandoned its assault on the beleaguered city. The failure of these mercenaries to fight well for their employers strengthened Machiavelli's conviction that hired soldiers were useless in military operations, and persuaded him to press for the recruitment of native soldiers. In 1506 he obtained the government's approval to hire and train men in the *contado* for military service. For the remainder of his tenure as *segretarius* he was very active in this enterprise, going out personally into the *contado* to supervise the enlistment and drilling of peasant soldiers. This militia was pressed into service against Pisa, whose starving citizens finally sur-

The preparation of gunpowder (left) and work in a cannon foundry (below) provide the subject of two frescoes in the Uffizi by Bernardino Poccetti that symbolize the development of the arms industry at the end of the 16th century. The artillery that had already appeared on the battlefields of the 14th century became firmly established during the 15th century with the introduction of the first rudimentary gun carriages. An enormous and very fine artillery piece of cast bronze is now displayed in the courtyard of the Museo Nazionale del Bargello. It is called "St. Paul's cannon" (opposite above) because of the gigantic head of the saint adorning its rear, which was modelled and cast for Ferdinando II de' Medici by the Florentine Cosimo Cenni in the 17th century. Opposite below, a folio from the Miscellanea Medicea (Archivio di Stato, Florence) shows a soldier armed with a "musket (…) a very good and everlasting weapon." The musket, which first appeared in Italy in the army of Charles V during the 1529-30 campaign, was a portable firearm, but so much heavier than the arquebus that it needed the support of a bracket resting on the ground; it had a maximum range of a little less than 100 meters (328 feet) and could fire a shot every five minutes.

rendered to Florence (June 1509). That was the high point of Machiavelli's career as a civil servant.

The Florentine government was so pleased with the role of the *contado* militia in Pisa's conquest that it decided to cease hiring foreign mercenaries, and to rely exclusively on its own subjects for defense. That policy was severely tested in 1512, when a Spanish army marched into Tuscany to attack Florence. Under Machiavelli's supervision, a militia force of some 12,000 was mustered to resist the invaders. Most of these soldiers remained close to Florence; a contingent of 3,000 troops defended Prato, where the Spanish army first struck. Those professionals easily routed the Florentine militia, killing more than 2,000; they entered Prato and sacked the city. This military collapse heralded the demise of the republican regime headed by Machiavelli's patron, Pier Soderini, the return of the Medici, and the exclusion of the *segretarius* from civic office.

The sack of Prato was only one (though the most serious) of many devastations inflicted upon the Florentine dominion during the troubled years following the first French invasion. The campaigns for the reconquest of Pisa had wrought severe damage, by friend and foe, in the Pisan *contado* and adjacent areas. Tuscany was a major thoroughfare for armies moving from Lombardy to the south; their troops were invariably undisciplined, burning and looting the unfortified villages and farms in the countryside. After the French (1494-95) came a Venetian mercenary force (1498), followed by Cesare Borgia (1501-02), whose troops marched from the Mugello past Florence to Piombino, and then to Arezzo and the Valdichiana, leaving a trail of desolation in their wake. Under Medici rule (1512-27), Tuscany did enjoy a brief respite of peace, while Lombardy bore the brunt of warfare between the rulers of France and Spain. But that peaceful interval ended with the sack of Rome (spring 1527) by an imperial army and the restoration of republican government in Florence. After the Medici pope, Clement VII gained his release from Castel San Angelo, he made an agreement with Emperor Charles V (June 1529), in which the emperor agreed to provide troops, at papal expense, for the recovery of Florence by the Medici. In Florence a citizen army was formed to defend the walls

against the besieging army. Under the leadership of Francesco Ferrucci, Florentine militia fought bravely against the imperial forces in the Arno valley west of the beleaguered city. But the superior numbers of the enemy finally overcame this heroic resistance. Ferrucci's army was defeated at Gavinana near Pistoia (3 August 1530),

Far left, detail of the wooden door of the Pandolfini chapel in the Badia Fiorentina; the arms of the family include three stylized dolphins. Left, a window set amidst the rustication of the Palazzo Gondi. Below, the stone commemorating the mule, an animal which proved its worth as a means of conveyance during the building of the Palazzo Pitti. Opposite, two lions flanking a window in the Torre degli Amidei (above); the walkway built by Vasari to link the Palazzo della Signoria and the Uffizi with the Palazzo Pitti (which had become a Medici residence) in the section where it skirts the tower of the Mannelli, who had opposed the demolition of their building (below).

and nine days later the Florentines surrendered to the head of the imperial army.

The granducato

The recovery of Florence and its territory from the ravages of war and the siege required several years, and very careful management by the Medici rulers. The political situation was not stabilized until 1537, when the young Cosimo de' Medici, son of Giovanni delle Bande Nere, was chosen as Duke of Florence in place of the assassinated Alessandro. During his long rule of nearly 40 years, Cosimo demonstrated a remarkable talent for government; he was certainly one of the most capable and energetic princes of 16th-century Europe. His primary objectives were to secure for himself and his successors the absolute control of Florence and her dominion, and to escape from the tutelage of his Spanish patrons and become the sovereign ruler of a Tuscan principality. Cosimo realized that he could achieve those goals only after he had developed an effective territorial administration and promoted an economic recovery. Building

upon the structure that he had inherited from the republic, he developed (for the age) a remarkably effective and efficient administration. He selected officials from the old Florentine elite; but also from the urban patriciates in the dominion, whose members were thus bound to the Medici by ties of loyalty and self-interest. When, on becoming duke in 1537, Cosimo appealed to the magistrates of these towns for support, these men responded enthusiastically. Their hopes that the duke would treat them and their communities more favourably than the republic had done were fully justified. Members of the Usimbardi family from Colle, the Pagni and Turini from Pescia, the Marzi from San Gimignano enjoyed high office and status from Cosimo and his successors. More than a thousand inhabitants of the dominion were granted Florentine citizenship during the 16th century, a dramatic change from earlier practice when only men of the stature of Leonardo Bruni or Poggio Bracciolini could aspire to that honour.

Cosimo's administrative policy was designed to centralize power in his hands and those of his closest advisers, who formed a *Pratica Segreta* with supreme executive and judicial authority. These officials in Florence supervised the activities of that army of bureaucrats – the *podestà*, captains and vicars – who were directly responsible for the administration of the territory. Although this administration was never as centralized nor as efficient as some admiring contemporaries (and some later historians) have believed, it did represent a significant improvement over the republican period. Cosimo's perspective was Tuscan, not Florentine, and his policies were designed to promote the welfare of the entire territory. He favoured the development of the woollen cloth industry and of sericulture in the dominion. He sought to attract skilled glassmakers and tapestry weavers into the territory to promote those industries. He expanded the port of Leghorn and built the new towns of Portoferraio on Elba and Terra del Sole near Faenza. These protomercantilist measures certainly contributed to the revival of the territorial economy in the middle decades of the 16th century.

Of all the social categories in the *granducato,* none benefited more from the rule of the Medici than the urban elites in the dominion. After

Amongst the coats of arms in Florence a frequent symbol is the golden lily on a blue background, similar to the red lily of the republic; it is, in fact, the emblem of Charles of Anjou, brother to St. Louis IX, who was summoned to Italy to raise the fortunes of the Guelf party when the Swabian king Manfred ruled in Italy. The city became smothered in this device, as can be seen by the ceiling of the Sala dei Gigli in the Palazzo Vecchio (opposite), which is the work of Benedetto da Maiano. Above, the ceiling of the Sala delle Udienze (The Audience Hall), also by Benedetto da Maiano, which bears the cross of the popolo *surrounded by seraphim to signify that popular justice had to be tempered by a burning desire for charity.*

centuries of disorder and upheaval, Tuscany finally enjoyed an era of internal peace and stability. The phenomenon of rebellion, so characteristic of the republican period, practically disappeared under the *granducato*. If residents of Pisa or Arezzo or Volterra resented the rule of the Medici, the sight of the massive and heavily garrisoned fortresses dominating their cities was sufficient to cool their rebellious impulses. Even the elites of Pisa and Pistoia became reconciled to Medici rule which, they recognized, was more sympathetic to their interests and sensibilities than the republican regimes of the 14th and 15th centuries. Landowners and merchants benefited from the economic policies of the Medici; members of the old town oligarchies obtained positions in the central administration and in the church. Like their counterparts in Florence, they built palaces as visible symbols of their wealth and status: the Avignonesi, Tarugi and Cervini palaces in Montepulciano; the Venuti, Marioni and Mancini-Sernini palaces in Cortona; the Formichini and Grifoni palaces in San Miniato; the Campana, Giusti and Usimbardi palaces in Colle Val d'Elsa.

Cosimo moved warily to disengage himself from the tentacles of imperial control. In the early years of his rule, when the exiles still represented a threat to his regime, he relied upon the Spanish garrisons that were stationed in the Fortezza da Basso and in other strategic locations within the dominion. In his foreign policy, he never wavered from his allegiance to Charles V, whom he recognized as his sovereign. But he did arrange for the withdrawal of Spanish advisers at his court, and for a reduction in the garrison at the Fortezza. In 1543 the emperor was in desperate need of money to finance his war with the French. He accepted Cosimo's offer of 100,000 *scudi* in return for the withdrawal of the imperial garrisons in Florence and Leghorn. Finally free from that foreign military presence, the duke wrote proudly to his ambassador in France to tell Francis I that "we are prince through necessity or obligation and recognize as our benefactor no one save God and, because we must, the emperor, but we do so not as a tribute, or an acknowlegement ... I am no vassal, like the Duke of Ferrara who pays homage to the pope ..."

The event that, more than any other, established Cosimo's reputation as an independent prince was his conquest of Siena (1554-55), which enlarged his dominion by one third, and gained for him the grudging respect of all Italy. Had he been alive to witness it, Machiavelli would surely have applauded Cosimo's strategy, and his exploitation of an opportunity, provided by fortune, to expand and strengthen his state. The occasion was an uprising by the Sienese populace against the Spanish garrison stationed in their city. That revolt would have been quickly and easily suppressed by imperial forces, had not these been heavily engaged in a Europe-wide struggle between Hapsburgs and Valois, between Charles V and Henry II of France. In Italy the French were again contesting Spanish hegemony in the peninsula, from bases in Piedmont and Ferrara; they accepted the Sienese offer to send troops to defend their city. The French king sent Piero Strozzi, a bitter enemy of the Medici, as his lieutenant to Siena, a move that Cosimo interpreted as a direct challenge to his state. Encouraged by the emperor to attack Siena and recover it for Spain, Cosimo launched a three-pronged assault on the city and its *contado* in January 1554. His troops seized a fortress outside

Florentine expansion reached its peak under Cosimo I with the capture of Siena in 1555. Regarded as the founder of the Tuscan state, Cosimo (below left, in a bust by Benvenuto Cellini) had in 1538 thwarted an attempt to restore republican rule by defeating the political exiles led by Filippo Strozzi at Montemurlo. Pursuing an expansionist policy, Cosimo built a fleet of warships and established the military order of Santo Stefano (left, a small painting by Biccherna from 1561 showing the duke being granted the insignia of Grand Master of the order). Opposite above: the republican lily of Florence in the refectory of the priors in the Palazzo Vecchio and, below, part of the niche and its statue of Alessandro de' Medici, the first Duke of Florence, by Baccio Bandinelli in the Salone dei Cinquecento. Above the niche can be seen the decoration conceived by Paolo Giovio: a rhinoceros accompanied by the motto "Non vuelvo sin vencer" ("I do not return without victory").

the Porta Camollia, but they were unable to take the city, which was tenaciously defended by the inhabitants. Ducal troops plundered the Sienese countryside and prevented food from entering the besieged city. In an attempt to lift the blockade, Piero Strozzi took his French army into Florentine territory, occupying towns in the lower Valdarno. In Lyons, in Rome and Venice, Florentine republican exiles were urged to provide money and troops for the French army. Piero Strozzi moved his troops back into Sienese territory in July 1554, followed by the ducal army. Near Foiano, east of Siena, Cosimo's forces decisively defeated Strozzi, who fled to Montalcino with the remnants of his troops, which included a band of Florentine exiles. In Siena the starving populace finally surrendered to Cosimo's forces on 17 April 1555.

Cosimo had accepted the Sienese surrender in the name of the emperor, who expected the duke to turn over the city and its territory to his officials. But Cosimo was determined to retain Siena for himself, since its conquest was achieved by his forces and his money. While the ducal army continued to fight against French and Sienese troops who still resisted in Montalcino,

Cosimo's diplomats were working hard to obtain imperial approval for his incorporation of Siena into the Medici state. To gain this concession, he had to give up the port towns of Orbetello, Talamone, Portercole, Monte Argentaro and Santo Stefano, that had been under Sienese control. Cosimo did not gain full possession of his Sienese prize until July 1559, when the last defenders of the republic of Montalcino surrendered, on honourable terms, to his officials. The final legal embellishment to his triumph and his status was the bestowal of the title of Grand Duke of Tuscany by Pope Pius V in 1569. The Tuscan state found and consolidated by Cosimo was bequeathed to his son Francesco (1574-87) and to his Medici successors, whose sumptuous tombs are visible in the Cappella dei Principi adjacent to the basilica of San Lorenzo.

A civic culture

The cultural artifacts from Florence's early medieval period, before the 13th century, are neither numerous nor easily accessible. In crypts and corners and on façades of monastic and parish churches – Santissimi Apostoli, Sant' Ambrogio, Santa Maria Maggiore, San Miniato al Monte – can still be seen parts of the ancient structures that have escaped the ravages of time and the attention of restorers. In the countryside too are scattered churches and rural monasteries, like the Badia a Settimo, that still retain their Romanesque exteriors, even though the interiors have been remodelled in the Renaissance or baroque style. Decorating the pages of the Rustici codex (now in the Seminario arcivescovile) are sketches by an unknown 15th-century artist of several Florentine churches, some of which, like San Tommaso in the Mercato Vecchio, have since been demolished. There does not exist in Florence a museum devoted exclusively to the medieval age, but in the Museo dell'Opera del Duomo are some architectural and sculptural fragments that have survived from the Romanesque period.

The written record from these early centuries is somewhat richer than the archeological, though it is in no sense abundant. The parchment collection in the Archivio di Stato contains many thousand documents, though only a handful from before the year 1000. Nearly all of the early parchments, from the 11th and 12th centuries, come from ecclesiastical sources, for the most part monastic, like the rich *fondo* of San Michele di Passignano, which contains records of property donations, bills of sale and rental contracts pertaining to the agrarian world in which that Vallombrosan convent was located. Scattered among those documents that describe the local

and the mundane are a few references – imperial charters, papal letters – to that wider world which occasionally touched these churches and monasteries. In the Biblioteca Nazionale, the Biblioteca Laurenziana and the Biblioteca Riccardiana, are parchment codices that once belonged to these ecclesiastical foundations. Their contents are varied: saints' lives, records of synods, monastic rules, a detailed record from the late 12th century (from the Biblioteca Riccardiana) of the schedule of religious *feste* held in Florence throughout the canonical year. It would be misleading to suggest that the education and literacy of the majority of the Florentine clergy were at a high level. Many priests did not know enough Latin to say Mass properly, and some who could be described as "literate" were only capable of reading a very simple prose.

The provenance and the contents of these sources demonstrate that, before the 13th century, Florentine culture was predominantly clerical. As it had been for centuries, literacy was a near-monopoly of the clergy, whose schools taught the rudiments of Latin to young men training for the priesthood and for the monastic life. A few Florentine laymen may have enrolled in these church schools and some apparently went elsewhere, to Ravenna and Bologna, to study law and medicine. Though the documentary evidence is ambiguous it is possible that by the early 13th century schools of grammar and law, in which laymen were enrolled, were established in Florence. By that time, however, the fame of the law school at Bologna had spread throughout Italy and across the Alps, attracting Florentine students interested in a legal career. The documents from these early centuries contain a few references to the vernacular

THE MONASTERY OF SAN MARCO

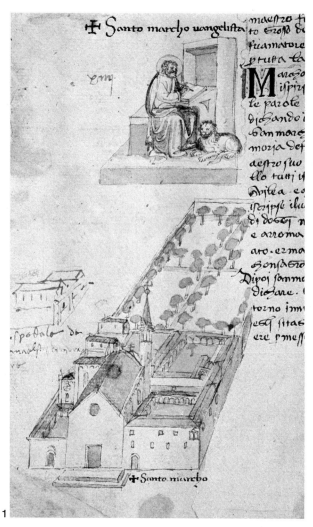

1

A Vallombrosan oratory used to stand on this site, and in 1299 the Silvestrines erected a monastery and church dedicated to St. Mark the Evangelist. In the 15th century the Silvestrines were expelled, and Pope Eugenius IV gave the monastery to the Dominicans. The buildings were then renovated and enlarged at the expense of Cosimo the Elder and his brother Lorenzo. The architect chosen by Cosimo (4) was the faithful Michelozzo Michelozzi, who later followed him into exile. According to Vasari, Michelozzo was, after Brunelleschi, the most sought-after architect of his day, the most skilled in designing palaces, monasteries, and houses, and the most judicious in seeing to their lay-out. He worked on San Marco from 1437 to 1452. The drawing (1) in the manuscript of the Florentine goldsmith Marco di Bartolomeo Rustici, begun in 1448 on his return from a pilgrimage to the Holy Land, shows the building almost finished. The monastery is set around three sides of a cloister (2), today the cloister of Sant'Antonino (10), to the right of the church seen from the front. On the ground floor are the pilgrims' hospice, the chapter house, and the refectory. Upstairs, the monks' cells (11) open off long corridors (9). The wing leading off from the cloister beyond the apse of the church, alongside the cloister of San Domenico (of which only one side is shown on the diagram), housed the guests' lodgings downstairs and the library upstairs (8) – the latter a long hall divided into three well-lit aisles by arches on Ionic columns. Everything is simple, neat, and imbued with the compact, uncluttered elegance typical of humanist sensibility. Prior of the monastery from 1439, Antonino Pierozzi left to become Archbishop of Florence in 1445, and on his death in 1459 he was canonized by Hadrian IV. As prior, Antonino was responsible for the decoration undertaken by one Guido di Pietro (born near Vicchio di Mugello), Brother John of Fiesole, who had come from the Dominican monastery in

Ground plan of San Marco

Ground floor:

1. Church
2. Cloister of Sant' Antonino
3. Large refectory
4. Washing room
5. Pilgrims' hospice
6. Chapter room
7. Small refectory
8. Guest house
9. Cloister of San Domenico

First floor:

10. Dormitory corridor
11. Library
12. Savonarola's cell
13. Savonarola's study cell
14. St. Antonino's cell
15. Double cell thought to be Fra Angelico's

2

3

4

5

6

7

8

9

10

11

Fiesole to the new community in Florence, and who is now known in English as Fra Angelico (in Italian, Beato Angelico – Blessed Angelico) (3). Another monk at San Marco was the Ferrarese brother, Girolamo Savonarola (7). Made to leave the monastery at one point, he returned there in 1490 and became prior. A brilliant and impassioned preacher, he inflamed reaction against the corruption and paganism of contemporary society by his own religious vision. The Medici were driven out in 1494, and for a time the friar had enormous political power in the city. He was finally arrested in one of the corridors of the monastery, and burnt at the stake in the Piazza della Signoria (1498). In July 1500 Baccio della Porta became a Dominican at San Marco: better known as Fra Bartolomeo (6), he had already worked as a painter, with his own *bottega,* in Florence for some years, and he was an important influence in forming the style and general taste of High Renaissance art.

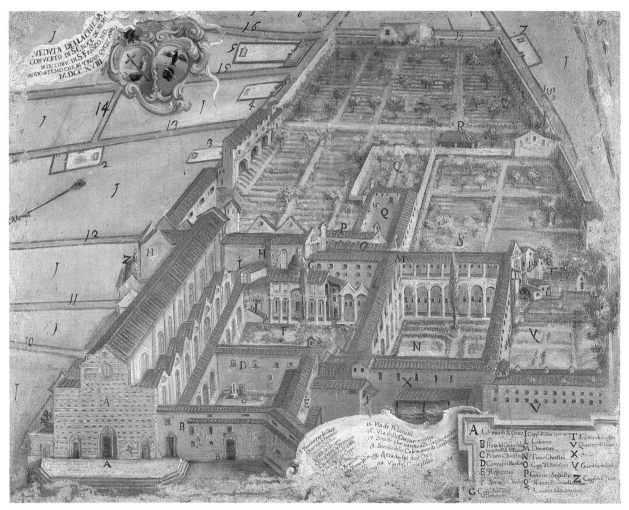

Before the 13th century, Florentine culture was mainly the prerogative of the church. As in the rest of Europe, religious institutions were the centers of knowledge and craft skills, where information was gathered and manuscripts stored. In the scriptoria, the copyists went about their slow and silent task, transmitting the precious knowledge of antiquity and paving the way for the renewal of learning that took place during the ensuing centuries. The Franciscans and Dominicans both had very important centers in Florence, which provided the impetus for an extraordinary religious upsurge. As early as the beginning of the 13th century the first companies of St. Francis arrived in the city, establishing themselves in 1228 in the small church of Santa Croce, not far from the banks of the Arno, which was later enlarged thanks to contributions from the faithful and from the commune. Around this first nucleus there developed one of the largest and most impressive religious establishments in all Italy, as can be seen in the fresco (left) painted in 1718 in the actual monastery.

and also include examples of poetry in the Tuscan dialect dating from the mid 12th century. But concerning instruction in the vernacular, the teaching of reading and writing that was essential for the mercantile class, the documents are totally silent.

By the early 1200s a flourishing lay culture had developed in Florence, in both Latin and the vernacular. Lawyers, notaries, physicians, teachers of grammar and rhetoric: these professionals read and wrote in Latin. An account book of a firm of bankers, dated 1211, is an early example of the utilization, by Florentine merchants, of the vernacular for their business activities. But the city's cultural life was, and was long to remain, predominantly and pervasively religious. The writings that have survived from that pre-Dante era are for the most part the product of clerics, and are devoted to religious topics. The majority of Florentines, of course,

were illiterate and they received their religious instruction from sermons, from the paintings that adorned the churches and monasteries, and from participation in the numerous processions that moved through the city on feast days. As early as the 1060s, when the founder of the Vallombrosan order, San Giovanni Gualberto, organized a popular uprising against a simoniac bishop, Florentines had demonstrated their strong interest in religious issues, particularly in the quality of the priests and monks in their churches and convents. Many became so disenchanted with their church and its representatives that they joined heretical movements like the Paterines, that swept through Italy during the 12th century.

No city in Italy, in Europe, was more profoundly influenced than was Florence by the great religious revival led by the Franciscans and Dominicans in the 13th century. The friars

brought Christianity to an urban population that had grown so rapidly that its religious needs were not met by the traditional ecclesiastical organization created for a society that was predominantly rural. According to legend, the first companions of St. Francis to visit Florence arrived in the city in about 1210, but they had no stable site until 1218, when the friars were given an *ospedale* on the Via San Gallo. Francis himself visited the city on several occasions, most notably in 1221, when he composed the *Regola dei terziari*. Shortly after the saint's death in 1228, the Franciscans established their headquarters near the small church of Santa Croce close to the river Arno. With the offerings of the faithful and donations from the commune, the friars constructed the great basilica and the convent that became one of the most important religious centers not only in Florence but in Italy as a whole. San Domenico and his friars were in Florence by 1219 and

From the 15th-century Rustici codex: the Benedictine Badia Fiorentina, founded at the end of the 10th century (above left); the church and cloisters of Santissima Annunziata, begun in 1250 for the order of the Servites of Mary and enlarged in the 15th century (above); Santa Maria degli Angeli (below).

probably earlier; they established their base in Santa Maria Novella in 1221. Based diametrically opposite their rivals in Santa Croce, the Dominicans developed their area of influence in the western part of the city but like the Franciscans, extended their influence and activities into Tuscany and beyond.

These friars were inspired by missionary zeal to preach to an urban populace that was hungry for religious instruction and inspiration. Their sermons were often delivered in the open air, in crowded squares where they attracted listeners from every stratum of society, from the wealthiest to the poorest. Addressing themselves directly to the concerns of their audience, they appealed to the Florentines to emulate Christ's love for his fellow men, to abandon their feuds and exchange the kiss of peace with their neighbours. In the Franciscan message, the themes of poverty and humility were emphasized; the Dominicans stressed religious orthodoxy and obedience to the Roman papacy. Together with their Augustinian and Carmelite brethren (and competitors), who had established themselves in Santo Spirito and Santa Maria del Carmine on the south side of the Arno, these friar preachers presented to their audiences a vision of the faith that was humane and consolatory. This world was indeed a vale of tears, full of tribulation; but it was also an arena in which laymen could achieve their salvation by living in accordance with Christ's precepts. The friars' message was tinged with hope and expectation, and the promise of salvation in the hereafter.

Florentines responded with great enthusiasm to the friars and their religious message. The flow of bequests to the mendicant foundations was enormous, enabling them to build their spacious basilicas, to accommodate the crowds at the sermons, and the convents designed to house hundreds of friars. Florence was a major center of recruitment for the mendicant convents and for their nunneries: the *Clarisse* (Poor Clares) of Monticelli and the Dominican nuns of Sant'Iacopo di Ripoli. Saint Francis's establishment of a third order, for women who wished to lead pious but uncloistered lives, responded creatively to the religious and social needs of this urban society. The mendicant churches became the most desirable sites for burial; this created an important link between these orders and the leading *consorterie* in their neighbourhoods.

The relatively few examples of pre-13th-century Florentine medieval art are overwhelmingly ecclesiastical in origin and relate mainly to religious life. This ivory cover from a Florentine copy of the Gospels, now in the Biblioteca Apostolica Vaticana, is a beautiful example of such work and dates from the 11th century.

In the church of San Miniato al Monte, one of the finest examples of Florentine Romanesque architecture, there is a vast crypt containing an altar, a magnificent example of 11th-century marble inlay work. It is also the resting place of the bones of St. Miniato (according to some an Armenian prince, according to others a Florentine), who lived as a hermit in a cave before suffering martyrdom during the reign of the Emperor Decius. According to tradition, the saint was thrown to the wild beasts in the amphitheater, but they refused to devour him; beheaded in the presence of the emperor, he is alleged to have gathered up his decapitated head with his own hands and replaced it on his shoulders, retiring then to die in his cave in the hills, where the church dedicated to him now stands.

Thousands of Florentines dictated testaments that provided for their burial in a mendicant church, often in the garb of the order; they also made bequests for masses and devotions on the anniversary of their death. Still another bond forged between the friars and the laity were the confraternities that were founded in each of the mendicant convents: such as the society of St. Peter Martyr in Santa Maria Novella and the Compagnia di Santa Maria in Santa Croce.

The Dominicans first, the Franciscans more slowly and reluctantly, the Augustinians and the Carmelites, were all involved in education, from the lowest to the highest level. In their convents they established schools for novices, which also attracted children destined for secular careers. To staff their schools, these convents sent their friars to Europe's leading universities, above all to Paris and Bologna, to study the humanities, theology, philosophy, civil and canon law. In Paris in particular, they absorbed the instructional method, based on Aristotelian logic, of scholasticism. Some Italian friars, like Thomas Aquinas, remained in Paris to teach in the university. Others returned to Italy as instructors in the *studia* which were located in the convents of major cities. In Florence in the late 13th century, the Dominican, Franciscan and Augustinian convents housed schools which gave advanced instruction in the major disciplines

then being taught at the unversities. The most dramatic evidence of the high level of learning sustained by these Florentine *studia* is not in the writings of the masters who taught there, but in the works of their most brilliant pupil, Dante Alighieri.

Dante was, first and foremost, a poet and his earliest intellectual work was the writing of love poetry in the style of the *dolce stil nuovo* (literally, sweet new style). It is not known when he began the serious study of philosophy and theology, possibly not until after Beatrice's death (1290). No direct evidence exists to document his attendance at specific schools, though he did write in the *Convivio* that for 30 months he went

to religious schools, and listened to the arguments of the philosophers. He was strongly influenced by the works of two Franciscans teaching at Santa Croce, Piero Olivi and Ubertino da Casale, and by a Dominican theologian, Remigio de' Girolami. As his references in the *Convivio* indicate, he had read the leading Christian theologians and philosophers of his age most intensively, Aquinas and Bonaventura. He was conversant, too, with the writings of Christian mystics: Bernard of Clairvaux, Ramón Lull, Joachim of Floris. He had mastered the intricacies of the scholastic method; he was well acquainted with the leading scientific and mathematical writers (Aristotle, Ptolemy, Pythagoras)

Almost at the same time as the Franciscans, who established themselves at Santa Croce, the Dominicans also put down roots in Florence, setting themselves up in 1221 in the church of Santa Maria Novella. The juxtaposition of Dominicans and Franciscans, rivals with a common religious goal, was a frequent phenomenon in Italian cities during the Middle Ages. They differed in their approach to Christianity: whereas the Franciscans in their preaching laid emphasis on the theme of poverty and humility, the Dominicans set themselves up as champions of religious orthodoxy and obedience to the pope. In the Santa Maria Novella complex, in the Cappellone degli Spagnoli, a cycle of frescoes created by Andrea di Bonaiuto and his pupils in 1335 provides a visual representation of the religious and cultural doctrines of St. Dominic and St. Thomas Aquinas. The underlying theme, that of the road to salvation through the Dominican order, is conveyed in the form of a series of images designed to instruct the faithful. The cycle is composed of a number of different scenes, portraying Christ and the Virgin Mary, saints, philosophers, the common people, and symbols of science and the liberal arts; its focal point is the allegory of the Church Militant *(left), whose background consists of a side view of Florence cathedral.*

Opposite, smiling figures of putti and angels with strong classical overtones, a detail from Donatello's choirstalls in the Museo dell'Opera del Duomo.

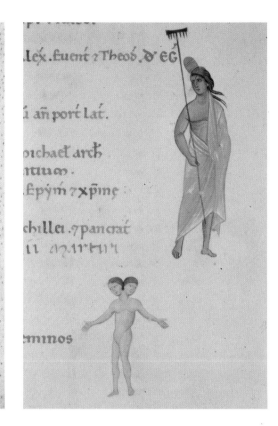

of antiquity, whose works were still viewed as authoritative. He immersed himself in the Latin poets (Vergil, Ovid, Lucan) and in the writings of Cicero and Boethius. He knew as much of Greek philosophy, and as little of the writings of their poets, dramatists and historians, as did most scholars of his time.

Dante's legacy to his contemporaries and to future generations was his great poem, the *Commedia*. He took the Tuscan dialect and fashioned it into a literary language, the most mature and sophisticated of the European vernaculars. His decision to write his masterpiece in Tuscan and not in Latin was doubtless influenced by his perception of his skills; as Leonardo Bruni noted a century later, he realized that he wrote better in the vernacular. But he also knew that his poem would reach a much larger audience if it were written in the language of the *popolo*. To those readers, and to countless others who could not read but who heard and memorized parts of the poem, he presented a vision of the Christian faith that embodied all of the knowledge that he had absorbed from years of study: a vision that appealed both to reason and emotion. Over the centuries, scholars have examined the *Commedia* canto by canto, line by line, word by word,

to understand its intellectual and theological order. But for most readers, the *Commedia*'s appeal has always been its evocation of a vision of the Christian faith in a human context. Through the depiction of characters like Paolo and Francesca in concrete and dramatic scenes, Dante invites his readers to understand the Christian message in terms of their own lives.

The parallels between Dante's vision of the human condition in the *Commedia* and Giotto's artistic achievement are very close. The two were contemporaries and acquaintances, both profoundly influenced by the Florentine religious environment, Giotto in particular by its Franciscan component. It is a visual shock to shift one's gaze in the Uffizi from the wooden, static, lifeless figures in the paintings of the 13th-century Byzantine style, to Giotto's dynamic characters, which convey a powerful sense of living, breathing, feeling people inhabiting a real world. The surviving fragments of Giotto's paintings of the life of St. Francis in Santa Croce tell a dramatic and emotional story, which affects the imagination as sharply and indelibly as Dante's vignettes in the *Inferno*. It may be, as some scholars have argued, that Giotto was not responsible for the Legend of St. Francis cycle in the upper church of

Written and illuminated probably in the scriptorium of a Florentine monastery, this calendar by an anonymous 11th-century copyist is now in the Biblioteca Laurenziana in Florence. The three pages illustrated above are dedicated to the months of March, April and May and their relevant astrological signs.

A further three pages from the 11th-century Florentine calendar. The figures and zodiacal signs relate to the months of June, July and February.

San Francesco in Assisi. But that artist, whoever he was, was a product of the same milieu as Giotto; a milieu profoundly influenced by Franciscan ideals of love, charity, peace and poverty. Those ideals were immensely popular among those Florentines who, like Giotto, were acquisitive, litigious, violent and often meanspirited.

The secular dimensions of this Florentine (and Italian) urban world of the early trecento have been portrayed most graphically and eloquently by Giovanni Boccaccio in the *Decameron*. Much has been written about the author's intentions in writing this immensely popular collection of stories, depicting life in the two worlds that Boccaccio knew intimately: the life of the court in Naples and in Forlì and Ravenna, and the bourgeois environment of Florence. The setting of the *Decameron* in the villa outside Florence during the great plague of 1348 created a very realistic context for the tales which are based on the author's personal experiences and fictional tales that he had heard or read in his wide-ranging journeys. The Florentine stories are filled with characters, some drawn from life, who might have been encountered in the city streets: knights and prelates in their fine garb, avaricious merchants, shrewd artisans, cunning peasants,

shrewish and licentious women, gluttonous and hypocritical friars. This is the same human society, seen from another perspective, whose members thronged the churches to hear sermons, and who participated in the penitential rites and ceremonies that could be seen nearly every day in the city.

The cult of antiquity

It is possible to imagine, in 14th-century Florence, the evolution of a vital culture based on the vernacular and expressing the thoughts, feelings and aspirations of the *popolo*. There were, indeed, significant manifestations of that culture in the late trecento and early quattrocento: in religious poetry, in the sonnets of Burchiello, in the *novelle* of Sacchetti, in *frottole* and other musical forms. But this popular culture, while never suppressed, had to compete with the revival of classical Latin which gained the allegiance of Florence's elite and became the dominant cultural force in Tuscany, in Italy, eventually throughout Christian Europe. The three crowns of Florence – Dante, Petrarch and Boccaccio – wrote both in the vernacular and in Latin, and thus addressed both that educated

minority of jurists, theologians and grammarians, and a much larger audience that was literate in the Tuscan idiom. In *De Vulgari Eloquentia* Dante argued for the legitimacy of the vernacular as a literary language. Boccaccio, however, was more defensive about his vernacular writings; his later works were composed in a heavy and prolix Latin style, modelled on the classical authors whom he admired so greatly. Petrarch's Italian sonnets are still read and admired today, and they were enormously influential in the development of European poetry. But in his own judgement, and in that of his contemporaries, his Latin writings were his greatest claim to fame. He was the prince of the humanists.

Though born of Florentine parents (his father was an exiled White partisan), Petrarch was not very closely involved with the city and its cultural life. He made clear his distaste for urban life in his diatribe against "that disgusting city of Avignon ..." He preferred the world of the courts and, even more, the solitude of his rural retreats at Vaucluse and Arqua. His mission was, first, to immerse himself in the literature of antiquity and then to promote that study among

his contemporaries through his writings. The cult of antiquity did not begin with Petrarch; others before him (Dante being the most famous) had studied and admired the writings of Vergil and Livy, of Cicero and Sallust. But no other scholar or school had been as successful in promoting and publicizing the *studia humanitatis* as Petrarch. He carefully nurtured his reputation as a poet and classical scholar; he cultivated patrons who supported him and his aims. His letters to friends and sympathizers, and occasionally to enemies and rivals, were widely circulated and they enhanced his reputation. From those letters emerges the portrait of a very complex personality: passionate, dedicated, combative, obsessed with the historical characters and literary works of antiquity. Not since St. Augustine in his *Confessions* had any Christian writer left, as his literary legacy, an autobiographical statement as full and revealing as that of Petrarch.

Petrarch spent little time in Florence, having rejected an invitation to teach in the university. But he had many friends in the city, who admired his work and shared his interest in classical studies. Among his correspondents were friars

The monastic orders, the sole guardians of learning during the Middle Ages, are also credited with having founded and maintained schools of an extremely high standard, which were open not just to clerics, but also to those embarking on secular careers. These schools provided the impetus for a sudden literary flowering in Italy, as well as being instrumental in launching its greatest poet, Dante Alighieri, the very embodiment of the spirit of medieval civilization and also the initiator of Italy's greatest linguistic tradition. The establishment of this Florentine writer as a catalyst in the development of a national language occurred at a time of extraordinary splendour for the city. In Florence, famous for its political influence, for its important trading companies and for its extraordinary artistic development, Dante's writings proved to be of crucial significance. When, during the 14th century, the magnificent poetry of his Commedia *began to reach an ever wider public, the future direction of the Italian language became clear. The advent of a second generation of writers, personified by Petrarch and Boccaccio, marked the completion of a trinity of authors who, in spite of their disparity, represent a milestone in the history of Italian culture; not only were their works literary masterpieces, they also became stylistic and grammatical models with a highly important role to play in the process of uniting the different dialects of the country into a single common language.*

The illustrations on these two pages relate to the three great men of letters who were instrumental in creating the Italian language. Right, a miniature from a 14th-century codex in Florence's Biblioteca Nazionale, which illustrates the second Cantica *of Dante's* Divina Commedia, *it portrays the poet himself, Virgil and Cato Uticensis, the guardian of Purgatory.*
Opposite below, the likeness of Petrarch in a Laurentian codex of the poet's works. He is portrayed in his study, writing and meditating, with a cat curled up at his feet and with large numbers of books lying at random on a bench and on a sort of revolving lectern, as though he had just consulted them. Although there are certain classical elements, such as the small columns on which his desk rests, the overall mood is that of a medieval study.
Opposite above, Giovanni Boccaccio seated at his desk, from a codex of the Egloghe *(Eclogues) in the Biblioteca Laurenziana, Florence.*

who taught in local convents, notaries from the *contado* who had moved to Florence to pursue their professional careers, lawyers and *literati* from the city's leading families. His two most prominent disciples were Boccaccio, who had known Petrarch since 1350, and a young notary from Stignano in the Valdinievole, Coluccio Salutati, who wrote an eloquent eulogy of the great humanist when he died in 1374. In that same year, Salutati was elected chancellor of the Florentine republic, a position that he used to promote humanistic studies. He arranged for the appointment of the Greek scholar, Manuel Chrysoloras, to a professorship in the university in 1397. Though intellectually less gifted than his master, he was a very important link between Petrarch's generation and the Florentine humanists of the quattrocento. Unlike the peripatetic Petrarch, he established his permanent residence in Florence, thus creating a stable environment for classical learning. He encouraged young scholars like Leonardo Bruni and Poggio Bracciolini to pursue their studies and their careers as professional humanists.

In the years around 1400, humanism established itself as an important educational and cultural movement in Florence, competing successfully with older traditions in the schools and in the streets. Several young men from prominent families – Palla Strozzi, Agnolo Pandolfini, Angelo and Antonio Corbinelli, Cosimo de' Medici – studied Latin authors with tutors hired by their parents, or in schools that specialized in classical literature. As the 15th century progressed, this educational curriculum attracted more and more students from the Florentine aristocracy. It became the fashion for these young men to read Cicero and Livy and Vergil, and to write letters in classical Latin to their friends. The merchant Giovanni Morelli, who himself could only read and write in the vernacular, advised his sons thus (c. 1400): "You should devote one hour each day to the study of Vergil, Boethius, Seneca or other authors ... You will be well served by a study of Vergil, Boethius, Dante and the other poets ... and by reading Cicero and Aristotle." The latter to be read, one may assume, in Latin translation, since the study of Greek was still very uncommon.

As an educational and cultural phenomenon, humanism flourished in every Italian city in the 15th century, but nowhere was its influence

203

From a letter by Poggio Bracciolini (1416): "By some happy chance, while I was at leisure in Constance, I was suddenly seized by the desire to visit the monastery of St. Gall (…) to amuse myself and also to see the books, of which there was said to be a large number. There, in the midst of a great mass of manuscripts, which it would take a long time to enumerate, we found a work by Quintilian that was still safe and sound, albeit covered in dust and mould. These books were in fact not in the library, as they deserved to be, but in a sort of dark and gloomy prison at the base of a tower, of a type in which not even those condemned to death would be incarcerated. And I am certain that anyone who, out of love of his forefathers, carefully searched through the prisons in which these great men are confined, would find that a similar fate has befallen many of those whose fate has long been despaired of…"

From the mid 14th to the mid 16th century, Florence played host to such an intense degree of cultural and artistic activity that the city became known as "the new Athens." A decisive part was played by the rediscovery of Greek and Latin authors, a process that was started by Petrarch's discovery of two of Cicero's speeches and then continued by Boccaccio. Suddenly, the 15th century became obsessed by a burning interest in pagan antiquity, and people began to track down the ancient manuscripts that provided the lifeblood of humanism. Each new discovery was a source of endless discussion, and the period became one of discourse and study, involving art, philosophy, literature, music and the sciences. Academies sprang up, inspired by Plato, whose goal was the furtherance of such studies.

stronger, and its devotees more numerous, than in Florence. Like their colleagues elsewhere, Florentine humanists were attracted to classical studies for reasons both personal and professional. They admired the stylistic elegance and the moral lessons of the Latin writings, which they sought to emulate. They were aware that humanistic training could lead to professional advancement, either in the church or in the secular world. Two humanist prelates, Tommaso Parentucelli and Aeneas Sylvius Piccolomini, became popes as Nicholas V (1447-55) and Pius II (1458-64). Leonardo Bruni, Carlo Marsuppini and Poggio Bracciolini succeeded Salutati as chancellors of the republic. Florentine humanists produced an extensive corpus of eulogistic writing, glorifying their city and its inhabitants, its government, its wealth, its culture. They traced parallels between the Roman republic of antiquity and their Florentine government. They praised the *vita attiva*, the life of the citizen; rejecting a deeply rooted medieval prejudice they found merit in the acquisition of wealth as

benefiting human society. Matteo Palmieri, in his *Della Vita Civile,* Giannozzo Manetti in his *De Dignitate Hominis,* and Leon Battista Alberti, in his *Della Famiglia,* formulated a coherent justification for the secular life, as an alternative to the friars' message exalting poverty and the renunciation of the ephemeral satisfactions of this world. In his classic work on the crisis of early Renaissance Italy, Hans Baron has described this "civic humanism" as a particular Florentine creation, inspired and shaped by the political struggles with the tyrants seeking to conquer the city, and by the need of its citizens for a secular ideology appropriate to their lives and activities.

There are parallels between the rise of humanism and the adoption of classical forms and motifs in sculpture, painting and architecture. In this cultural development, too, Florence was the site of the most significant innovations in the early quattrocento. Common to both movements was the conviction by humanists and certain artists that the culture of antiquity

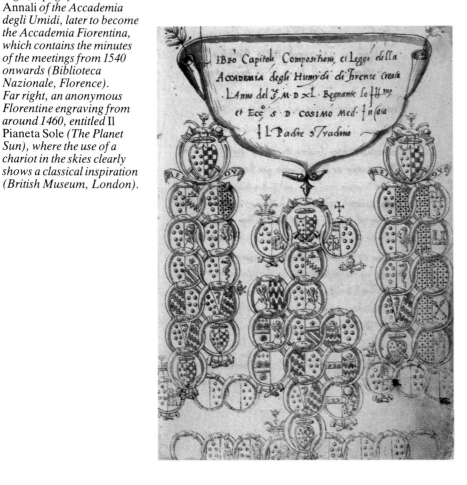

"WHAT A DELIGHTFUL THING IS THIS PERSPECTIVE!"

1

2

3

Vasari tells a story of Paolo Uccello (2) showing his friend Donatello examples of *mazzocchi* (among other things, caps worn by the *gonfalonieri*), both pointed and square (perspective drawing of a *mazzocchio* (11) attributed to Uccello) "all drawn in perspective under various aspects, his spheres having seventy-two facettes, like diamond points, with a morsel of chip bent upwards on each plane ..." Donatello replies, "Ah, Paolo, with this perspective of thine, thou art leaving the substance for the shadow. These things are serviceable to those only who work at inlaying of wood ..." Nevertheless, as we know, first with Giotto, and then conclusively with Brunelleschi, perspective was one of the most intensely explored areas of artistic interest in 15th-century Florence. "Distance can be suggested by correct handling of foreshortening or by graduation of colours to black and white," writes Eugenio Battisti. "Some cultures, such as the Chinese and that of the Flemish artists, have an intuitive feel for distance which they develop with great expertise; others need to rely on rational theories, as happened in the Renaissance." Brunelleschi's anonymous biographer mentions two perspective experiments. Brunelleschi (1) painted two small pictures – now lost – of perspective views of the octagonal Baptistery (frontal) and the Palazzo Vecchio (from an angle). These two pictures had to be looked at from behind, in a mirror, through a small hole which was presumably placed at the "vanishing point." When positioned in the correct place, the viewer could then check the accuracy of the picture against the original, by removing the mirror. Manetti adds that the top of the pictures was not painted to resemble the sky, but had a reflecting silver surface which would mirror the actual sky and clouds.

The problem which Brunelleschi was at pains to

vanishing point (three *braccia*)

distance seven *braccia*

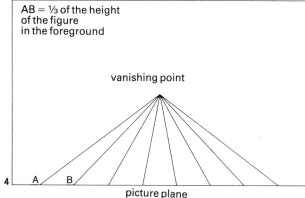

AB = ⅓ of the height of the figure in the foreground

vanishing point

A B

picture plane

4

7

scale of points to be transferred proportionally

viewing point (three *braccia*)

distance of viewer from picture plane, in this case seven *braccia*

5

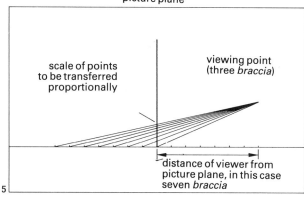

viewing point

scale of points transferred proportionally

6

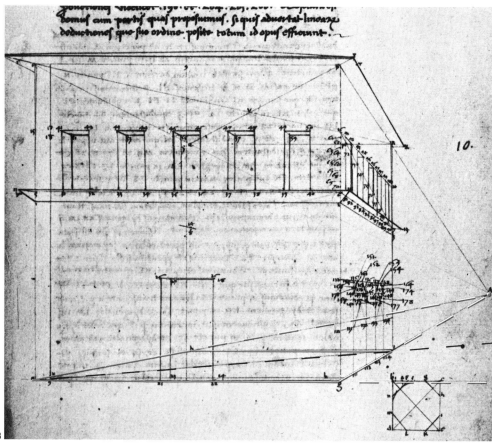

10.

8

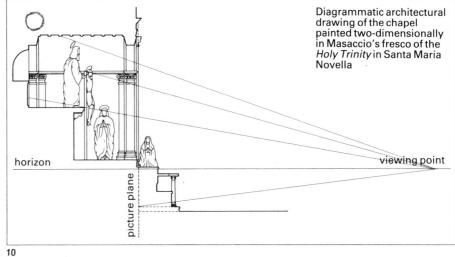

Diagrammatic architectural drawing of the chapel painted two-dimensionally in Masaccio's fresco of the *Holy Trinity* in Santa Maria Novella

horizon

viewing point

picture plane

10

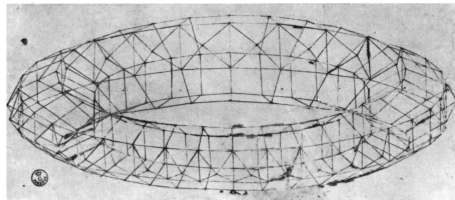

11

tance between the painting and the viewer's eye is established as the viewing point (in this example, at a height of three *braccia,* corresponding to the height of the vanishing point, and at a distance of seven *braccia*). Straight lines join the viewing point and all the points marked along the base line to the left of the vertical picture plane (i.e. "behind" the surface of the picture). These straight lines dissect the picture plane at points progressively closer together the higher up they are. If one then proportionately

points of intersection that have been thus formed, one can be sure that one has not made a mistake. This, therefore, is Alberti's method. From it, however, derives a rather quicker system, illustrated here by the square subdivided into 25 equal squares in (7). Having established the vanishing point as being three *braccia* up, and the viewing point as being at the same height seven *braccia* from the vanishing point, one draws a line between the viewing point and the point farthest away on the base line: and where this in-

pectiva Pingendi on the method just described, as can be seen by determining the viewing point in one of his own drawings (8). The first artist to use Brunelleschi's constructional perspective seems to have been Masaccio, in his fresco of the *Trinity* (9) in Santa Maria Novella (1428). The illusion of depth is noted by Vasari, when he describes the wall as appearing to have had a hole knocked into it. The architectural dimensions of the imaginary chapel in which the subject is presented can be reproduced

show he had solved by means of a geometrical system concerned three different visual illusions: the way objects at a distance look smaller, the apparent joining up of parallel lines as they recede, and the apparent lessening of equal distances the closer they get to the horizon. For the study of these, the regular chessboard paving of a *piazza* was an ideal subject. Leon Battista Alberti (3) suggests a practical method in his *Della Pittura* (1436, although there was an earlier Latin edition). At the base of the surface to be painted (4) one marks two points at a distance related to the size of the figures to be placed in the foreground; one then decides the point at

cia (to use the old Italian measure) up from the lower edge of the picture (one *braccio* being the distance between the two initial points). All the points marked along the base of the picture can then be linked through the vanishing point. Alberti now suggests that a secondary drawing be made on a sheet of paper (5), to scale. On the bottom line of this, one marks equidistant points (which one agrees to call one *braccio* apart). The vertical line represents the surface to be painted: the section of the bottom line to the right is the distance at which the painting is to be seen; the section to the left, the distances to be conveyed in the painting – the required visual "depth."

marks the scale thus obtained up one side of the picture surface, one can obtain the lines parallel to the base of the picture which we see in (6). The first line up

tersects the lines departing from the vanishing point, one draws the various horizontals that represent the different distances.

Renaissance artists did not

diagrammatically (10). Perspective had become part of the painter's craft – a tool of the trade for some, for others a veritable passion in itself. Vasari again tells how Uccel-

B

VANISHING POINT

which one wishes the lines to converge – the vanishing point (this can be wherever one likes, but should be at the viewer's eye level rather than related to the size of the figures in the foreground). In the example (4), the vanishing point is three *brac-*

The geometrical construction that results reveals the paintings as a slice through the visual pyramid formed by the lines of convergence ("visual rays") between the objects depicted and the eye of the viewer. The height of the viewer's eye and the dis-

shows where to place objects conceived as being one *braccio* away from the picture plane; the second, where to place objects that are two *braccia* away, and so on. If one can then draw a straight diagonal line passing through the various

theorize further than this. The elaboration of the general principles of perspective as part of descriptive geometry did not occur till much later. For all his masterly use of perspective, even Piero della Francesca based his detailed *De Pros-*

lo's wife complained that her husband spent his nights "in his study, poring over perspective theories, and when she called him to bed, he would exclaim, "What a delightful thing is this perspective!"

was superior to their own, and that excellence in the plastic arts – as in poetry, history and philosophy – could only be achieved by imitating the ancients. Just as humanists searched the monastic libraries for copies of unknown works by classical authors, so did two young goldsmiths, Filippo Brunelleschi and Donatello, visit Rome (if we accept the authority of Antonio Manetti's account) to study and measure the columns, capitals, architraves, cornices and pediments of the Roman buildings, whose ruins dotted the landscape. Their knowledge of Roman sculpture was enhanced by their inspection of the friezes, busts and sarcophagi that were unearthed in Rome and elsewhere; only the painters were deprived of any classical models.

In this revolution that created (or recreated) a classical style that would dominate Western art for four centuries, the key figure is Filippo Brunelleschi, whose architectural masterpieces (the Ospedale degli Innocenti, the cupola of the cathedral, the Pazzi chapel, the interior of San Lorenzo) made him the most renowned architect of his age. A contemporary, Giovanni Rucellai, wrote of him: "There has been no one since the days when the Romans ruled the world, so accomplished in architecture and geometry and sculpture; he is a man of much genius and imagination …" After he lost to Ghiberti in the competition for the Baptistery doors (1401), Brunelleschi abandoned sculpture to concentrate on architecture. But he remained a close

A window framing the city of Florence as it stretches over the plain, dominated by the massive dome created by Brunelleschi for the cathedral: linear purity, perspective perfection and a sublime sense of balance characterize this detail (left) from Pollaiolo's Annunciation, *which acts almost as a symbolic embodiment of the themes of the Florentine Renaissance (Staatliche Museen, Berlin). A famous work by Andrea del Verrocchio (opposite): the funerary monument of Piero and Giovanni de' Medici (1472) in the old sacristy of San Lorenzo, which was commissioned by Lorenzo and Giuliano for the burial of their father and uncle. The porphyry sarcophagus, which rests on lion's claws, is decorated with ornaments made of cast bronze and finished by hand. A pure bronze grille in the form of a rope lattice shields the space behind. As Vasari tells us: "… nor would it be possible to discover a more perfectly executed work, whether cast or chiselled; on this occasion the master also gave proof of his skill in architecture. Having erected the tomb in question within the embrasure of a window, five* braccia *in breadth, and about ten high, and placed the sarcophagus on a basement which divides the above-named chapel of the sacrament from the old sacristy (…) he then (…) constructed a grating in bronze …"*

Trinità in Santa Maria Novella, or the frescoes he painted in the Brancacci chapel of the Carmine, marvelled at the realistic portrayal of the figures, their geometric location in space, the artist's effective use of light and shadow and, above all, the dramatic power of those religious scenes.

Brunelleschi was the main personal link connecting Florentine artists who were developing the new style *all'antica* during the early quattrocento. He was also in close contact with members of the city's elite, who individually and collectively were the patrons of these sculptors, painters and architects. Brunelleschi was the only *maestro* of his age to qualify for high civic office, being chosen to the *Signoria* in 1425. His stunning achievement in building the cathedral cupola won him the admiration of his fellow

In 1420, Brunelleschi presented his plans for vaulting the cupola of Santa Maria del Fiore (the cathedral). From Vasari: "Filippo [Brunelleschi] alone declared that the cupola might be erected without so great a mass of wood-work, without a column in the center, and without the mound of earth (…) very easily, without any frame-work whatever (…) The cynics (…) felt convinced that Filippo had talked like a mere simpleton; they derided him (…) they bade him discourse of something else, for that this was the talk of a fool or madman …"

friend of Donatello and surely encouraged him to create those pioneering works, the sculptured figures of San Marco and San Giorgio based on Roman models, for the niches outside Orsanmichele, and the statues of the four Old Testament prophets for the cathedral campanile. Brunelleschi's contribution to the new style of painting is more direct, for he was the inventor of perspective, the geometric technique for creating an illusion of three dimensions (and thus a sense of depth) on a flat surface. Using this technique and his sense of the human form derived from Donatello's sculptures, the young painter Masaccio created a series of paintings that combined the natural and monumental qualities of Giotto's art with the order and harmony derived from classical models. Florentines who viewed his

citizens, some of whom had been associated with him on that project, as members of the commission *(operai)* responsible for its construction. It was the common practice of these *operai* to invite specialists to give professional advice on their projects, thus creating a regular channel of communication between patrons and *maestri*. One can be certain that Brunelleschi was consulted frequently about the numerous civic projects of building and decoration that were being undertaken in Florence in the 1420s and 1430s. Brunelleschi was also employed by the commune to supervise fortifications on the Sienese frontier, and he was apparently responsible for an ill-fated project (1430) to flood the city of Lucca during the republic's war with that city. In addition to these civic responsibilities, the architect was employed by ecclesiastical and private patrons: Cosimo de' Medici, the Pazzi family, Luca Pitti, the *operai* of Santo Spirito and the monks of Santa Maria degli Angeli.

Brunelleschi's career spanned one of the most active and creative phases of building and embellishment in Florentine history. The civic projects in which he was involved were part of a massive plan to enhance the beauty and grandeur of the city. This had begun in the 1300s, with the rebuilding of the cathedral and campanile, the enlargement of the Piazza della Signoria (with its adjacent loggia), and the construction of Orsanmichele. After 1400, the authorities concentrated on the completion of unfinished projects and their decoration: the cathedral cupola; the guild statues of Orsanmichele; the sculptures for

The cupola, despite the disbelief of its opponents, was erected effortlessly, an architectural masterpiece that marked the end of the Middle Ages and the launching of Renaissance ideals.
Opposite, some of the equipment used in the construction of the cupola (Museo dell'Opera del Duomo, Florence).
On this page, right, drawing of the scaffolding erected for the lantern (Galleria degli Uffizi, Florence).
Below left, drawing of a man by Michelangelo, annotated with the canons of proportion that were applied by Renaissance artists.

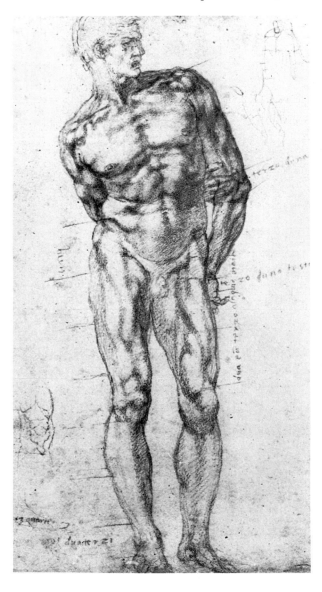

the campanile and the cathedral façade; the bronze doors of the Baptistery. Some of these projects were assigned to the guilds, which received public funds to subsidize them and those charitable foundations, like the Ospedale degli Innocenti, built in the 1420s under the auspices of the guild of Por San Maria. The Augustinian church of Santo Spirito was rebuilt with communal funds, the project supervised by *operai*, some of whom were appointed by the commune. Other monastic foundations were the beneficiaries of private patronage; most notably, Cosimo de' Medici, responsible for the rebuilding of San Lorenzo and San Marco. Private chapels proliferated in these monastic complexes: the Pazzi chapel in Santa Croce's cloister; the Rucellai chapel in San Pancrazio; the Sassetti chapel in Santa Trinita.

No clear distinction can be made between public and private patronage in this period, since the same men were responsible for commissioning and supervising most of the building and decoration in the city. These prominent citizens gained knowledge and expertise from participating in the decisions of communal and guild *operai*, which may explain their receptivity to the new style, and their willingness to hire innovative artists. Until about 1430, a rough balance was maintained between civic and private patronage of the arts, but the heavy military expenditures of the 1430s and 1440s substantially reduced the scale of communal investment in public projects. By the middle of the 15th century, the construction and decoration of private palaces for wealthy Florentines was the most dynamic branch of the building industry, employing thousands of craftsmen and labourers, and contributing to the development and specialization of the decorative arts.

One of these palaces was built for the rich merchant, Giovanni Rucellai, in the 1450s; he employed Leon Battista Alberti to design its façade. Rucellai made no specific mention of his new palace in his *Zibaldone,* but he did obliquely suggest one motive for the enterprise: He quoted the reference, in Cicero's *De officiis,* of a Roman citizen, Gnaeus Octavius, "who was the first in his family to be made a Roman consul, because of the beautiful palace built for him on the Palatine Hill, which was renowned and dignified, and secured for him the admiration and goodwill of the people."

Thousands of volumes, 12,000 manuscripts, 4,000 incunabula and first editions: such are the riches of the Biblioteca Laurenziana, a library which is unique in the world for the quality of its priceless contents. Founded by Cosimo the Elder, extended by Lorenzo the Magnificent, entrusted to the priests of San Marco following the fall of the Medici, ransomed and carried off to Rome by Cardinal Giovanni de' Medici, later Pope Leo X, it was finally restored to Florence as a gift by Pope Clement VII, the other Medici pope, who commissioned from Michelangelo the splendid building that now houses it. Planned for the conservation and study of documents, it is an outstanding example of the Humanist concept of culture. Cosimo I opened it to the public in 1571, enriching his city with a library to which was subsequently added the one already in existence at San Marco, founded in 1444.

Above, the reading room of the Biblioteca Laurenziana, designed by Michelangelo, as were the benches with lecterns. Among the texts preserved in the Laurentian Library is Lorenzo the Magnificent's 15th-century Book of Hours, *of which we illustrate a page with miniatures of the Assumption and Nativity (right). Opposite, other priceless manuscripts in the collection: the opening of the 14th-century* Liber Iudiciorum Alphodol Philosophi Saraceni *(above); an illuminated page of Dante's* Divina Commedia *from the end of the 14th century (below).*

The Laurentian Era

Eugenio Garin has written that during the age of Lorenzo, "Florence was probably the foremost cultural center in the world." A distinctive quality of that rich cultural environment was its variety and complexity, its receptivity to diverse and even contradictory ideas and ideologies. Before the university was transferred to Pisa in 1473, the professional disciplines of law and medicine were taught in Florence as they had been for three centuries. Theological instruction in the *studia* of the Franciscan and Dominican convents had changed little since Dante's time. The study of rhetoric and Latin poetry continued to flourish under the aegis of such distinguished scholars as Cristoforo Landino and Poliziano. The serious study of Greek philosophy was a recent innovation, promoted at the university by Joannes Argyropulos, and by Marsilio Ficino at his Careggi villa, where he worked on the translation of Platonic texts and attracted disciples from all over Europe: Giovanni Pico della Mirandola, Lefèvre d'Etaples from Paris, John Colet from London. Still another scholarly tradition, the study of natural science, was represented by Paolo Toscanelli (1397-1482). Toscanelli had trained in medicine at Padua; on returning to Florence, he had pursued an active scientific career. He practiced and studied medicine, and wrote treatises on mathematics, optics, astronomy and philosophy. Like his friend, Leon Battista Alberti, and like the young painter and student of nature, Leonardo da Vinci, Toscanelli was interested in both theory and practice. His famous letter (1474) to the Portuguese cleric, Fernam Martins, suggesting the viability of a voyage to the Orient by sailing west, was a result of his study of ancient geographical treatises and maps, and conversations with travellers.

Leonardo da Vinci was a product of this pluralistic cultural environment. His formal education in the vernacular was rudimentary. He did teach himself some Latin in his later years, but he was never fluent in the language. As *un omo sanza lettere* (a man of no letters), he was unable to read with ease the literary or the scientific works of classical antiquity and the Middle Ages that had not been translated into Italian. But he compensated for this deficiency by exploring for himself the natural world that, as an artist, he had learned to view with a meticulous attention to detail. What he could see interested him most; what he could not see interested him least or not at all. Hence his fascination for plants and animals, including men, and his interest in anatomy, revealed by those marvellous drawings of the human body that surpassed anything done before his time. His interest in landscape was also stimulated by his artistic training. And his studies of landscape may have inspired him to think about the earth's formation, and about the geological implications of seashells found on mountain tops. Leonardo's fascination with moving water, with floods, is well documented in his drawings, and these reflect his perception of a physical world in constant flux. Unlike many of his contemporaries, Leonardo had no strong interest in cosmology. The movements of celestial bodies did not interest him, nor did he speculate much about the physical properties of matter, as did the alchemists of his day. Despite his lack of formal training and his limited knowledge of natural philosophy, he did grasp a fundamental principle concerning scientific method, which he formulated more clearly than any of his contemporaries:

On the ceiling of the Salone dei Cinquecento in the Palazzo Vecchio, Vasari painted a balustrade on which a number of figures appear; they are the carvers, decorators and gilders who helped in creating those grandiose surroundings that glorify Florentine history through art (above). Below, a detail from Andrea del Sarto's Story of Joseph, which illustrates the stylistic characteristics of Tuscan architecture. Opposite, at the end of the narrow Via dei Servi, which still retains echoes of its former glory, the traveller arriving from the Piazza della Santissima Annunziata is confronted by the massive bulk of the cathedral and the cupola that moved Vasari to observe that it was a work of such beauty that it alone inspired faith.

'Knowledge which is born of experience is (...) called mechanical, and knowledge which is born of the mind scientific, whereas knowledge which is born of science is called semi-mechanical (...) for it is not born of experience, the mother of all certainty, (...) and does not end in experience (...) Such knowledge does not pass through any of the five senses (...) Real knowledge is that which has penetrated the five senses by means of experience, silencing the tongues of its opponents and taking care to feed those who investigate it not on dreams but on principles...'

ANDREA DEL VERROCCHIO: A MASTER AND HIS WORKSHOP

His name was Andrea di Cione, and he was born in Florence in 1435. The great innovator Brunelleschi was then 58, and the other towering genius of the day, Donatello, was 49. The 46-year-old Cosimo de' Medici had returned from his brief exile in Venice the previous year and was now in undisputed power in Florence.

The name by which the artist is now known – Andrea del Verrocchio (1) – is believed to have been taken from the master goldsmith Giuliano del Verrocchio. His teachers are thought to have been (2, from left to right) the unascertainable Giuliano, the sculptor Desiderio da Settignano, who was only five years his senior, Donatello, and – some historians think – Filippo Lippi. André Chastel tells us that "the 15th century in Italy was the age of the *bottega,* firms organized around small workshops, with directors and assistants." Verrocchio's *bottega* was typical. From 1465 to 1467, now in his thirties, he worked on Cosimo the Elder's tomb in San Lorenzo. In 1463 he had already received from the Tribunale di Mercanzia the commission for his *Incredulity of St. Thomas,* a bronze composition which was to stand outside Orsanmichele in a niche where a statue by Donatello had been removed (however, this work was not unveiled until 20 years later). Thus the patrons for his *bottega* – public institutions and the Medici family – were already commissioning work from him. The Medici indeed commissioned his earliest known works: the lavabo in the old Sacristy of San Lorenzo (3), then the wonderful tomb of Giovanni and Piero de' Medici (4) in the same church, completed in 1472; the terracotta relief *Resurrection* (5), for which we have no firm date, and which was originally in the Medici Villa Careggi; and the bronze *David* (6), which Lorenzo and Giuliano de' Medici sold to the *Signoria* in 1476.

The *bottega* undertook all kinds of work (for example, in 1468 it cast the copper globe for the lantern on the dome of Santa Maria del Fiore, which was installed in 1471 and destroyed by lightning in the 17th century), and the degree of collaboration on paintings was such that it is difficult to draw up a precise Verrocchio catalogue. Not everyone agrees that the Berlin *Madonna and Child* (7) is his; while in the case of the *Baptism of Christ* (8, detail), painted for the monastery of San Salvi, what is disputed is not whether Leonardo had a hand in it, but how much of it is his. Seventeen years younger than Verrocchio, Leonardo da Vinci was the most celebrated of the master's pupils (14, from left to right): these included the great Sandro Botticelli; perhaps also Botticini; certainly Pietro Perugino – who in turn taught Raphael; and Lorenzo di Credi. It was to the last of

these (his executor according to the terms of his will, dated 25 June 1488 – the year of his death) that Verrocchio left his *bottega,* with the commission to complete the equestrian statue of Bartolomeo Colleoni. The bust known as the *Lady with Primroses* (9) is thought to be of Lorenzo the Magnificent's mistress Lucrezia Donati, which would of course make it another Medici commission. In 1477 came

GIULIANO DEL VERROCCHIO

DESIDERIO DA SETTIGNANO

1

3

5

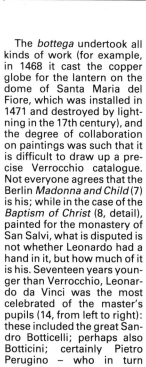

4

6

the commission for the only known sculpture in precious metal by Verrocchio, the relief *Beheading of St. John the Baptist* (10) for the silver altar of the Baptistery. It took three years to complete. Meanwhile also in 1477 Verrocchio's model for the monument to Cardinal Forte-

13

10

11

12

9

guerri in the cathedral at Pistoia had been chosen; and though it was still unfinished at the time of his death, the terracotta *Angel* (11), now in the Louvre, is thought to have been intended for this monument.

The *Incredulity of St. Thomas* (12), of which mention has already been made, was finally placed in position in 1483; two years previously a model of the work had been put there to placate those who had commissioned it, and who for some time had been paying advances. That same year (1481) saw the model of the horse for the Colleoni monument (13), commissioned by the Venetian senate. Verrocchio moved to Venice, but died in 1488 before the work was finished. It was eventually completed, not by Lorenzo di Credi, but by the Venetian Alessandro Leopardi (1495), who also designed the pedestal with its columns and bas-reliefs.

14

FRANCESCO BOTTICINI

Leonardo's argument identified a significant problem: the relationship between elitist and popular culture. Ever since Dante wrote his *Commedia,* that issue had preoccupied Florentine intellectuals, who had to choose either to write in Latin for a small minority of educated men or in the vernacular for a wider audience. In the early quattrocento, the enthusiasm for classical Latin was so great that many humanists refused to write in the Tuscan idiom, and they criticized Dante and Petrarch for composing their poems in the vernacular. In an age when social distinctions were becoming sharper, the adoption of humanism as the educational curriculum for the elite could be interpreted as a reinforcement of stratification, comparable to the aristocratic penchant for building large palaces. Marsilio Ficino's Neoplatonic treatises, and Botticelli's *Primavera,* are illustrations of this elitism carried to extremes; only a handful of their fellow citizens could understand their meanings. But this trend to-

The Building of a Palace, *an oil painting by Pietro di Cosimo (John and Mable Ringling Museum of Art, Sarasota, Florida).*
"Because drawing, the father of the three arts, is a product of the intellect, it derives its view of the world from many factors, like a representation or rather an imagined representation of all the elements in Nature, which is itself endlessly varied in its

dimensions. As a consequence, not only when dealing with human figures, but with plants as well, and buildings and sculptures and paintings, it knows the proportions of the whole to its parts and also of the different parts of the whole" (Vasari).

wards the exclusive and the esoteric came up against resistance from within the humanist camp. In the prologue of the third book of *Della Famiglia* (c. 1434), Leon Battista Alberti had written an eloquent defense of the Tuscan vernacular: "The wise, indeed, are more likely to praise my zeal if, by writing so that all could understand, I have made an effort rather to educate many than to please a few, for you know how few these days are the educated." The distinguished rhetorician Cristoforo Landino

justified the use of the vernacular which should be enriched by the assimilation of Latin forms. Lorenzo de' Medici also wrote a defense of Tuscan, when he was only 17. He argued that it was the equal of Latin in its capacity to treat eloquently a broad range of topics and moods. But his own poetry was the most effective weapon in this competition between classical Latin and popular idiom. His contribution leads to Bembo, and the final resolution of the *questione della lingua* (the question of the

Above, the model of the Medici theater set up in 1508 in a room in the Palazzo degli Uffizi created by the architect C. Livi.
The 16th century saw an extensive revival in the theater, which became a cultural entertainment for the upper classes. Performances took place in the rooms of patrician palazzi.

Signoria. He had received the standard humanist education, supplemented by rhetorical studies with Landino and Greek philosophy with Argyropoulos. His correspondence with Marsilio Ficino demonstrated his ability to write in a good Latin style; he was familiar with the commentaries and translations of the Neoplatonic scholar. Lorenzo and Ficino's pupil, Giovanni Pico della Mirandola, became close friends; it was Pico who persuaded *Il Magnifico* to arrange for Savonarola's return to the city in 1490. Without solid evidence, one can only speculate about the intellectual rapport between these two men, and the extent to which Lorenzo understood Pico's bold plan to integrate the world's philosophies and religions into a single harmonious system. Lorenzo died before he could read Pico's *Oration on the Dignity of Man,* with its powerful statement about man's freedom to determine his

language) in the 16th century, with the adoption of Tuscan as the literary language of Italy.

Lorenzo himself is an appropriate symbol of this late quattrocento culture, in all its complexities and tensions. He was conversant with and knowledgeable about every intellectual current in the city. The remarkable range of his interests and experiences is reflected in his poetry which includes love sonnets, *laudi* on religious themes, pastoral verse, and carnival songs with their vivid description of *il mondo popolare.* By training and inclination, however, Lorenzo was an elitist, who preferred the rarified intellectual atmosphere of Careggi or the privacy of the Medici palace, to the public life of the streets, the *botteghe* and the council halls of the Palazzo della

own fate. Lorenzo's experience had taught him about the limites of human endeavour, and the role of fate in thwarting man's hopes and expectations. He was stricken with a mortal illness while only 43; two years later (1494), his friend Pico was dead at the age of 31.

Though a connoisseur of refined taste and sensibility, Lorenzo was not a major patron of the arts, although he did commission Botticelli to paint frescoes (later destroyed) for his villa at Spedaletto, and he engaged Verrocchio to design the tomb in San Lorenzo for his father Piero. Most of his expenditure on the arts was confined to the purchase of antique gems. He did not himself promote or favour the commission of any civic monument, which might have stimulated republican yearnings that he did not encourage. Two business associates, Francesco Sacchetti and Giovanni Tornabuoni, commissioned

Domenico Ghirlandaio to paint fresco cycles in Santa Trinita and Santa Maria Novella, but these contained no overt political message.

Crisis

In the whole course of Florentine history, there have been few transformations more sudden and dramatic than that marked by the coming of the French, the expulsion of the Medici and the emergence of Savonarola as a religious and political leader. There had been signs of unrest and discontent in the city during Lorenzo's last years; these intensified when Piero de' Medici succeeded his father. But no one could have predicted the sudden collapse of that regime as a consequence of the French invasion, nor Italy's inability to resist future attacks from foreigners bent on her conquest. The self-confidence of the

In the last decade of the 16th century, an event took place that had far-reaching effects on the future of music and the theater. The theories formulated by a group of musicians and literati, *known jointly as the* Camerata fiorentina, *came to theatrical fruition in* Dafne, *with a libretto by Ottavio Rinuccini and music by Jacopo Peri. Performed in 1597 and regarded as the first example of an opera,* Dafne's *immediate antecedents were the* intermedi *or musical and theatrical interludes that were inserted between the acts of plays (opposite right and on this page right, drawings by Bernardo Buontalenti for the intermezzi of* La Pellegrina, *1589). The musical score of* Dafne *has been lost, and the earliest opera to have survived in its entirety is* Euridice, *which is by the same composers and was performed in 1600 at Palazzo Pitti (above, the frontispiece of the opera).*

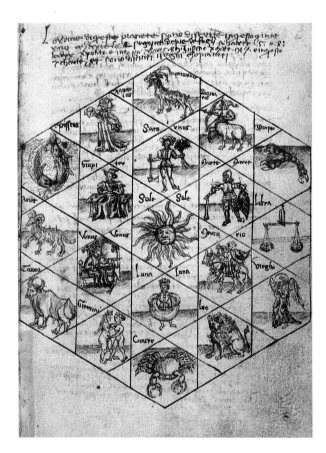

citizenry was eroded, replaced by fear and a sense of vulnerability. Florentines no longer believed that they could control their own destinies, individual or collective. They realized that their fate would be determined, not in the Palazzo della Signoria, but in the chanceries of foreign princes.

This mood of pessimism and anxiety provided the background for Savonarola's career. He appeared on the scene at the precise moment when the Florentines had lost their equilibrium, their sense of controlling their destiny. The friar's preaching, filled with warnings of imminent doom, struck a responsive chord in the hearts of thousands who flocked to churches to hear him, who marched in his processions, and who supported his plans for reform and rejuvenation. In his early sermons, before the French invasions, the friar had emphasized the traditional theme of repentance. Then, as the French armies marched towards the city, the prophetic element became more pronounced, and many citizens were persuaded that Savonarola's words were divinely inspired. In his later sermons, he offered the Florentines a very sanguine vision of their future. God had chosen Florence to be the new Jerusalem, the center of a rejuvenated Christian community. If the Florentines accepted his will, reformed their lives and their state, God would reward them with victory over their enemies, and with great wealth. This view of Florence's central role in the divine scheme won many converts, and enhanced the friar's popularity.

Of contemporary judgements on Savonarola, none was more positive than that of the historian Francesco Guicciardini: "His efforts to maintain the observance of good behaviour were holy and admirable; there was never such goodness and religion in Florence as in his time . . ." Guicciardini, in particular, commended the friar for his efforts to reform public morals: by closing the taverns, prohibiting gambling, enforcing sumptuary laws, and mobilizing the city's youth in religious processions and as enforcers of the moral code. The bonfires of the vanities during carnival in 1497 and 1498 were the most dramatic manifestations of this plan to cleanse the city of corruption. But like most efforts to reform public behaviour, Savonarola's campaign was only temporarily and superficially successful. While many Florentines publicly supported him, though

Left, a page from the 15th-century Zibaldone Andreini *(Biblioteca Laurenziana, Florence) shows a fantastical composition of zodiacal signs round the sun. The contrast between the geocentric system of Ptolemy and the heliocentric intuitions of Copernicus, exercised the minds of scientists and theologians, as well as troubling their consciences, for a long period stretching from the 16th to the 17th century. It was an invention of seemingly limited importance that gave substance to Copernicus' brilliant theory. The telescope, perhaps invented in Holland, became in the hands of Galileo, who perfected it, both an instrument for exploring the skies and also the symbol of a fundamental revolution in philosophy: the triumph of experimentation over blindly accepted tradition. "We were walking round blind and you opened our eyes and showed us a new heaven and a new earth," the philosopher Tommaso Campanella wrote to Galileo.*
Opposite, two sheets of notes on Galileo's heavenly observations; the examination of sunspots, "the death" in Galileo's words "of pseudo-philosophy" because they contradicted the Aristotelian assumption of the incorruptibility of heavenly bodies (above); the satellites of Jupiter, discovered by Galileo in 1610, whose movement he cited as a possible model for the solar system (below). Galileo also devoted himself to perfecting a sort of slide rule, illustrating it in his work Operations of the Geometric and Military Compass, *whose frontispiece is illustrated below left.*

more from fear than conviction, they reverted to their traditional habits after his death. A minority of "true believers" did become converts to his cause. They clustered around the friar in the last months of his ministry, gained comfort from their close association with him and his fellow Dominicans. They escorted him on his public appearances from San Marco to the cathedral and back; they ignored his excommunication, attended his last sermons, and took communion at his hands. After his martyrdom, they kept his memory alive and continued to believe that he was truly a man of God who died for them. One of these disciples may have been Sandro Botticelli, whose later paintings (the *Mystic Nativity,* the *Mystic Crucifixion*) reflect the artist's preoccupation with the themes of reform and redemption.

Some Florentines had responded to the turmoil of the 1490s by seeking solace in religion; others, like Machiavelli, became ardent republicans, committed to the *governo largo* that Savonarola had promoted. The visible symbol of that popular regime was the Sala del Maggior Consiglio that was built for the 3,000 citizens who were members of the Great Council. To decorate the hall, the government of Piero Soderini, the standard-bearer of justice, commissioned Leonardo da Vinci and Michelangelo to paint two battle scenes, commemorating the republic's victories over the Pisans at Cascina (1364) and over the Milanese army at Anghiari (1440). Neither fresco has survived, though sketches and later copies provide some clues to the artists' intentions. Just before receiving that commission, Michelangelo had completed his giant statue of *David* which, originally planned to adorn the buttress of the cathedral, was later moved to a site in front of the Palazzo della Signoria. This move was approved after lengthy consultation with the city's leading artists. For the Florentines, David had long been a symbol of their city as a bastion of republican liberty. Michelangelo's *David* was the most powerful statement of that concept that the city's artists had ever created. That point was not lost on the republican leadership, which determined to locate that magnificent monument to the human spirit next to the city's political heart.

The heroic figure of *David* was the last major artistic commission to be completed under a Florentine republican regime; and so it may be viewed as the culmination of a 300-year-old tradition of civic culture that died with the republic in 1530. The *Signoria* had asked Michelangelo to create a statue of Hercules as a companion to the David, but he never finished the work. The statue was eventually completed under Medici auspices, by the sculptor Bandinelli (1534). Though suspicious of those symbols of republican Florence (the *Marzocco,* Donatello's *Judith and Holofernes,* the *David*), the Medici grand dukes did not remove them from their locations in front of the Palazzo della Signoria. Instead, they commissioned their own monuments to glorify themselves and their dynasty: the Neptune fountain (1565-75), Cellini's *Perseus* (1554), Vasari's frescoes in the Sala del Maggior Consiglio (1563-71); the equestrian statue of Cosimo I by Giambologna (1591).

In his long professional career spanning seven decades, Michelangelo lived and worked in two worlds: the Florentine civic world of his Buonarroti ancestors; and the courtly world of princes, popes and prelates. He grew up in Medicean Florence, living for a time in the Medici palace where he was exposed to the cultural influences of the Laurentian circle. He first visited Rome in 1496, but was soon back in Florence to work on the David and on the fresco for the battle of Cascina. Pope Julius II persuaded him to return to Rome in 1508, where he completed the ceiling of the Sistine chapel and began work on the pope's tomb. In 1516, he was back in Florence, where for a decade he was employed by the two Medici popes, Leo X and Clement VII: designing a façade for San Lorenzo and a new sacristy for that church to serve as a Medici burial chapel, carving the sculptures for two Medici tombs and building the Laurentian library. The expulsion of the Medici in 1527 left him without a patron, and provided him with a last opportunity to participate in a civic enterprise. Placed in charge of fortifications by the republic in April 1529, he worked at that task for six months, and then abruptly fled the city and went to Venice. He was declared a rebel, but returned to Florence two months later (November 1529), to serve the republic in its last days. The tower that he designed to strengthen the city's defenses on its southern boundary still looms over the church of San Miniato. It is an appropriate memorial for this last heroic moment of Florence's civic life.

After the Medici restoration, Michelangelo

Founded in 1582, under the protection of the Medici, the Accademia della Crusca was dedicated from its inception to the study of the Italian language, with the intention of preserving its Florentine quality and of preparing the famous dictionary. The word "crusca" (bran), is possibly a light-hearted agricultural reference to the separation of the good and bad in language. Its present seat, in the Medici villa of Castello, photographs of which are shown on these two pages, preserves furniture and plaques bearing the enterprises and mottoes of the old cruscanti. *In keeping with the Academy's name, the old seats were made in the shape of the panniers used for carrying bread, with their backs in the shape of the peels used by bakers.*

was again employed by the Medici in San Lorenzo, but his heart was not in his work. In 1534, he left Florence for Rome, where he painted the *Last Judgement (1535-41)* in the Sistine chapel for Pope Paul III. His ostensible reason for rebuffing Duke Cosimo's numerous invitations to return to Florence was his hostility to Medici tyranny. But his decision to live permanently in Rome was motivated as much by personal and professional considerations, as by political conviction. Michelangelo found the religious environment in Rome congenial, and the commissions (the new St. Peter's and the Campidoglio) more challenging than any he could have found in Medicean Florence. After his death (February 1564), Duke Cosimo arranged for his body to be transported to Florence, where it was buried in Santa Croce. A few months later, a service was held in San Lorenzo to honour the memory of this greatest of Florentine artists.

FLORENTINE FURNITURE

1

2

3

chests still survive, with a number of front panels painted by celebrated artists – such as the famous one portraying the *Adimari Wedding*. One style of *cassone* made in Florence in the first half of the 15th century had curved sides (16), with decorative panels featuring the heraldic depiction of ermine (symbolizing chastity). The style known as "vasarian"

4

5

6

Almost all the furniture shown on these two pages belongs to the Museo di Palazzo Davanzati, the beautiful 14th-century house that used to belong to the Davizzi family. There is no better place to study the art of the furniture maker, which developed first of all in Florence the Renaissance styles that then quickly spread throughout Italy. The rooms in medieval and Renaissance houses took the fireplace as their focal point, and the fixed seating arrangements were dictated by the distribution of light and heat. Paintings show seats in window embrasures, for instance. Wall openings with shelves were used for storage purposes – one common function of furniture. Movable furniture as we know it did not exist: individual items

were too large and heavy. The lighter styles to which we are accustomed only appeared much later.

A common article for storage in the late Middle Ages and early Renaissance was the large chest known as a *cassone*. This was used to store the bridal trousseau, and many splendidly decorated examples of such

(17) dates from the following century, and the compartmentalization of the front panel into rectangles and ovals, and the lion's paw feet, illustrate the influence of the contemporary taste for classicism and Mannerism. Arms and backs came to be added to the chest, and probably from this developed the bench-chest designed to stand against a wall. Imposing and monumental in size (14), with a substantial base (in draughty houses it was warmer to rest one's feet on wood rather than a stone floor), and scroll-shaped arms, this still remained a dual-purpose piece of furniture, but nevertheless clearly anticipates the modern sofa. This example was made in a Florentine *bottega* in the 16th century. A further type, without backrest (15), has less storage space and is supported by three brackets; dating from the same period, it is a variation, for indoor use, on the stone benches on the streets outside the *palazzo*.

The use of chairs instead of benches or stools increased in prosperous Italian households during the 16th century. Illustration (13) shows a somewhat unusual 16th-century chair, with X-shaped legs and a sloping back, covered in leather like other types of seat. More common was the large straight-backed armchair with straight legs joined by transoms. One interesting type of chair was the typical 16th-century folding armchair (12), known as "Dantesque" (though it only acquired this name in the 19th century). Probably of Spanish origin, the style nevertheless derives from the Roman *sella curulis*. In the way of beds, we know of a variety of styles. The example with different sized headboards (4), standing on a dais forming three bench-chests, dates from the 15th century. A striking feature is the regular pattern of square panels. Similar beds appear in paintings of the period. Another style of bed was the fourpos-

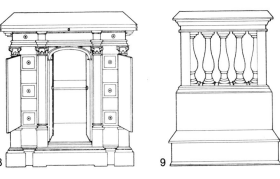

7

ter. The 16th-century example shown here (6) has a scrolled headboard, and dolphins supporting a coat of arms; the four bedposts are carved into ostrich feather shapes at the top. This magnificent style of bed could be hung with curtains all round for warmth and intimacy – both of which were rather

8

9

10

11

scarce in the house of this period. The bed with decorative bedposts was a humbler version of the fourposter. This one (5) probably dates from the turn of the 16th century. The posts are beautifully carved, and the scrolls on the coping of the headboard and on the transom at the foot of the bed are finely carved. An accessory that began to appear in Renaissance houses was the wall mirror. The style of the frames followed the fashions of the day. Shown here is a 16th-century "shrine" type

(2), with a carved coat of arms supported by scrolls at the bottom, and a heavy curving tympanum surmounting it on top. The overall severity of the frame is offset by the delicate

inlaid leaf patterns.

While mirrors gained popularity as objects of wordly vanity, they were complemented at the same time by that other vital piece of bedchamber furniture, the prie-dieu. The 16th-century example here (9) features a rather odd, severe kind of balustrade – typical of the contemporary trend for designing furniture along architectural lines. The top surface slopes slightly, to facilitate the reading of the prayer book, and the step on which one would kneel may be lifted up. This is perhaps an appropriate moment to mention the fine cinquecento lectern (11). This was made for a church, but we know from paintings that lecterns were also found in private houses, especially those of humanist scholars or lawyers and notaries. Among the various types of table it is worth noting the so-called *fratino* (little monk), which was used in the refectories of regular communities. Drawing (7) is a magnificent example of a table from a nobleman's house: of walnut, almost three and a half meters long, it is the work of a Florentine *bottega* of the second half of the 16th century. The plain top is edged with a border of tooth patterns and semicircles. In the *fratino* style, it is supported by two massive leg ends resting on lion's paw feet and bearing coats of arms set in cartouches. Somewhat more sober, but very elegant, is the little table (1) with a beautiful fluted band below the top, containing a drawer, and with four turned legs strengthened by transoms.

Dating from the second half of the 15th century, or the early part of the 16th, is the superb wardrobe (3), with its balanced composition. It is divided into two sections, each of which is subdivided by four panels. Crowning the wardrobe is a cornice. The central panels are doors, with bronze knobs, inside which are two shelves. The wood is mostly walnut, with strips of inlay, while the four outer panels have vases of flowers executed in inlay. Of particular value is the 16th-century writing desk (8) with composite columns and pilasters, made to resemble a triumphal arch. The "vault" opens up through doors that slide round inside; in the sides are both visible and "secret" drawers; the top surface is extendable, being hinged, and can be moved to give

access to more drawers by means of a "secret" unlocking device. Finally, to give an idea of the sumptuous elaborateness of furniture in the baroque period, it is worth studying the cabinet (10) presented by Cosimo III to his daughter Anna Maria Luisa (1667-1743), made of ebony, gilded bronze, and Florentine mosaic work.

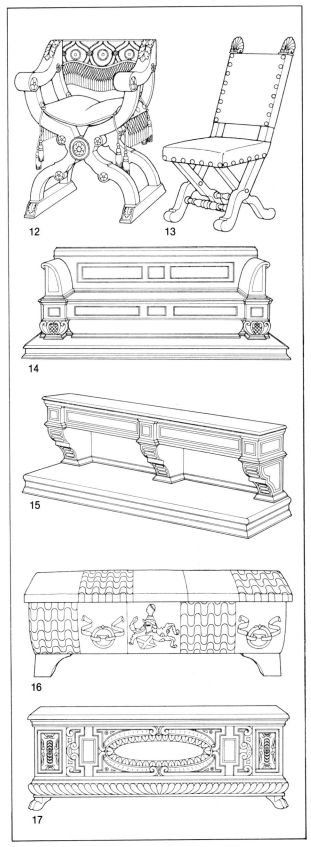

12 13

14

15

16

17

Florence under the principato

The bustle of Florentine street life is captured in Giovanni Maria Butteri's painting The Return *from the Palio. It contains a portrayal of the horse called "Il Seicento," presumably the winner of the race, being led in triumph through the streets of the city (National Gallery of Ireland, Dublin).*

Two themes, crisis and decline, have dominated the historical writing on Florence, and on Italy, in the years after 1494. In his *Storia d'Italia*, Francesco Guicciardini presented his theory of crisis, a sudden and dramatic change in Italy's historical development, as a result of the invasions. Prior to the coming of the "barbarians," Italy was a land of peace and prosperity, "teeming with inhabitants, merchandise and much wealth ..." But the French, Spanish and German invaders destroyed that terrestrial paradise, bringing with them destruction, diease and death. Guicciardini and the other historians who wrote about "the calamities of Italy" described the disintegration of this once-flourishing civilization. Italian states that had been independent fell under the control, direct or indirect, of the Spanish crown. Republican regimes, like Florence's, were crushed and replaced by despotic authoritarian governments. The Italian economy, once the most advanced in Europe, suffered a serious and permanent decline, particularly in its industrial and commercial sectors. Italian society, influenced (so it was thought) by the Spanish model, became increasingly rigid and hierarchical. But the most dramatic change was seen, by both contemporaries and modern historians, in Italy's cultural life. The point was made most forcefully by Benedetto Croce: "From the middle of the 14th to the beginning of the 15th century one senses that Italy was not really alive ..."

What, or who, was responsible for these calamities, which culminated in Italy's subjugation to foreign domination? Savonarola viewed the initial French invasion as God's punishment for Italy's depravity; this interpretation was popular with the clergy, and with some laymen, who accepted this traditional medieval explanation for Italy's plight. But for those who, like Machiavelli and Guicciardini, sought to understand these events in a secular context, the responsibility for the invasions lay primarily with the rulers of the Italian states, who had not taken appropriate measures to secure their rule and furthermore, had failed to unite to repel the foreign invaders. Viewing this problem in a longer historical perspective, Machiavelli identified the papacy as the institution primarily responsible for the political fragmentation of the peninsula, and blamed the ruling elites of the city-states for their incessant feuding, and their failure to place their country above private interest. Modern historians have been as prone as their 16th-century counterparts in searching for scapegoats for the so-called "Italian calamities." Their explanations are more complex and sophisticated, but the villains in this historical scenario are still the members of Italy's ruling class. The princes, and the social elite from which they came, were so preoccupied with self-interest that they had lost all sense of the common good. By their tenacious resistance to change, the elites have also been accused of blocking Italy's transition from a feudal to a capitalist society.

More plausible than these "conspiracy" theories are interpretations that stress the enormous burden of tradition in conditioning and limiting the nature of the Italian response to the crisis precipitated by the invasions. The key element in that tradition, for northern and central Italy, was the city-state. Parochialism was so strong, so pervasive, that very few urban dwellers could look beyond their walls to the wider world, or identify with any community other than their own. The city-state experience

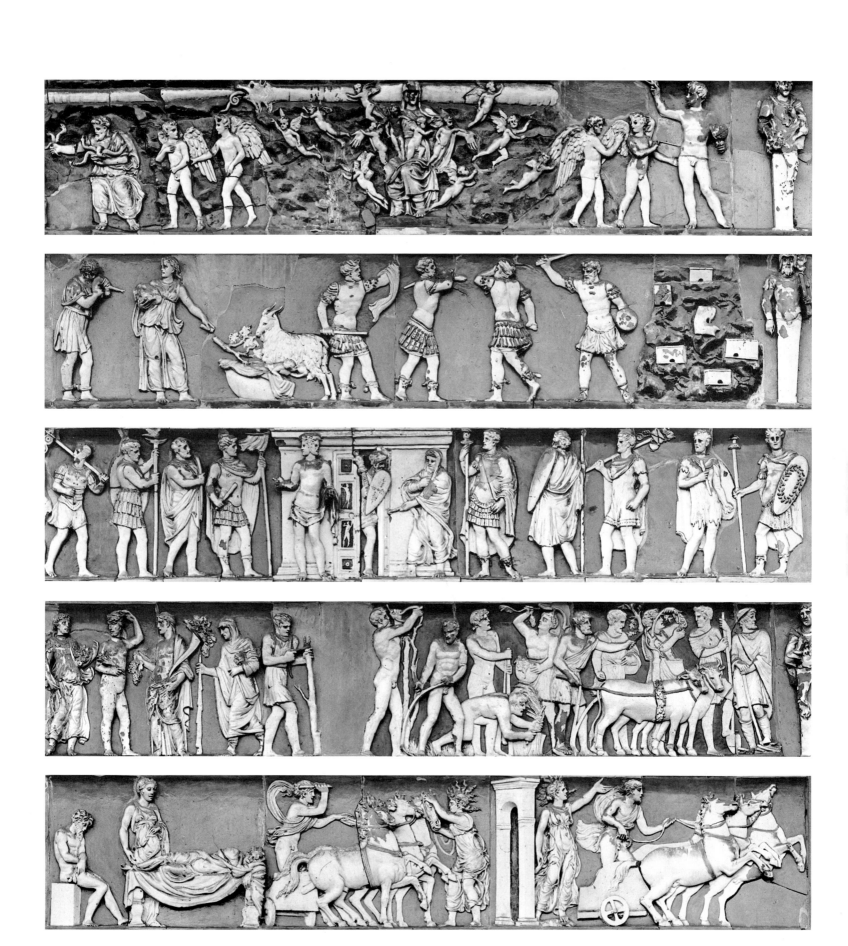

Opposite, a glazed terracotta bas-relief in the form of a frieze on the façade of the Medici villa of Poggia a Caiano, attributed to Giuliano Sangallo, who, at the request of Lorenzo the Magnificent, between 1480 and 1485 carried out the reconstruction of the villa, one of the most magnificent

Medici properties. The villa of Artiminio, known as La Ferdinanda, was commissioned by Ferdinando I and built around 1594 to a design by Buontalenti. Access to it is gained via a broad flight of steps (below) and it gives out onto a panoramic view of the surrounding countryside.

Above, a plan by Ludovico Cigoli (1559-1613) for a triumphal arch. One of the most representative painters and architects of the late 16th century in Tuscany, Cigoli created many important works in Florence, among them the courtyard of the Palazzo Nonfinito.

had also created a wide gulf between elites and masses, between those who ruled and those who were ruled. Imperial authority had been so ineffective for so long that it could command no loyalty among Italians. Political legitimacy was claimed by communes, and by the *signori* who had replaced those republican regimes, but that claim was tenuous and frequently challenged. Though some efforts were made in the late quattrocento, notably, by Lorenzo de' Medici, to promote mutual cooperation among the Italian states, those efforts were only marginally successful. These palliatives did not change the institutions and the mentality that had been inherited from the past. Machiavelli's vision, described in the last chapter of *The Prince,* of a ruler endowed with virtue who could unite Italy was a fantasy. More realistic were the views that he expressed (August 1513) in a letter to his friend, Francesco Vettori: "As to a unification

with other Italians, you speak in jest; there are no leaders for such a purpose, there are no weapons worthy of mention, and there is no unity between the leaders and the ordinary people (...) a conflict would instantly arise, with the people seeking to supplant their peers and take their place ..."

For nearly two centuries, a politically fragmented Italy had been immune from foreign occupation because her neighbours were too weak to take advantage of her vulnerability. In the early 15th century, the revenues of Venice, Florence and Milan were comparable to those of Europe's largest monarchies. During the late 15th century, the development in France and Spain of strong monarchies capable of mobilizing large armies, and of collecting the revenues to support them, decisively changed Italy's situation in Europe. After 1494, the question was not whether Italy would be controlled by a foreign

GAMES AND FESTIVITIES

Florence's biggest celebrations were those on the feast day of her patron saint, John the Baptist (24 June), which were described on page 114. In the afternoon there was a horse race, for which the prize was a cloth or *palio* – similar to the famous races still run in Siena. The painting opposite (6), the front panel of a chest (*cassone*) gives a lively impression of this occasion. If the city happened to be at war, the *palio di San Giovanni* was held under the walls of the besieged city. In his record of communal expenditure, Villani details that the "*palio di sciamito* (*sciamito* was a

prized coloured cloth) ran annually at the feast of St. John, and the lesser *palii* of St. Barnabas and St. Reparata cost one hundred gold florins per annum." The attractive circular painting (1), possibly a birth tray, depicts a popular game called *civettino* (little owl). It was a tough game of skill, said to "require good reflexes, an eye for dodging and parrying," and speed. The point of the game was that the players had to stay within a certain distance of each other – as can be seen from the picture, the right foot of

one participant having to touch the other's left. Both the paintings referred to date from the 15th century.

During the period of the *granducato* the monarchic structure of society led to more displays of collective life. The competitors in these games were the courtiers (or men playing for them), for whom they perhaps compensated for the absence of political rivalry. Great ceremonial celebrations were arranged for important visitors or events in the lives of the princes. The joust at the quintain (5, from a fresco in the Palazzo Vecchio) involved charging on horseback and striking with a lance the shield of a dummy which, at the blow, would swing round with a whip: the art, of course, was to avoid the whip. This traditional game still survives in Arezzo. Such jousts took place in Florence in Piazza Santa Croce, Via Larga, or on the bridge of Santa Trinita. The game in illustration (8), here taking place in Via de' Tornabuoni, consisted of similarly charging with a lance, and striking a ring hanging from a sort of gallows. These games were imbued with romantic nostalgia for a bygone age of chivalry, more imaginary than real – hardly surprising in a society that had adopted the ways of chivalry, yet whose roots were those of bourgeois trade rather than the sword. Thus in Stradano's decorations for the apartments of Eleanora of Toledo in the Palazzo Vecchio we see a full-blown tournament, complete with armour and plumed helmets (7). A more literary form of nostalgia, going back to classical times, were the naumachia (4, in the courtyard of the Palazzo Pitti, specially flooded and covered) and the military displays held in the public squares. For the visit of Prince Federico of Urbino in 1616 an amphitheater was erected in Piazza Santa Croce for a *festa a cavallo:* a mock battle with 42 horsemen. Allegorical floats rode into the arena, a ballet was danced, and "another battle was shown on foot" involving 300 combatants (2). Of all Florentine games the best known is that of *calcio* (football). It is debatable – and on the whole it is thought not to be the case – whether, for all

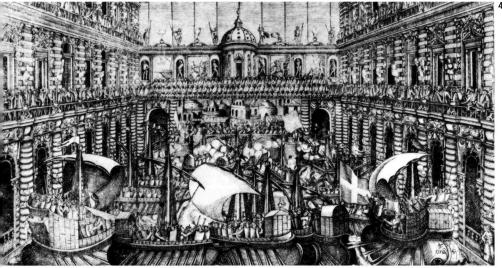

its slight similarities with the modern game, this was a forerunner of football as we know it. The object of this extremely rough game was to send a large ball into the opponents' "goal," so it may be said in this respect that it anticipates modern football. In the detail from an anonymous 17th-century painting reproduced here (3) we see a match taking place in Via de' Tornabuoni. The spectators at the windows of the *palazzi* certainly had as good a view as any modern stadium can provide.

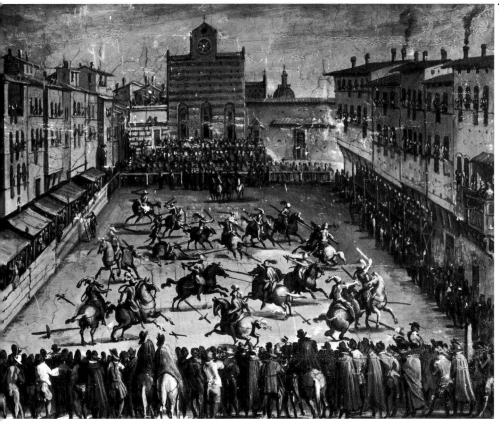

The childless bride of the Elector Palatine William of Neuburg, Anna Maria Luisa, the last of the Medici, died in Florence in 1743, at a time when the house of Lorraine had already taken possession of the granducato (1737), following the death of her brother Gian Gastone without heirs. The story of the Medici now ends, but not before Anna Maria Luisa had achieved her final wish: that the family's priceless collections should remain forever in Florence. Whilst arranging to hand over to the new rulers of Tuscany "all the furniture, effects and rarities of the estate of the most serene duke, my brother, such as galleries, pictures, statues, libraries, jewels and other precious objects, the reliquaries and their ornaments in the palace chapel," she stipulated "the express condition that nothing which is for the ornament of the state, for the use of the public and for the attraction of outsiders' curiosity, will be taken out of the capital or out of the territory of the granducato." This pact has earned her the gratitude not only of the city of Florence, but of the whole civilized world. A belated funerary eulogy of this great family is contained in the words of Alexandre Dumas père: "Let the Medici rest in peace in their tombs of marble and porphyry, for they have done more than any king or prince or emperor for the glory of the world." The last of the Medici is portrayed (left), together with her husband, dancing to the accompaniment of the court orchestra in a painting by Johannes Franciscus van Douven.

power, but rather which state (France, Hapsburg Spain, the Ottoman Empire) would succeed in the competition. City-states, even if joined in alliances, could not compete with the vast resources of a French or Spanish monarchy. Fernand Braudel reminds us that Italy was a Mediterranean country, poorly endowed by nature, severely constrained by geography and climate, rich only in human resources and *ingegno*. For three centuries, the intense concentration of those human and financial resources in her cities had sustained a flourishing civilization. Through skill and chance, Italy (or rather, some Italians) had temporarily escaped from the impoverishment that was the "natural" condition of their world. By the 16th century, however, the balance of wealth and power was gradually but inexorably shifting to the north.

Though influenced by her particular traditions and experiences, Florence's fortunes in the aftermath of the invasions were largely determined by these historical trends of the *longue durée*. In particular, the political settlement finally achieved in the 1530s, Cosimo I's *principato*, was a compromise between imperial and local interests, and between Medici supporters and the old civic aristocracy. There were brief moments, during the two republican interludes (1494-1512 and 1527-30) when Florence's political community was united; more commonly, however, it was divided and weakened by factional discord. By the 1530s, an exhausted aristocracy was reconciled to some form of authoritarian government, and the Medici were the logical candidates for the role of *signori*. Death eliminated several incompetents before young Cosimo was given the opportunity to establish his regime. Cosimo was intelligent, shrewd, astute, diligent; he understood that politics was a difficult and demanding profession. He satisfied most of the criteria that Machiavelli had formulated for his ideal prince. His main goal was the creation of a stable dynastic state under his personal control, a state that was militarily strong and diplomatically autonomous. Before his death in 1574, he had taken great steps towards achieving that objective.

Cosimo retained many features of the republican administration that he had inherited, adapting that system to the requirements of autocratic rule. He chose qualified officials, scrutinized their performance, and rewarded them for their loyalty and devotion. Unlike French kings and Roman popes, Cosimo did not sell offices, and thus maintained effective control over his subordinates. Moreover, he and his successors increased the number of permanent officials, while reducing those short-term appointments that had been characteristic of the republic. The result of thesee sensible policies was a professional, experienced bureaucracy, possibly the most efficient in 16th-century Europe. Its size was sufficient to permit an unusually large degree of control over this provincial society. These officials administered justice with severity if not equity, suppressed unrest and rebellion, enforced ducal legislation, and ruthlessly col-

The collections of Lorenzo the Magnificent, added to by his successors, mark the beginning of modern art collecting. In the Museo degli Argenti in the Palazzo Pitti, which conserves artifacts that come mainly from the grand ducal crown, one of the rarest objects is a white onyx cameo bearing portraits of Cosimo I, his wife and his children, which was carved by Antonio De' Rossi in around 1575 and whose center once contained a picture of Florence.

This drawing by Federico Zuccari (above) shows visitors busy drawing inside the New Sacristy that contains Michelangelo's tombs of the Medici in the church of San Lorenzo. During the 18th century, a visit to Florence was de rigueur for travellers, artists and men of culture from all over Europe. Armed with notebooks and pencils, they wrote down their thoughts and observations and sketched buildings, paintings, sculptures and views. In 1773, King George III of England, in order to please his wife Charlotte, commissioned the artist Johann Zoffany to travel to Florence and execute a painting of the Tribune in the Uffizi. The result was a large canvas (a detail of which is illustrated on the page opposite) that depicts a number of the masterpieces in the Uffizi collection and acts almost as a symbolic representation of the cultural heritage bequeathed to Florence by the Medici.

lected the taxes to pay for the administrative and military system of the *granducato*.

The efficiency of this bureaucracy was most clearly demonstrated during the rule of those Medici princes who were less talented, and less strongly motivated, than the first grand duke. Cosimo I's oldest son Francesco (d. 1587) was a recluse, who had no interest in governing his state and devoted little effort to the task. Fortunately for the dynasty and for the duchy, his brother Ferdinando (d. 1607) possessed a measure of his father's political skills and energy, and bequeathed some to his son Cosimo II, who died (1621) when he was only 30 years old. His young heir, Ferdinando II, eventually became an effective ruler, but after his death (1670), the quality of Florence's Medici rulers plummeted. Only a dedicated group of officials could have kept the state functioning under the rule of inept princes like Cosimo III (d. 1723) and the last Medici ruler, Gian Gastone (d.1737).

The efforts of Cosimo I and his successors to stimulate the Tuscan economy were only partially successful. While some of their schemes were well conceived, e.g. the promotion of specific industries, their policies did not attack the most important obstacles to economic growth; specifically, the internal restrictions on trade and manufacturing, the inequitable tax system, and the unproductive utilization of capital. The grand dukes were no more successful than other European rulers in devising mechanisms to protect their subjects against the ravages of famine and disease. The deadly cycle of poor harvests, high grain prices, malnutrition and plague was repeated again and again in these years. The duchy's population had risen to over half a million in 1552, but this increase was reduced by periodic visitations of plague, most virulent in 1575, the 1590s and the early 1630s. In the terrible decade from 1622 to 1633, Tuscany's population fell by 17 per cent; thereafter, it increased only slightly for the remainder of the century. Mercantile and industrial activity remained at a relatively high level during the second half of the 16th century, but it declined dramatically after the 1620s. Florentine cloth could not compete in European and Levantine markets with that produced elsewhere and this once-thriving industry ceased to provide work and sustenance for more than a handful of the city's poor residents. Those who could not find employment as servants in the *palazzi* of the aristocracy begged for alms outside the churches and monasteries. These scenes of penury were noted by many foreign travellers who visited the city.

Between rich and poor, the gulf was perhaps greater than ever before; the progressive rigidification of the social order effectively eliminated any possibility of upward mobility by the lower classes, or even the artisans and shopkeepers. In their city *palazzi* and country villas, the nobility were concerned with preserving their wealth and status through court connections, marriages, and cautious investments in land and government bonds. Some nobles served honourably in the granducal administration. A minority preferred to live on their rural estates; of these, a few took a personal interest in the cultivation of their land and in the welfare of their peasants. Some members of the aristocracy, like the *savant* Lorenzo Magalotti (d. 1712) devoted their lives to intellectual pursuits. The cultural sophistication of the nobility was frequently mentioned by foreign visitors. Charles de Brosses wrote (1739) that "literature, mathematics and the arts are still much cultivated in this city, which I have found to be full of men of letters, both among the nobility and among those who make literature their profession. Not only are they conversant

The city, its inhabitants, their customs and their activities are sympathetically observerd by Giuseppe Zocchi (1711-67) in these details of prints.
Left, the lively Piazza di San Firenze and a foreshortened view of the façade of the Badia Fiorentina.
Below, the Arno beyond the Porta alla Croce and the San Niccolò weir near the Ponte alle Grazie.

with the literature of their own country, they also seemed to me to be knowledgeable about French and English literature too."

The apex of Florentine society was the court, established in the Pitti palace, and gradually evolving into that highly formalized and ceremonial life style reflected so brilliantly in Bronzino's portraits. The prevailing influence was Spanish, imported by the duchess, Eleanora of Toledo, and her Castilian entourage. The formal, indeed artificial, atmosphere of the court suited Cosimo's temperament, which had little of the affability of his Medici predecessors. Court protocol defined that strict hierarchy of orders that was slowly evolving in Florentine society. Though initially with reluctance, the old urban aristocracy was drawn into this system, seeking the pensions, benefits and titles that the dukes could bestow upon their favourites. That struggle for advantage and precedence fostered an atmosphere that was intensely competitive and occasionally perilous for the participants.

The congenial, relaxed milieu of the Urbino court in the early cinquecento, idealized by Castiglione in *The Courtier,* had become the rigid and neurotic world described in the last part of Cellini's autobiography. Cellini reported a statement by the French monarch, Francis I, that might well have been uttered by Cosimo I: "It is something extraordinary, Benvenuto, that you men of genius are not sensible of your inability to display your talents without our assistance,.and that you show yourselves great only by means of the opportunities that we afford you; it would become you to be a little more humble and less proud and opiniative (...) I must therefore repeat it to you, that I insist upon your showing yourself obedient, when I lay my commands upon you; because, if you continue obstinate in your whims, you will only run your head against the wall."

Cosimo sought to harness the talents of Florentine artists and writers for his, and his dynasty's, aggrandizement and, incidentally, for the beautification of the city. Under the direction of his "minister of culture," Giorgio Vasari, the duke developed an elaborate building plan, which focused on the redecoration of the Palazzo della Signoria (transformed into "a pictorial genealogy of his [Medici] forebears"), and the building of the Palazzo degli Uffizi. Sculptors and painters were employed on these and other

A washerwoman at the river's edge, the Ponte alle Grazie and, in the background, the tower of the Palazzo Vecchio, as seen in a drawing by Giuseppe Moricci.

A man sharpening knives, a horseman and a dog barking at the horse riding by: an everyday scene along the Arno embankment, as depicted in an engraving by Giuseppe Zocchi.
The last of the Medici, Anna Maria Luisa, had travelled extensively in Europe. She had carefully observed a variety of famous cities, and her touching conclusion was that "… in order to want these cities to appear beautiful one would have to have been born somewhere other than Florence."

projects: in the Piazza della Signoria, in the cathedral, in San Lorenzo and Santa Maria Novella. Cosimo favoured a uniform cultural style in the arts and in literature. To that end he established, in 1540, the Accademia Fiorentina, which became the official organ of Florentine literary activity. In 1563, the Accademia del Disegno was established under ducal patronage, its mission to enroll and control the artists who were among the least disciplined of Cosimo's subjects. With such effective mechanisms of cultural control, reinforced by a state security system, Florence had little need for the Inquisition and the Index, the newly created institutions for preserving religious orthodoxy.

Florentine culture during the *principato* was perhaps not as moribund as Croce had suggested, but it had lost its civic core which, for more than three centuries, had been the prime source of its vitality and creativity. The sense of belonging to a community with a glorious past and a bright future was the link uniting the generations of Florentines from Brunetto Latini to Machiavelli. With the demise of the republic and the emergence of a dominant Spanish power in the peninsula, that spirit had died. After 1530,

Florentine writers could extol the benefits of Medici rule and of the *pax hispanica*. But they could not experience the sanguine mood of Giovanni Villani when he described how his visit to Rome in 1300 had inspired him to write the history of his native city, "considering that Florence, child and product of Rome, was in the ascendant, while Rome was declining …" Florentines living under the *principato* did possess their monuments and memories of their city's past, but they could not imagine a future in which they would participate as citizens in a rejuvenated community. That future would indeed emerge in a form that no one of that age could have foreseen.

Chronology,
Illustrious families,
The Medici family tree,
Glossary,
Index

Chronology

The double foundation; Roman Florence; third century B.C. – third century A.D.

Florence was first founded by the Etruscans from Fiesole in the period of peace following the second Punic War (c. 200 B.C.): its name (Florentia, place of flowers) did not seem to bring luck, however, for as punishment for the participation of the people of Fiesole on the side of the popular party in the Civil Wars, Sulla completely destroyed Florence in 82 B.C. The city was then refounded by Caesar in 59 B.C. as a colony enclosed within a square perimeter wall some 500 meters (1,600 feet) across. It was traversed by two streets, the *cardos* and the *decumanus,* the characteristic layout of the Roman *castrum.* Geographically well placed, on the Via Cassia, having links with both the Tyrrhenian and the Adriatic, the city developed as a center for the wool and copper businesses. In the third century A.D. it became the administrative center of Tuscia, expanding beyond the limits of the walls, and acquired magnificent temples, baths, and an amphitheater.

From the Ostrogoths to the Lombards; the spread of Christianity: fourth – eighth century

The city declined along with the Roman Empire. Christianity spread only slowly here, as is attested by the limited degree of persecution in the third century (the martyrdom of St. Miniatus, 250). By 313, however, there was a Bishop of Florence, and the process of Christianization accelerated with the presence of St. Ambrose (393) at the time of the foundation of the church of San Lorenzo. The spread of the cult of St. Reparata and the founding of the church dedicated to her (on the site of the present cathedral) coincided with the siege by the Ostrogoth Radagaisus – who was driven back by Stilicho in 406. Little has come down to us from the period after the fall of the Roman Empire, but we know that the city declined as a commercial and manufacturing center. The Graeco-Goth war hit Tuscia hardest in 539, when the Byzantines besieged the Goths in Fiesole. The Byzantine victory ensured some decades of peace, until the Lombard occupation, under which Florence became a duchy. Records from the Lombard period are mostly ecclesiastical: the activities of bishops and the foundation of new churches and monasteries on the outskirts of the city.

A slow recovery: ninth – tenth century

The Carolingian era is usually given as the time at which Florence began its slow political and economic recovery. Fiesole and Florence – two separate sees – were united in 854, forming the largest political unit in Italy. During the same period the textile industry in the monasteries of Sant'Andrea and San Michele and the acquisition of land by Florentines in the surrounding region testify to an undoubted economic boom. Under Otto I opposition to the corrupt secular clergy was raised by hermits such as Romualdo, the founder of the hermitage of Camaldoli. Under Otto III the economic expansion spread to the nearby cities of Lucca and Siena. In his lexicon compiled in Byzantium in the 11th century, Suidas quotes Florence in the same breath as Pisa in his discussion of Tuscan cities; neither Lucca nor Siena warrant so much as a mention. By now Florence was also experiencing a period of agricultural and industrial growth, so that in 1018 a new market had to be built, to replace the old one on the site of the Roman forum.

City of the empire and council seat: 1055

The movement of reform within the church found one of its earliest centers in Florence. Already in 1011-34 Abbott Guarino of Settimo had challenged the simoniac Bishop Ildebrando; and in 1035-37 Giovanni Gualberto had publicly preached reforming ideas in the squares of the city before retiring to the hermitage of Vallombrosa. Emperor Conrad II supported the new ideas when in Florence in 1037, as did his successor Henry III, who had favoured Victor II's election to the papacy. It was this pope who spread the name of Florence throughout Christian Europe, when in 1054 he called on the council for the following year (to be held in Santa Reparata) to review the degree of corruption in the church, to put an end to the sale and purchase of ecclesiastical positions and to check concubinage among the clergy. Henry also placed the city directly under his own authority, releasing it from the "local" power of the *marchese* of Tuscany.

The second circle of walls: 1078

Until halfway through the 11th century Florence still retained its Roman walls, although houses and above all monasteries had spilled out beyond their confines. To the north now was Borgo San Lorenzo, to the south Borgo SS. Apostoli, to the east Borgo San Pietro, and to the west Borgo San Pancrazio: these suburbs, together with Borgo del Parione, were defended by temporary ditches and stakes. In 1078 a new circle of walls was decided upon, that would take in these *borghi,* and transform the original Roman square into an irregular octagon, with new gates at each corner. The new defenses included the built-up area on the left bank of the Arno. Here gates were built but no walls, since these were made up by the houses standing side by side in a row with their backs to the hill. It was not until the third circle of walls that the defenses of the city could be said to extend beyond the Arno.

The alliance with the pope and the siege of Henry IV: 1082

The proud behaviour of Matilda, Countess of Tuscany, during the investiture struggle between empire and papacy is well known in history. Emperor Henry IV was made to wait for three days in the snow outside the stronghold of Canossa before being received by Gregory VII, to appeal against his excommunication, which had created serious instances of rebellion among his subjects (1077). Excommunicated once again in 1080, the emperor reacted differently: having elected an antipope, Clement III, he went to Rome in order to receive the imperial crown, but was unable to gain admittance to the papal capital enclosed within the city walls. He therefore journeyed north and, while other Tuscan cities opened their doors to him and welcomed him with great honours, Florence alone, faithful to the papacy and the Countess Matilda, refused him admission. In July 1082 Henry besieged the city: after just one month, as a result of the valour of Florence's defenders and the intense heat which weakened Henry's men, he abandoned the plan and left. Florence's stand in favour of the papacy on this occasion was the basis of the city's ensuing good fortune which was linked to a profitable alliance with the church.

The first crusade: the economic gains

The crusade to liberate the Holy Land from the hands of the heathen, called by Pope Urban II in 1096, met with enthusiasm in Florence, especially from the monks of Vallombrosa. Many Florentines followed east in the wake of Godefroy de Bouillon, and legend has it that a

Florentine, Pazzino de' Pazzi, first raised the crusaders flag over the walls of Jerusalem. Of more significance, however, were the lucrative trade links established with the Orient. The populous city center was connected to the surrounding countryside by a comprehensive network of streets, which made it an important crossroads (and hence place of trade) for the whole peninsula. The principal road between Tuscany and the Po Valley now no longer passed through Lucca, but through Florence.

The first period of expansion: 1107-23

The first Florentine wars – dictated by the need to protect the traffic of agricultural and manufactured goods to and from the city – date from the same period in which we first hear of the formation of an autonomous form of government by consuls (1138). The year 1107 saw the destruction of the castle used by the Adimari, a feudal, imperial family, to control and raise tolls on the stretch of the Arno at Signa. A similar castle owned by the Alberti which blocked the way to Pistoia was conquered that same year. In 1115

Florence and Pisa launched a joint "Tyrrhenian crusade" against the Saracens in the Balearic Islands. Fearing occupation by Conrad, *marchese* of Tuscany, the Florentines attacked their ancient mother-town Fiesole in 1123-25, taking it and razing it to the ground. Between the 12th and the 13th century the Florentines took a number of castles: Montebuono, Montegrossoli, Pogna, Frondiglioso, Semifonte, Combiata, Montemurla, Montelupo. "And thus the commune of Florence began to expand," writes Giovanni Villani, "either by force or by argument, increasing its territory and bringing under its jurisdiction all the country nobility, and destroying the castles." The dispossessed feudal lords moved into the city, attracted by the profits to be made through trade and industry.

The struggle against the Guidi: 1143-47

The expansion of Florence was bound to clash with the interests of the ancient Tuscan feudal family of the Guidi, who owned land in the Casentino, the Mugello, and much of Romagna. The castle they owned at Cuona (situated near the modern Pontassieve) which impeded free traffic

to Romagna was besieged and destroyed, together with an adjacent monastery (1147) after a series of attacks spanning four years. The seizure of another Guidi castle, Monte Croce, however, cost the Florentines a papal interdict, and they were obliged to return the manor to its owner, Guido Guerra. Guido rebuilt and refortified it, and the Florentines re-took it just 75 years later.

The failure of the imperial restoration: 1160-77

Frederick Barbarossa's dream of restoring imperial authority in Italy was shattered by the now well consolidated autonomy of the communes. Directly engaged in the conflict with the rebel communes in northern Italy (with the disastrous outcome at Legnano, 1176), Barbarossa approached Central Italy by means of legates. Welf of Bavaria, who had been nominated *marchese* of Tuscany, called a diet of Tuscan cities at San Genesio. The Florentines did not attend. San Genesio, at the foot of the hill of San Miniato, afterwards known as San Miniato al Tedesco, (*tedesco*, German) then became the base for the

Shrine of the Arte dei Pellicciai *(the guild of furriers) in Orsanmichele. The beheading of St.* *Jacob, a 15th-century work attributed to Niccolò Lamberti.*

emperor's representatives – one of whom, Christian of Mainz, started a war in which Pisa and Florence fought Pistoia, Lucca and Siena, the latter backed by imperial forces. The eventual victory of the Florentines at Ascanio (1177) put an end to the most critical phase of interference by Barbarossa in the life of the Central Italian communes.

The first stirrings of civil strife: the consuls versus the Uberti: 1177-78

"Thus in the said year (1177) there began in Florence dissension and fighting among citizens, the like of which had never been seen in Florence. The cause was excessive wealth and leisure, and the haughty arrogance of the Uberti, the most powerful and greatest citizens of Florence, together with their followers both noble and common, who started a war with the consuls, who were the lords and leaders of the commune" (Villani). The fight between the Uberti – noblemen recently arrived in the city, with towers in the present Piazza della Signoria – and the commune government, drawn from the oldest aristocratic families in the town, ended in 1178 with the defeat of the Uberti, who were also forced to surrender their castle of Altafronte. It was a full-scale war (to quote Villani, "many people died, and the city experienced great danger and damage") yet at the same time it was almost a rehearsal for Florence's later civil wars. Bloody though these were, they nevertheless alternated with periods of reconciliation, so that "one day the Florentines would be fighting, the next they would be eating and drinking together, vaunting each other's exploits in battle" (Villani).

Semifonte; new danger: 1182

The emperor's power had been weakened in the city, but in the country it still had supporters, namely the imperial feudal families. One of these, the Alberti, who had already crossed swords with the Florentines, decided to found a new town, Semifonte, near Certaldo, as the new imperial capital of the region. Twice, in 1182 and 1183, the Florentines mobilized for action against the Alberti, destroying the entrenchments and walls of the city under construction. They were, however, stopped by Barbarossa who restricted Florentine jurisdiction to within the city walls, denied the Alberti any authority in the country, and placed the commune consuls under an imperially appointed *podestà*. Under these conditions it was finally possible to build and extend Semifonte. Not until 1198 were Florentine troops able to march against the imperial citadel and destroy it once and for all in 1202.

Gherardo Caponsacchi, podestà of Florence: 1193

Caponsacchi would not warrant a mention in a brief historical summary such as this, were it not for the fact that he is the first named *podestà* to be recorded in Florentine history. Only in 1207 were foreigners admitted to the office of *podestà* – as a guarantee of non involvement with internal city factions, since the office was held just for a year. The job was above all concerned with law and order, and under the terms of the appointment the *podestà* had to supply his assistants from his own city of origin. He was also in charge of the army in time of war. In 1207 the post was held by Gualfredotto of Milan; but he was soon outshone by another Milanese, Rubaconte da Mandello (1237), who erected a new bridge across the Arno and paved the streets of the city, which until then had been for the most part dirty and miry. Thus, as Villani tells us, the town of Florence became cleaner, healthier and more beautiful.

Guelfs and Ghibellines: 1216

The terms Guelf and Ghibelline did not initially signify pro-pope and pro-emperor respectively, the meaning they later acquired; they were simply Florentine translations of the names of two German parties supporting different claimants to the imperial crown: Otto IV (*Welf,* Guelf) and Frederick II (*Waibling,* Ghibelline). Despite the incidental cause for the splitting of Florence into two factions, it was also part of an ongoing struggle among the various families of the aristocracy to gain control of the city. At the source of it was the insult of young Buondelmonte Buondelmonti to the Amidei family caused by his refusing the hand in marriage of a young woman of that family. Allies of the Amidei (the Arrighi, Fifanti, Uberti, Alberti and Lamberti families) met with the insulted party to decide on a suitable punishment. They agreed to Mosca de' Lamberti's suggestion that Buondelmonte should die. The young man, "nobly dressed in a new white robe, and riding a white palfrey" (Villani), was assassinated on Easter Day, 1216. The crime shook the entire city. The relatives and allies of the victim appealed to the *podestà* for justice, but the plotters appealed to imperial law, thus refusing to recognize the power of the *podestà*. While the Ghibellines turned to Frederick II, the Guelfs embraced the opposing party of the papacy, and so the ancient rivalry between imperial aristocracy and urban obligarchy found a fresh lease of life in the rivalry between emperor and pope.

St. Francis and St. Dominic meet in Florence: 1221

Preceded in 1209 by three of his disciples, who

had introduced the Franciscan ideals and way of life to Florence, St. Francis himself arrived in the city in November 1211. After a short stop in Oltrarno he entered the city center, followed by a small crowd of onlookers, and had soon welcomed a number of Florentines among his brothers. A Franciscan convent was founded at Monticelli, first under St. Agnes then under the Florentine Avegnente di Albizzo, and it was in Florence, in 1221, that the Rule of the Franciscan Tertiaries was issued. Two years after Francis's death, pope Gregory IX granted privileges and protection to the Franciscans who met outside the walls, on the site where Santa Croce was later to

Monastery of San Marco. The interplay of light in the white corridors and the cells of the dormitory situated round the cloister of Sant' Antonino.

The war with Siena: 1230-35

In 1220-22 Florence and Pisa had fought a minor war, out of which Florence had emerged the victor, although the conflict had not changed the political geography of the region. More protracted was the war against Siena, despite opposition from both the emperor and the pope. In 1230 Florentine troops occupied Porto Ercole; in 1233 they besieged Siena. Villani records that the corpses of donkeys and other beasts were catapulted over the enemy walls as a gesture of contempt. Peace was signed in 1235, the Sienese having to surrender the castle of Montalcino to the victors.

The battle of Signa; the Umiliati in Florence: 1239

Though severe with the Lombard communes allied under the League of San Zenone, whom he had defeated at Cortenova in 1237, Frederick II treated the Florentines differently, giving them various guarantees and privileges, and even allowing them to mint their own money, despite his monopoly over coinage. He was counting on the dominance within the city of the Ghibellines, whose loyalty he commanded, and such imperial benevolence could not but enhance the prestige of that party. Their opponents, however, were encouraged by the excommunication of the emperor by Pope Gregory IX, and fought a battle against the Ghibellines at Signa in 1239. The latter, helped by the imperial army, won a resounding victory. That same year the order of the Umiliati established a house in the monastery of San Donato a Torri. A mixed order of monks and nuns, who worked as weavers and dyers, the Umiliati created the foundation on which the later textile industry was based (prior to their arrival Florence had lagged behind neighbouring cities in this area) when, with their move to the monastery of Ognissanti, they increased the number of looms and were able to teach more skills.

A winged putto *holding a dolphin, a magnificent bronze sculpture by Verrocchio, formerly part of the small fountain in the first courtyard of the* Palazzo della Signoria. *The original is now preserved in one of the rooms in the* palazzo.

Fra' Pietro da Verona and the Paterines: 1244-45

The fight against heresy evolved alongside the political struggles, not merely because it coincided chronologically with a period of intense rivalry between the papacy and the empire (culminating with the deposition of Frederick II in 1245), but also because the Paterines in Florence, led by two brothers, Pace and Barone, were backed by the Ghibellines. Leading the party of Catholic orthodoxy was the Dominican Fra' Pietro of Verona – better known as St. Peter Martyr, after he was murdered by heretics in northern Italy. Fra' Pietro managed to win over

be built. Meanwhile, worried by the spread of the Paterine heresy, St. Dominic in 1219 had sent a preacher, Giovanni da Salerno, to Florence. This preacher had based himself in the little church of Santa Maria *inter vineas,* outside the city walls, granted him by the cathedral chapter in 1221:

here the great edifice of Santa Maria Novella would later be erected. In the same year, 1221, St. Francis and St. Dominic – the two most famous figures in the religious history of the 13th century – are said to have met in Florence, in the hospice of San Paolo, near the Porta di San Pancrazio.

the people both close to the mother church of his order and in the city center. It was said that in the Piazza San Giovanni he had miraculously saved the crowd listening to him from a crazed black horse supposed to have been sent by the devil. Two religious factions developed: the *Società della Fede* (fellowship of faith) founded by Fra' Pietro, and a group led by the Ghibelline *podestà.* Words gave way to force when, on 24 August 1245, the Paterines attacked the church of Santa Reparata, where their opponents were assembled. The attack was repulsed, and Pace and Barone had to flee to the villa of San Gaggio.

From the Ghibelline victory to the primo popolo: 1247-50

The "defeat" of Santa Reparata did not weaken the Ghibellines, who indeed took on a new lease of life with the appointment as *podestà* of Frederick of Antioch, King of Apulia, the son of Frederick II. Harassed by their adversaries, the Guelfs revolted in 1247 and stormed the houses and towers of the Ghibellines, starting with those of the Uberti. The *podestà* Frederick arrived with his army from Prato, forcing the Guelfs to leave the city. In Tuscany, however, imperial authority waned. In 1250 the Guelfs defeated their enemies at Figline and entered the city once again. The new constitution promulgated on 20 October 1250 ratified a state of affairs that was socially and economically very different from what had prevailed before. The new regime, known as the *primo popolo,* gave a share of power to the wealthy trading classes, organized into corporations. Alongside the *podestà* and his council now was a *capitano del popolo* and council of elders, whose job it was to defend the people, and who were able to mobilize an army drawn from the 20 *gonfaloni* into which the citizenry was divided. The era of the *primo popolo* was recalled nostalgically by both Dante and Giovanni Villani. The latter writes: "the citizens of Florence led sober lives, eating simply, spending little, their clothes and ornaments rough and crude (...) Many went bare-headed (...) and the Florentine women wore plain shoes (...) And one hundred lire was a normal dowry, and two or three hundred lire was thought a grand fortune (...) but they were honest and loyal to each other and to the commune, and for all their unsophisticated life and poverty, they achieved more than we have done and led more virtuous lives than are led in our own times of greater luxury and wealth."

The birth of the gold florin: 1252

At the time of the new constitution promulgated on the return of the Guelfs, the city acquired some splendid new buildings. Built for the *capitano del popolo,* the Bargello was Florence's first public *palazzo;* and a new bridge, the Ponte di Santa Trinita, was added to the Ponte Vecchio, the Ponte alla Carraia (1220), and the Ponte Rubaconte (1237, later called the Ponte delle Grazie). Yet the clearest symbol of Florentine economic power in international markets was the new coin, the gold florin, first minted in 1252. Struck with a lily and an image of St. John the Baptist, the patron saint of the city, the florin was the first gold coin to be minted in large numbers in Western Europe since the Carolingian age. It spread throughout the then known world, wherever the great Florentine banking and trading companies operated, and was accepted everywhere both for its stability in value and for the quality of the metal itself. Villani records that the King of Tunis, who only dealt with Pisa and had never heard of Florence, when shown an example of the new coinage by a Florentine merchant, "...welcomed the Florentines with open arms on account of the florin, provided the citizens with dwellings and churches in Tunis, and honoured them on a par with the Pisans."

New expansion; Ottavio degli Ubaldini: 1253-60

Guelf Florence enlarged its territories, waging war with Siena and Pisa. Occupying Pistoia (1253), then Poggibonsi and Volterra (1254, it went on to defeat Pisa at Ponte sul Serchio in 1256, wrestling land from that powerful maritime republic in exchange for peace. An attempted coup by the Ghibellines, who had unsuccessfully tried to make *podestà* one of their allies, Cardinal Ottaviano degli Ubaldini, ended bloodily with the execution of the chief plotters: Uberto degli Uberti and Mangia degli Infangati. The Ubaldini were deprived of the castle of Montaccianico, which threatened the passage of foodstuffs to Romagna. The powerful Ottaviano, formerly Bishop of Bologna, and owner of extensive property in Mugello, was then the object of a concerted Guelf "smear campaign" – being described as a heretic as well as a shameless epicure. Half a century later Dante would portray him in the *Inferno,* in a tomb together with Frederick II, among those who "With the body make the spirit die."

Montaperti: 1260

Reneging on sealed agreements, Siena had welcomed the exiled Florentine Ghibellines. The "city of St. John" now marched against its bellicose neighbour to teach it a lesson. Laying siege to Siena, the Florentines followed their tradition of catapulting a donkey into the enemy city, as a gesture of contempt. They had underestimated their Ghibelline compatriots, however, in particular the proud Farinata degli Uberti. Appealing to Manfred of Apulia for reinforcements, the Ghibellines had been sent a squad of about 100 men, with the imperial banner. This meager outfit was cunningly exploited and was to prove extremely useful, if only to gather up further reinforcements. After being fortified with generous quantities of wine, the men were sent out against the Florentine forces who greatly outnumbered them and who not surprisingly defeated them and seized the banner. This was a direct insult to Manfred, who immediately sent a much stronger force. The trap now began to close around the Florentines. Siena announced that she would meet Florence openly, and despite warnings from those who suspected a trick, the Florentines mustered an army 70,000 strong, including men from other Guelf cities – Lucca (an allied city), and Pisa, Pistoia, Arezzo, and Volterra (all subject cities). The two armies met in battle on 4 September 1260 at Montaperti: the Sienese supported by the emperor, and the Guelfs politically weakened both by a papal interdict issued as a result of violence inflicted against Florentine clergy, and by treachery from Ghibelline infiltrators within their own army who, at the moment of attack, created confusion amongst the ranks. Dante recounts an imaginary altercation with one of these traitors, Bocca degli Abati, in the terrible circle of hell reserved for traitors. Most of the defeated Guelfs were taken prisoner and taken back to Siena; many others were slaughtered, turning the waters of the little river Arbia, which ran close by the battlefield, red with their blood.

Farinata degli Uberti: 1260

Meeting at Empoli to discuss whether they should destroy Florence, the Ghibelline leaders were persuaded to milder action by Farinata degli Uberti – the only one who, as is recalled by Dante in a memorable passage from the *Inferno,* spoke out boldly in its defense. With the Guelf leaders now in exile, the imperial and Ghibelline victors entered Florence and plundered the shops, houses, towers, and castles of the vanquished. The constitution of the *primo popolo* was abrogated, and power was placed once again in the hands of an imperially appointed *podestà* – Guido Novello (a member of the Guidi family), the Ghibelline leader at Montaperti

Benevento: 1266

Once again, external political developments affected the course of internal Florentine life. The

The Isolotto *(Islet) pond with its figure of the mythical Perseus, in the Boboli Gardens. Magnificent fountains, statues and greenery* *combine to form one of the most beautiful Italian-style gardens.*

12 *Buonomini* (good men), was charged with protecting the interests of the faction. The Ghibellines were exiled to Siena, Pisa and elsewhere and their property sacked. Charles was appointed *podestà* for six years. Seldom in Florence, he governed by means of *vicári* – representatives. The next pope, Gregory X, tried to reconcile the factions by mounting a spectacular ceremony of peacemaking six years after the return of the Guelfs. Held on the shore of the Arno, in the presence of both Charles and the Emperor of Constantinople, the ceremony was backed by a threat of excommunication for anyone who broke the agreement. The papal reconciliation lasted only a few hours, however. That very night the Ghibellines were obliged to flee from Florence and resume a life of exile.

The government of the guilds: 1282

A second grand ceremony of pacification between the two factions was organized in 1279 by Pope Nicholas III, outside the Dominican church. Once again the concrete results were scant – all the more so since the now all-powerful Guelfs had become divided among themselves. Quarrels among the aristocracy, coupled with Charles's difficulties in Sicily allowed the Florentine populace to create a new constitution, which was ratified by Cardinal Latino (whom the pope had despatched to resolve the civil strife). The positions of *podestà* and *capitano di Parte Guelfa,* with their respective advisory bodies, remained as before, but alongside them there now appeared representatives of the guilds, testifying to the henceforth decisive importance of such corporations in the political and economic life of the city. These delegates were known as priori. Three at first, then six, there was one for each administrative district of the city. Guelfs for the most part, who had acquired wealth through trade or banking, the *priori* established a smooth and effective mode of government, constituting as Villani put it, "the wisest and most influential citizens of Florence." Just as the Guelf and Ghibelline parties were gaining official recognition, the common people of Florence came to the fore, through representatives from the greater guilds (the judges and notaries, the cloth refiners, the money changers, the woollen cloth manufacturers, the doctors and druggists, the silk merchants and haberdashers, and the furriers) and the five middle guilds (the *baldrigari,* the butchers, the cobblers, the masons and woodworkers, the blacksmiths). For the present the lower guilds did not supply any representatives (these included the vintners, the innkeepers, the oil merchants, the armourers and sword makers, the saddlers, the bakers, the locksmiths, the leather workers, and the second-hand dealers). Florence now entered a

new pope, Clement IV, a Frenchman by birth and hostile to Manfred, not only warmly welcomed the exiled Guelfs, offering them favours and economic help, but also called on the King of France, Charles of Anjou, to come to Italy and take the Sicilian crown from Manfred. When Dante describes meeting Manfred in the afterlife, he describes his body as disfigured by a wound in the chest, the mortal would received at Benevento (16 February 1266). The Angevin army at this battle had been swelled by the Florentine Guelfs who, having been rejected by Signa and expelled from Lucca (1262), were thirsting for revenge. At Benevento, hundreds of miles from Florence, they finally found their revenge. The Florentine government did not change immediately, though. To begin with, two prelates, Loderingo degli Andalò and Catalano de' Malavolti, were sent by the pope to take charge of the city and pacify the

rival factions. Only when the Ghibellines attempted an armed return did the people force Guido Novello to flee. And although the pope would have preferred peace between the factions to the dominance of one over the other (even if this dominant party were to favour the papacy), a new Guelf government now emerged under the protection of Charles of Anjou.

The Guelf government: 1267

While apparently similar to the *primo popolo* government, the new regime supported by Charles in fact introduced substantial changes, inasmuch as official recognition was accorded to the victorious party (which was unprecedented) with the magistracy of the *capitano di Parte Guelfa.* This official, together with a "cabinet" of period of prosperity, "a happy and good state of rest and calm, a state of peace, profitable to both merchant and craftsman, and of great benefit to the Guelfs who ruled the land" (Villani).

Campaldino: 1289

Pisa was once again defeated by Florence in 1268, and forced to cede Porto Pisano and Motrone. Then in 1269 at Colle Val D'Elsa the Sienese, together with exiled Florentines who were hoping for another Montaperti, were beaten. In 1289 the Florentine army moved against Arezzo – a Ghibelline refuge – and marched towards Casentino, its ranks swelled by Guelfs from all over Tuscany. Leading the army were Neri De' Cerchi and Corso Donati, and among their men was one Dante Alighieri. History mocks the commander of the Aretines, Guglielmo degli Ubertini, as an inept and myopic *condottiero* (he was apparently so short-sighted that he mistook the shield-bearing Guelfs who suddenly appeared in the night for a wall.) The Florentine victory was due to Corso Donati, the captain of the reserve, who without waiting for the order (thus risking his own head) led his cavalry into battle, thereby decisively establishing the outcome of the conflict. Over 1,700 Aretines lost their lives, while 2,000 were captured.

The Ordinances of Justice: 1290

"When the citizens returned to Florence, the people for some years enjoyed great power and influence, but the nobles and leading citizens in their arrogance mistreated the common folk, beating them and committing other such outrages" (Villani). The Ordinances of Justice proposed by Giano della Bella went against the magnates and favoured the upper and middle bourgeoisie as represented by the guilds. Appointed prior, after introducing a law allowing members of the lower guilds to participate in government, Giano in the Ordinances deprived 250 noblemen and their relatives of the right to hold public office the same law curtailed the abuse of power by magnates over their dependents, and created a new government office, that of *gonfaloniere di giustizia,* the holder of which would be backed by a militia of 1,000 men, to ensure that the Ordinances were carried out. Only those nobles who were professionally within the guild system could take part in politics. Any Ghibelline aristocrats who failed to comply with the people and opposed this law suffered severe punishment (the death penalty or confiscation of possessions). The Ordinances came to be applied with excessive rigour, to the anger of both the magnates (who spoke of "Ordinances of Iniquity") and the middle classes. Discontent in the city

The Artichoke Fountain, by Francesco Tadda and Francesco Susini, erected in 1641 for Ferdinand II in the magnificent courtyard by Ammannati in the Palazzo Pitti.

mounted, until a riot erupted and the *podestà*'s residence was attacked. Excommunicated and condemned to death, Giano della Bella just managed to flee to France (1295).

Architectural renewal: 1290-98

The last decade of the 13th century saw a great flurry of building activity in all spheres, religious, private, and public. The streets and bridges were paved. Churches were extended. The Dominican Santa Maria Novella, already under construction, received large grants from the commune (1294); and even the Franciscans, hitherto loath to burden themselves with fine buildings, decided to extend Santa Croce (1295). In 1290 work began on the grain market in the central Orto di San

Michele, as a safeguard against future shortages, while the exterior of the Baptistery of San Giovanni acquired a new ornamental marble "casing." The enlargement and decoration of the cathedral was entrusted to Arnolfo di Cambio, who was responsible for all major building enterprises. Somewhat later, in 1298, the priors also commissioned a new building – the Palazzo dei Priori (later, the Palazzo Vecchio) – on the edge of the area where the now demolished houses of the Uberti had stood. With its asymmetrical proportions dictated by the nature of the site, and its tall tower built up from the tower which formerly belonged to the Della Vacca family, the Palazzo dei Priori was a perfect symbol of Florentine autonomy. In 1284 it had already been decided to expand the city walls, since now as well as the new *borghi*, the churches of both the Franciscans and the Dominicans and many magnates' houses lay unenclosed. The first section of wall to be completed was that bringing the church of the Santissima Annunziata into the city; then in 1299, the Ognissanti area was walled round.

Whites and Blacks: 1296-1300

Efforts by the magnates to destroy the new constitution were fiercely countered, but fresh discord began to emerge between certain family groups – reminiscent in some ways of the earlier Guelf-Ghibelline antagonism. The neo-Guelfs, led by Corso Donati and supported by the Pope, were called Blacks, while the neo-Ghibellines, led by Vieri de' Cerchi and including Dante and Villani, were called Whites. The trouble started in 1296. Feelings had risen to such a pitch that the *stilnovista* poet Guido Cavalcanti, who had sided with the Cerchi, tried to assassinate Corso Donati. The situation came to a head in 1300, the year of the great Jubilee proclaimed by Pope Boniface VIII, when during the course of the May Day festivities the Cerchi and the Donati clashed in one of the city squares. Nobody was seriously injured, although Ricoverino de' Cerchi had his nose cut off in the skirmish, but to avoid further bloodshed the leaders of the two factions were exiled.

Dante in exile: 1302

Boniface VIII openly supported the Blacks. He sent the French prince Charles de Valois, the champion of international Guelfism, to Florence. Charles was not popular with the Florentines, who felt their autonomy might be threatened, the Whites being temporarily in the ascendant in the city. Corso Donati also returned. Accused of conspiracy, the Whites had heavy fines imposed on them. Dante Alighieri was among those fined, though he was out of the city at the time. He had sat on the *Consiglio del capitano del popolo* in 1295, the *Consiglio dei cento* in 1296, and the *Consiglio del podestà* in 1297; finally in 1300 he had been a prior, and as such one of the strongest opponents of the interference of Boniface and Charles in Florentine affairs. Charged on political grounds, but also for administrative misconduct and embezzlement, the poet did not return to Florence. On 10 March 1302 the fine was changed to the death penalty. Cut off from the other exiles and disillusioned with their inefficiency, Dante now embarked on his hard period of exile in northern Italy. As the guest first of Bartolomeo della Scala in Verona, then of Gherardo da Camino in Treviso, and of the Malaspina in Lunigiana, he wrote his greatest works: the *Divina Commedia,* the *Convivio,* and the *De Vulgari Eloquentia*. After supporting Henry VII's activities in Italy, he then stayed with Cangrande della Scala in Verona, and eventually went to Ravenna, to Guido Novello da Polenta, for whom he acted as ambassador. He died in 1321 without ever having returned to his native city.

Donateschi and Tosinghi: 1304-08

One group of exiled Whites had assembled in the Mugello, at the castle of the Ubaldini. Other Whites who had remained in the city fled to the Chianti region after a terrible fire that destroyed much of the city center, only to be captured and brought back. A further group led by Vieri de' Cerchi was expelled after an attempted coup. The capture of the Ubaldini stronghold of Montacianico, and then the taking of Pistoia in 1306, were a sort of scorched earth policy against the Whites. The walls of Pistoia were destroyed and the surrounding land was divided between Lucca and Florence. Meanwhile, however, the Blacks had split into two rival groups themselves – the Donateschi and the Tosinghi. The latter, under Rosso della Tosa, succeeded in expelling their opponents from the city. Corso Donati was captured as he fled towards Rovezzano, and killed.

Henry VII: 1310-13

The surviving Whites, based in Siena, Arezzo, and other cities of Tuscany, repeatedly begged the Hapsburg emperor Albert to march into Italy and restore imperial authority. Their pleas were heard by Henry's successor, Henry VII, who entered Italy in 1310. Florence sent no representatives to Lausanne when the other Italian cities sent ambassadors to pay homage to the emperor, instead receiving as her ally Robert of Anjou, King of Apulia and Sicily. Avoiding Florence (which he intended to make "our chamber, and the best in our empire") for the time being, Henry proceeded to Rome to receive the imperial crown, and only started back north in 1312, determined to conquer once and for all the Guelf cities whose armies had mustered at Florence. On discovering their defenses, however, he did not dare attack; after travelling around Tuscany, as far as Pisa, he then decided to head south once again, to attack the Kingdom of Naples. The enterprise ended at Buonconvento near Siena, where Henry died on 24 August 1313, dashing the hopes of the Florentine exiles.

The dangerous Castruccio Castracani: 1325-28

Under Robert of Anjou for eight years, Florence embarked on a war with the newly revived Ghibelline cities of Tuscany. The war against Pisa (the Pisan commander being Uguccione della Faggiola) ended in the disastrous defeat of Montecatini, where some 2,000 Florentines lost their lives (1315). Ten years later an even more dangerous adversary appeared in the shape of the new lord of Lucca, Castruccio Castracani, "a brave and noble tyrant," according to Villani, "wise and shrewd, active and conscientious, a fine soldier and well prepared for war." In 1325, having occupied Pistoia and defeated the Florentines at Altopascio, Castruccio went on to plunder the countryside as far as Careggi and Rifredi, coming dangerously close to Florence. Robert of Anjou's son, Charles of Calabria, under whose protection the city had placed itself for ten years in 1324, was slow in coming to their aid, and the Florentines lay within their city walls, "cowering stunned with fear." When he did finally arrive he proved unequal to the situation, being more interested in revelry at his hosts' expense. The city was saved only by the deaths of Castruccio, after a return from Rome, on 3 September 1328, and of Charles on 9 December of the same year. Of the two, their ally, the Duke of Calabria, had perhaps been the greater threat: his 19-month stay had cost the city a good 300,000 florins.

The flood: 1333

The years following Castruccio's death were among the happiest in Florence's history. At the height of its industrial and commercial power, and governed by an elite of merchants, bankers, and industrialists with Guelf sympathies, the city reached a population of almost 100,000, excluding the 80,000 in the surrounding countryside. Florence took Pistoia (1331), Cortona (1332), Arezzo (1337, and Colle Val d'Elsa (1338), and expanded into the Mugello and, in the opposite direction, beyond the Appennines, into the Po Valley, founding the castle of Fiorenzuola (1332). The Florentines lived luxuriously: sumptuary laws were passed to curtail the extravagance of women's fashions. Monks and preachers condemned such elegant living, and warned of divine retribution. Many saw the flooding of the Arno in 1333 as just such a punishment. After several days of rain, "as though the cataracts of the heavens had opened" (Villani), the river overflowed, first at Ripoli and San Salvi, then in the city center, destroying the four bridges connecting it to the Oltrarno.

The foundations of Giotto's campanile: 1334

On 12 April 1334 Giotto was put in charge of the building work on Santa Reparata, and appointed architect in charge of the city walls and fortifications. On 18 July the foundations were laid of the famous campanile which now bears his name (although it was not actually built entirely according to his design). He personally supervised the work on the lower part, up to the first relief sculptures (executed in Andrea Pisano's workshop), some of which are thought to be based on models of his own design. Though his greatest picture cycles are not in Florence – notably the celebrated works in Assisi and Padua – Giotto did spend many years in Florence being admitted in 1327 to the guild of doctors and druggists. During the 1330s he frescoed the Peruzzi and Bardi family chapels in Santa Croce, with the *Lives of St. John the Baptist* and *St. Francis* respectively. In these works his style – at once both monumental and naturalistic – shows full maturity. With dramatic economy of conception, and magnificent spatial effects, these works give expression to the worldly, secular, rational ideals of the Florentine upper middle class.

Rise and fall of the Duke of Athens: 1342-43

Having in 1336 allied herself with Venice and Milan against the Scala dynasty, Florence was plunged into a long war to gain possession of Lucca. Finally taking Lucca in 1341, the Florentines were then forced by the Pisans to abandon it. On 10 September 1342 Walter of Brienne, Duke of Athens, was proclaimed governor and installed in the Palazzo della Signoria. A friend of the King of Naples, he could have averted the bankruptcy of the major Florentine bankers, whose capital had been depleted by the war with Lucca, by ensuring that the Neapolitans did not withdraw their capital. A clever and very cunning man, he was disliked in Florence, where he had his coat of arms displayed everywhere, where he introduced burdensome taxes, dispensed arbitrary sentences, and supported the lower guilds to the detriment of the greater guilds. One year after his appointment there was a revolt. "Every citizen was armed," Villani wrote. "All were out, either mounted or on foot, and went to their *contrado* or neighbourhood, bringing out the flags of the locality, and the people, as ordered, shouted 'Death to the duke and his men, long live the people, the commune, and liberty!'" Political prisoners were freed, the duke's collaborators killed (one was actually eaten alive by the enraged mob), and an emergency government deposed Walter.

The abortive coup of the magnates: 1343

Assisting in the expulsion of the Duke of Athens were the magnates, who were still excluded from public posts of government. The Bardi, Frescobaldi, Strozzi, Donati, Pazzi, and Adimari now determined to continue the struggle to abolish the Ordinances of Justice. There thus emerged a government in which the magnates were also included, albeit in a minority (which did not however necessarily imply less political muscle). The common people rebelled, besieging the Palazzo dei Priori and destroying the houses of the Bardi. The Ordinances came back into force, and there was a reshuffle of government positions, the magnates being excluded and representatives of the lower guilds included. The upheavals of that year were thus summarized by Villani: "Before the arrival of the Duke of Athens the *popolo grasso* (i.e. the members of the greater guilds) held the reins of power; their bad government led to the tyranny of the duke's regime, which sparked off a reaction from both great and small ... Now it is the government of the artisans and common people."

The great crash of the Bardi and the Peruzzi: 1346

Since 1270 Florentine banking companies had done business with the English court, particularly for trading purposes: much of the wool woven in Florence was imported from England. These banking institutions lent sums of money to the English crown which were only repaid much later. In 1335 the Bardi, the Peruzzi and the other great banking houses were obliged to lend a vast amount of money to Edward III to finance him in the war against Philip VI of France – had they refused, they would have lost all their previous loans. The war went against Edward, who found himself unable to pay his debts (1,365,000 florins according to Villani's calculations – or, as he put it, the value of an entire kingdom). All the banks' customers then withdrew their capital, and the companies could not meet their commitments. The consequent bankruptcies precipitated an economic crisis for the whole city, since its wealth depended on the commercial and banking activities of just a handful of houses. Here Villani is a valuable source of information (he too found himself in debt, and was imprisoned): he talks of the "ravening she-wolf, avarice," which had led the Bardi and the Peruzzi, without guarantees, to lend capital which was not theirs but belonged to "a number of citizens and foreigners." He adds that the crash jeopardized the security of the entire city, for "with the bankruptcy of the said two companies, which were two bastions, so strong in their time that they controlled the traffic of much of the trade of Christendom, and so to speak fed all and sundry, every other business became suspect and discredited ..."

The Black Death: 1348

The bankruptcies were followed by particularly bad harvests (1346), while the following year the crops were damaged by an exceptionally severe hailstorm. In the summer of 1348 a terrible epidemic of bubonic plague killed roughly half of the population of Florence. This was the worst natural disaster ever to have struck the city, and was not to be parallelled even by the two later epidemics of 1363 and 1374. Nobody was spared in 1348: those who escaped the disease themselves all had family and friends to mourn. In fact, as Boccaccio writes in the *Decameron,* few people now mourned the dead, since all felt they could themselves be struck down at any moment. Corpses were buried in their hundreds in vast graves, stored, as Boccaccio tells us, like merchandise in the holds of ships, layer after layer, covered by a sprinkling of earth. The epidemic had unexpected consequences, both spiritual and material. Many people became obssessively religious, while others threw themselves into a life of pleasure – as Matteo Villani records, "giving themselves up to obscene and riotous living such as they had never indulged in before ..." Some citizens, including some members of the middle classes, found themselves very wealthy, having come into several legacies at once. A great influx of immigrants brought thousands of new workers and craftsmen to the city, who had little experience of the traditional ways. Immediately after the plague the population was 25,000-30,000 but by 1351 it had grown to 45,000, then by 1375 to 60,000, and by 1380 to 70,000. Among the casualties of 1348 was Giovanni Villani.

The War of the Eight Saints: 1375-78

The years following the plague saw various attempts by the *Parte Guelfa* to defend the *popolo grasso* at the expense of the plebeian *popolo minuto*. Outside the city, after a war with Milan (concluding with the Peace of Sarzana in 1353), and a longer war with Pisa which had been threatening Florentine trade (a conflict won by Florence in 1364), a more menacing danger now loomed with the War of the Eight Saints, in which Florence confronted the papacy. Provoked by an anti-Guelf faction, the war was opposed by the Guelfs, since the interdict put on the city by Gregory XI was damaging to Florentine trade throughout Europe. Leading the war was a group of eight citizens popularly known as the Eight Saints, who displayed considerable astuteness. They bribed the mercenary John Hawkwood (Giovanni Acuto), whom the pope had sent against Florence, to join them, fomented anti-papal revolts in the other Tuscan towns; and confiscated the possessions of the church in Florence. Gregory despatched St. Catherine of Siena as a peace envoy, who, despite alienating the *popolo grasso* and the *Parte Guelfa,* succeeded in opening negotiations for the peace which was finally signed at Tivoli in 1378.

The Ciompi Revolution: 1378

The economic difficulties arising from the war, the loss of political power among the Guelf upper bourgeoisie, and the discontent of the workers belonging to the various guilds, who had no rights of union or political representation, all contributed to the great explosion of 1378. The Ciompi – those who worked in the textile industry – had already organized protests at their wretched standard of living (1345, 1368). In 1378, thanks to the support of the *gonfaloniere di giustizia* Salvestro de' Medici, an opponent of the great Guelf families, there evolved a huge political movement. On 19 July they burned down the Palazzo dell'Arte della Lana, the headquarters of the wool guild, and hanged the *Bargello* (chief of police). Breaking into the Palazzo dei Priori, they established a new government with Michele di Lando, the movement's leader, as the new *gonfaloniere*. This government included three new guilds (doublet makers, dyers, and cloth workers, known as Ciompi), thus giving the higher and lower guilds equal representation. The higher guilds rallied against the Ciompi and closed down the workshops; the lower guilds, taking fright at the situation, joined the higher guilds. On 31 August the men of the corporations defeated the Ciompi in the Piazza della Signoria, and dissolved both their government and the guild which they had founded barely six weeks before.

The oligarchy: 1382

Between 1378 and 1382, after the failure of the Ciompi, the minor guilds and the two new ones which had risen with the Ciompi retained considerable influence. At the same time, however, there were on the one hand sporadic attempts by the cloth workers to regain power, and on the other efforts by the aristocratic families excluded from government to topple the regime of the corporations. The magnates succeeded in 1382, when a committee of 82 passed a new constitution, very different from that which had preceded it. The magnates were now allowed to hold political posts, while the greater guilds gained absolute control of the *Signoria* – inasmuch as the *gonfaloniere* had always to be chosen from among their number, and the priors were divided equally between the higher and lower guilds. The Guelf upper bourgeoisie had now gained a decisive advantage, through dominant families such as the Albizzi, the Peruzzi, the Capponi, the Soderini, the Rucellai, and the Strozzi.

The war with Milan: 1389-1402

The regime of the oligarchy was further bolstered by the threat of the Milanese Giangaleazzo Visconti, who in the last 20 years of the 14th century extended his hegemony beyond the inherited frontiers of his dominions, into the Veneto, Piedmont, Emilia, and Tuscany. Pisa, Siena, and Perugia gave themselves over to him. Florence, hemmed in and in a clear position of weakness, offered resistance by sending the troops of John Hawkwood (who was to die in 1394) to fight Visconti in Lombardy and the Veneto, and by seeking allies in Rome and Naples. At the head of the Florentine situation at this time was Maso degli Albizzi, along with one Nicolò da Uzzano, who acted as advisor, soldier, and diplomat all in one. In 1398 the Florentines were beaten at Casalecchio, leaving the city an easy prey to the enemy. As on other such occasions, though, the situation was altered by an unexpected external factor, namely an outbreak of plague, which ravaged first the city of Florence, then spread to the area around Milan, claiming Giangaleazzo Visconti as one of its victims (3 September 1402). His death put an end to the dream of creating a single huge state out of northern and central Italy.

The capture of Pisa: 1405-06

The Visconti territory was divided between three heirs. Gabriele Maria Visconti, who received Pisa, sold it to the Florentines, as if it were a chattel, for 200,000 gold florins in 1405. However, the Pisans did not intend to remain the property of their detested neighbours. The Florentine army, led by Maso degli Albizzi and Gino Capponi, laid siege to Pisa, hoping to starve the city into submission. The siege developed into an orgy of cruelty on both sides; "useless" mouths to be fed – the elderly, women and children – were driven out of the city, to be caught and killed by the Florentines (in an attempt to demoralize the enemy). Finally on 9 October 1406 the Pisans surrendered, and the Florentines entered the city, thus realizing a dream which was at least 200 years old – the liberation of the mouth of the Arno and the resultant setting up of an independent maritime trade outlet.

War with Naples; the papacy in Florence: 1409-19

The church was in a state of schism, with two mutally hostile popes, Gregory XII and Benedict XIII; further confusion was now created when a council held in Pisa in 1409 elected a third pope, Alexander V. Approving of Alexander, the Florentines allied themselves with him against Ladislaus, King of Naples, who had attempted to follow Charles and Robert of Anjou in interfering in the politics of Central Italy. They entered Rome, and in 1411 seized Cortona. But then Ladislaus mounted a counterattack in Tuscany. Yet again, Florence was saved only by the death of her foe (1414). That same year the Council of Constance deposed the three popes and elected Martin V. Unable to take possession of the Papal States, occupied by local barons and lesser lords, the pope settled in Florence, at Santa Maria Novella – to the great profit of the Florentine banking houses (especially the Medici), who entered into highly lucrative negotiations with him. While taking full advantage of these economic possibilities, the Florentines nevertheless had little respect for a pope who could not control his own state.

Filippo Brunelleschi and the cathedral cupola: 1420

The *Arte della Lana* had been in charge of the construction of the cathedral since 1331; the nave had been finished in 1380, after which preparations for the cupola started. On 19 August 1418 a competition for a design for the dome was announced: the entries chosen were those of Filippo Brunelleschi and Lorenzo Ghiberti. After a further competition they were both appointed, along with Battista d'Antonio, to supervise the building of the cupola. From 1423 Brunelleschi was sole designer and supervisor of the great cupola. First and foremost was the sheer complexity of the engineering problem: how to cover a circular area over 40 meters (130 feet) in diameter – the largest space ever to be covered in this way until then – with a structure that would be self-supporting at every stage of its construction. The result was a two-layered cupola: one inner, smaller in diameter, the other outer, "more magnificent and full-blown" in the architect's own words, on an octagonal base, with eight white ribs projecting from the red brick surface to set off the curvature and volume of the structure. In 1436 Brunelleschi then designed the crowning lantern: set at the summit of the cupola, where the ribs meet, this was built between 1446 (the year of Brunelleschi's death and 1471. The difference between Brunelleschi's vast "cup" and the gothic *tiburium* beneath it is emblematic of the cultural break with the previous century brought about by, among others, Brunelleschi, Masaccio, Donatello, Fra Angelico, and Paolo Uccello.

The acquisition of Leghorn; The dominance of silk production: 1420

The port of Pisa having become silted up, it was no longer a real maritime base for the Florentines. Only with the purchase of Leghorn from Genoa, for 100,000 gold florins in 1421, was Florence able to establish real sea trade links without having to hire Genoese, Venetian, or Neapolitan vessels. The office of Sea Consul was introduced in 1421, and the following year the first Florentine ship sailed for Egypt. This access to the sea, resulting in the greater availability of the raw materials required for the silk industry, hastened the decline of the wool trade (20,000 articles produced in 1420, compared with 60,000-80,000 in 1336). Introduced to Florence in 1314 by refugees from Lucca, silk weaving had developed very rapidly in the workshops around Por Santa Maria. The secrets of the trade were handed down from father to son, and silk workers were forbidden to emigrate, so that the technical innovations developed in Florence should not be revealed abroad and unwanted competition instigated.

War and the crisis of the oligarchy: 1424-33

The long war which Florence fought in alliance with Venice against Milan brought no territorial gain. In 1425 the Florentines were defeated at Anghiari; a long siege of Lucca, defended by Milanese forces under Francesco Sforza and Nicolò Piccinino, proved fruitless (1430). The Florentines had even tried to flood Lucca, following a bold plan devised by Brunelleschi, to divert the river Serchio; the plan failed however, and the result had been the flooding of their own camp. The Peace of Ferrara in 1433 was hard for the Florentines to swallow. The fighting, together with a long wrangle over fiscal matters, had split Florence into two factions – the oligarchic party of the Albizzi, and the "popular" party of the Medici. Given the concentration of power in the hands of just a few men, and the de facto disintegration of the republican political system, the outcome of this conflict would entail nothing less than political supremacy for the winners. Giovanni de' Medici had won popular sympathy in 1426 by opposing the plan of Maso degli Albizzi's son Rinaldo to suppress the 14 lower guilds, which still had some political muscle. On 3 October 1433 a henchman of Rinaldo's, the gonfaloniere Bernardo Guadagni, succeeded in banishing Giovanni de' Medici's son Cosimo from the city for ten years.

The return of Cosimo de' Medici: 1434

Cosimo was given a princely welcome in both Padua and Venice. A move to ruin him financially was thwarted by his transfer of his bank to Venice. This not only testified to remarkable financial soundness, but also precipitated a serious economic depression in Florence. Pope Eugenius IV, who like his predecessor was installed at Santa Maria Novella, foiled the attempt by Rinaldo degli Albizzi to prevent the

commune summoning Cosimo back to Florence. Rinaldo was banished for eight years. The triumphant Cosimo re-entered Florence on 6 October 1434. "Rarely was any citizen, returning triumphant from victory, received by his country in such great crowds and with so great a show of good will as he received on his return from exile, hailed by all as benefactor of the people and father of his homeland" (Machiavelli). Though maintaining the façade of a republic, Cosimo was now in reality lord of Florence. He banished his enemies (including the wealthy and cultivated Palla Strozzi, who had had no part in the intrigues of the Albizzi) and appointed his friends to government positions, himself wielding power behind the scenes. Imposing heavy taxes on the other magnates, he made substantial profits by granting them loans through his bank.

The Council of Florence; the Battle of Anghiari: 1439-40

At first Cosimo maintained Florence's traditional alliances – with Venice and the papacy – against Milan. He arranged for the council which had opened in Ferrara in 1438, to discuss the reunification of the Western and Eastern Churches to be moved to Florence – a clever political tactic, if one considers the money the Florentine merchants would have made through trade with the East, had the Council been successful in its aims, and the personal fortune Cosimo himself might have made as banker to the pope. In 1439 Pope Eugenius IV, Patriarch Joseph of Constantinople, the highly cultured Cardinal Bessarione the Byzantine Emperor John VII Palaeologus arrived in Florence, all agreeing on the points of controversy between the Western and Eastern Churches, including the existence of Purgatory and the primacy of the see of Rome. The fall of the Byzantine Empire (1453) then nullified the political results that had been achieved, but the contacts established with Greek culture were of untold importance for the humanist culture of both Florence and the whole of Italy. Meanwhile the war with Milan had resumed, provoked by Cosimo's enemies, led by Rinaldo degli Albizzi, who urged the Duke of Milan to conquer Florence. Ill advised by the political exiles, the Duke of Milan hoped the Florentines would revolt against Cosimo; this did not happen, and when the Lombard army led by Piccinino neared the city, the gates remained shut. The conclusive battle of this stage of the war, fought at Anghiari on 29 June 1440, resulted in a resounding victory for Florence. It was a curious battle, fought by mercenaries whose concern for their own lives overrode their desire for victory; Machiavelli records that after 24 hours of combat "only one man had died, and not from wounds or any other heroic enterprise, but from falling from his horse

and being trampled to death." Tuscany was saved, and the Florentines now also acquired the Casentino from the Guidi di Poppi, allies of the Milanese.

The reversal of alliances and the Peace of Lodi: 1454

The death of Filippo Maria Visconti, Duke of Milan (1447), shook the political equilibrium of the entire peninsula. The greatest threat to Florence now came from Venice rather than Milan. Taking Bergamo and Brescia, and absorbing Ravenna, Venice set her sights on Milan as well. At the same time Florence's success in sea trade and the silk business made her a direct rival of the Most Serene Republic. Cosimo thus opposed Venice, whilst welcoming the mercenary condottiero Francesco Sforza as ruler of Milan. The fall of Constantinople to the Turks dealt Venetian interests in the Levant a severe blow, leading to the end of war and the Peace of Lodi (1454), which recognized the legitimacy of Francesco Sforza in Milan. The new Milan-Florence axis was the decisive element in a political balance of the peninsula which, with some sporadic interruptions, was to remain basically the same for more than 40 years.

The open vote: 1458

The cost of the wars prior to the Peace of Lodi had been borne by the great families of Florence, who now found themselves impoverished, and forced to sell their properties to pay the crippling taxes imposed on them – Cosimo's friends buying the said properties at derisory prices. The Serragli, Baroncelli, Mancini, Vespucci, and Gianni were all ruined. Opposition reared its head once more with demands for political reforms, freedom of speech in the councils, and administrative parity. Cosimo's response to criticism and to the plots hatched against him (such as that devised by Piero Ricci) was to call a popular assembly dominated by his own supporters, who approved the creation of an emergency council holding extraordinary powers. This body exiled all opponents and introduced the open vote in the councils, in order to unmask the anti-Medicean "rebels" within the government hierarchy.

The turbulent accession of Piero de' Medici: 1464-68

On 1 August 1464, "greatly ravaged by age and gout" as Lorenzo the Magnificent later wrote in his Ricordi, Cosimo died in the Medici villa of Careggi. The Signoria acclaimed him as pater patriae. He was succeeded by his son Piero, known as il Gottoso (the Gouty) a weak and sickly man, neither very able nor very experienced in government. Opposing him was the Poggio party, under Luca Pitti, which included among its members Agnolo Acciaiuoli and Nicolò Soderini (an attempted revival of the houses dispossessed by Cosimo). In the summer of 1466 the Poggio marched on Florence, supported by Ercole d'Este of Ferrara. With the aid of his son Lorenzo and the Milanese, Piero the Gouty defeated them; he then displayed magnanimity towards his enemies, some of whom (including Luca Pitti) he pardoned and restored to citizenship. The exiles turned for help to Venice, which under Bartolomeo Colleoni opened hostilities with Florence. The Battle of Imola (1468) ended inconclusively, but put a stop to the war – thanks to which Florence had gained the fortresses of Sarzana and Sarzanello, both of great strategic value.

The rise of Lorenzo the Magnificent: 1469-70

On the death of Piero the Gouty (1469), Lorenzo writes: "though I, Lorenzo, was very young, twenty-one years of age, the leading men of the city and the state came to our house to mourn and to comfort me, asking me to take care of the city and the state as my grandfather and father had, and … I unwillingly accepted." An attempted anti-Medicean revolt led by Diotisalvi Neroni was

Bust of Gian Gastone, the last Grand Duke of Tuscany of the Medici family.

nipped in the bud at Prato, and the rebels were hanged. Trained for the political leadership of the state, and a keen observer of the events and cultural developments of his time, Lorenzo like his predecessors retained the formal structures of a republic, while in fact ruling Florence as its lord – on a par with the Sforza in Milan, the d'Este in Ferrara, and the Gonzaga in Mantua.

The Pazzi conspiracy: 1478

Despite their slightly unfortunate name (*pazzo* in Italian means mad), the Pazzi had considerable support from Rome, from Pope Sixtus IV, who had entrusted the papal treasury to their bank (this had previously been administered by the Medici bank). The pope's aim was to install Cardinal Gerolamo Riario in Florence. The conspiracy planned by Jacopo and Francesco de' Pazzi, Bernardo Bandini, and Giovan Battista Montesecco was part of a wider political scheme involving the proposed murder of Piero de' Medici's two sons, Lorenzo and Giuliano. A convenient opportunity presented itself in the shape of a solemn mass to be held in the cathedral on 26 April, at which both brothers would be present. The assassins struck at the very moment of the elevation of the host. Giuliano died, riddled with stab wounds but, because of the inexperience of his attackers, Lorenzo was only slightly wounded, and was able to defend himself and flee from the cathedral. Francesco Salviati, Bishop of Pisa, an accomplice of the Pazzi, had meanwhile taken possession of the Palazzo dei Priori, while the conspirators' supporters swarmed through the city. Lorenzo wrote in his own hand requesting help from the Sforza ("My brother Giuliano has been killed and I am in extreme danger; so now, my lord, the time has come for you to help your servant Lorenzo…"), and was soon able to return – partly because of the refusal of the Florentine people to accept the Pazzi. The conspirators were all hanged from the windows of the Palazzo dei Priori. Bandini delayed his execution by fleeing to Constantinople, only to be arrested by the sultan and sent back to Florence, where he was duly executed, a year and a half after the others. The Pazzi possessions were confiscated. So intense was the hatred felt for Jacopo de' Pazzi that his body was disinterred, carried around the streets of Florence, thrown into the Arno, fished out, hanged anew, and thrown into the river once more to be carried away by the current.

Balancing the scales of Italian politics: 1478-92

An important factor in the myth that grew up around Lorenzo de' Medici was his proven ability

to resolve the never-ending squabbles between the various states of Italy by diplomatic – and usually peaceful – means. After the failure of the conspiracy, the pope adopted a new tack in his attempt to topple Lorenzo: a declaration of war, in alliance with Ferdinand of Aragon, King of Naples, leading to the battles of Trasimeno and Poggibonsi. Florence allied herself with Milan and Venice. A hazardous diplomatic mission in Naples undertaken by Lorenzo himself, with the collaboration of the Aragonese banker, the Florentine Filippo Strozzi, successfully brought about peace. Between 1482 and 1484, during the War of Ferrara (in which Venice attacked the d'Este state), Lorenzo then joined in an alliance with Milan and Naples, forcing the Venetians to agree to the Peace of Bagnolo. Subsequently the Milan-Florence axis foiled an attempt by Pope Innocent VIII to dethrone Ferdinand I of Aragon and create a state for his own relatives, the Cybo. Meanwhile all important matters of internal policy were dealt with personally by Lorenzo, who modified the republican statutes to his advantage by a reform reducing the number of magistrates, so that they could all be selected from among his supporters. The zenith of the family's glory coincided with that of the city, as Lorenzo observed in one of his most lucid political documents: the letter-cum-testament given to his son Giovanni, on the latter's departure for Rome as a cardinal in 1492. On 8 April 1493, plagued by the traditional family disease, gout, Lorenzo died in the Medici villa of Careggi.

Piero de' Medici, Savonarola, Charles VIII: 1492-94

Lorenzo's son Piero broke the "system" of government evolved by his forebears, whereby they contrived to be *primi inter pares* in an officially republican city – forming ties with the great Florentine families through public appointments, skilful matrimonial tactics, and the granting of privileges. In his internal politics, Piero tried to over-centralize power, thus alienating even those aristocrats – such as Bernardo Rucellai or Paolo Antonio Soderini – who had supported his father. The situation was further complicated by Savonarola, the prior of San Marco, who had arrived in Florence in 1489 and preached religious and political reform, finding a ready audience among the middle and lower classes. Piero then made the mistake of opposing the French when, summoned by Ludovico il Moro, Duke of Milan, Charles VIII of France entered Italy in September 1494 to conquer the Kingdom of Naples. Arriving at the borders of Florentine territory, Charles seized Sarzana. Piero was forced to enter into negotiations, ceding Sarzanello, Motrone, and Ripafrutta. He was accused of treachery. A popular revolt made him flee the city, and the Medici palace in Via Larga was sacked. Towards the end of 1494 the magistracies created by Lorenzo were replaced by a new republican constitution.

"... and we shall ring our bells": 1494

Pisa surrendered to Charles, thus freeing itself from the Florentine yoke. "Small of build, ugly of countenance with big shoulders and an aquiline nose," as an eyewitness described him, Charles marched back up the Arno and made a triumphal entry into Florence, where he lodged in the Medici palace on the Via Larga. The thousands of people who made up his retinue established themselves in private houses about the city. Their hosts were not overjoyed to receive them. There was mutual mistrust between the Florentines and the French, while the Florentines secretly gathered their weapons. Charles offered to leave, on condition that he should receive 150,000 gold florins, retain possession of Pisa, and keep men in the Florentine fortresses. The proud Florentine ambassador Pier Capponi rejected these demands with the famous challenge that if Charles sounded his war trumpets, the bells of Florence would call the citizens to arms. Conditions changed. The king set off south, towards the defeat of his expedition.

Girolamo Savonarola: 1494-96

A Dominican born in Ferrara in 1452, Savonarola was the moving spirit and instigator of the first stage of Florence's revival as a republic. His exhortations to *renovatio* combined medieval prophecy with the humanist myth of the golden age. Although he found listeners among the upper classes and intellectuals (indeed he had originally been recommended to Lorenzo the Magnificent by the celebrated Neoplatonic philosopher Pico della Mirandola), his followers came mostly from the lower classes, among whom religious fervour and loyalty to the tradition of the republican commune were strong. For Savonarola the common people were the heroes of a renewal that had to come from below, from the "people of God" of Florence, the "city of God." The new republican constitution was inspired by his political ideals, modelled on those of the Venetian doge and council. A *Maggior Consiglio* (Great Council) of over 1,000 men would elect the magistrates from among the citizens, some 80 of whom would then form the *Minor Consiglio* (Lesser Council): both councils would have to approve the resolutions of the *Signoria*. Started in 1495, a new chamber was built in the Palazzo dei Priori for the Great Council (later called the Salone dei Cinquecento – Hall of the Five

The ceiling of the Mars Room in the Palazzo Pitti, frescoed by Pietro da Cortona and Ciro Ferrari (1645-47). The central element is the Medici coat of arms. Mars is portrayed kindling the flame of battle.

Hundred). On 20 August 1496, after an opening speech by Savonarola, the first solemn session was held. The city was swept by a wave of puritanism, with the *piagnoni* (whimperers), Savonarola's followers in the forefront. Feasting, sporting, and luxury were now replaced by christian "virtue," liturgies, and the "burning of vanities," i.e. the public incineration of sinful objects.

Savonarola's death; Pier Soderini appointed gonfaloniere for life: 1496-1502

Those who opposed Savonarola were not united among themselves. They included the secular clergy, the religious orders, the supporters of the Medici (the *bigi*, greys), and above all the so-called *arrabbiati* (angry ones). This latter group comprised the aristocracy who had led the 1494 revolt; they were against both the tyranny of the Medici and the democracy envisaged by Savonarola and represented by the Great Council, and had been hard hit by the expenses incurred by the King of France and the war for repossession of Pisa. They had also suffered financially from the clash with Rome. The anti-French league, including Milan and the papacy, was against Florence and Savonarola. Accusations of heresy were raised against the Dominican by the Franciscans close to Pope Alexander VI. He was summoned to Rome to answer these charges, but did not go. Opposition to him grew, fuelled by the serious food shortage and plague of the summer of 1496. Finally in 1498 the opposition movement succeeded. San Marco was besieged, and the friar was arrested, along with his supporters Fra' Domenico Buonvicini and Silvestro Maruffi. A highly irregular trial ensued, involving trumped up evidence and confessions extracted under torture, and the accused were duly hanged and then burned in the Piazza della Signoria on 25 May 1498. The death of Savonarola did not solve Florence's problems, though. The war for repossession of Pisa had now dragged on for two years, the Pisans putting up a dogged resistance; in 1499 the commander of the Florentine forces was executed for his Medicean sympathies. Pisa was to be retaken only in 1509. Once again the need was felt for a strengthening of executive powers. The new constitution introduced the post of *gonfaloniere* for life (1502), and appointed Pier Soderini to the office. Soderini's support of the popular classes provoked a renewal of opposition from the *ottimati* (the upper classes and aristocracy), who lent their support to the Medici.

The anti-Medici plot and the exile of Machiavelli: 1513

The election of Giovanni de' Medici as pope (Leo X) in 1513, and the commissioning of Giuliano as *gonfaloniere della Chiesa* (prince defender of the Church) in Rome, left Florence in the control of Lorenzo de' Medici, under the aegis of Giulio (now bishop of the city). A plot hatched against the Medici by two Florentine aristocrats, Pietro Boscoli and Agostino Cappeni (both supporters of Savonarola, and inspired by the tyrannicides of ancient Rome) was easily uncovered and quashed, with the execution of its leaders (22 Feburary 1513). Among the victims of the subsequent stringent protective measures taken by the Medici was Niccolò Machiavelli, the famous political theorist, historian, and playwright, who was exiled to the villa of the Albergaccio, near San Casciano in Val di Pesa. From 1498 to 1512 he had been secretary of the second *cancelleria* of the republic, conducting important state business, being sent abroad as ambassador on several occasions, and meeting the foremost figures of the day: from the King of France to Emperor Maximilian. During his exile at Albergaccio his life consisted of the humble business of everyday existence and long hours of study, in which he "divested himself of his court finery," writing his most famous works, *The Prince* (1513-14), the *Discourses* (1513-21), and *The Art of War* (1519-20). Submitting the main forms of ancient and modern government (republic, oligarchy, and principality) to strict critical analysis, singing the praises of the ancients, and presenting the ideal of an active, astute prince able to create a strongly centralized state in Italy, Machiavelli bequeathed to posterity the basic notion that politics are

divorced from ethics, and showed how the practical application of religious and humanitarian ideals are instrumental in the wielding of power.

Lorenzo and Giulio de' Medici: 1516-19

A sudden reversal of the political situation – the reconquest of Milan by the French under François I (Battle of Marignano, 1515) – once again wrought changes in Italy. Leo X went to Bologna to meet the king. Lorenzo de' Medici, with the pope's approval, marched on Francesco Maria della Rovere, Duke of Urbino, whom he defeated easily in 1516. However, the young Lorenzo was clearly aiming to make himself Duke of Florence also, and this presumption alarmed the Florentines, and jeopardized the sympathy which the Medici had regained among the aristocracy. Lorenzo's premature death, and the takeover of power by his uncle Cardinal Giulio restored the Medici position in the city. Ensuring that his nephew's death did not lead to revolt, Giulio re-established correct legal procedure in the election of members of the magistracies. His wise government of the city won him the approbation of even the most fervent republicans.

A new anti-Medici plot: 1522

On the death of Leo X (1521) the political situation changed yet again. The French had been driven out of Milan, and the hegemony of the young Spanish Hapsburg Charles V was growing (the vast Spanish kingdom, stretching from Europe to America, was already said to be one on which the sun never set). Florence experienced an unusual period of tranquillity with Giulio de' Medici ably applying the "system" devised by Cosimo the Elder – namely, the maintenance of formal republican structures with a discreet autocracy. He was obliged, however, to end a long political debate on liberal reforms when a plot was hatched among the Orti Oricellari circle, in which the memory of Savonarola and the traditional humanism of the commune still lived on. For the conspirators – Jacopo da Diaccete, Luigi Alamanni, Zanobi Buondelmonti, and Antonio Brucioli – the plot ended in flight and death (1522).

The results of the sack of Rome: 1523-27

The "reign" of Giulio de' Medici continued even after his elevation to the papal see (as Clement VII) in 1523. His proxy in Florence was the unpopular, uncouth Cardinal Passerini, and two young illegitimate Medici – Ippolito and Alessandro. Though a good administrator of Florence, Clement VII was an inept pope, uncertain

whether to ally himself with France or Spain, and switching from one to the other because "he himself did not know where to turn" (Francesco Guicciardini). When he joined the French alliance of Cognac (1526), an army of lansquenets in the imperial service took and sacked Rome (against the wishes of Charles V) in 1527. This had great repercussions in Florence. Already before the sack of Rome the populace had occupied the Palazzo della Signoria during the so-called Friday Riot on 26 April 1527. After this the opposition to Passerini (orchestrated by Pier Capponi, Francesco Vettori, and Filippo Strozzi) hardened. On 17 May the cardinal and Alessandro and Ippolito de' Medici had to concede defeat and leave the city.

Leonardo and Michelangelo; the "Battles": 1503-06

Under Soderini a project of enormous artistic importance was launched: the decoration of the new council chamber of the Palazzo della Signoria, with scenes depicting Florentine military victories. Though unfinished (until completed by Giorgio Vasari half a century later), the two greatest artists in Florence in the first five years of the 16th century worked on it: Leonardo da Vinci, who had returned from 20 years' service with the Sforza in Milan, now at the height of his powers and working for Florence as both an architect and a military engineer; and Michelangelo, who though younger was also introducing revolutionary new ideas to art, having already to his credit works such as the statue of *David* (commissioned by the *Arte della Lana* for Piazza della Signoria). The cartoon for *The Battle of Anghiari*, which Soderini commissioned from Leonardo in April 1503, was drawn during the course of 1504, with work on the final fresco starting in June 1505. Because of the technique employed the paint would not hold on the wall, and in June 1506 Leonardo abandoned the job and returned to Milan. Meanwhile in August 1504, in competition with Leonardo, Michelangelo had been commissioned to produce a cartoon for *The Battle of Cascina* (a Florentine victory over the Pisans in 1364). Interrupting the project in 1505 for a visit to Rome, Michelangelo resumed work in the spring and summer of 1506. Yet his fresco too was destined never to appear on the walls of the Palazzo Vecchio. In 1508 Michelangelo was to begin his decoration of the Sistine chapel in Rome. These two battle scenes were radically different in character: Leonardo's work was a kind of dense vortex of men and horses, with a powerful exploration of the relationship between physical movement and the movements of the mind and will which they express; Michelangelo's work on the other hand was an "anthology" of sculptural figures in an endless variety of poses, an affirmation of supreme mastery of an artistic medium. Studied and copied by younger painters whilst on show in Florence, the two cartoons were seminal models for the Renaissance and baroque "modernism" of the 16th century.

The return of the Medici: 1512

The main reasons for the fall of Soderini's republic were the opposition of the *ottimati,* and above all his pro-French foreign policy. A council of French cardinals at Pisa (1511) ended in failure, and a massive alliance – the Holy League – was formed against Louis XII of France. Led by the vigorous Pope Julius II Della Rovere, and embracing Switzerland, Spain, and Venice, this alliance was later joined by Henry VIII of England. Florence had refused to join or to allow the Medici back into the city, so a combined Neapolitan and Spanish army under Raimondo di Cardona surrounded the Florentine plain in the summer of 1512 and on 29 August pushed through to Prato, massacring the population. Soderini abdicated and fled from Florence. On 1 September the Medici troops entered the city and occupied the Palazzo della Signoria. The Medici returned *en masse* – Cardinal Giovanni (the son of Lorenzo the Magnificent), his brother Giuliano (who was to become Duke of Nevers), with his son Giulio, and Piero's son Lorenzo (later the Duke of Urbino). The life *gonfalonierato* was abolished, Soderini was banished, the *Maggior Consiglio* and the *Minor Consiglio* or *Consiglio degli Ottanta* (Council of Eighty) were removed, and the advocates of republicanism dismissed. Legislative and executive power was now concentrated in the hands of a body of 65 men, drawn from the great aristocratic families of Florence.

The Last Republic: 1527

A republican government was set up, led at first by Nicolò Capponi, who was elected *gonfaloniere.* He hoped to be able to form an aristocratic republic, but opposition presented itself from the Medici faction on the one hand and from the democrats on the other. In his foreign policy Capponi endeavoured to mediate between France and the emperor, but the democratic opposition (who soon came into the ascendant) forced him into an alliance with France just at the point when François I, his armies ravaged by plague, was leaving Italy. The introduction of taxes on church property and the removal of Medici insignia from houses and churches further aggravated the tension with the papacy. Accused

of having secret dealings with the papacy, Capponi was forced to resign in favour of Francesco Carducci of the democratic faction. That same year, 1529, the pope signed the Treaty of Barcelona with Charles V. This promised imperial help in reconquering Florence. Meanwhile, by the Treaty of Cambrai, François I deserted his Italian allies. Florence found herself alone. Her government was distinctly anti-aristocratic, the nobles were classed as rebels, and the fiercest opponents of the Medici pope took command of the armed forces.

The siege of Florence: 1529-30

In the summer of 1529 the imperial troops under Philibert de Chalon marched on Florence, and began to besiege the city in October. The aristocratic faction (the Guicciardini, Pazzi, Acciaiuoli, Rucellai) had left the city. Preparations for defense included the levelling down of the towers (already begun in 1526) to remove potential targets for cannon fire, and the flattening of the land around the walls to make it impossible for the enemy to hide. As in Savonarola's day, a civic militia was set up alongside the mercenary army, and the defense of the republic acquired quasi-religious overtones. Two preachers, Fra' Benedetto da Foiano and Fra' Zaccaria da Treviso, urged moral reform, at the same time calling for a commitment to manning the walls. Michelangelo, one of the elected *Nove della Milizia,* was put in charge of the fortifications, and busied himself in particular with an emplacement at San Miniato. The fighting, together with hunger and plague killed off tens of thousands, but the city refused to yield, seeing itself as the last bastion of the republican communal tradition. For the carnival of 1530 a football match was organized in the Piazza Santa Croce, to deceive the enemy about the state of morale and the efficiency of the defense. The vital element in the latter, however, was the action of Francesco Ferrucci, who controlled Empoli and Volterra, and who managed to get food supplies into the city. And it was his defeat at Gavinana (3 August 1530) that brought about the final collapse of the city: wounded and taken prisoner, Ferrucci was executed by the imperial commander in person (as a result the surname of this commander, Fabrizio Maramaldo, entered the Italian language as a term of abuse). The Florentine commander, Malatesta Baglioni, who was initially accused of treachery, was then recalled to negotiate an honourable surrender with the new imperial general, Ferrante Gonzaga. A sack of the city was averted, the lives of the defenders were spared, and the city retained its independence. Florence formally capitulated on 12 August 1530.

Alessandro de' Medici, Duke of the republic: 1532-37

The foremost figures of the republic (including the painter Bartolommeo Carducci) were imprisoned and then executed; many were exiled and either attempted a subsequent show of force or, after some years and by agreement with Cosimo de' Medici, returned (among the latter, Benedetto Varchi, Piero Vettori, Silvestro Aldobrandini, Nardi, and Michelangelo). The city placed itself under the emperor. The aristocrats returned from banishment and filled the posts in the magistracies (banishment and war having ruined them financially, destroying their agricultural and commercial businesses, they were willing to comply with the wishes of the Medici). The population had been halved by war, starvation, and plague. With 120,000 inhabitants in 1529, the city was now reduced to 60,000; food was still short, and prices rose. At first a republican government was instituted, controlled by emissaries of Clement VII, and only in 1532, under the advice of the leading members of the aristocracy, who were overwhelmingly in favour of creating a principality, did Clement introduce a constitutional change. The *Signoria* and *Gonfalonierato* were abolished; the councils of the *Duecento* and the *Quarantotto* were born; and the executive consisted of four councillors elected by the *Quarantotto* to assist Alessandro de' Medici – who had returned as duke in 1531. Alessandro's power was ostensibly checked by the councils, but in practice he ruled the city, and the councils played only a consultative role. For the first time in its history Florence minted a coin (designed by Benvenuto Cellini) struck with the head of a sovereign (Alessando de' Medici). Alessandro's policies tended to benefit the lower classes, however, at the expense of the aristocracy (with the exception of those close to him, including the famous Francesco Guicciardini). This, together with certain tyrannical measures – a personal guard, and arbitrary justice – provoked intense hostility among the upper classes.

The activities of the exiles; the assassination of Alessandro de' Medici: 1537

The internal opposition of the aristocracy led by Filippo Strozzi joined forces with the republican exiles. The accusations of tyranny were such that emperor Charles V, who was in Naples, was eventually forced to open public proceedings to investigate the charges. Guicciardini defended the duke. Charles finally came down in favour of Alessandro (1535), but the exiles were to be allowed to return and to recover their confiscated possessions. With this imperial backing, and with the added alliance of marriage to the emperor's daughter, Margaret of Austria, Alessandro was now unassailable. Assassination was the only course open to his opponents. The tyrannicide was in the event a younger member of the Medici family, and an advisor of the duke, Lorenzino de' Medici. Alessandro often stayed with Lorenzino, who procured mistresses for him. And it was there, as he waited in bed for one of these mistresses, that he was stabbed to death by Lorenzino and a hired assassin called Scoroncolo (6 January 1537). Fleeing to Venice, the murderer was hailed by the exiles as another David or Brutus – the Biblical and historical comparisons emphasizing the religious and literary impulses of the murder, which followed in the tradition of the plots of 1513 and 1522.

Cosimo, Duke of Florence; the defeat of the exiles: 1537-39

Alessandro's death put the autonomy of the city in danger, for it was now controlled by imperial troops and threatened from outside by the republican exiles. Secretly, for fear of uprisings, the duke's corpse was carried to the cemetery of San Lorenzo wrapped in a carpet, and hurriedly buried there. The *Consiglio dei Quarantotto* offered power to the young Cosimo de' Medici, son of Giovanni dalle Bande Nere, and a descendant of a brother of Cosimo the Elder. The condition, however, was that he should be head of the government rather than duke of the city. Cosimo handled the situation well, given that he lacked both the imperial investiture and the support of the pope, the Farnese Paul III (who would have preferred his own candidate, Pier Luigi Farnese). The exiles meanwhile prepared for war. Cosimo was able to delay their action – or at least, their alliance with the powerful banker Filippo Strozzi – up until the moment when he was refused imperial recognition and the support of Spanish troops. He then met them in battle at Montemurlo and defeated them (1 August 1537). The exile leaders (Valori and Albizzi) were executed. Strozzi, imprisoned in the fortress of San Giovanni, committed suicide the following year, leaving a famous document declaring how he wished to imitate the action of Cato Uticensis. Cosimo's position was consolidated. He received the title of duke from the pope, then later also from the emperor (1543). On 29 June 1539, now undisputed ruler of the city, he married Eleanora of Toledo, daughter of the Viceroy of Naples, in a magnificent ceremony at San Lorenzo.

Absolutism affirmed: 1540-50

Cosimo created an absolutist state of Florence for the first time. Though he retained the 1532 constitution, he took more and more of the power of the *consigli* to himself; he then appointed *auditori* ("listeners") as intermediaries between himself and the *consigli,* with a common bond of "secret knowledge." His assistants were not picked from among the aristocracy or his own family, but were chosen for their intelligence and political flair regardless of social class. Similarly, in dealing with the various lesser towns of the state he did not base his authority on support from individual internal factions – indeed he resolved disputes and insisted on reconciliation. At the same time these lesser cities were developed on a par with the capital, and not economically handicapped. In 1540 he moved his residence to the Palazzo della Signoria, indicating symbolically that he was now the supreme authority in the state (over the next few years Giorgio Vasari decorated the Salone dei Cinquecento, the apartments of Eleanora of Toledo, Leo X, and the *Elementi* with a succession of landscapes). In 1549 Eleanora bought the Palazzo Pitti in the Oltrarno, and built it up into one of the most sumptuous courts in Europe (work on the exquisite Boboli gardens began that same year). In 1543, desperate to fill the coffers of his vast empire, Charles V gave Cosimo, in exchange for 200,000 gold *scudi,* Pisa, Leghorn, and the fortress of San Giovanni in Florence (from which the imperial garrison was withdrawn). With the murder of the tyrannicide Lorenzino de' Medici in Venice in 1548, by assassins hired by Cosimo, the danger of conspiracy by the exiles was averted.

The fall of Siena: 1554-55

While having to be on his guard where France was concerned (the Florentine exiles found a warm welcome on French territory), Cosimo also had to tread carefully in his relations with the emperor, whose representatives were apprehensive about a strong independent state (albeit an ally) in Central Italy. Spain did not take kindly to the thought of the Florentines seizing Siena, the only Tuscan town still independent from Cosimo. However, since Siena had allied herself with the French, she had become an open enemy of the emperor and it was on the strength of this that Cosimo, with the agreement of his allies, marched on the city. While negotiations were still under way, an army secretly left Florence on 26 January 1554. Taking three different routes, it occupied the fortresses held by the Sienese and ravaged Grossetano and the Val di Chiana. Help from France was delayed, and the Sienese were defeated at Scannagallo. The Florentine general was Marignano, and this battle was the only major one fought by the army of Cosimo de' Medici. Siena, besieged and on the verge of starvation, continued to resist; even the women helped defend the walls. Meanwhile all who tried to take food into the city from outside were hanged. On 17 April 1555 Siena surrendered. The exiles fled to Montalcino, which for a few years – until their eventual defeat in 1559 – they ran as a tiny Sienese state. Charles V's son, Philip II, having succeeded to the Spanish throne, Cosimo finally received the feudal investiture of Siena in 1557, even though the city nominally belonged to Spain.

Ducal splendour; social and economic change: 1560

The death of Henry II of France and the election of a Medici pope (Pius IV) granted Cosimo a degree of security such as he had not previously enjoyed. In 1558 he had acquired Castiglione della Pescaia and the Isola del Giglio from the Piccolomini; and the following year saw the eradication of the last pocket of Sienese resistance (Montalcino). The year 1560 was a year of good fortune for Cosimo: his son Giovanni was made a cardinal, and his daughter Lucrezia married the Duke of Ferrara, Alfonso II d'Este. Work started on the Uffizi, under the direction of Vasari. In October 1560 Cosimo was given a triumphal welcome in Siena (his first visit), and in November he went to Rome, where for two months he was regally entertained by the pope, the cardinals, and the Roman aristocracy. During these same years the Florentine economy underwent a change. The wool industry continued to decline, while the silk business expanded, strengthened by the duke's protectionist policies. These policies were not enough to support an industrial state, however. There was thus an ever greater tendency, which had already begun to be noticeable in the 15th century, to divert capital that had once gone into trade and industry into financial ventures and farming. Trade and industry began to be looked down on as not suitable for the nobility. Such attitudes were reinforced by the creation of a court – so alien in concept to the bourgeois ideals that had led to the flowering of the Florentine economy. The Tuscan nobility had a craving for titles and coats of arms. Cosimo created the Order of St. Stephen, the members of which, in exchange for their title, protected the coast from pirates. As the historian Rudolf von Albertini has observed, there thus occurred "a transformation of the Renaissance city-state, based on bourgeois institutions, into a territorial principality, based on fiefs and a court aristocracy."

Misfortune and the hand over of power: 1561-64

If 1560 had been a year of triumphs, the following years were a bitter period in which some of the closest members of Cosimo's family died. The first to die was his 17-year-old daughter Lucrezia, the wife of the Duke of Ferrara. Then between November and December 1562 two sons (including Cardinal Giovanni) died, while his third son, Ferdinando, only just recovered from a serious illness. Finally his greatly beloved wife Eleanora also died. Two years later, weary and disillusioned, Cosimo made his son Francesco regent. This was not an actual abdication, in that Cosimo retained the ducal titles, but rather an interim handing over period, prior to his son's formal accession.

Joan of Austria; Cosimo, Grand Duke of Tuscany: 1565-70

One of the greatest diplomatic triumphs of Cosimo's principality was the marriage of his son Francesco to Joan of Austria, Emperor Ferdinand's daughter. Though she was not particularly beautiful, her lineage brought considerable prestige to the small Italian duchy. Immediately prior to her arrival Florence was a hive of building activity. The courtyard of the Palazzo della Signoria acquired stuccoes, a new fountain crowned by a delightful putto by Verrocchio, and frescoes of the main cities of the empire, in homage to Joan. The Palazzo Vecchio and the Palazzo Pitti were connected by a corridor designed by Vasari, running through the Uffizi, across the Ponte Vecchio, and along the present Via Guicciardini. Celebratory arches, statues, and columns were set up to form a triumphal entry into the city for her. The bride and groom met at Innsbruck in October 1565; and on 16 December, having been met by Cosimo at Poggio a Caiano, Joan of Austria entered Florence, through the Porta al Prato. The wedding celebrations lasted several months, after the ceremony itself in the Duomo on 18 December. Recently built, beside the Palazzo della Signoria, was the splendid *Fountain of Neptune* by Bartolomeo Ammannati: this was a reference to Florentine naval strength, which Cosimo had taken great pains to build up, with the fortifying of the port of Leghorn. Cosimo's career reached its zenith when in 1569 Pope Pius V offered him the title of Grand Duke – a highly significant title, raising him above all the other princes of Italy. He received this title officially at a solemn ceremony in St. Peter's in Rome on 8 March 1570.

Francesco I de' Medici, Grand Duke of Tuscany: 1574-87

On Cosimo's death (21 April 1574) Francesco assumed the title of Grand Duke – which to all intents and purposes he had already been for some years. A cultured man, and a lover of both the natural and the occult sciences, in particular alchemy, as well as a collector of antiquities, Francesco had received the title of Grand Duke also from the Emperor Maximilian II (doubtless because of his marriage to Joan of Austria in 1576). His first wife died in childbirth in 1578, and he then married a Venetian noblewoman of great beauty, Bianca Cappello, who had already been his mistress for some time. Ardently interested in culture, and enjoying the company of intellectuals (the historian Pietro Vettori and the geographer Ignazio Danti), Francesco was less than enthusiastic about the machinations of politics. While Cosimo had striven to enhance the prestige and independence of the Florentine state, Francesco was more inclined to obey Spain: there thus emerged a political subservience to the Iberian monarchy that was to characterize Florence for the next century and a half.

From the Medici dynasty to the first Grand Dukes of Lorraine: 1587-90

The history of Florence in the 17th and 18th centuries was the same as that of the Tuscan state. Under the Medici grand dukes – Ferdinando I (1587-1609), Cosimo II (d. 1620), Ferdinando II (d. 1670), Cosimo III (do. 1723), and Gian Gastone (d. 1737) – all traces of the former communal regime were dispersed. Along with the other parts of Italy under Spanish dominion, Tuscany, under its landed aristocracy placed ever greater importance on agriculture, to the detriment of trade and the manufacturing industries. The population of the capital increased only very slowly – from 59,000 in 1551 to 72,000 in 1701. Passing into the Grand Duchy of Lorraine, under Francis II (1737-65) and, most particularly under Peter Leopold (1765-90), within the Austrian orbit of power, Tuscany experienced widespread economic, political, and administrative reforms. These were put into effect with the collaboration of Florentines inspired by the Enlightenment ideas of the Accademia dei Georgofili (founded in 1753). Tuscany was the first European state to abolish the guild restrictions, and the first to adopt a penal code (based on the ideas of Cesare Beccaria) which included abolition of the death penalty (1786). The customs taxes that hampered internal trade were removed (1783), and in 1774 the independence of individual cities from the capital was established. An effort to create a class of small landowners was made by distributing portions of land owned by the Grand Duke or the Order of St. Stephen; land was also gained by reclamation. Ecclesiastical privileges and immunities were reduced. Not all these reforms had the intended results. For instance, the abolition of the guilds, which was necessary for the evolution of modern industry, initially brought about a serious crisis among artisans; the land reclamation, especially at Maremma, was limited, and the redistribution of land ultimately favoured the nobility and upper bourgeoisie – the farmers having to accept harsh contracts involving payment of rent in kind. This was the system that prevailed in the Tuscan countryside up to the 20th century.

Illustrious Florentine families

Acciaiuoli

Near the Lungarno which still bears their name, the Acciaiuoli (a Brescia family who arrived around 1160 in Florence) owned *palazzi*, houses, and towers. Metal workers at first, they subsequently acquired their wealth through the wool trade and banking, and were involved in the bankruptcy of the Bardi and Peruzzi. Nicolò di Acciaiuolo Acciaiuoli (1310-65), a senior official at the Neapolitan court, built the Certosa (charterhouse) of Galluzzo; Agnolo became Archbishop of Florence (1342). The Florentine branch of the family died out with Filippo, Bishop of Ancona, who died in 1766.

Adimari

A very old line, originally founded by an Adimaro who was one of Charlemagne's knights. Guelfs, the Adimari were active in the rivalries of the different factions, with varying fortunes. They lived in the San Giovanni quarter, where they also built churches. A prior of this family called for the exiled poet Dante's house to be confiscated, only to be rebuffed by the venom of the poet's tongue: "The o'erweening brood,/That plays the dragon after him that flees,/But unto such that turn and show the tooth,/Ay, or the purse, is gentle as a lamb ..." (*Paradiso*, XVI, 113-116) – bullying towards the weak and docile to the powerful.

Agli

Guelfs, garlic merchants, excluded from government by the *Ordinances* of Giano della Bella, but active in Florentine politics during the 15th century. The line ended with Antonio di Francesco degli Agli in 1652.

Alberti

An extremely powerful family, originally from Lombardy, who resided throughout Tuscany. They owned houses, a *palazzo*, loggia, and tower near the old Porta dei Buoi (where a Canto is still named after them). This Florentine branch of the family, from Catenaia, produced no fewer than 50 *priori* and 9 *gonfalonieri di giustizia* (leaders of the *Signoria*) between 1289 and 1528. Another scion of this branch was the famous Renaissance architect and writer Leon Battista Alberti – born

in Genoa in 1406, son of an exiled member of the family. The line finally ended with another Leon Battista in 1836.

Albizzi

In Florence from the 13th century, the Albizzi settled in the Borgo di Por San Pietro (now Borgo Albizzi). Lords of the castle of Nipozzano, they were bitter enemies of the Medici. They produced 13 *gonfalonieri* and 98 *priori*, starting with Compagno degli Albizzi (*priore* in 1282) and Filippo di Lando degli Albizzi (*gonfaloniere* in 1317). Rinaldo degli Albizzi, who exiled Cosimo de' Medici (1433), was exiled in turn by his enemy the following year. With the death of Vittorio at the beginning of the 19th century the family died out.

Aldobrandini

Successful merchants, possibly descended from the Lombard king Ildebrando. They gave the republic six *gonfalonieri* and 28 *priori*. In 1592 Ippolito Aldobrandini became Pope Clement VIII.

Alepri

Said to be descended from Catiline. Bearers of many titles of chivalry presented by Charlemagne and the Emperor Conrad. Ghibellines, they soon disappeared from Florentine public life.

Alfani

Owned property in the present Via degli Alfani and produced two *gonfalonieri* and six *priori* between 1291 and 1360. The line ended with Pier Forese di Giovanni Alfani in 1694.

Allegri

This family produced four *priori* between 1348 and 1529. Domenico di Antonio Allegri (exiled from Florence in 1434) was said to be the grandfather of the painter Antonio Allegri, better known by his pseudonym derived from his place of birth: Correggio.

Altoviti

The founder of this family from the upper Arno valley was Altovita di Longobardo (11th-12th century). Ghibellines, the Altoviti produced members of the commune government in the 13th century.

Amidei

An ancient family owning towers in the city and castles in the countryside. As leading Ghibellines they were banished from Florence after the battle of Benevento, and were never able to return.

Anselmi

Guelf merchants, descended from Anselmo Fighineldi, who was knighted by Charlemagne. Between 1283 and 1433 they produced two

gonfalonieri and 28 *priori*. Hated by the Medici, they went into exile in France. The last of the family, Angelo Domenico, died in Sesto Fiorentino in 1732.

Antellesi

Lords of L'Antella, a village close to Florence, from which they took their name. They boasted both politicians (15 *gonfalonieri* and 42 *priori*) and religious leaders, including Beato Manetto, one of the "seven saints" who founded the Order of the Servites of Mary. The line died out in 1698.

Antinori

The founder of his lineage was Antinoro di Rinuccino. Originating perhaps from Lucca, they settled first in the Oltrarno quarter, then moved to a magnificent *palazzo* in Piazza Antinori. Able silk merchants and bankers, they also played a part in the government of the commune (three *gonfalonieri* and 23 *priori*). Giovan Francesco di Raffaello, known as *il Morticino* (the dead child) degli Antinori, led the armed citizenry during the siege of 1529-30.

Bagnesi

A Guelf family from Bagni di Montici. It died out in 1635, with *senatore* Giuliano Bagnesi.

Baldovinetti

Guelf family descended, with Baldovinetto, from a branch of the Guidi di Poppi. They gave the republic five *gonfalonieri* and 34 *priori*. Another member of the family was the celebrated painter Alessio Baldovinetti (1425-99).

Barbadori

Guelf family which produced two *gonfalonieri* and 18 *priori*. The family had a turbulent history: Donato Barbadori, ambassador to Avignon during the War of the Eight Saints, was beheaded in Padua, while one of his descendants suffered a similar fate as a result of his enmity with Cosimo the Elder. On the death of Alessandro di Giovan Donato the family inheritance passed to Maffeo Barberini (Pope Urban VIII).

Bardi

Arriving in Florence in the 11th century, from the castle of Ruballa, near L'Antella, they settled in the Oltrarno. By the 13th century their banking business extended from the Kingdom of Naples to England. Indeed it was as a result of the insolvency of Edward III of England that the spectacular bankruptcy of the Bardi (along with the Peruzzi, the Acciaiuoli, the Antellesi, and the Castellani) occurred.

Belfredelli

Guelfs. 11 times *priori* from 1322. Famous especially for two very different characters: Lambertone, who killed a rival from the Vescovo family in a feud, and Pietro (born c. 1340), a Jesuit, whom the people acclaimed as a saint.

Bentaccordi
Originally from Fiesole, they settled in the Oltrarno then in the present Via Bentaccordi. Deo di Bentaccorda was the first of 15 *priori* from this family. The line became extinct in the 16th century.

Boni
Immensely wealthy silk merchants from Gubbio, who produced 12 *priori*. The family died out in the 18th century.

Boscoli
A Ghibelline family with political power (*priori* and ambassadors) only in the 15th century. Ruined by the failure of the anti-Medici plot organized by the young Pietro Paolo Boscoli in 1513. Pietro Paolo was executed, and shortly afterwards the line died out. Their old tower has survived, incorporated into the Palazzo del Bargello.

Buondelmonti
Buondelmonte Buondelmonti was a central figure at the start of the long Guelf-Ghibelline feud. Guelfs from Montebuoni (hence their anagrammatic name), they shared in the ups and downs of their faction, producing a number of political figures between the 14th and the 16th century. The scholarly Giuseppe Maria was a member of the Accademia della Crusca in the 18th century, shortly before the family died out.

Canacci
Descended from Lapo di Dino, known as Canaccio, this family originated from Santo Stefano ad Usignano. Though it produced many politicians, it is remembered chiefly for the Bartolomeo Canacci who in 1638 killed and dismembered his stepmother, following a rather shady love affair. The line ended in 1777 with Giovan Cosimo Canacci.

Cerchi
Wealthy merchants from Acone in the Sieve valley, who lived in the *sesto* of San Pier Maggiore. Their *nouveau riche* vulgarity drew savage criticism from Dante and Giovanni Villani ("uncouth and ungrateful men, typical of those who have only recently acquired great position and power"). Leaders of the White Guelfs with Vieri de' Cerchi, they disappeared from the political scene after the defeat of their party until the time of the *granducato*. We then find Vieri (b. 1588) and Alessandro (d. 1708) among the scholars and *consoli* of the Florentine Academy. The family died out in the 19th century.

Cerretani
This powerful family came to Florence from Castello di Carreto near Monte Morello in the 12th century. They supplied the republic with both *gonfalonieri* and *priori*. The line became extinct in 1737.

Compiobbesi
Ghibellines, they vanished from politics after the defeat of their faction, and died out in the 15th century. In 1308 their tower was incorporated into the Palazzo dell'Arte della Lana.

Corsi
Originally furnace makers from Fiesole, the Corsi came to Florence very early on. They became rich and produced nine *gonfalonieri di giustizia* and 28 *priori*. The first performance of *Dafne* (with a libretto by Ottavio Rinuccini) was given in 1591 in the *palazzo* of Jacopo Corsi – a philanthropist known as "the father of the poor."

Corsini
This powerful family, a branch descended from the Counts of Gangalandi, settled in the Oltrarno (13th century) and was prominent in Florentine politics from 1290 to 1530. The family also included some notable religious figures: Andrea di Nicolò (1304-73), Bishop of Fiesole, later declared a saint, and Amerigo di Filippo Corsini, first Archbishop of Florence in 1420. During the pontificate of Lorenzo Corsini (Clement XII), starting in 1730, many grandiloquent titles were conferred upon the family.

Da Filicaia
A powerful family from the castle of Filicaia at Pontassieve, which produced 12 *gonfalonieri* and 60 *priori*. Vincenzo (1642-1707) was a poet as well as a politician, and belonged to the Accademia della Crusca.

Davanzati
Merchants descended from Davanzato Bostichi. Bernardo di Antonfrancesco Davanzati (1529-1606) was a historian, famous for his translations of Tacitus. Carlo di Giuseppe, the last of the Davanzati, committed suicide in 1838.

Della Bella
Already in the 12th century one Riniero Della Bella achieved the position of *console*, but the family is noted particularly for Giano, who issued the Ordinances of Justice. The line died out in the 16th century.

Della Vacca
Ghibellines who joined the Uberti and the Foraboschi in a separate faction. The Palazzo della Signoria was built on the site of their property, the new tower rising above the old.

Donati
A proud family of ancient lineage. Having achieved titles of nobility in the crusades, they never deigned to join a guild. Corso Donati, leader of the Black Guelfs, was killed in a riot in 1308; while a relative of his, Gemma Donati, was the wife of his political opponent, Dante (who exchanged sonnets with his brother, Forese). The line ended with Giovanni di Piero in 1616.

Federighi
Having become wealthy through trade, this family moved to Florence from the castle of Sovigliana at the end of the 13th century. It died out on the death of Mattia Federighi in 1838. Prominent in politics (nine *gonfalonieri* and 35 *priori* between 1346 and 1528), the Federighi also produced Benozzo, Bishop of Fiesole (d. 1450), whose tomb, by Luca della Robbia, is in Santa Trinita.

Fifanti
An ancient Ghibelline family descended from Fante (*figli di Fante*, the children of Fante, was contracted to *fi' Fanti*), banished from the city in 1265, never to return. Some of their names were rather unfortunate: Bieco (sinister) and Truffa (fraud), to name but two.

Filipetri
Guelf merchants descended from one Pietro (*filii Petri*). The family died out with Franesco Filipetri in 1671. Talano Filipetri was a leader of the Guelfs.

Foraboschi
Descended from the Ormanni, notable already by 1165, this family formed a faction with the Uberti and the Della Vacca. Razzante Foraboschi was *podestà* of Bologna and *priore* of Florence in 1321, thus consolidating the family's position in public life.

Foresi
One of the Foresi towers still stands in Via Porta Rossa. Rinuccino di Forese entered the *Consiglio comunale* in 1197. Guelfs, they produced five *gonfalonieri* and 18 *priori*.

Gherardini
Descendants of the Adimari. Many members of this family lost their lives in the great Florentine wars: at Montaperti, at Campaldino, and in Florence itself in 1529-30. They spread throughout Europe – to France and England, and even to Cracow. Baccio Gherardini, Bishop of Fiesole (1614-20) was a disciple of Galileo.

Gianfigliazzi
The founder of this dynasty, Giovanni son of (*figlio di*) Azzo, achieved prominence in 1201. Allies of the Guelfs, they gave the city ten

gonfalonieri and 30 priori, also fulfilling functions during the time of the granducato. The line ended in 1764.

Ginori
Came to Florence from the castle of Galenzano in Val Marina, and made their fortune as notaries, also participating in the political life of the commune. It is said that Bartolomeo Ginori, a soldier of Herculean build, was a model for Giambologna's *Rape of the Sabine Women*. Carlo founded the famous porcelain factory at the Villa di Doccia near Sesto Fiorentino in 1735.

Girolami
Merchants prominent in Florentine politics between 1296 and 1529, producing ambassadors, prelates, and soldiers, as well as gonfalonieri and priori. St. Zanobi, Bishop of Florence in the fourth century, was said to be a member of this ancient family.

Gondi
Although principally remembered for the great palazzo commissioned from Giuliano da Sangallo in 1488, this was an ancient family dating back to the Carolingian period, and already in the 13th century one Gondo di Ricovero was prominent in government. Giuliano Gondi, known as *il Magnifico* (the Magnificent), was advisor to the King of Naples.

Iudi
Arrived in Florence with Barbarossa; they then became Ghibellines, and later White Guelfs. Owing to persecution by their political opponents they changed their name to Nozzi. The line died out in the 16th century.

Lamberti
Hailed as one of the greatest noble families of Florence as far back as the 12th century. Their palazzo in the Piazza San Biagio became the headquarters of the Guelf capitani after the Ghibelline defeat. The family was at the source of Florence's internecine strife: Mosca Lamberti precipitated the murder of Buondelmonte Buondelmonti (1215) which split the city into the two rival Guelf and Ghibelline factions.

Lanfredini
An old feudal family which achieved prominence in 1160. Active in the commune government, they became allies of the Medici. The family died out on the death of Cardinal Leopoldo Lanfredini in 1741.

Macci
This very wealthy Ghibelline family owned towers and a loggia in Via Calzaiuoli and Orsanmichele. They fell from power after the defeat of

their party, but survived in modest circumstances until the 17th century.

Magalotti
Descended from Magalotto di Bonaccorso, this family gave the commune three gonfalonieri di giustizia and 34 priori. The most eminent member of the family was Lorenzo (1637-1712), a scholar and councillor of state under Cosimo III, and secretary of the Accademia del Cimento.

Mannelli
Soldiers and politicians, some Guelfs and some Ghibellines. Initially against Cosimo I de' Medici, then in the following century courtiers of the Medicean grand dukes. Their family tower survives still at the Oltrarno end of the Ponte Vecchio.

Marignolli
Guelf family. The last member of the line, Curzio, was court poet to Maria de' Medici (Marie de Médicis), and lived and died in Paris (1606).

Marsili
Guelf family (one gonfaloniere and 15 priori) with houses and towers in Via Toscanella and Borgo San Jacopo. Luigi, an Augustinian monk, in the 14th century was at the center of one of the earliest humanist groups. With the death of another Luigi in 1650 the line came to an end.

Martelli
Arrived from Val di Sieve in the 13th century. Martello Ghetti, a sword maker, made a fortune, and his son Ugolino started a big silk business. From the 14th century on they played an important public role, with seven gonfalonieri and 40 priori.

Monaldi
Ghibellines, originally from Orvieto, mentioned by Dante. Bonfigliolo Monaldi (d. 1261), a hermit, was one of the founders of the Servites of Mary, and was canonized. Piero di Giovanni, the last Monaldi (d. 1629), wrote a history of Florentine families.

Mozzi
A Guelf family resident in the Oltrarno. As papal bankers, one of the richest families in Florence. In 1273 Pope Gregory X stayed in their palazzo on his way to Lyons. Andrea de' Mozzi, Bishop of Florence, was moved to Padua on account of his scandalous behaviour, and is listed by Dante among the sodomites. Important politically both during the republic and the granducato. After economic difficulties in the 19th century they had to sell their family palazzo and its entire contents.

Nelli
Merchants from Mugello, owning houses near the present Canto dei Nelli. Worthy of note were Bartolomea, the mother of Machiavelli, and Plautilla di Pietro, prioress of the convent of St. Catherine of Siena, who was also a painter.

Nerli
Old family from Latium who arrived in Florence in the 12th century. Their firm political and religious alliances (as Ghibellines and Paterines) sometimes made life difficult for them. Dante records their good life through the words of his ancestor Cacciaguida: "The sons I saw/Of Nerli, and of Vecchio, well content/With unrobed jerkin; and their good dames handling/The spindle and the flax ..." (*Paradiso*, XV, 109-112). Members of the family held important religious posts until the 18th century: Benedetto, Bishop of Volterra from 1543; Francesco (d. 1670), Bishop of Pistoia; and Francesco (d. 1708), Archbishop of Florence.

Pandolfini
From Signa, descendants of the notary Pandolfino di Rinuccino. Rich merchants who boasted senior administrators (12 gonfalonieri and 28 priori), ambassadors, and eminent clergymen.

Pazzi
Owned houses, towers, and a loggia in the present Borgo degli Albizzi. Roman by origin, according to tradition, the family achieved renown in the crusades: Pazzo di Ranieri was the first to enter Jerusalem in the first crusade (1088). They are known above all for their part in the plot against the Medici in 1478, in which Lorenzo the Magnificent's brother Giuliano was killed. The family's possessions were confiscated, and the conspirators' relatives banished. The conspirators themselves were caught and hanged.

Pecori
Descended from one Dino di Giovanni di Ildebrandino, known as *il Pecora* (the sheep), recorded as a member of the butchers' guild in 1296. Between 1285 and 1512 this family produced 32 priori and seven gonfalonieri.

Pepi
Traders, though not in pepper (*pepe*), as was once thought because of their name. A powerful commune family. Their descendants still lived in their original palazzo (bought in 1653) at the beginning of the 20th century.

Peruzzi
A very powerful family, originally from Rome, at first called Della Pera, who owned property in the present Piazza Peruzzi and in the country. Weathering the famous bankruptcy of 1342, they con-

tinued as bankers, though on a rather smaller scale, and also remained active in politics until the end of the republic. Temporarily exiled by Cosimo the Elder, they put down roots in Volterra; it was into this branch of the family that Baldassarre Peruzzi (1481-1536), the famous Renaissance painter and architect, was born. Worth mentioning too is the family chapel in Santa Croce, frescoed by Giotto.

Pitti

Immensely rich merchants from Semifonte in the Val d'Elsa, who produced 13 *gonfalonieri* and 47 *priori*. As well as the historians and chroniclers Buonaccorso (14th century) and Jacopo (1519-79), posterity remembers Luca (1395-1472), an ally of Cosimo the Elder, who commissioned Brunelleschi to build the great *palazzo* on the left bank of the Arno which was then to become, under the Medici, one of the most splendid courts of Europe.

Pucci

Old Florentine family: a cabinetmaker called Puccio di Benintendi is recorded in the 13th century. Puccio di Antonio, a *gonfaloniere di giustizia* who favoured the Medici, was the founder of the family fortune to which the great family *palazzo* built by Alessandro in the 18th century testifies.

Ricasoli

A very ancient Lombard family, with a powerful fief in the Chianti region in the ninth century. The Palazzo Ricasoli in Florence was an acquisition of 1684. The most famous member of the family is Bettino (1809-80), the great statesman and patriot of the Risorgimento.

Ricci

An important family with houses and towers in the Corso, they gave the commune more than 50 *priori* and 14 *gonfalonieri*.

Rondinelli

Guelf merchants from Castello di Rondine near Arezzo. The Franciscan Giuliano Rondinelli offered himself for trial by ordeal in 1498 to prove that Savonarola was a heretic. Alessandro di Giovanni betrayed first the republic then Cosimo I de' Medici – who killed him for his pains. Members of this family were honoured with the title of *marchese,* and the line survived until the end of the 19th century.

Rucellai

Owners of the exquisite *palazzo* built by Leon Battista Alberti. An old trading family, previously called Oricellari, because they imported orchil (Italian, *oricello*) from the Levant. Bernardo (1448-1514), a humanist and patron of the arts,

organized meetings of men of letters at the Orti Oricellari. The politician and writer Giovanni (1475-1525) wrote a didactic poem entitled *Le Api* (The Bees) and a number of tragedies.

Sacchetti

Possibly of Roman origin, but the first we hear of the family is when Brodaio Sacchetti became consul in 1203. His descendants (Guelfs) produced eight *gonfalonieri* and 32 *priori*. Franco (c. 1335-1400) was both a politician and, more importantly, a writer – author of the *Trecento Novelle* (Three Hundred Tales). In the 18th century the family made a great deal of money in Naples and Rome.

Salterelli

White Guelfs, from Castello di Monte Croce. Lapo Salterelli was well known as a harsh judge, drawing criticism from Dante and Boniface VIII, who described him as *"non Lapus, sed lapis offensionis et petra scandali."* The family died out in the 15th century.

Sassetti

Ancient family, supporters of the Medici, who produced many prominent citizens. Matteo Sassetti commissioned Ghirlandaio to fresco the family chapel in Santa Trinita. Filippo (1540-88) was sent by Francesco I to India to find ways of beating the Portuguese trade monopoly; his records contain many observations about the habits and customs of those distant regions. The family died out with Cosimo di Filippo in 1651.

Serristori

Descended from Ristoro di Jacopo, a notary of the *Signoria* in the second half of the 14th century. Originally from Figline Valdarno, they settled first in Santa Croce then in the Oltrarno, moving in the 16th century to the *palazzo* on the Arno which bears their name. Merchants, loyal to the Medici, they had also been active in the political life of the republic. The line ended in 1873.

Soderini

This family, who arrived from Gangalandi in the 12th century, produced 16 *gonfalonieri* and 32 *priori*. Piero (1453-1513), who was *gonfaloniere* for life in the troubled years of transition between the 15th and 16th century, was deposed by a Medici plot, and died in Rome.

Strozzi

A family of vast wealth, traceable to the tenth century (though the first name we have, Ubertino, dates from 1282), it produced 16 *gonfalonieri* and 94 *priori*. Filippo di Matteo Strozzi, who made his fortune through trade between Palermo and Naples, commissioned the famous family *palazzo* from Benedetto da Maiano. Begun in

1489, it was taken over by Simone del Pollaiolo known as *il Cronaca*. Palla Strozzi, an opponent of Cosimo the Elder, was exiled to Padua. The anti-Medici tradition was then continued by the cultured Filippo, translator of Polybius and Plutarch and an ardent republican. Captured at Montemurlo, he committed suicide in his cell in the Fortezza da Basso.

Torrigiani

Leading wine merchants from Lamporecchio, at the time of the republic they were more interested in business than politics. The Torrigiani family produced important clergymen in the 17th and 18th centuries. Members of the family were given the title *Marchese di Decimo* in 1719, and the line ended in 1777.

Ubriachi

Ghibellines, banished in 1265, widely known as usurers. Dante includes one of them among the usurers in the *Inferno*.

Velluti

Descended from Piero di Berto, who came to Florence from Castello di Semifonte in 1202 the Valluti were a family of wealthy merchants, politically active between 1283 and 1519. Donato di Lamberto Velluti (d. 1370) wrote a *Chronicle of Florence from 1300 to 1370*.

Visdomini

Vices Domini of the Bishops of Florence, standing in for them when they were away from the city, or when the office was vacant following the death of the prelate. This office remained in the family for many years: as Dante observes, it is quite lucrative; he inveighs against "the sires of those, who now,/As surely as your church is vacant, flock/Into her consistory, and at leisure/ There stall them and grow fat." (*Paradiso*, XVI, 110-13).

The Medici family tree

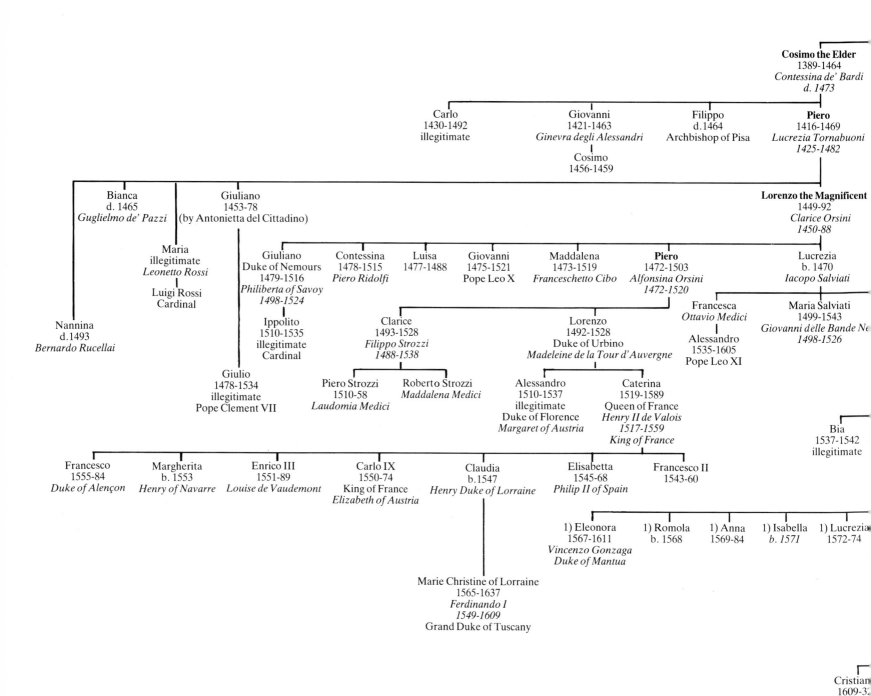

Cosimo the Elder
1389-1464
Contessina de' Bardi
d. 1473

Carlo
1430-1492
illegitimate

Giovanni
1421-1463
Ginevra degli Alessandri

Cosimo
1456-1459

Filippo
d.1464
Archbishop of Pisa

Piero
1416-1469
Lucrezia Tornabuoni
1425-1482

Bianca
d. 1465
Guglielmo de' Pazzi

Giuliano
1453-78
(by Antonietta del Cittadino)

Lorenzo the Magnificent
1449-92
Clarice Orsini
1450-88

Maria
illegitimate
Leonetto Rossi

Luigi Rossi
Cardinal

Giuliano
Duke of Nemours
1479-1516
Philiberta of Savoy
1498-1524

Contessina
1478-1515
Piero Ridolfi

Luisa
1477-1488

Giovanni
1475-1521
Pope Leo X

Maddalena
1473-1519
Franceschetto Cibo

Piero
1472-1503
Alfonsina Orsini
1472-1520

Lucrezia
b. 1470
Iacopo Salviati

Nannina
d.1493
Bernardo Rucellai

Ippolito
1510-1535
illegitimate
Cardinal

Clarice
1493-1528
Filippo Strozzi
1488-1538

Lorenzo
1492-1528
Duke of Urbino
Madeleine de la Tour d'Auvergne

Francesca
Ottavio Medici

Alessandro
1535-1605
Pope Leo XI

Maria Salviati
1499-1543
Giovanni delle Bande Ne
1498-1526

Giulio
1478-1534
illegitimate
Pope Clement VII

Piero Strozzi
1510-58
Laudomia Medici

Roberto Strozzi
Maddalena Medici

Alessandro
1510-1537
illegitimate
Duke of Florence
Margaret of Austria

Caterina
1519-1589
Queen of France
Henry II de Valois
1517-1559
King of France

Bia
1537-1542
illegitimate

Francesco
1555-84
Duke of Alençon

Margherita
b. 1553
Henry of Navarre

Enrico III
1551-89
Louise de Vaudemont

Carlo IX
1550-74
King of France
Elizabeth of Austria

Claudia
b.1547
Henry Duke of Lorraine

Elisabetta
1545-68
Philip II of Spain

Francesco II
1543-60

1) Eleonora
1567-1611
Vincenzo Gonzaga
Duke of Mantua

1) Romola
b. 1568

1) Anna
1569-84

1) Isabella
b. 1571

1) Lucrezia
1572-74

Marie Christine of Lorraine
1565-1637
Ferdinando I
1549-1609
Grand Duke of Tuscany

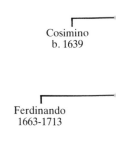

Cristian
1609-32

Cosimino
b. 1639

Ferdinando
1663-1713

The two branches of the Medici family, which ruled Florence and subsequently Tuscany as a whole, are derived from two brothers, sons of one Giovanni di Bicci, who thanks to the Medici bank, laid the foundations for the family's continued prosperity: Cosimo the Elder, the grandfather of Lorenzo the Magnificent, and Lorenzo the Elder, great-great-grandfather of Cosimo I, the first Grand Duke of Tuscany. It is interesting to note that the two branches of the family tree are joined through the latter. Indeed, Cosimo was the great-great-grandson of Lorenzo the Elder on his father's side (Giovanni delle Bande Nere), and great-grandson of Lorenzo the Magnificent on his mother's side (Maria Salviati). In this family tree, names given in italics denote spouses of the people named immediately above; 1) and 2) before a name denotes the spouse (and respective offspring where applicable) of a first or second marriage.

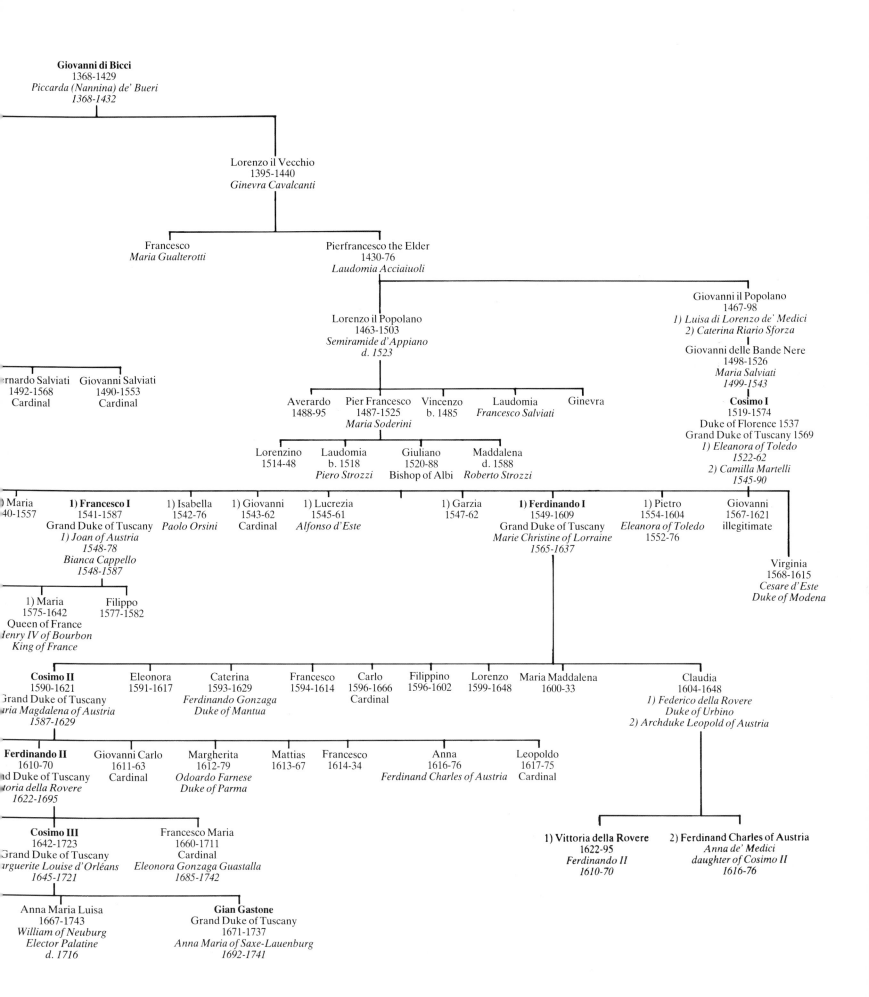

Giovanni di Bicci
1368-1429
Piccarda (Nannina) de' Bueri
1368-1432

Lorenzo il Vecchio
1395-1440
Ginevra Cavalcanti

Francesco
Maria Gualterotti

Pierfrancesco the Elder
1430-76
Laudomia Acciaiuoli

Lorenzo il Popolano
1463-1503
Semiramide d'Appiano
d. 1523

Giovanni il Popolano
1467-98
1) Luisa di Lorenzo de' Medici
2) Caterina Riario Sforza

Giovanni delle Bande Nere
1498-1526
Maria Salviati
1499-1543

rnardo Salviati
1492-1568
Cardinal

Giovanni Salviati
1490-1553
Cardinal

Averardo
1488-95

Pier Francesco
1487-1525
Maria Soderini

Vincenzo
b. 1485

Laudomia
Francesco Salviati

Ginevra

Cosimo I
1519-1574
Duke of Florence 1537
Grand Duke of Tuscany 1569
1) Eleanora of Toledo
1522-62
2) Camilla Martelli
1545-90

Lorenzino
1514-48

Laudomia
b. 1518
Piero Strozzi

Giuliano
1520-88
Bishop of Albi

Maddalena
d. 1588
Roberto Strozzi

) Maria
40-1557

1) Francesco I
1541-1587
Grand Duke of Tuscany
1) Joan of Austria
1548-78
Bianca Cappello
1548-1587

1) Isabella
1542-76
Paolo Orsini

1) Giovanni
1543-62
Cardinal

1) Lucrezia
1545-61
Alfonso d'Este

1) Garzia
1547-62

1) Ferdinando I
1549-1609
Grand Duke of Tuscany
Marie Christine of Lorraine
1565-1637

1) Pietro
1554-1604
Eleanora of Toledo
1552-76

Giovanni
1567-1621
illegitimate

Virginia
1568-1615
Cesare d'Este
Duke of Modena

1) Maria
1575-1642
Queen of France
Henry IV of Bourbon
King of France

Filippo
1577-1582

Cosimo II
1590-1621
Grand Duke of Tuscany
Maria Magdalena of Austria
1587-1629

Eleonora
1591-1617

Caterina
1593-1629
Ferdinando Gonzaga
Duke of Mantua

Francesco
1594-1614

Carlo
1596-1666
Cardinal

Filippino
1596-1602

Lorenzo
1599-1648

Maria Maddalena
1600-33

Claudia
1604-1648
1) Federico della Rovere
Duke of Urbino
2) Archduke Leopold of Austria

Ferdinando II
1610-70
Grand Duke of Tuscany
Vittoria della Rovere
1622-1695

Giovanni Carlo
1611-63
Cardinal

Margherita
1612-79
Odoardo Farnese
Duke of Parma

Mattias
1613-67

Francesco
1614-34

Anna
1616-76
Ferdinand Charles of Austria

Leopoldo
1617-75
Cardinal

1) Vittoria della Rovere
1622-95
Ferdinando II
1610-70

2) Ferdinand Charles of Austria
Anna de' Medici
daughter of Cosimo II
1616-76

Cosimo III
1642-1723
Grand Duke of Tuscany
Marguerite Louise d'Orléans
1645-1721

Francesco Maria
1660-1711
Cardinal
Eleonora Gonzaga Guastalla
1685-1742

Anna Maria Luisa
1667-1743
William of Neuburg
Elector Palatine
d. 1716

Gian Gastone
Grand Duke of Tuscany
1671-1737
Anna Maria of Saxe-Lauenburg
1692-1741

A short glossary of Florentine place names

Acqua: water. The street now called by this name runs into via dell'Anguillara. The name possibly recalls the existence of a well (known as the Anguillara) at this junction, where water used to be drawn.

Agnolo: angel. This name is very old in origin. On this street in the Santa Croce quarter, at the junctions with Via delle Conce, the Compagnia di San Michele had its headquarters. Carved on the outside was the company's crest – an effigy of the archangel Michael.

Albero: tree. Many street names retained in modern Florence relate to the vegetation that used to grow in the old city. The tree recorded in this case grew in the garden of the Spedale di Santa Maria della Scala, which gave on to this street.

Alloro: laurel. Another plant name, but this time not directly pertaining to a laurel growing in this street. The street in fact led to a postern in the second circle of walls, the name of which was Dell'Alloro.

Altafronte: the name of a castle which stood on the site of the present Piazza dei Giudici. Owned by the Altafronti family, it was destroyed by the flooding of the Arno in 1333 and then rebuilt by the Castellani. The name survives in the street leading to the castle square.

Amorino: cupid. Diminutive of the old name, Amoricchio, the street leading from the Piazza Madonna degli Aldobrandini. So called due to its proximity to a street named Amore (love), the modern Via Sant'Antonino. It was here that the romantic adventures which provided the basis for Machiavelli's play *La Mandragola* took place.

Anconella: a small religious panel painting. There may have been such a painting in a shrine on this street.

Anguillara: joining Piazza Santa Croce and Piazza San Firenze, this street is named after Baldaccio d'Anghiari, the Count dell'Anguillara, a famous soldier of the Florentine republic (15th century), who lived behind the church of San Firenze.

Aranci: oranges. Fragrant orange trees used to grow in the large garden of a *palazzo* owned by the Lioni, a wealthy Florentine family, at the corner of Via Verdi and Via Ghibellina. Hence the present-day name of this Canto.

Arazzieri: tapestry weavers. In the street of this name stood the hospital and hostel for priests who were passing through Florence. In 1545 Cosimo I used the site to lodge the weavers working at his newly founded tapestry workshop. The museums in Florence still display many of the tapestries woven for the Medici court.

Archibusieri: arquebus makers. The Lungarno formerly known as Dei Castellani (after a Florentine family who lived there), housed the workshops of the manufacturers of arquebuses from the 14th to the 16th century. The street only later acquired its present name.

Arcolaio: the reel or frame used in winding a skein of wool. Many streets in the city were named after the villas – now no longer in existence – to which they led. The Villa dell'Arcolaio belonged to the Da Filicaia family. The origin of the name is not known.

Arcovata: Traces of the great Roman aqueduct which carried water from the Settimello hills to the baths were still visible in the 18th century. The arches (*arcovate*) of this aqueduct followed the line of this street, giving their name to it.

Ardiglione: the metal point of a buckle. This street used to be called Via della Fibbia (buckle), because of its shape – turning at a right angle towards Via dei Serragli, and intersected by Via Santa Monaca.

Ariento: *argento*, silver. Since before the 15th century silversmiths manufactured silver thread in the Via dell'Ariento. A narrow street, it was widened in 1874.

Arte della Lana: in the street of this name stood the headquarters of the powerful guild of wool workers (*Arte della Lana*), which played so prominent a part in the political and economic life of medieval Florence. In the 14th century the wool trade accounted for some 200 workshops and 30,000 workers.

Artisti: a relatively recent name for the street running between Piazza Donatello and Piazza Vasari, where artists and sculptors had their workshops. The sculptor Jean Dupré (1817-82) worked at no. 9.

Avelli: tombs. The cemetery of Santa Maria Novella was one of the most important in Florence. The tombs stood in rows within a rectangular wall, each carved with the arms of the deceased. Formerly called *Via dietro gli Avelli* (literally, the street behind the tombs), the Via degli Avelli was widened in 1867, and the tombs were repositioned to run alongside it.

Badessa: abbess. Beside the basilica of San Piero Maggiore (destroyed in the 18th century) was a Benedictine convent, giving onto the present Via delle Badesse, which runs into Via Pandolfini. On the site of the present Canto alla Badessa, at the junction of Via Pandolfini and Via Verdi, stood the house of the Mother Abbess of the convent. Every new bishop in the city went through an "episcopal marriage ceremony" – a symbolic wedding with the Abbess here – as a symbol of the oneness of the ecclesiastical community in Florence.

Balla: package. The Canto di Balla, at the junction of Via dei Pucci and Via dei Servi, was close to the second circle of city walls, near a gate of the same name, through which bales of wool were carried to textile workshops just outside the city.

Ballodole: the etymology of this name (which is the name both of a single street and of a whole district of Careggi) is unknown. The plague cemetery used to be here, hence the local Florentine expression *"si va alle Ballodole,"* (going to the Ballodole), i.e. to die.

Banchi: counters. In 1324 the *Signoria* ordered that "the new street begun at the Canto di Panzano, leading to Piazza Nuova (the present Piazza Santa Maria Novella) be completed." The street acquired this name in the 16th century because of the number of traders who were based there.

Bandino: the name both of a single street and of a whole area close to the abbey at Ripoli, derived from a villa there belonging to Giovanni Bandini (who betrayed and besieged his own home city, with imperial troops, in 1529-30).

Barriera del Ponte alle Mosse: one of Florence's toll gates, located outside the Porta al Prato, near the Ponte sul Mugnone – the bridge from which the starting signals (*mosse*) for the horse races through the city (*palii*) used to be given.

Bellariva: the literal meaning of this name (beautiful bank) speaks for itself, for this street leads to the river Arno. The origins of the names Piazza di Bellosguardo (literally, fine view) and the Fortezza di Belvedere ("the castle with the fine view"), and the similarly named street leading to the castle, are equally self-evident. Built by Bernardo Buontalenti in 1590-95, the Belvedere towers over the city on the hill above the Palazzo Pitti.

Bersaglio: target, shooting range (a recent name). This street runs between Via Maffei and Via Sacchetti. In the years immediately after Florence became annexed to the Kingdom of Italy the National Guard had a firing range nearby.

Bisarno: this avenue acquired its name in 1900, as a reminder of the branch of the Arno that used to traverse the city, making the Piazza Santa Croce an *"isola d'Arno"* (an island of the Arno). The 1966 floods showed that, even very high, the river tends to try to retrace its old course.

Boboli: the magnificent gardens flanking the Palazzo Pitti. The name in fact applies to the hill on which they are laid out, and is itself a corruption of a Florentine family name, Bogolesi. In the same way, Via dei Biffi recalls a family that died out in the 18th century, the Biffoli (elevated on several occasions to the *priorato* between 1345 and 1431). Another such street is the Via delle Bombarde, named after the Bombarda family.

Borgo: a number of streets in Florence bear witness to their original location: *borghi* were suburbs or clusters of houses built outside the first or second circle of city walls, which then became integral parts of the city as it grew.

Brache: trousers. This street links Via dei Neri and Piazza Peruzzi. It used to be called Chiasso Calabrache, though the reason for this strange name is not known. (*Chiasso* literally means din or uproar and *calabrache* might be translated as "trousers falling down.")

Burella: Via delle Burella between Via Torta and Piazza Peruzzi, is where the Roman amphitheater used to be. The *burelle* (underground passages) were artificial caves, probably the vaulted tunnels created by the banked seats of the amphitheater, where the wild animals for the arena were kept. These "caves" still existed in the Middle Ages, after the amphitheater had disappeared, and were used for shelter by prostitutes, or occasionally also as prisons. The 740 prisoners taken at the battle of Campaldino were confined there.

Caldaie: boilers. Piazza Santo Spirito, when the wool industry spread to across the Arno, was the dyers' quarter. Large boilers were used in the dyeing process, hence the name of this street.

Calimala: it was from this street that the *Arte dei Setaioli* (the silk merchants' guild) took its name. The merchants who owned shops and warehouses here bought material from abroad, to be worked and finely finished and then resold. At one time it was thought that the old name, Kalimala, stemmed from an Arabian import (*kali*) used for giving a shine to fabrics. In fact it probably derives from the Latin *callis malus* (bad road): a smart residential area in the Middle Ages, it had previously been a haunt of prostitutes.

Calza: stocking. The Ingesuati were known as "brothers of the *calza*" (stocking), as the mark of the order was a long white hood somewhat in the shape of a stocking. After 1529 their house was in the Conventino, by Porta Romana, the site of the present Piazza della Calza.

Calzaiuoli: hosiers. Before being connected by the straight Via dei Calzaiuoli in 1842-44, Piazza della Signoria and Piazza del Duomo were linked by short sections of street each named after the shops housed therein. Thus this name only applied to the section as far as Orsanmichele. The street then became Via dei Caciaiuoli (makers and sellers of cheese), then, among other names, Via dei Farsettai (makers of flags and doublets).

Camerata: a corruption of *Ca' Marte* (House of Mars). In Roman times there was a temple to Mars here, of which no trace survives.

Campidoglio: running between Via Brunelleschi and Via dei Pescioni, Via del Campidoglio crosses the site of the old Roman Capitol, the fortified center of the city, where Santa Maria del Campidoglio, after which this street is named, was later built.

Campo d'Arrigo: this street winds around the area where Emperor Henry VII encamped while besieging Florence in 1312. His camp would then have stood about a mile outside the city walls.

Canto: corner. Vernacular Italian word of Latin derivation, still common today in Florentine street names.

Capaccio: standing in the vicinity of the old baths, where the aqueduct came to an end, was a medieval *palazzo* known as *caput aquae*. This name evolved into "Capaccio," and was then given to the street joining Via delle Terme and Piazza del Mercato Nuovo.

Careggi: the hill on which Cosimo the Elder built one of the most beautiful of the Medici villas was formerly royal land, (in Italian, *campo regio* – by contraction, "Careggi.")

Carrozze: coaches. In Via delle Carrozze, which runs from Lungarno degli Archibusieri to Via Lambertesca, Cosimo I built the ducal coach houses. Of more recent date is the name Via delle Carra, beyond Porta al Prato, where the builders and repairers of transport wagons worked.

Casaccia: hovel. A flood in the 15th century destroyed a house belonging to the Organi family, and the ruins remained for some considerable time, giving rise to the name of both an area and a particular street.

Cascine: dairies. This famous park, created by Cosimo I, initially in the possession of the Medici, then of the Lorena, finally becoming public in the second half of the 18th century, used to house the ducal dairies. It was also known as Tenuta dell'Isola (the island holding), as it was completely surrounded by water (the Arno, the Fosso Macinante, and the Mugnone).

Castellaccio: literally, "unsightly castle" (-*accio* lends a pejorative sense to any noun to which it is appended). The street joining Via dei Servi and Via degli Alfani. At one time a *palazzo* of unprepossessing appearance stood here – perhaps reduced to ruins through civil strife during the medieval period. By the 14th century, though, the *Arte della Lana* already had stretching sheds here known by the name of Castellaccio.

Catena: chain. The Canto alla Catena derives its name from a chapel erected in 1370 by Nicolò di Jacopo Alberti, which featured the family crest: four links of a chain enclosed within a ring.

Catinai: bowl makers. Via dei Catinai leads to Impruneta, and was used by the carts carrying bowls and earthenware from the furnaces there.

Cavallari: couriers. The name both of a piazza and a *vicolo* (alley). The *cavallari* handled mail and transported the personal belongings of ambassadors and businessmen on their travels.

Ceci: Leading off from Via Settignanese, this street is named after an ancient family.

Cella di Ciardo: here was the wineshop of Ciardo di Betto, who was condemned to death for leading the Ciompi Revolution. *Celle* was the old name for wineshops.

Chiasso: an ancient noun derived from the Latin *classis,* applied to several narrow lanes in Florence.

Cimatori: one vital stage in the production of woollen cloth was known as *cimatura* – when the roughly worked cloth from the farms was cleaned, dried and finished off. The people who performed this work were based in the piazza which is now named after them.

Condotta: the job of the four officers of the *condotta* was to enrol men into the republic's militia. Their headquarters were in this street, between Piazza San Firenze and Via dei Calzaiuoli.

Corso: course, road. At the time of the republic horse races were run from the Ponte alle Mosse to Por San Piero, taking in the present *corso* (formerly known as Corso di Por San Piero) on the way. The word *palio,* by which these races came to be known, originally meant the rich cloth embroidered with silk and gold and edged with ermine which was given to the winner.

Piazza Davanzati. Metal brackets to support poles on which washed or dyed cloth was hung.

Costa: hill. This is the name of the hilly area dominating the city across the Arno. Some of the streets that lead up to the Costa have names relating to the steep gradient. Thus Via della Costa Scarpuccia resembles an escarpment (in Italian, *scarpata*), and there is a street near the Palazzo Pitti called Sdrucciolo (steep path).

Diavoli: devils. Canto del Diavolo (Devil's Corner) was the name given to the spot where a frenzied black horse, thought to have been sent by the devil, broke up a crowd that had gathered to hear the anti-Paterine Fra' Piero da Verona. It was renamed in the plural, Canto dei Diavoli, on account of the flag holders carved in the shape of demons by Giambologna, on the *palazzo* of Bernardo Vecchietti, on this very street corner.

Drago: dragon. One of the areas of the Santo Spirito quarter had as its emblem a green dragon on a yellow background. Via del Drago lies in this area. Similarly, Via del Sole (sun), takes its name from the flag of the Santa Maria Novella quarter, which had a golden sun on an azure background.

Farine: flour (*farina*). The present Via delle Farine housed the offices of the *Provveditore della Gabella delle macine e delle farine,* the tax office which controlled the profits made by the flour milling industry.

Forbici: shears. Via delle Forbici, in the Santa Croce quarter, recalls the crest of the Della Tosa family, who had a villa there: silver sheep shears on an azure field. Via dei Fiordalisi likewise derives its name from a *palazzo* owned by the Nobili, whose arms showed lilies and fleurs-de-lis.

Ghibellina: after the Ghibelline victory at Montaperti (1260), Guido Novello, *vicario* to King Manfredi, named a new gate built in the second circle of city walls Porta Ghibellina. This name was subsequently given also to the street running through it.

Giudei: Jews. A street in Florence's ghetto area, the origins of this name are self-explanatory. Jews were invited to Florence in the 15th century to lend money at low interest rates, in order to bring down the very high interest demanded by Florentine bankers. They were later subjected to fierce discrimination: Cosimo I – sadly anticipating Nazi practice – made them wear an identification patch of yellow material (men had to wear this on their hats, women on their sleeves).

Grazie: mercies. A chapel dedicated to Our Lady of Mercy (Madonna della Grazie) used to stand on the Ponte delle Grazie. Built by Jacopo degli Alberti in 1374, it was pulled down when the

bridge was widened. The Via delle Grazie in Settignano is similarly named after a shrine to Our Lady of Mercy.

Guelfa: it is not known when this street (connecting Via Cavour and Piazza del Crocifisso) acquired its name. It may have been when the church of San Barnaba was built. St. Barnabas was the Guelf patron saint at the victorious battle of Campaldino (1289) against the Ghibellines and the Aretines.

Isola delle Stinche: the prison, work on which was begun in 1296, on the site of the present Teatro Verdi. It was called after the castle of the same name. The owners of the castle, the Cavalcanti, were among the first inmates of the Stinche (1303), having been betrayed in the town. Cut off from the city by its huge walls, the prison gave its name to the present street.

Lanzi: the famous Gothic loggia in Piazza della Signoria, housing magnificent works of sculpture, including Cellini's *David* and Giambologna's *Rape of the Sabine Women.* The name recalls the 200 lansquenets of Cosimo I's personal guard, who were barracked here in 1541.

Larione: the winding Via del Larione derives its name from Ilarione Buonguglielmi, who had a villa here in the 15th century.

Laura: a pavilion built by Lorenzo the Magnificent gave its name to the street than ran by it. Via Laurenza or Laurenziana then became contracted to the present Laura. It thus bears no reference to any woman and has no connection with the Laura who inspired Petrarch.

Leoni: lions. There used to be a lions' den in this street behind the Palazzo della Signoria. Goro Dati records 24 animals. Lions continued to be bred until 1777, though under Cosimo I they were moved to San Marco.

Lupo: wolf. Via del Lupo recalls a celebrated Florentine artilleryman, Giovanni di Antonio, nicknamed Lupo, who defended the city in the siege of 1529-30. As Varchi recalls, every time the great Lupo fired at the enemy, "one or more of them would be killed instantly."

Madonna della Tosse (Our Lady of the Cough): this street leads to the church of the same name, built for the veneration of an image of the Virgin which Christine of Lorraine (wife of Grand Duke Ferdinand I de' Medici) considered had miraculously cured her and her children of a cough.

Malcontenti: malcontents. Public executions were held in a field known as the Prato della Giustizia (the field of justice), outside the city gate of the same name. Spectators would line the street to watch as the condemned passed by on their way to the Prato, hence the name Via dei Malcontenti.

Mantellate: cloaked women. Like the Piazza della Calza (see above), this street name also derives from a religious order. The sisters of the Servites of Mary had a convent here (from 1787), and their voluminous cloaks earned them the nickname *Ammantellate*.

Marzio: of Mars. A Roman statue of Mars used to stand in this lane close to the Ponte Vecchio. It was destroyed when the Arno flooded in 1333.

Mercato Nuovo: new market. The arcaded gallery of the Mercato Nuovo, built by Bernardo del Tasso in 1547, was for the buying and selling of luxury goods and for the moneychangers. Its name, Loggia del Porcellino (the arcade of the little pig), comes from a statue of a wild boar by Tacca commissioned by Ferdinand II de' Medici – a copy of an antique original in the ducal collections.

Moro: mulberry. Mulberry trees in the various gardens of Florence provided the names of both the Via del Moro in the San Giovanni quarter and the Via de' Mori in that of Santo Spirito.

Morte: death. Leading into the Piazza del Duomo is the street which housed the buildings of the *Arciconfraternita della Misericordia* (Archconfraternity of Mercy), whose emblem was of a funerary nature. It is also said, however, that in the 15th century a newly buried woman, Ginevra degli Amieri, walked this street. Having in fact not died, she returned to her husband – who, thinking she was a ghost, repulsed her.

Murate: immured women. The Florence prison owes its name to an enclosed convent called the Monastero della Murate (because the sisters were forbidden any contact with the outside world). Originally on the Ponte alle Grazie, the convent moved in the 15th century to the Via Ghibellina, and subsequently became the prison.

Ninna: child's sleep. The *Madonna della Ninna* was a painting by Cimabue in the church of San Per Scheraggio (demolished to make way for the Uffizi). The painting shows the Child asleep in the Virgin's lap. Hence the name of this street, which debouches into Piazza della Signoria.

Oltrarno: literally, across or beyond the Arno. The crowded quarter on the left bank of the river. When Florence acquired its second circle of walls in 1078, the Oltrarno already boasted three large *borghi* (Piazza, Pitiglioso, and San Jacopo).

However, these were not enclosed within the walls. Only later, after *palazzi* and craftsmen's workshops had been built there, was the area protected by walls.

Onesta: honesty. The *Magistrato dell'Onestà*, comprising eight citizens, monitored public morals and the crime rate. Its premises were in Orsanmichele, near the present Vicolo dell' Onestà.

Orsanmichele: the loggia of Orsanmichele was begun in 1284 as a grain market, where the church of San Michele Arcangelo stood in the middle of an *orto* (garden) – hence San Michele in orto, which was eventually contracted to Orsanmichele. With the addition of the upper floors this loggia became a church in 1381. The shrine by Orcagna was already there, and over the following three centuries the guilds commissioned the statues that still adorn the external walls of the building.

Orti Oricellari: the gardens owned by Bernardo Rucellai (flanking the present Via degli Orti Oricellari) were until 1522 the meeting place of the *Accademia platonica*. The Rucellai were the first to import orchil (Italian, *oricello*), used for dyeing wool.

Palancola: plank bridge. This street led to such a bridge across the Mugnone.

Panzani: bogs. Both an area and a street name. Outside the second circle of walls, this area was called *Pantano* (swamp) as it was low-lying and was often flooded by ditches.

Parte Guelfa: in this square, in a *palazzo* confiscated from the Ghibelline Lamberti family in 1267, the *capitani* of the *Parte Guelfa* had their headquarters. This body of three looked after the interests of the *Parte Guelfa* and disposed of the property acquired from its opponents.

Pergola: this name derives from an extensive trellised walk beside a wool shed. There were also a *vicolo* and a theater of the same name, the latter erected by the *Accademia degli Immobili* in 1652.

Pignone (cutwater): a large cone-shaped construction (*pigna*) protected a stretch of the bank of the Arno, forming a small harbour for commercial vessels from the sea. The name Pignone applied to the whole area as well as to the Lungarno at that spot, and to a street away from the river. A nearby alley was called Vicolo Pignoncino (a diminutive of Pignone).

Pinzochere: women who took vows yet still remained secular (men who did the same were

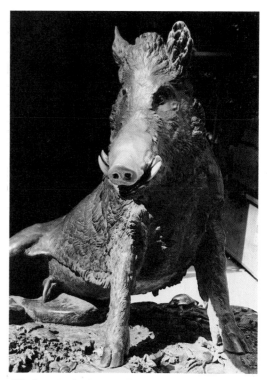

The boar in the Loggia di Mercato Nuovo. A magnificent cast-bronze work by Pietro Tacca (c. 1612), it was inspired by an earlier, marble version, part of the Medici collections and now in the Uffizi.

called *Pinzocheri*). Sometimes they formed a community. Cosimo I closed down all such houses, which were a source of endless scandals. In the present Via delle Pinzochere, between Via Malcontenti and Via Ghibellina, was a house of Franciscan tertiaries, connected to the Santa Croce friary.

Poggio Imperiale: imperial hill. On top of this hill was a villa owned first by the Pandolfini, then by the Salviati and the Orsini, then finally by Cosimo II's widow, Maria Magdalena of Austria. Her imperial lineage gave the hill its name.

Ponte alla Carraia: built in 1218, rebuilt in 1264, then again in 1559, and then widened in 1867, this bridge led to a gate in the third ring of city walls called the Porta Carría – so named after the carts (*carri*) that used to pass through between town and country.

A ring for holding banners, one of the very numerous examples still to be seen in the city.

Saggio: sample. In a corner of the Mercato Nuovo called the Canto del Saggio was the building which housed the *Saggio della Mercanzia*, responsible for reviewing the quality of the goods being offered for sale.

Serpe: one of the few surviving towers of the fourth circle of city walls, named after a well-known officer of the guard who lived there.

Speziali: apothecaries. Here the purveyors of chemicals, medicines, and spices, members of the guild of doctors and druggists, had their shops. Formerly known as Via degli Speziali Grossi (literally, street of the big chemist's shops).

Stufa: public baths. In this street, leading off Piazza San Lorenzo, was the old Stufa di San Lorenzo. In the 15th century this was administered by the Lotteringhi, who thereby earned the named Della Stufa.

Tempio: temple. The year 1336 saw the foundation of the *Compagnia di Santa Maria al Tempio*, whose task was to minister to those awaiting execution at the nearby Prato di Giustizia. The Lungarno del Tempio marks the site of the Company's chapel, which Alessandro de' Medici later incorporated into defense ramparts.

Tintori: dyers. The dyers' workshops were concentrated near the Ponte alle Grazie, but the main headquarters of the Guild, with its school, hospice, and hospital, were in the present Corso dei Tintori. It was called *corso* (course) because the *palio* of the Feast of St. Ornuphrius (9 June), the dyers' patron saint, passed along it. The heavy draught-horses used for transporting materials would be entered in this *palio*, provoking hoots and catcalls from the onlookers.

Tiratoio: stretching shed. *Tiratoi* were large sheds in which pieces of fabric were hung on wooden frames to dry after being washed and dyed, and to be stretched to the desired size. A *tiratoio* still in existence in the Santo Spirito quarter in 1874 supplied the name for a *piazza*, a street, and an alley.

Uffizi: the famous art gallery, but also the name of a *piazzale*. Originally built by Giorgio Vasari for Cosimo I de' Medici, who wanted to bring together the *uffizi* (offices) of the civil, judiciary, and fiscal magistracies.

Vacchereccia: running into Piazza della Signoria, this was the street where the Della Vacca family lived. Later the commune government buildings stood here.

Vagellai: a *vagello* was the great boiler used by dyers, who from the 14th to the 16th century congregated around the present Via dei Vagellai (although this name originally referred to the present Via Torta).

Vigna: vineyard. Two street names in Florence recall the existence of vineyards within the city walls: Via della Vigna Vecchia, where the gardens of the abbey were situated inside the second circle of walls; and Via della Vigna Nuova, which ran up to the land cultivated by the monks of San Pancrazio, inside the third circle of walls.

Ponte Vecchio: old bridge. The oldest bridge in Florence, dating from 1345 (though it is not known when the very first bridge was built here). The goldsmiths and jewellers who still have their shops on the Ponte Vecchio first moved there in 1594, when the *capitani* of the *Parte Guelfa* evicted other humbler traders – butchers, greengrocers, etc.

Porta a Faenza: the city gates that still stand, dotted around the *viali* of Florence belong to the fourth circle of walls (the walls themselves were demolished in 1865). The road that passes by this gate does not lead to Faenza; its name derives from a convent that used to exist there, founded by St. Faenza.

Presto: loan. From 1495 the Monte di Pietà (official pawnshop) was in Via del Presto. Another such establishment near the church of San Martino Vescovo gave its name to the Via del Presto di San Martino.

Ricorboli: a very old *borgo,* named after a small canal that ran through the area, the Rio di Corbolo (or Corbulo) – by contraction, Ricorboli.

Rifredi: another *borgo* named after the Terzolla which flows through it, the old name of which was Riofreddo or Riofrigido.

Select bibliography

Albertini, R. von, *Firenze dalla repubblica al principato. Storia e coscienza politica,* Turin, 1970.

Baron, H., *The crisis of the Early Italian Renaissance,* Princeton, 1966.

Bertelli, S., *Il potere oligarchico nello stato-città medievale,* Florence, 1978.

Brucker, G., *The civic world of Early Renaissance Florence,* Princeton, 1977.

   Renaissance Florence, Berkeley California, 1983.

Caggese, R., *Firenze dalla decadenza di Roma al Risorgimento d'Italia,* three vols., Florence, 1912-21.

Capponi, G., *Storia della Repubblica di Firenze,* Florence, 1875.

Cochrane, E., *Florence in the Forgotten Centuries, 1527-1800,* Chicago, 1973.

Conti, E., *La formazione della struttura agraria moderna nel contado fiorentino,* three vols, Rome, 1965-66.

Davidsohn, R., *Storia di Firenze,* eight vols., Florence, 1956-65.

De la Roncière, C., *Florence: centre économique régional au XIVe siècle,* four vols., Aix-en-Provence, 1978.

Diaz, F., *Il Granducato di Toscana. I Medici,* Turin, 1976.

Doren, A., *Le arti fiorentine,* two vols., Florence, 1940.

Garin, E., *L'umanesimo italiano,* Bari, 1952.

Goldthwaite, R., *The Building of Renaissance Florence,* Baltimore, 1980.

Guidi, G., *Il governo della città-repubblica di Firenze del primo Quattrocento,* three vols., Florence, 1981.

Herlihy, D., Klapisch-Zuber, C., *Les Toscans et leurs familles,* Paris, 1978.

Hoshino, H., *L'arte della lana in Firenze nel basso medioevo,* Florence, 1980.

Kent, F.W., *Household and Lineage in Renaissance Florence,* Princeton, 1977.

Martines, L., *Lawyers and Statecraft in Renaissance Florence,* Princeton, 1968.

—*The Social World of the Florentine Humanists,* Princeton, 1963.

Melis, F., *Aspetti della vita economica medievale,* Siena, 1962.

Ottokar, N., *Il Comune di Firenze alla fine del Dugento,* Florence, 1926.

—*Studi comunali e fiorentini,* Florence, 1948.

Rodolico, N., *I Ciompi,* Florence, 1945.

Rubinstein, N., ed., *Florentine Studies,* London, 1968.

—*Il governo di Firenze sotto i Medici,* Florence, 1971.

Salvemini, G., *Magnati e popolani in Firenze dal 1280 al 1292,* Turin, 1960.

Sapori, A., *Studi di storia economica,* three vols., Florence, 1967.

Spini, G., ed., *Architettura e politica da Cosimo I a Ferdinando I,* Florence, 1976.

Sznura, F., *L'espansione urbana di Firenze nel Dugento,* Florence, 1975.

Trexler, R., *Public Life in Renaissance Florence,* New York, 1980.

Index

Picture sources

The abbreviations a, b, c, l, r, refer to the position of the illustration on the page (above, below, center, left, right).

The following sources of illustrative material relating to Florentine history and customs have been referred to in the present volume:

The *Rustici Codex*, named after its author Marco di Bartolomeo Rustici (1392-c.1457). A goldsmith, he had a *bottega* in the Mercato Nuovo and practiced his craft until the early part of 1448, when he undertook a journey to the Holy Land. The codex compiled on his return from this pilgrimage contains numerous miniatures of Florence; it is preserved in the Biblioteca del Seminario Maggiore (illustrations on pages 11b, 66ar, 111, 192a, 195). The *Croniche* (Chronicles) of Giovanni Sercambi. The author (1347-1424), a writer and politician from Lucca, also wrote 155 *Novelle*. The richly illuminated manuscript of the *Croniche* (which cover the years 1164 to 1424), is preserved in the Archivio di Stato, Lucca (illustrations on pages 77a, 77c, 125a, 125b, 127a, 127b, 129al, 159, 163b, 170, 171).

Trattato sull'arte della seta. This treatise on the silk workers' guild, an impressive technical manual, illustrated with highly evocative water colours, is preserved in the Biblioteca Laurenziana (illustrations on pages 78, 79).

The *Cronica* (Chronicle) of Giovanni Villani. The author (1280-c.1348), a Florentine merchant, also held important public posts. The idea of writing the *Cronica* (which spans the period from the Tower of Babel up to 1346) came to him on a journey to Rome in 1300. The manuscript (Chigi codex, L. VIII. 296) contains 332 illustrations executed by several artists, notably members of Pacino di

Bonaguida's workshop, and is preserved in the Vatican Library (illustrations on pages 46r, 121al, 124, 132, 162al, 167ar).

Photographers and photographic agencies

Alinari, Florence, 37a, 84, 85c, 118a, 143l, 146a, 165c, 173ar, 230.
Cortopassi, Lucca, 77a, 125b, 127, 129al.
Corvina, Budapest, 14.
Costa, Milan, 12, 13, 16, 17, 25cr, 32, 40b, 67, 68r, 70-71b, 72, 77c, 79c, 95b, 99, 102b, 104a, 125a, 128ar, 129ar, 129c, 152a, 159, 168b, 169, 170, 171, 188a, 206b, 238, 239, 240.
ItalfotoGieffe, Florence, 37b, 66al, 66bl, 66br, 70ar, 71ar, 74, 81, 105b, 117a, 120cr, 120b, 144, 147b, 232b, 233br.
Niccolini, Milan, 3, 8, 28a, 29a, 33, 49, 53a, 57, 62, 63, 73al, 73ar, 80, 97, 108, 112, 113a, 113bl, 117b, 120cl, 131b, 136, 138, 139bl, 139br, 146b, 153, 168a, 174b, 176ar, 178, 179, 183a, 184, 185, 186, 187, 189, 190, 193, 197, 199, 209, 210, 215, 224, 225, 231l, 244, 245, 248, 249, 254, 255, 268, 269.
Pineider, Florence, 36a, 47b, 51, 78, 79ar, 92, 177ar, 177br, 200, 201, 202, 204b, 205bl, 212a, 222.
Publiaerfoto, Milan, 174.
Quattrone, Florence, 48br, 61a, 93, 123, 204a, 211r, 231r, 232a, 233ar.
Scala, Florence, 2, 11, 18-19, 22, 23, 24, 30ar, 30al, 35, 36b, 44, 45, 53b, 54a, 55ar, 60a, 66ar, 68l, 69, 75, 76l, 89, 90a, 90bl, 98r, 100al, 102al, 103, 106, 107, 111, 114a, 114-115, 118b, 119, 121c, 131a, 135, 139a, 142, 143a, 145, 148, 149, 156, 161, 173al, 175al, 175b, 182, 188b, 192a, 194, 195, 198, 203, 207a, 213l, 214, 217al, 232c, 233ar, 235.
Archivio Arnoldo Mondadori Editore, Milan, 9, 10, 15, 20a, 20br, 20bl, 21, 25ar, 25bc, 29b, 34, 40, 41, 42, 43b, 48a, 48bl, 50, 52, 54b, 55al, 56b, 58, 59, 64, 70cl, 73b, 76r, 85r, 91, 94, 95a, 98l, 100r, 101a, 104l, 105a, 110, 113br, 121al, 121ar, 122, 124, 132al, 132ar, 132b, 137, 140ar, 141, 143br, 147a, 150, 151, 154c, 158, 162ar, 162b, 164, 165al, 165b, 176al, 176b, 177l, 180, 181a, 192b, 206a, 212b, 213r, 216a, 217b, 220, 221, 223, 233bl, 234, 236.

Museums, churches and collections
Amsterdam, Rijksmuseum, 26.
Arezzo: Duomo, 102r; San Francesco, 173ar.
Berlin: Staatliche Museen, 34b, 134, 217cl.
Budapest: Museum of Fine Arts, 14.
Cleveland: Museum of Art (Holden

Collection), 233c.
Coblenz: Landeshauptarchiv, 166, 167al, 167c.
Dublin: National Gallery of Ireland, 48a, 228.
Ferrara: Palazzo Schifanoia, 165c.
Florence: Archivio di Stato (by permission of 3/5/83, no. 1958) 47a, 70ar, 71ar, 86, 90br, 116, 117a, 126, 128l, 130, 133, 152b, 154b, 155a, 160, 183b; Antico Setificio Fiorentino, 81; Biblioteca Laurenziana, 47b, 73b, 76, 78, 79, 200, 201, 202, 204b, 212, 213r, 222a; Biblioteca Nazionale Centrale, 15, 51, 58, 59, 177ar, 177br, 203, 205bl, 220b, 222b, 239; Biblioteca Riccardiana, 68r, 92, 94, 104b; Biblioteca del Seminario Maggiore, 11b, 66ar, 111, 192a, 195; Bigallo, 23, 45r, 118b, 119; Casa Buonarroti, 175ar; Galleria dell'Accademia, 43, 46bl; Galleria Palatina, 214b, 234; Galleria degli Uffizi, 10, 30al, 42al, 46a, 90b, 149, 180b, 182, 217al; Galleria degli Uffizi (Gabinetto dei Disegni e delle Stampe), 25a, 48br, 61a, 93, 110, 123, 204a, 207c, 211r, 232a, 233al; Galleria degli Uffizi (Raccolta Topografica), 12, 13, 16, 17, 32, 67, 95b, 104a; Istituto Geografico Militare, 163a; Museo degli Argenti, 22, 235; Museo del Bargello (or Nazionale), 3, 8, 49, 53a, 114-115, 120b, 131a, 164b, 216cr, 216br; Museo Firenze com'era, 9, 11a, 20bl, 24, 54a, 55ar, 60a, 66al, 66bl, 66br, 68l, 74, 100al, 144, 148, 175al, 175b, 238, 240; Museo dell'Opera del Duomo, 84, 85, 114a, 118a, 199, 217ac; Museo Opificio delle Pietre Dure, 143a; Museo di San Marco, 142, 151b; Palazzo Medici Riccardi, 34a, 42ar, 69; Palazzo Vecchio, 18-19, 106, 107, 121c, 139a, 139, 145, 176b, 180a, 181a, 214a, 233ar, 233bl; Villa medicea di Poggio a Caiano, 230; Santissima Annunziata, 75; Santa Croce, 194; San Lorenzo, 216cl, 216bl; Santa Maria Novella, 2, 35a, 35bl, 53b, 141, 164ar, 165ar, 198, 207a; San Martino dei Buonomini (or del Vescovo), 44, 45a, 45bl, 89; San Miniato, 6, 197; Santo Spirito, 161; Santa Trinita, 35br, 90a, 135; Collezione Giuntini, 232b, 233br.
London: British Museum, 64, 96, 122, 205br, 208; National Gallery, 41, 172; Watney Collection (Charlbury, London), 41, 172.
Lucca: Archivio di Stato (by permission of 24/2/82, no. 659; of 9/3/83, no. 1155; of 6/4/83, no. 1522), 77a, 77c, 125a, 125b, 127a, 129al, 159, 163, 170, 171.
Milan: Biblioteca Ambrosiana, 206b; Biblioteca del Presidio Militare, 206b.

Munich: Graphische Sammlung, 52b.
Oxford: Bodleian Library, 100b.
Padua: Cappella degli Scrovegni, 31, 36b.
Paris: Bibliothèque Nationale, 55al, 101l, 101r, 181b, 217c; Louvre, 173b, 221; Louvre (Cabinet des Dessins), 56a.
Pisa: Composanto, 103; San Nicola, 162ar.
Prato: Archivio di Stato, 105b; San Francesco, 98.
Rome: Palazzo Madama, 143l.
Sarasota (Florida): John and Mable Ringling Museum of Art, 218-219.
Siena: Archivio di Statio, 40b, 99, 102b, 128r, 129ar, 129c, 152a, 154a, 168b, 169, 188a.
Stuttgart: Staatsgalerie, 48bl.
Vatican City: Biblioteca Vaticana, 46r, 88, 121al, 124, 132, 162al, 167ar, 196; Pinacoteca Vaticana, 30ar, 30b.
Windsor Castle: Royal Library, 52a, 158, 211l; Royal Collections (by gracious permission of Her Majesty the Queen), 237 (copyright reserved).

Acknowledgements

The Publishers would like to thank the following for the kind assistance given them during the course of their picture research: the Archivio di Stato, Florence and its director, Professor Giuseppe Pansini; Dr. Francesca Klein; the Archivio di Stato, Lucca, and its director, Professor Vito Tirelli; the Archivio di Stato, Prato, and its director, Dr. Paola Benini; the Biblioteca Laurenziana, its director Dr. Antonietta Morandini; the Biblioteca Nazionale Centrale, and its director, Dr. Anna Lenzuni; the Biblioteca Riccardiana, and its director, Maria Jole Minicucci; the Museo Firenze com'era and its director, Dr. Fiorenza Scalia.